3.

CREATIVE ADVERTISING:
Theory
and Practice

Sandra E. Moriarty

University of Colorado

PRENTICE-HALL, ENGLEWOOD CLIFFS, N.J. 07632

Library of Congress Cataloging-in-Publication Data

Moriarty, Sandra Ernst.
Creative advertising

   Includes bibliographies and index.
    1. Advertising. I. Title.
HF5821.M62 1986   659.1   85-16879
ISBN 0-13-188947-8

Editorial/production supervision and
  interior design: Eve Mossman
Cover design: Lundgren Graphics, Ltd.
Cover photograph by Lou Odor Photography
Manufacturing buyer: Ed O'Dougherty

© 1986 by Prentice-Hall
A Division of Simon & Schuster, Inc.
Englewood Cliffs, New Jersey 07632

Printed in the United States of America

10 9 8 7 6 5 4 3 2 1

ISBN 0-13-188947-8   01

Prentice-Hall International (UK) Limited, London
Prentice-Hall of Australia Pty. Limited, Sydney
Prentice-Hall Canada Inc., Toronto
Prentice-Hall Hispanoamericana, S.A., Mexico
Prentice-Hall of India Private Limited, New Delhi
Prentice-Hall of Japan, Inc., Tokyo
Prentice-Hall of Southeast Asia Pte. Ltd., Singapore
Editora Prentice-Hall do Brasil, Ltda., Rio de Janeiro
Whitehall Books Limited, Wellington, New Zealand

Contents

Preface

This book is intended to be an introduction to the creative side—both foundation theories and practical application. In advertising it is not enough to know *how*, you also need to know *why*. Advertising is a changing field—it thrives on novelty and originality and new situations. In order to be able to cope with changing conditions, you need an understanding of basic principles, as well as basic practices.

Most advertising books that discuss the creative side focus on practice. They teach you *how to do it*. You will find few books that present theory *and* principles. That's not the fault of the textbook writers. In reality, there is little theory that has been compiled and synthesized and applied to the creative side.

The theories and their supporting research are there; they are just buried in psychology, sociology, aesthetics, education, public opinion, and consumer behavior. One of the big tasks ahead for advertising scholars is to synthesize the theory and research from these areas and develop an actual body of theory for the creative side.

This book will make a small attempt at theory building for the creative side. At the same time, however, we will also include the very necessary practical information and, where possible, will use the theory as explanation for the practice.

Part of the problem is the breadth of the field. The creative side includes the two professional areas of copywriting and art direction. Those areas are distinct enough that most textbook writers align with either one or the other. We will attempt to cover both sides of the creative side.

Creative thinking is very important to the creative side of advertising, and this topic is also discussed in this book, along with message strategy and management of the creative function.

All of these subjects are important, but most of the books in the field focus only on one topic or perhaps a few of these topics. What is needed is a book that covers the entire creative side. It may sound impossible to do all of that in one book—copywriting, design, creative thinking, strategy, and management as well as other necessary topics such as production and research. However, many of our courses do, in fact, approach the creative side as a comprehensive topic. Furthermore, there are professionals in advertising who have to figure out objectives, come up with ideas, write copy, design their own layouts, and critique the work of others—strategy, creativity, copywriting, art direction, and management—they are responsible for it all.

The material in this book covers all media from print to broadcast and specialized areas such as brochures and Yellow Pages. The creative side is exciting because you never know what you will be working on next. We try to maintain that same spirit.

This book is dedicated to all those people, students and professionals as well as their teachers, who are well rounded, well read, and excited about the creative side—theory as well as practice.

ACKNOWLEDGMENTS

Among those who have contributed to this book, I would like to acknowledge the help of my colleagues and students at Kansas University, Michigan State University, and the University of Colorado. In particular, I would like to thank Bruce Vanden Bergh and Ed Scheiner at MSU, Charles Frazer at CU, and Ted Vaughan at the University of Wyoming for their contributions.

The book has been in process for many years, and during that time a number of students have commented on the material and brought ads to my attention. I would particularly like to thank all the students who have shared their enthusiasm with me in the beginning, advanced and graduate level creative strategy and copy and layout courses at all of the universities.

For ideas, insight, and anecdotes I would like to thank the fine people I worked with at Campbell Ewald. In particular, I would like to thank Rhoda Parkin and Tom Tucker for opening all the doors.

Another group of dedicated people have reviewed the manuscript at various stages and their suggestions have helped to sharpen its focus. For their extremely helpful comments, I would like to say thanks to Charles Frazer, Leonard

Reid, George S. Anderson, Jr., Ron Lane, Gary Wilcox, and Florence Feasley, as well as Dean Krugman and Tony McGann.

With a great deal of appreciation I would like to acknowledge the tremendous amount of work produced by two of my Colorado students, Jenny Reising and Stacey Grezelewski. Jenny was my library assistant and Stacey drew the illustrations in the graphics chapter. They also contributed a script and storyboard for the television advertising section.

A number of people were involved with the production and preparation of the manuscript, including most of the staff in the Jayne Media Center at the University of Wyoming. In particular, I would like to say thanks to Del Hastings, Rhonda Frazier, and Dianne Nordmann. A special thanks to Kevin Vaughan for his computer work. Others I have leaned on at the University of Colorado include Phil Emery and Ron Claxton for typesetting help and Garda Meyer for keeping everything afloat.

I would like to acknowledge the host of editors, publishers, account executives, advertising managers and other executives who supplied facts and made available quotes, illustrations, and copies of the ads that are used to illustrate the theory and the practices described in these chapters.

Finally I would like to gratefully acknowledge the support, encouragement, and patience of Elizabeth Classon, marketing editor at Prentice-Hall; Eve Mossman, production editor; and Lionel Dean, copy editor.

Creative
Thinking

Chapter One

Ideation. Creative thinking is the process of getting ideas—but getting ideas is not limited to the creative side of advertising. Everyone in the field is responsible for solving problems (a very practical form of getting ideas). That includes media, research, traffic and production, even account management. The entire field of advertising is an idea field, so everything that is said here relating to creative thinking can apply to just about every side of the business.

Getting ideas is formally called *ideation*. To "ideate" is to imagine, to conceive thoughts. *Creativity* is the ability to produce original ideas or thoughts. In a publication of the Creative Education Foundation,[1] creativity is defined as "a quality possessed by persons that enables them to generate novel approaches in situations, generally reflected in new and improved solutions to problems." The key word here is "novel," which is described in advertising as new, fresh, or original. Novelty, the "one-of-a-kind" approach, is what makes your idea creative.

You might also note the problem-solving orientation of this definition. Much of the early theory building in the area of creative thinking came from such diverse fields as engineering and industrial design, business administration, education, and psychology. Engineers look at ideation as a way to design new gears and production techniques. It's practical, not artsy.

1

Novelty. Creative is defined as work that is characterized by novelty, originality, or imagination. *Original* is something that has not been done before, something novel. Ideation is linked with creativity through the common use of the concept of *imagination*, which is the ability to form a mental image of something that is not seen. In other words, you get ideas by forming mental images, and they can be considered creative ideas if they are unlike ideas previously produced by you or anyone else. Everyone gets ideas; that's not exclusive to people on the creative side. Furthermore, everyone is capable of producing creative ideas—ideas that they have not thought of before.

We've already mentioned that an idea can be original in the sense that *you* have never thought of it before. It also can be original on a higher level in the sense that *no one* has ever thought of it before. Just because it's an original idea to you, however, doesn't mean it is original to anyone else. In advertising we look for the people who produce ideas that are not only original to them, but that are also novel. That's both the challenge and the test of your aptitude for advertising.

Clichés. Having defined creative, original, and imaginative, we've also opened the door for definitions of uncreative, unoriginal, and unimaginative. *Unimaginative* suggests there is no clear focused picture in the mind. *Unoriginal* is the common idea that everyone comes up with, the "pat" answer, the obvious. *Uncreative* is producing work that is not original or imaginative.

A *cliché* is a particular type of uncreative idea; it is an idea that at one time had some unexpected phrasing or imagery. The first time it was used it was novel, but it quickly became worn out with overuse. So a cliché is an expression that was original but has become unoriginal through overuse. While a cliché is uncreative because of overuse, a cliché with a twist can resurrect the original magic of the phrase and imagery.

A creative idea, then, is built on some unusual combination using either association, metaphor, or clichés. The ideas are creative because the association is unexpected.

Ways of Thinking

The development of an advertising strategy is a very careful and logical process. It is a rational process aimed at arriving at conclusions using either inductive or deductive thinking. With advertising strategy, which will be discussed in the next chapter, reasoning is critical and logic must be unassailable. A creative idea, however, doesn't evolve the same way strategy does. Ideation involves entirely different ways of thinking.

Many people think that creative ideas come from out of the blue. In reality, there is a process to creative thinking, too—and we'll discuss that shortly—but for now please note that when we talk about creative thinking, as opposed to strategic thinking, we are talking about a radically different way of reasoning.

So what kind of reasoning is it? There are several terms used to describe the type of thinking used to generate ideas.

Divergent thinking.   J. P. Guilford is a scholar who has developed a complicated three-dimensional model of the intellect.[2] He sees creative thinking as extremely complex, but suggests that most of the creative thinking abilities are grouped around an aptitude that he calls divergent production. Convergent thinking is the logical (inductive, deductive) type of thinking that leads to what Guilford calls "logical imperatives" or conclusions. Divergent thinking, however, starts at a common point and shoots off in many directions, arriving at what he calls "logical alternatives."

Guilford's Structure-of-the-Intellect model is based upon decades of factor analysis of hundreds of traits. As a result of this work he has identified three specific types of traits that are common in people of high creative ability: fluency, flexibility, and originality. *Fluency* is the ability to rapidly produce ideas and *flexibility* is the ability to produce original, divergent solutions in a number of categories or areas. *Originality* is a function of frequency of occurrence—how often does your idea show up on someone else's list? If it doesn't, then you have produced an original idea.

Associative thinking.   James Webb Young's definition of the word *idea* is "a new combination of old elements."[3] He is referring to a process of seeing new connections in old relationships, or juxtaposing two previously unrelated thoughts. That's the basis of the association process. To many people, associative thinking is like waiting for the lightning to strike, and creative people are simply targets where creative ideas happen to strike with more regularity. The complexities of associative thinking are rarely understood or appreciated.

Associative thinking, more commonly called free association, involves opening up your mind and expressing the thoughts as they come. The association process has been described by Mednick,[4] a psychologist, who developed a test called "The Remote Associates." With this type of thinking the thought pattern will not be a logical one but an associational one—in other words, one thought makes you think about something else.

The connection is there but it is embedded deep in your experiences, rather than in your reasoning. The associative pattern is distinctively your own, and someone else listening to the seemingly random spray of ideas may see no logic to them at all. But the ideas only appear to be random. The associations, however deep, are still there.

The importance of acquiring facts for association was stressed in an article presenting a model of associative thinking in advertising.[5] The authors commented that "the more you know about the consumer's perception of the problem, the better will be your chances of creating ads that elicit the desired response." The association process needs lots of facts as raw material.

Lateral thinking.   Edward de Bono in his book, *Lateral Thinking: Creativity Step by Step*,[6] develops his theory of thinking focusing on a process that is a form of associative thinking. De Bono describes it as *lateral* thinking, or jumping around without any apparent structure, like a dog digging for a bone. He contrasts lateral thinking with *vertical* thinking, which is reasoned, more like the thinking we have called "convergent." Vertical thinking is linear and uses either induction or deduction. People can "follow you" as you reason through a chain and arrive at a conclusion.

Everyone utilizes both types of thinking. You do it subconsciously, without even thinking about it. People who are considered creative have unusually well-developed and well-practiced lateral thinking or associative powers. They can jump around, like de Bono's dog digging for a bone, and dig in hundreds of unlikely places until they find something unexpected.

The differences between creative thinking and analytical thinking, as presented by de Bono, were summarized in an article by two Michigan State University professors, Bruce Vanden Bergh and Keith Adler.[7] Their list of differences is as follows:

VERTICAL THINKING	LATERAL THINKING
1. Selective	1. Generative
2. Needs direction	2. Seeks direction
3. Analytical	3. Provocative
4. Sequential	4. Jumps, leaps
5. Judgmental—correct every step of the way	5. Not judgmental—no need to be correct at every step
6. Negative—blocks certain paths	6. Positive—investigates all possibilities
7. Excludes the irrelevant	7. Welcomes chance intrusions
8. Categorical, classifying, labeling	8. Does not categorize, classify, or label
9. Follows most likely paths	9. Explores least likely paths
10. Finite	10. Probabilistic

Analogical thinking.   This type of associative thinking uses metaphors and analogies. A metaphor lifts an idea out of context and uses it in another context to suggest resemblance to some other concept. When a hand is described as "fluttering in the wind," the writer is using a leaf metaphor to suggest a delicate or perhaps hesitant gesture.

An *analogy* is similar to a metaphor. It indicates a resemblance of form, process, or relationships. An analogy can be used to help in the reasoning process because it explains steps and procedures. Many times an analogy may be a story rather than an image. Both metaphors and analogies are creative tools because they trigger the associative response. A metaphor may be even stronger than a statement of fact because the audience becomes involved in the message as they complete the association from their own experiences. They are participating in the creation of the idea.

William J. J. Gordon has developed a program to train creative thinking based on the idea of forcing metaphors and analogies. His think-tank training program, called Synectics,[8] is structured around three types of analogical approaches. *Direct analogy* is a metaphorical comparison between a key element of the problem and a roughly similar concept in a new context. A *personal analogy* is developed by expressing an empathetic identification with the problem, like trying to imagine how an umbrella would feel opening in a driving rainstorm. Synectics also uses a technique called *compressed conflict* by developing two-word descriptions using words that contradict each other, such as "delicate aggressor."

The concept behind analogy is basically mathematical. The Synectics exercises are built around this simple formula: "A is to B as C is to what?" That's the foundation for analogical thinking. It becomes creative by using free association to stimulate the wildest possible connections. The credo of creative innovation through Synectics is to "make the strange familiar and the familiar strange." Gordon says that, with a structured program of metaphor construction, you don't have to wait passively until the creative muse strikes, that there are definite metaphorical weapons with which you can hunt and track down the muse.

(216)

Right brain/left brain. Another way to describe how we think is based on the physiology of our brains. The brain is two separate compartments, or hemispheres, connected by a thin tissue. Recent research and neurosurgery has found that, when this connection is cut, we have two separate brains, each capable of quite different ways of thinking and remembering. As explained in a book called *Drawing on the Right Side of the Brain,* by Betty Edwards, the left brain is verbal and controls speech, writing, and all thinking that is logically determined. This is similar to convergent or lateral thinking. The right brain is nonverbal and controls emotions, intuition, psychomotor skills, and things that you learn *to do* and develop a *feel for.*[9]

The left brain thinks in linear and sequential steps; the right brain thinks in sensory images and grasps the "whole picture." When you recognize a face, you are using right-brain knowledge and thinking patterns. According to Thomas Blakeslee in *The Right Brain,*[10] the right brain "manipulates complex images" rather than comparing feature by feature, as the left brain does.

Blakeslee uses "catching a ball" as an example of the sophistication of right-brain thinking skills. Intuitively a kid who has no background in physics can calculate speed, targeting, wind, and velocity. However, the same kid would probably not be able to estimate this complicated set of activities on paper. Conversely, someone who could breeze through the calculations might not be able to catch the ball at all. You can know how to do something intellectually, such as play tennis, and not be able to perform it physically.

We all have left- and right-brain capabilities, but one-half of the brain may be more developed than the other. Typically, our society and education values the verbal and logical patterns of the left brain. Consequently, most of us have mastery of those skills and some people are totally dominated by left-brain thinking. Right-brain thinking is largely unrecognized and untaught in our society, although not in others, and only a few people have well-developed skills in those areas—such as painters and musicians.

Research has indicated that the right and left brains have a working relationship, even though their thinking and remembering systems are completely separate. Sometimes we use both halves at the same time. When you have a conversation, for example, your left brain responds to the literal meaning of the words while your right brain responds to the inflections, tone of voice, gestures, and facial expressions.

Sometimes one side of the brain has to translate for the other. For example, if you ask someone who skis, golfs, dances, or paints how he or she does it, the person will probably say "like this" and show you. That's a right-brain response. If you want a verbal explanation, then the left brain has to do the translating. The person will probably perform the action while his or her left brain "watches," and then the left brain will try to come up with words to express this basically nonverbal knowledge.

That's why creative ideas are so very difficult to express. They are the product of right-brain thinking and essentially nonverbal, but the left brain has to do the translating in order to communicate them to bosses and clients.

In terms of applying these theories to creativity, obviously the right brain is largely the center of most creative thinking. That's where the mental images are stored. Visual thinking and imagery are basic to creative thinking. Blakeslee explains, "An ability to recognize things in an altered form or context is the basis of creative thinking." He points out that "creative breakthroughs are generally a result of finding hidden relationships—patterns that are obscured by their context." Verbal thinking, he says, "is inherently limited in its ability to make these kinds of abstract connections."

The right brain is also the source of intuition and inspiration. Blakeslee explains that "in most intellectual fields the real breakthroughs are the result of intuition." He points out, however, that "intuition itself is generally useless until it can be verified and described verbally and logically."

Intuition is our ability to make estimates based on past experience. Blakeslee describes intuition as a "catch-all word for thinking processes that we can't verbally explain." A calculated estimate is determined methodically—point by point. In contrast, Blakeslee explains that "intuitive judgments are not arrived at step by step, but in an instant. They typically take into consideration a large mass of data in parallel, without separately considering each factor." He points out that, with experience, the intuitive judgments can be just as accurate as the methodical ones.

Not only is the right brain important to creative thinking, it is also important as a receiver of information. In advertising, many of our messages are aimed at emotions, and that's a right-brain message. The graphics are complex visuals that have to be read and understood by the right brain. Many of our messages try to stimulate the association process and, as Blakeslee explains, symbolization and free association are right-brain thinking patterns. Maybe someday we will be able to target predominantly left-brain and right-brain audiences and design messages specifically for them.

Visual Thinking

The word *visualization* is used in several different ways in advertising. One way is to refer to a presentation piece, called a comprehensive, that is executed by artists to depict what the advertisement will look like after it is produced. This is a visualization of the complete ad, making the idea visible so others can "see" it while it is still in the talking stage. Comprehensives will be discussed in the section on layout.

Another use for the word involves referring to the process of turning the creative concept into a visual—either photograph or artwork. The words are translated into an effective piece of art that is both arresting and memorable. This type of visualization calls for a sound understanding of the principles of visual communication—what you can and can't do with a visual as well as knowledge of how a visual communicates its message. The chapter on graphics discusses the production as well as the perception of visual images.

Visualization is also used to refer to the process of mentally "seeing" the solution to an advertising problem. This calls for a well-developed ability to think visually using the powers of mental imagery. Being able to think visually is characteristic of many people who work in advertising—artists as well as writers. Advertising calls for imagination in all areas on all levels and imagining means being able to see things in "the mind's eye." That's another way to define visualization.

In order to appreciate how advertising works and how people in advertising work, we need to consider how people think. Different people process information in different ways and that's because people think differently. Educators know that some people are primarily visual in terms of learning styles; other people are primarily verbal. A good individualized teaching strategy will communicate using a person's strongest mode.

You can test this out by saying some common word to yourself like "car" or "house" and observing what comes to your mind—a mental image of the word or a mental image of its physical appearance. *Visual* and *verbal* are the two most common ways of perceiving information and thinking about it. There is a third: *kinesthetic*. If you can feel the motion of a car while you say the word to yourself, you are a kinesthetic thinker.

Most people think in all three modes—depending upon the nature of the stimulus. If you ask someone to remember what it is like to take off roller skates after skating for several hours, most people will describe the tingling sensation in their feet. That's a kinesthetic response.

While most people adjust their thinking style to the stimulus, some people think totally in one mode or the other. Researchers using the Edmunds Learning Style Inventory (ELSI) have found that 17 percent of the people tested can't think visually at all while at the other extreme they found that 17 percent only think visually.[11] In between are people who are more or less visual and use a variety of thinking modes. The important thing to note from this research, however, is that while 17 percent can't think visually, 83 percent can and do—and that has a tremendous impact on how we see the world and process information.

In thinking, the image comes before the word. We see before we speak, both in terms of developmental psychology and communication. Words are the tools we use to translate what we see and feel; communication substitutes for reality. By necessity, words are abstract and have to be learned. Because of that, our minds are able to absorb images more quickly than words. There are some who say that images are not just "translations" of thought, but thought itself.

Imagery. "Imagery" is a word used to describe this process of thinking visually. We know that certain people have highly developed powers of imagery. This is an attribute valued highly in advertising. The people who work on the creative side tend to be very strong in imagery. Writers as well as artists are able to see "pictures in the mind." While artists sketch their images with pencils and felt tips, writers paint with words.

Imagery is our ability to recall sensory impressions—what something looks, feels, smells, tastes, and sounds like. Visual imagery is the ability to recall appearances; audio imagery recalls sounds. Both are important in advertising and audio imagery is particularly important for people who work with radio.

Thinking in words tends to be slower and more plodding. How many times have you found yourself with a thought, but have to search for the right words to express it? Translating thoughts into words can slow down the thinking process—but the mental images tend to leap into the mind. That's because there is no translation step involved. It is also helpful if management people in advertising are strong in imagery. Account executives, for example, have to critique creative concepts. They also have to sell a client by painting pictures with their words. They need to be able to translate a concept and make it come to life for people who sometimes—even oftentimes—have limited powers of visual thinking.

While some people have more imagery power, some concepts are more easily communicated using imagery. The old saying, "a picture is worth a thousand words," applies only to certain kinds of information. If you want to give directions, you look at a map or draw a map. Location and geography need pictures in the mind. (See Exhibit 1–1.)

Things that you have known or experienced are often filed in memory

EXHIBIT 1-1:   **The Maxell "500 plays" advertisement was created by Scali, McCabe, Sloves, Inc.** (Courtesy of Maxell/Scali, McCabe, Sloves, Inc.)

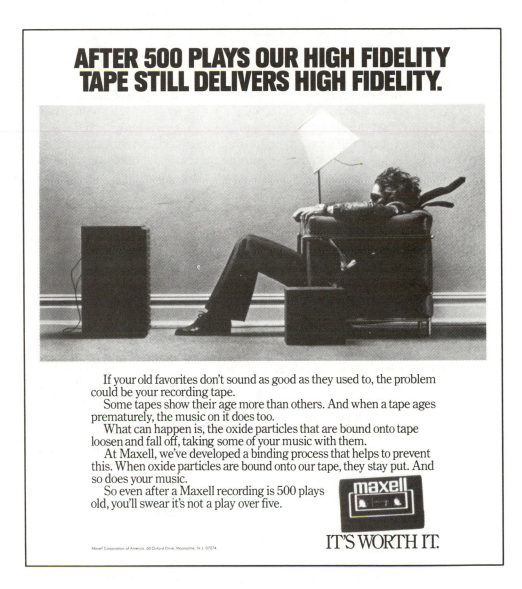

as a picture. Think back to the house where you grew up, your first car, your first date—most of these come back as pictures, not as words.

Quantified relations, particularly in size and amount, are often best expressed as visuals. Anyone who has had a basic course in math knows that a pie chart explains the relative size of pieces much easier than words or even numbers. Most statistical findings are graphed for presentation, and analysis using graphs shows the results far faster than columns of numbers can.

Some kinds of concepts are naturally expressed in words. Abstractions, for example, are verbal constructs—they can be symbolized but never depicted. There is no way, for example, to draw a picture of "loyalty," "good value," or "quality." You can symbolize them, but you can't show them. Consequently, discussions of such abstractions tend to be verbal.

In this section we are trying to stress the value of visual thinking to overcome some of the word-oriented emphasis of your previous education. It is true, however, that the strongest message is one that uses both verbal and visual channels to express the same thought. In a *Journal of Advertising* article on visual imagery,[12] the researchers explain the theory of "dual coding," in which information is encoded both verbally and visually. They call this a "dual loop" and stress that using both pictures and words can exert more of an effect on attitudes than either one alone. That's why it is important for you to realize that a strong creative concept is a perfect blend of word and picture with each one reinforcing the other.

Creative Process

A number of advertising scholars have tried to describe the creative process and, while the steps don't work in the same way for everyone, they at least provide some ideas on how to get started.

Graham Wallas as early as 1926 developed an outline of the ideation process identifying the following four steps: preparation, incubation, illumination, and verification.[13] *Preparation* means research and study. *Incubation* means getting away from it and letting the ideas jell on their own. *Illumination* is that point where the light dawns. *Verification* is the process of applying the great idea to see if it fits the requirements of the strategy.

James Webb Young, a former creative VP at J. Walter Thompson, wrote a little book titled *A Technique for Producing Ideas*, which outlines his theory of the creative process.[14] He believes that creative thinking is based on two factors: combining old elements into new combinations and seeing the relationships between them. We've talked about combining ideas in terms of associative thinking.

His second factor, the ability to see the relationships, seems obvious but, in fact, it is a real stumbling block to creativity. Many people come up with creative ideas (or have creative ideas presented to them) and have a difficult time comprehending the essence of the novel relationship. This is a judgment problem, and you can train yourself to improve this evaluation skill by comparing your responses with others.

Immersion.   Beyond these two factors, he also describes a five-step process that summarizes how most people "get" ideas. The first step is *immer-*

sion, where you gather raw materials through background research, totally immersing yourself in the problem. We'll talk about techniques of backgrounding in more detail later in this chapter.

Digestion.   The second step is *digestion,* where you are mentally chewing the cud. It's a type of fooling around with the information—turning it over, looking at it from different angles, doodling, making lists of features and phrases. This digestion step often ends with something Young calls "brainfag" when you reach the hopeless stage. At this point everything is probably in a jumble. Have you ever concentrated on a word until it no longer makes sense? That's the state of "brainfag."

All writers on this topic agree that you have to immerse yourself in the problem and wrestle with it until you think you have hit a blank wall. When you are close to the point of giving up in exasperation, you may reach that final pressure point where the ideas start to bubble to the top.

Sometimes a good idea will come easy and early, but more likely the ideas that come first are the obvious approaches, the tried and true, the common, the unoriginal, the clichés. Still, getting all these obvious ideas out in the open is a necessary first step. Let them come, sort through them looking for little glimmers of possible great ideas, and dump the rest.

Incubation.   Young's third state is *incubation,* where you put it all out of your mind and go for a walk. In effect, you are turning it over to your subconscious. Most people intuitively turn to something that stimulates the imagination. Sherlock Holmes used to play his violin or drag Watson to a band concert. There is debate on the incubation phase. Many creative thinkers report anecdotes about the great idea that strikes when they put the problem away for a while. None of the research, however, has been able to prove the value of this step. Some people working in advertising believe in incubation and, when they hit the wall, they will drop everything and go walk around the block or ride up and down on the elevator. There are others, however, who feel the only way to proceed is to work against pressure. Who has time to go sit in a movie when the copy has to be on the boss's desk in two hours?

One point of agreement is that the ideas come after a period of sustained effort. You have to plant the garden and weed it before you can harvest the crop. Most creative people agree that it is hard work coming up with ideas—even though the idea itself may come at some unexpected, nonwork, relaxed time.

Rollo May, in *The Courage to Create,* makes the point that insight not only comes after a period of effort, it also tends to come at a moment of transition—usually the transition between work and relaxation.[15] It comes at the point when you put away the books and start to walk to the bus or right before falling asleep. Creative people often sleep with paper and pencil next to the bed for that reason.

Illumination.   In the fourth stage the light goes on. Out of nowhere, when you least expect it, the idea will appear—showering, shaving, half dozing, bathing.

That's the "Eureka phenomenon." What happens is that you turn your attention elsewhere and let your subconscious work on the problem without all the tension and anxiety. It solves the problem while you are occupied with something else.

Reality.   Young's last stage is *reality,* the cold gray dawn of the morning after. Does the great idea still look so great? Does it really solve the problem? More important, in advertising, does it fit the strategy? Sometimes (often) it doesn't, and you're back to starting over again at the beginning. Many creatives tell about when they got a really great idea, looked at it the next day, and wondered how they could come up with something so silly. It happens all the time.

Osborn's description of the creative process[16] is similar to the process described above: specify the problem, gather information, generate possible solutions, evaluate the solutions, and select one. His approach differs in that he emphasizes solving a problem by developing lots of options as opposed to seeking one good one.

Getting started.   Osborn describes a preliminary stage that he calls "setting the working mood." Essentially, it's a mind-opening process. Some writers use special techniques to flex or stretch their imaginations. One writer will make lists of words on a yellow pad with magic markers. Another writer takes all the pencils out of his desk, walks to the pencil sharpener, and sharpens them one by one, the grinding of the sharpener serving as a physical metaphor for the grinding of the gears in his mind.

Some people close the door, others find a chair in the middle of the bustle. Some like wide-open areas; others like dark cramped spaces. Some work with pencil or felt tips, others sit down to the typewriter. The setting-the-mood stage is as personal for most people as their signatures. It's something that you develop over time, and it serves as an internal cue to your brain that the system is on line and locked in.

Rollo May describes a mental state of intensity of awareness, a type of heightened consciousness.[17] He calls it suprarational (not irrational)—using intellectual, volitional, and emotional abilities. This state of intense concentration and arousal even has neurological responses, such as a faster heartbeat, higher blood pressure, narrowing of eyelids, lessening of appetite—in general, an obliviousness to things around you. In terms of imagery, he also notes that everything you encounter in this state becomes more vivid. You are more able to see unexpected patterns in what before was mundane.

The heart of the creative process for Rollo May is this intense encounter. He explains that a hobby is not a creative encounter because it lacks the intensity and the seriousness. He also notes that you can't will creativity or insight, but you *can* will the encounter and the intensity and, in that sense, you can train, manage, and improve your creative abilities.

Unblocking.   A phase similar in some ways to the setting-the-mood stage is *unblocking.* When you block, your ideas simply won't come. To a certain extent, that's a normal and expected part of the creative process. We've mentioned the role of "brainfag," the desperation you feel as you try to trigger the flow of ideas. Most creative people report having to wrestle through that familiar phase of desperation, and all have different ways of doing it.

Real blocking occurs when panic sets in. We know from previous discussions of obstacles that fear precludes creativity. That's the difference between the creative stage of "brainfag" and the dysfunctional stage of blocking. The panic has to be dealt with first. Sometimes incubation can be useful. Turn your attention to something else and let the adrenalin drop. If you have to keep working, then find something routine to do—something that's easy and rhythmic. Many writers work their way out of a block by making a list—lots of repetition of an activity that takes minimal brain effort. It's another adrenalin dropper. Another technique is to do something physical like exercise, jogging, lifting weights, moving furniture, running up and down stairs. It's a way to siphon off the adrenalin overcharge that comes from the panic.

1.2 BACKGROUND RESEARCH

One common denominator in all theories of creativity is the fundamental need for background research. Ideas just don't come from out of the blue. Backgrounding is hard work. Larry Plapler, executive VP and co-creative director at Levine, Huntley, Schmidt, Plapler, and Beaver in New York, says, "Instead of instant inspiration, it's long-term perspiration." He explains, "Ideas don't come in a vacuum. You have to do your homework. You must be armed with research, competitors' advertising and every other piece of information the marketplace has to offer."[18]

You will need tons of information to find the elusive fact that ultimately will be the foundation for the advertising strategy or the creative theme. You can't build a brick wall without bricks, and the little bits of information gathered in the backgrounding process are the bricks used to build the creative strategy. Foote Cone & Belding's Ron Hoff says, "I tell my writers they should never start writing until they have seven times as many facts as they will actually use in an ad."[19]

Attitudes.   People who work on the creative side of advertising are inquisitive. What's the difference in the two brands? Why does it work that way? Why did she choose that style? This curiosity shows up in the fact-finding effort. In an *Advertising Age* interview, Joel Raphaelson, executive creative director at Ogilvy and Mather, said, "The most productive people are always the most curious. They are the ones who have the most ideas, good and bad."[20] Creative people are dilettantes; they float from one topic, one fashion, one fad to another. They sponge up ideas and absorb the scene around them almost unconsciously. Their interests are broad.

There are sound psychological reasons for these personality characteristics. In an article on copywriters and their associative thinking abilities, the
authors speculated that creative people are better at incidental learning.[21] They
explained that incidental learning is a process by which "previously unrelated
facts or ideas are associated. Consequently a more creative person displays better
incidental learning than a less creative individual." The more miscellaneous information you carry around, the more material you have to work with when it
comes time to develop new ideas.

Fact-Finding Techniques

Read.   Advertising people are known for taking books to bed with them.
Late night reading, as well as reading on the bus or train, reading while waiting
in line, reading over a sandwich, reading in the bathtub, and, when there's time,
reading in the office at the desk. Reading is the number one source of information.
     Copywriters read published research reports, focus group transcripts,
books, trade magazines, general interest articles, scholarly journal articles, traffic studies, annual reports, profit-and-loss statements, interviews, medical
reports, technical studies—everything they can get their hands on related in any
way to the product they've been assigned. Somewhere in all that reading there
will be the elusive, unrecognized fact that will spark a creative theme or lock
the strategy together.

Ask.   Interview everyone involved with the product—the designer, the
engineer, the home economist, the accountant, the programmer, the systems engineer, the line worker—and, most of all, the user. Just like in reading, you're looking for that isolated remark that makes the bells ring.
     Bud Robbins describes his fact finding for a piano account in an ad that
runs for the Kresser & Robbins ad agency. He describes how he discovered the
Capo d'astro bar and wrote an ad about it that created a six-year wait in orders
for the piano company. (See Exhibit 1–2.)
     An interview can take a number of forms. You can go out with a pad
and pen, like a reporter, and interview people on the street, in their homes and
offices, or in the store. The interview can also be a formal questionnaire designed
for gathering large quantities of responses. You can also use open-ended surveys for in-depth probing of motives and reasons. Open-ended surveys don't lend
themselves to "number crunching," so you will talk to a smaller number of people and probe deeper into their reasons and opinions.
     Learn how to interview, ask questions, draw people out, follow up on
an aside. Look for random clues. People like to talk about what interests them;
the knack is to get them started. Believe it or not, most people are flattered when
you ask them their opinion.

Listen.   Listen to what they are talking about among themselves. Haunt
stores, malls, restaurants, kitchens, pinball places, and other hangouts. Listen
to the employees on coffee break. Most of all, listen to your client. Listen be-

EXHIBIT 1-2:   "Looking for the Capo d' astro bar" was a house advertisement written by Bud Robbins for Kresser & Robbins, Inc. (Courtesy of Kresser & Robbins, Inc.)

"Looking for the Capo d'astro bar."
By Bud Robbins

Back in the sixties, I was hired by an ad agency to write copy on the Aeolian Piano Company account. My first assignment was for an ad to be placed in The New York Times for one of their grand pianos. The only background information I received was some previous ads and a few faded close-up shots...and of course, the due date.

The Account Executive was slightly put out by my request for additional information and his response to my suggestion that I sit down with the client was, "Jesus Christ, are you one of *those*? Can't you just create something? We're up against a closing date!"

I acknowledged his perception that I *was* one of those, which got us an immediate audience with the head of our agency.

I volunteered I couldn't even play a piano let alone write about why anyone would spend $5,000 for *this* piano when they could purchase a Baldwin or Steinway for the same amount.

Both allowed the fact they would gladly resign the Aeolian business for either of the others, however, while waiting for that call, suppose we make our deadline.

I persisted and reluctantly, a tour of the Aeolian factory in Upstate New York was arranged. I was assured that "we don't do this with all our clients" and my knowledge as to the value of company time was greatly reinforced.

The tour of the plant lasted two days and although the care and construction appeared meticulous, $5,000 still seemed to be a lot of money.

Just before leaving, I was escorted into the showroom by the National Sales Manager. In an elegant setting sat their piano alongside the comparably priced Steinway and Baldwin.

"They sure do look alike," I commented.

"They sure do. About the only real difference is the shipping weight—ours is heavier."

"Heavier?" I asked. "What makes ours heavier?"

"The Capo d'astro bar."

"What's a Capo d'astro bar?"

"Here, I'll show you. Get down on your knees."

Once under the piano he pointed to a metallic bar fixed across the harp and bearing down on the highest octaves. "It takes 50 years before the harp in the piano warps. That's when the Capo d'astro bar goes to work. It prevents that warping."

I left the National Sales Manager under his piano and dove under the Baldwin to find a Tinkertoy Capo d'astro bar at best. Same with the Steinway.

"You mean the Capo d'astro bar really doesn't go to work for 50 years?" I asked.

"Well, there's got to be some reason why the Met uses it," he casually added.

I froze. "Are you telling me that the Metropolitan Opera House in New York City uses this piano?"

"Sure. And their Capo d'astro bar should be working by now."

Upstate New York looks nothing like the front of the Metropolitan Opera House where I met the legendary Carmen, Risë Stevens. She was now in charge of moving the Metropolitan Opera House to the Lincoln Center.

Ms. Stevens told me, "About the only thing the Met is taking with them is their piano."

That quote was the headline of our first ad.

The result created a six year wait between order and delivery.

My point is this. No matter what the account, I promise you, the Capo d'astro bar is there.

I found it hidden inside Burlington Mills' stay-up sock.

I found it within the rough, tough skin of the Baggies' Alligator.

Equitable's computers stored it and Master Charge built it into their convenience.

It was there in the 1,001 uses of Handi Wipes and saturated amongst the tangles and split ends of Clairol's world.

I found it in people. People like Ernest Gallo who, during my three year stint as Y&R's Creative Director, proved to be as dedicated to perfection in his art as I am to mine.

And most recently, I found it in Bob Kresser.

Bob's total involvement in our clients' marketing is as vital to him as the air he breathes.

Maybe that's how we've managed to attract the finest caliber of talent in the country. People who understand the trust our clients place in us.

In short, no one at Kresser & Robbins is in advertising because it beats heavy lifting.

That's why we practically doubled our billing in the past year alone.

If you put the same care into your product as we put in ours and no one has been gutsy enough to dig it out, call Bud Robbins at (213) 553-8254 and just say, "I'm looking for my Capo d'astro bar."

Kresser & Robbins, Inc.
2049 Century Park East / Los Angeles, California 90067 / Advertising & Public Relations

Home of the Capo d'astro bar.

tween the words. Surprisingly, many advertising people miss the point of the assignment because they have preconceived ideas about the problem. Clients may also be sitting on an answer, but can't see it because they are too close. That's where your outside viewpoint is valuable.

Hal Newsom, president and creative director of Cole and Weber, said in a *Wall Street Journal* advertisement, "No one has ever found an advertising solution by talking. But thousands of brilliant solutions are discovered by listening, by hearing what people have to say." He points to the critical task of listening to the client. "Clients can give you the answer, if you can listen and hear."[22]

A more formal way to listen is to use a focus group. Get people together, set up a tape recorder, develop a list of topics, and then let the people talk. Focus groups are useful because you can use the synergism of different people's comments to elicit responses beyond anything you might think to ask. People bounce off one another in a group interview—one idea leads to another. Copywriters spend hours listening to tapes of focus groups. Often, they sit in on the sessions and watch from behind one-way windows. In some situations they can even send follow-up questions to pursue interesting lines of thought.

Use.   A cardinal sin for creatives is to develop advertising for a product with which they are not personally familiar. Use it, taste it, drive it, touch it, test it. In a tribute to Bernice Fitz-Gibbon, when she was named to the Advertising Hall of Fame, Reva Korda tells a story about the importance of familiarity with the product. Fitz-Gibbon was head of advertising at Gimbels in New York and was a legendary figure in retail advertising. Korda recounts: "I remember Fitz fired a girl because the poor wretch didn't know if the belt on a dress she had written about was a self belt, or a leather belt. It turned out she had actually written about the dress without ever having seen it."[23]

The necessity to know the product explains why Campbell Ewald people drive Chevys. And the loyalty lasts. There are still people at Foote Cone & Belding who drive Edsels. A story is told about Leo Burnett, who, later in his life, suffered from low blood sugar that caused him to grow faint. At an annual Kellogg's marketing meeting, he grew weak and collapsed into a chair whispering "candy bar." One of his staff ran to a vending machine and Burnett called after him: "Geno, make sure it's a Nestle!"[24]

Work.   Foote Cone & Belding has a program of consumer research involving both the creative and the research departments. Called "Know the Consumer,"[25] the FCB program puts the creatives out "on the street" to meet the person they must persuade, either in person, in groups, in face-to-face dialogue, over the phone, or in any of a dozen other types of encounters.

One copywriter went back to an inner-city neighborhood where he grew up to shoot baskets with the kids. He was working on the Sears Winners gym shoes account. And he learned that the hero figures in the youngsters' lives were their big brothers; this little piece of understanding became the heart of an advertisement that "sold shoes like crazy."

FCB won the Pizza Hut account because the creatives actually worked in a Pizza Hut and found that "eating pizza is a sensual, gratifying, sharing, uninhibiting experience," according to Bill Baker, executive creative director. They observed what in retrospect seems obvious—that eating pizza is gooey, that you eat it with your fingers and smear sauce and cheese on your face and hands. It's a totally uninhibited experience. From this work experience came the theme for the winning speculative campaign: "Let yourself go at Pizza Hut."

Types of Information

The preceding discussion of ways to get information also outlines the type of information needed: marketplace, product, and consumer. Advertising should operate under a marketing plan. Some of the information you need will be in that document, although often not to the depth you need to develop a creative strategy.

Marketplace.   What's the economic health of the industry? Is it growing, declining, maintaining? Is it crowded? Is there room for growth or for a line extension? Obviously, you need the standard marketing information about share of market—who leads, who's moving up, who's declining. No market is static, always try to flesh out the share-of-market data with a picture of the dynamics of the market.

Hal Riney, the head of Ogilvy and Mather's west coast offices, developed such a feel for the marketplace for one of his clients, Blitz Weinhard, a popularly priced regional beer, that he was able to suggest a line extension. Riney felt the time was right for the company to market a superpremium brand. It took two years for the brewmaster to develop the beer, Henry Weinhard's Private Reserve, but when it hit the market it became a major success story in the beer industry. The firm's president said, "Hal just orchestrated everything along the line. He had a feel for the market that, frankly, we just didn't have."[26]

The company is another subject for backgrounding. Start with corporate history. Describe the staff and key executives. What are the sales objectives? Investigate the company's pricing and profit picture. What are the gross profits, total advertising expenditures, and advertising costs per unit? Is this a profitable line? How is distribution handled? Is there a geographical factor? How is the distribution system organized—retailers, distributors, sales reps, franchises, dealers? Analyze the packaging decisions and options. What is the prospect's image of the company? Collect all the client's past advertising.

In addition to finding out about the industry and the company, you also need to know everything there is to know about the competitive situation. Who are the competitors—both direct and indirect? If you ask people who Hallmark's competition is, they will probably respond with the name of other greeting card companies. The real competitor for Hallmark, however, is the telephone, and Hallmark and Bell have been locked in a serious battle for the "sentiment" market. You have to dig beyond the surface to understand the complexities of the competitive situation.

Investigate the competition's promotional strategies. What attributes are they featuring, what positions are they taking? What are the various product images—both yours and the competition's? Build a file of all advertising by all competitors. You need to know every headline, every copy point, every slogan that's in use or has been used. There's nothing more embarrassing than to propose a great new idea to a client only to find that it is something that was discarded by the competition five years ago.

Product.   When you do background research for your product, get excited about it. There is no such thing as a dull product. Someone invented it, and to invent it they had to see a need. It was created to solve some problem. In doing your research, you want to reexperience the excitement of creating that product. Develop the initial enthusiasm that the product's inventor must have felt as the product was being developed.

Shirley Polykoff, the first "living lady" to be elected to the Advertising Hall of Fame, is best known for her work with cosmetics and hair color. She legitimized the idea of women coloring hair. Prior to her famous campaign, "Does she, or doesn't she?", women who colored their hair were thought to be "loose."

Polykoff said in an interview in *Advertising Age* that "for me the reality of the product's performance has always been of vital importance."[27] But it goes further than just performance. She also believes in the product. Polykoff explains, "I really do believe in the promise of cosmetics—hair coloring and all those things I usually write about." She continues, "I believe cosmetics do make me look prettier. What's even more important, they make me feel prettier—and younger."

In order to develop convincing advertisements, *you* have to be convinced and the degree of your conviction is often dependent upon the adequacy of your research—how much you know about your product. Investigate the details. You would be surprised how much there is to know about something as simple as a pencil, a nail, or a paperclip. There are lots of features designed into every single object. If a hairpin is complicated, think how much more challenging a tire must be—or a television set.

Consumer.   When you do background audience research, you are trying to find out everything you can about the potential prospects. At this point in the process, you are not making any decisions about targeting—that comes later in the strategy stage. What you're doing here is spreading your net and sweeping up every little bit of information you can about people who might be your prospects.

Look at your present users—are there any differences between light and heavy users? Who are the nonusers and why are they not using your product? Who uses your competitor's product, and is there any difference between their users and yours? If it's a new product, then you will be looking for people who face the problem, whatever it is, that this product was designed to solve.

Know your audience intimately. You want to know everything from demographic characteristics like age, sex, income, level of education, and marital status to the psychographic characteristics that describe their personality and lifestyle. The demographic data are the essential first step. They identify your prospects in terms of certain "locater" variables. Demographic data draw boundaries around groups of people. They discriminate between those who are in and those who are out.

But demographics are not enough. Creatives, in particular, need a richer picture of their potential prospects. Middle income, for example, just doesn't mean much. Professors may make less than plumbers, but they see themselves in different ways—and their interests are likely to be quite different even though they are both "middle income."

In order to see the critical patterns in those statistics, you need to get psychographic information as well. Psychographic data consider such factors as lifestyle, activities, interests, opinions, personalities, and buying behavior.

Creatives don't always get to work on product assignments where they identify with the prospects. That's one of the biggest challenges in advertising—how can basically white, well-educated, urbane, upper middle-income copywriters write copy to people in other, sometimes radically different, social strata?

Bill Baker, executive creative director at Foote Cone & Belding, commented, "All of us in advertising seem to work in tall, air-conditioned buildings downtown. We spend an awful lot of time talking to each other on and off the job."[28] Baker is describing a form of social myopia, a serious disease that affects many in advertising. He continues, "We are probably—by traditional demographic definition, not to mention lifestyle—quite different than the persons we must persuade."

There are some who say that David Ogilvy was so successful, in part, because he was working with clients like Hathaway, Rolls-Royce, and Guinness, clients that matched his lifestyle. That's unusual in this business and rarely true for fledgling creatives. More likely, you'll be in Bill Baker's position when he commented: "The members of this focus group are as foreign to me as the people in the bar scene in Star Wars."

Self-image is a critical part of the psychographic profile. It may well be that self-image is the most important variable in the customer's purchasing decision. Find out who *they think* they are. An example of that is the change in the motorcycle market. In the sixties only "bikers" in black leather jackets rode motorcycles. Then Honda came along, said, "Nice People Ride Hondas," and changed the marketplace. It became okay for people who don't see themselves as "bikers" to ride motorcycles.

E. E. Norris, executive VP at BBDO, described in an *Advertising Age* article a BBDO research technique called "Problem Detection."[29] The first step is to develop a list of potential consumer problems related to a product. Norris comments, "As a generality, we can now come up with more than 100 possible problems for virtually every product or service in existence."

Step two is to determine the "Big Problem" by interviewing 150 prime prospects. The consumers are asked to rank each problem in terms of whether the problem is important, whether it occurs frequently, and whether the solution to the problem has been offered by some other product or service. The bigger the score, the bigger the opportunity.

Norris explains that most traditional consumer research is done in terms of consumer benefits and product attributes. He criticizes this kind of research because it tells you only what consumers have been hearing in other advertising. As an example, he cites BBDO research into the dog food market. The attribute/benefit studies found that consumers identified *balanced diet, good nutrition,* and *contains vitamins* as the three most wanted attributes. In contrast, "Problem Detection" found that the three biggest consumer problems were: *it smells bad, it costs too much, it doesn't come in different sizes for different dogs.*

Norris also points out that Problem Detection lets you monitor an advertising strategy and change it when the market changes. For example, when BBDO got the Burger King account, the research indicated that one of the consumer problems was that the burgers were too small. BBDO's promotion of the "whopper" turned that problem around. But then all the burger places started advertising burger size. The continuing research indicated that a new salient problem for consumers was that the hamburgers were all prefabricated with the same lettuce, pickles, and ketchup. BBDO spoke to that problem with the campaign, "Have it your way."

Beyond demographics, psychographics, self-concepts, and consumer problems, there's still more to audience analysis. To write believable advertising copy you will need to get a fix on the whole person. The details mentioned above are important, but so is the total picture. Why do Tom and Bob buy different cars (or any other relevant product) when they are the same age, income, educational level, profession, and live in the same neighborhood? Dig deep and probe the psyche of the whole person to explain these differences in buying behavior.

There are packaged research sources, like Simmons, for demographic information. Sometimes your client will have its own market research that includes demographics. But most psychographic data has to be obtained directly from the source. That means interviews—in-depth interviews, projective studies, focus groups, and street corner surveys.

Another source of audience information is your own intuition. Most experienced copywriters will warn you against projecting your own needs and views into the minds of your target, but your own intuition is still a good source for "crap detection." You can spot phony lines and insincere statements. And, as you become more skilled at audience analysis, then you will be better able to rely on personal intuition as an information source.

Shirley Polykoff explains, "It's only when you know yourself—when you can dig deep into your own motivations and recognize them—that you can understand what it is other people want."[30] You are a reservoir of personal experiences.

While you may not be able to decide the best appeal for a target entirely unlike yourself, you do share certain universal needs and face universal problems. In those areas your own intuition is a valuable resource.

Hand in hand with intuition is empathy. Leo Burnett put it bluntly, "If you can't turn yourself into your customer, you probably don't belong in the business."[31] Empathy means you have to be able to project yourself into other people's minds, lives, needs, and problems.

Alton Ketchum, in an article titled, "Creating Under Pressure," describes an exercise called "imaginative empathy," used to tutor actors. Ketchum says, "The copywriter who sets out to sell toothpaste must project himself into the whole state of mind of the prospect who has just risen and, bleary of eye and furry of mouth, is fumbling in the medicine closet for the tube and brush. He must feel the glad glow that accompanies the ritual of brushing."[32]

The ability to empathize was cited by Carl Hixon, in an *Advertising Age* article on Leo Burnett, as one of the advertising giant's greatest strengths. Hixon explains, Leo Burnett was a small shy boy from a small town in Michigan. "Perhaps in his shyness he learned to 'imaginate' himself out of himself and into the identities of other people, where he could feel their feelings and understand their wants." Hixon describes this ability to "imaginate" as an almost mystical sensitivity. People who have it have "this odd, sad experience of being extra-social, detached from their own society and therefore able to travel easily in their imagination to another, where—like watchers from a distant planet—they observe and relate but never belong."[33]

Background research is hard work. It calls for ability to read technical documents, puzzle out profit-and-loss statements, interview prospects, probe insights, identify beliefs and problems, and empathize with people from all walks of life. Like all first steps, background research is critical. If it isn't thorough, then your strategy may very well stumble and your creative ideas may be totally off target.

In an article on associative thinking,[34] the authors put it all in perspective when they observed that creative people need research in order to be creative. "The highly creative person has more ability to associate research data into problem-solving communications than has the less creative person." They explain that this relationship accentuates the importance of research to the creative process since facts are essential to association.

1.3 CREATIVE THINKING TECHNIQUES

There are a number of things you can do to improve your associative abilities. First of all, practice. Free association is a loosening up exercise, a way to get mentally limber. Many copywriters doodle with words when they first sit down to write copy. All they are doing is "wordstorming"—free association with words.

If you are sitting on a bus or in a car, you can do the same exercise with a pencil and piece of scrap paper.

Free association is a serendipity process—anything that comes to mind is relevant. Anything goes. What you are doing is unleashing your subconscious. This does take some practice because most of us have learned to keep our subconscious tightly controlled, chained, and restrained. In free association you take the chains off.

The associations are pieces of ideas, fragments—not well-turned phrases and constructed essays. Cultivate the ridiculous idea; search for nonsense. You loosen up when you laugh, so humor is a useful part of the mindset. When you feel relaxed and loose, then try for some exaggerated ideas. Push for the zany, crazy, totally unrealistic ideas. You can tone down the off-the-wall idea, but it's impossible to pump life into a tired one.

Quantity.   One thing you can do to improve your free association ability is to strive for quantity. Relax and practice until your lists get longer and longer. The idea is that the more material you have to work with, the more chances you will have of finding an idea with some potential. So work fast and push yourself to come up with more and more associations.

A study of free association conducted at Michigan State University found that the more ideas you come up with, the better your chances of having "good" ideas.[35] Students were asked to come up with one, three, five, and eight ideas. The researchers found that "increasing the number of creative alternatives increases the chance of finding the 'best' creative idea."

Chains and breaks.   Study how the free association process works. Look at your lists of words. Can you see the chaining process that holds the associations together? Notice how the words move along on one track, and then all of a sudden jump to an entirely different topic. That's called a break in the chain.

Cultivate those breaks in the chain. When you jump tracks from one category to another, you're beginning to develop what de Bono calls "lateral thinking." There are some who define creativity as the ability to break away from conventional sequences of thought. That's exactly what happens when you break the association chain. You're in a rut if you continue to move down the same track.

You may not realize it, but what you are doing with these exercises is developing the two aptitudes of *fluency* and *flexibility* that Guilford's Structure-of-the-Intellect model equated with creative thinking.[36]

Imagery.   Another way to improve your associative skill is to try associating, not with words, but with visual images. What pictures do you see in your mind when you think of words like "bank," "bush," and "guide"? When you do visual associations you write down, not words that come to mind, but descriptions of the pictures you see in your mind. Obviously, what is happening here is that you are expanding your capacity for visual imagery.

Once you feel comfortable with visual associations, move through the other senses. What do you hear in your mind's ear when you think of music?

What do you smell when you think of spring or the ocean? What do you taste when you think of ice cream? What do you feel when you think of roller skating? Tune in to your senses and develop your ability to make note of the sensations that come to mind. That's the hardest part—training yourself to make note of your own responses and then finding words to express them. It gets easier, but you have to practice. The point of all this is that the association ability can be developed. Some people have tremendous ability to begin with, but everyone has some talent in this area and we can all improve. Regardless of whether you have great musical ability, you can improve your ability to play the piano or sing— with practice. You have creative ability and you can come up with ideas.

Brainstorming

The discussion so far has focused on individual thinking. Individual ideation is important but advertising also uses a type of group ideation called brainstorming. This concept was developed in the late 1930s by Alex Osborn,[37] president of BBDO. His agency, along with many other agencies and corporations, has used brainstorming for group problem solving and generating ideas.

Brainstorming uses the brainpower of a number of people to intensify divergent thinking and increase the number of available ideas. It's a synergistic approach using free association in a group environment. Like a chain of fire-crackers, my idea bounces off yours and both of our ideas spark other ideas in other people's minds. It's a game of compound interest with the number of ideas exceeding any one person's contributions in an equivalent amount of time. Both the fluency and flexibility of a group is thought to be higher than that of one individual.

There is still a very important role for individuals. Groups don't write copy or design ads. They may be able to generate ideas, but the implementation and development is still left to the lonely individual at the board or the typewriter.

Brainstorming groups are used to teach individuals how to free associate so they can work on their own. Brainstorming is useful in situations where a number of people have pieces of the puzzle and you have to get them together to sort it all out. Also, ideas generated by a group tend to have a higher level of acceptance than do ideas contributed by individuals working alone. There is more participation and less ego involvement.

Collaboration. Ideas, after all, still come from one mind at a time, so the individual is still the heart of the ideation process. *Collaboration* is useful primarily as a supplement to the individual effort.

The most common collaboration is the partnership between a copywriter and an art director. Two people who work well together are teamed in most agencies, and work assignments are distributed to get the maximum use of a talented combination. Some people are on the same "wave length" and stimulate each other. Others couldn't find their way out of a paper bag together. Agencies encourage the natural teams.

Group collaboration may be planned or extemporaneous. An individual or team working on a particularly difficult problem may get a group of kindred spirits together to kick ideas around. Anyone who walks by is part of the group.

Defer judgment.   Osborn outlined four rules to guide brainstorming. The first and most critical is to defer judgment. Brainstorming feeds on a positive environment and, to make it work, all criticism must be ruled out. That doesn't mean there is no place for evaluation—in fact, evaluation is very important—but it comes at the end of the process. Osborn mentions that a number of research projects have shown that a group will produce twice as many good ideas in a spirit of cooperation and contagious enthusiasm when judgment is deferred. The idea is to separate idea generation from idea evaluation.

Quantity.   Osborn's second rule is to go for quantity. Pile up as many ideas as possible. Each one stimulates another line of thought and every one might possibly have the clue to a final solution. Brainstorming groups can easily compile 80 to 100 ideas in a 15-minute session. Hour-long sessions report ideas in the thousands. Fill the board, fill the pad, fill the wall—keep pushing your group to come up with more and more and more.

Playfulness.   This rule relates to attitude. Osborn insists that free-wheeling is welcome. Osborn suggests a spirit of playfulness. Shoot wild. Push yourself and the group to come up with wild and zany, off-the-wall ideas. Remember there's no evaluation at this stage, so nothing is inappropriate or foolish. Use humor, cultivate exaggeration. The truly original solution is more likely to be developed from a wild and zany idea than from a routine comment. Work on the edge of the silly.

Reprocessing.   Osborn's fourth rule is a suggestion for procedure: combine and improve. Ideas grow on one another and good ideas can become better. Every idea can be reconsidered in terms of how it can be improved. Osborn calls this "reprocessing." Can it be modified, combined, twisted, applied in a different context, and so on? Piggyback your ideas.

Group spirit.   In addition to Osborn's four rules, there are a number of other suggestions on how to make a brainstorming session work. The important thing is the spirit of the group. There needs to be a spirit of mutual encouragement. Nothing is taken personally; no one's ego is at stake. No one is trying to show off or score points.

The group spirit depends on a delicate balance of intensity and relaxation. Osborn says it should be a mental set where everyone is relaxed but trying hard. That's more difficult than it may sound. You have to be relaxed for the free association process to work, but you need a spirit of intensity to move beyond the partying mentality. It's like getting serious about playing a game—or making a game out of hitting a target.

Size.   Most formal brainstorming groups operate with 10 to 12 members, although they can function with as few as six and still be productive. Most research has found that the more people, the more ideas. However, the more people, the fewer the number of contributions per person. If you're working with a larger group, try to keep the group cohesive and avoid breaking up spontaneously into small groups.

Leader and recorder.   Appoint a leader, preferably someone skilled at leading brainstorming sessions. This person directs the effort in the beginning while you're trying to get the group momentum up as well as during the periods when the pace slows. The leader should also find ways to get everyone involved as well as limit the influence of any dominant individuals who might try to take over the session. One way to control participation is to use a technique called group sequencing, where everyone gives an idea in turn, ending the series with the person who has tried to dominate.

In terms of group composition it is useful, especially at the beginning, to have a few people in the group who are self-starters. They serve as spark plugs and their enthusiasm tends to ignite everyone else.

A recorder is needed to keep track of the ideas—*all* of the ideas. Sometimes you may work with a visual recording system—writing on a blackboard, a big piece of kraft paper taped to the wall, or a newsprint pad. The public recording is useful because it stimulates the reprocessing function. You often get new ideas from something that was said earlier.

The leader can function as recorder, although it is easier to have a second person doing the writing. If a visible recording system isn't available, then the recorder can make notes on a yellow pad.

Evaluation.   When the idea generation session is over, then it's time for evaluation. It's a good idea to maintain the same positive attitude in this stage as well. Sort the ideas looking for "possibles." In other words, avoid criticizing any of the ideas. Don't look for losers. There's no point in pointing out weaknesses. Focus only on the ideas that have potential. And keep sorting on that basis, each time narrowing the field.

Getting started.   One of the biggest problems with group sessions is getting started. A common technique used in advertising is attribute sorting. By simply listing the features of the product or service, you're beginning to get everyone's mind in gear. Next, move to benefit sorting, which is another way of listing features, this time in terms of the user. All of that is pretty dry, so you will have to throw in something to pull them away from rational "strategic" thinking. One way is to use the Synectics method of metaphor building.[38] Take each attribute or feature and ask what it's like in terms of an analogy or a metaphor. You can force free-wheeling by locating the metaphor. For example, ask how each attribute relates to something in a zoo or a garage or a schoolroom, and so on.

De Bono has a number of interesting techniques for overcoming inertia.[39] One of them, of course, is analogy. His other techniques all attempt to force divergent thinking. One method is random stimulation. He suggests you let group attention wander at random. You can move from item to item in the room you're in and see if there is any connection between that and the topic. Dictionaries and other books are useful. Open it to any page and put your finger on a spot—how does that word relate to your topic? Is there any trigger? Any connection?

De Bono also suggests two techniques relating to the product itself. The first is to *fractionalize* it by breaking it into pieces. Dissect it. Use each individual feature as a trigger. The other approach is *reversal*. Discuss the product in terms of what it isn't. Look at opposites. That's the approach that resulted in the highly successful "Un-cola" campaign.

Blocks.   There are blocks to brainstorming, just like there are to free association and other types of creative thinking. Now all those personal fears are compounded by public attention. Most of the fears that gum up brainstorming relate to the group environment: "What will the others think of me?" *The Universal Traveler*[40] details the debilitating effects of these fears. Here are some of the fears listed in *The Traveler:* fear of making mistakes, fear of being seen as foolish, fear of being criticized, fear of being misused, fear of being alone (any person with a new idea is automatically a minority of one), fear of disturbing traditions, fear of being associated with taboos, fear of losing the security of habit, fear of losing the respect of the group, fear of truly being an individual. These are mostly internalized fears and have to be worked on by the individual alone.

The only way to get over this kind of fear is to go to the wall with it—alone. If you practice free association while you are walking or riding, no one knows what's going on in your mind. So deliberately try to associate ideas, looking for the most stupid ones you can find. You will find out it isn't easy to come up with stupid ideas and, when you do, they may be the wild and zany ones you envied in others.

There are a few things the leader and the group members can do to help overcome the fright. First, stick absolutely to the principle of *defer judgment*. If there's no finger-pointing, no one can be made to look foolish. Mutual encouragement may help overcome some of these fears. Lots of positive responses ("that's good") may help. Develop the list of ideas, the raw materials, then go back and review them. Don't try to evaluate as you go because it dampens the spirit.

You can force people to venture and see that the experience isn't threatening by using the group sequencing technique where everyone speaks in order. Most of these fears can be overcome simply through experience. Once you've tried it and didn't get hurt, then it's easier the second time.

Alex Osborn described a number of cramps to creativity in his book, *Applied Imagination.*[41] In addition to the problem of ill-timed criticism, he also points to enthusiasm and positive attitude. It takes lots of alternatives to find a good idea. Someone who is negative minded will usually give up too soon. Osborn also mentions the fear of feeling foolish, timidity, and self-discouragement.

Rollo May in *The Courage to Create*[42] describes rigidity as another obstacle to creativity. Rigidity is seen in a lack of flexibility in thinking. May explains that insight always destroys something—something that was previously believed. It breaks through and tosses out old ideas and preconceptions. There's always resistance to new ideas. That's why so much advertising uses tried-and-true approaches. It's easier to copy an old formula than to fight the anxiety generated by a new idea. Keep this in mind: if it is truly a new idea, it will always create tension and resistance. Remember also that a bad idea will generate resistance. You have to be able to see the difference.

A common type of rigidity that shows up in advertising comes from an overdependence on strategy and research findings. Strategy is just a place to get started, it's rarely the expression of an inspired idea. John Fiedler, senior VP and executive director of research at Ted Bates, recognizes the limitations of research-bound creativity: "Carefully analyzed, beautifully charted, intelligently presented research briefings rarely inspire creativity." He continues, "I don't know of a single creative problem which, when it was surrounded by research, surrendered." He explains, "Creativity often arises from and flourishes in an atmosphere of inconsistency and incongruity, which is why creatives often want to see pieces of information, not compiled, but separate."[43]

Breakthroughs.   One of the biggest advantages of brainstorming in groups as opposed to working alone is that it can be an exhilarating, exciting, almost surrealistic experience. When a number of people loosen up and start associating, the ideas generated will astound you. And one or two zany thinkers can pull everyone into the deep water of unselfconscious spontaneous associaiton—an experience some individuals will never know on their own. There's something magical about being part of such a group. It's a real emotional high.

1.4 THE CREATIVE CONCEPT

With this discussion of creative thinking and visual imagery, you are probably wondering how all this relates to the daily work of the advertising professional. People in advertising, particularly people who work on the creative side of advertising, have to come up with the "Big Idea." Behind every ad, behind every campaign, behind every sales promotion, is a Big Idea. We'll refer to this as the creative concept. Every type of creative advertising assignment will revolve around the development of a dynamic creative concept. "Revolve" is a good term to use here because, until you come up with the creative concept, you will feel like you are going in circles.

A *creative concept* is hard to define in anything other than generalities. Marybeth Lareau, formerly a senior VP/creative director at Norman Craig & Kummel, discussed it in an article in *Madison Avenue*.[44] She defined it as "the central idea conveyed by the advertising." She further described it as "ideally pre-empting the competition. Usually, it either describes a product-related idea based on a product attribute or benefit, or it conjures up an image of a product." She concluded, "Naturally, it must stem from the strategy."

Sometimes you can identify the central idea from a slogan or headline used in the advertising, such as Frank Perdue's "It takes a tough man to make a tender chicken." Perdue is featured in the print and television ads as a tough-talking businessman/farmer who is a fanatic about quality in his chickens. Quality, of course, is expressed as tender meat.

The Samsonite Survivor luggage picks up on the Indiana Jones craze and uses an adventurer in jungle settings. The name of the line, Survivor, labels the concept and the various creative messages use the exotic adventures to dramatize the concept.

Comprehension.   You should be able to look at any ad or any ad proposal and ask yourself: *What's the point?* Whatever the point is, that's the creative concept. If you can't puzzle it out, either it isn't clearly communicated or it simply isn't there. Believe it or not, there are pointless ads being developed and sold to clients. A greater problem, however, is that the message is too complicated or too fragmented to deliver a coherent idea. The idea might be great, but it can also be too complicated to communicate easily in an advertisement. Another problem is an ad that's trying to do too many things. A single-minded ad rarely has a problem with its creative concept. The creative concept should be simple and clear and obvious. No matter how involved the execution, you should be able to put your finger on the heart of the message without any hesitation. What is it that you, or this ad, is trying to say?

Attention and memorability.   There are two other critical dimensions of an effective creative concept. It should be attention getting and memorable. Both of these factors are a product of the execution. Attention and memorability are created by the words and the pictures and the music. Creative concepts are also defined as "unique treatments," and it is the magic of the execution that makes these treatments unique.

The Samsonite campaign just mentioned uses "borrowed interest" to create advertising that is totally unique in the category of luggage advertising. As the Indiana Jones phenomenon spreads through the culture, then this particular idea may no longer be unique. As a matter of fact, that is a common problem for truly unique ideas. They are arresting while they are fresh; they become clichés after they have been borrowed too many times.

Gimmicks and "twists" on clichés are often used to create unique treatments for a message. In addition to becoming old, they have another problem. As Leo Bogart explained in his book *Strategy in Advertising,* "Advertising ideas misfire when the gimmickry buries or overwhelms the product or contradicts its appeal."[45] Be careful of glitzy, dazzling executions that mask an empty message.

An example of a campaign that uses a high level of gimmickry to create a novel and arresting creative concept is one by the American Museum of Natural History. This campaign used brochures, coloring books, subway posters, and other unconventional media to promote museum attendance. The idea was to create mythical dinosaurs with twentieth-century characteristics. The creatures come in parts and you can even assemble your own. Some of the creatures created by the advertising team and used in the promotions included "Thesaurus Rex," which they described with the following copy:

> A dinosaur with a vocabulary of 1,000 words?
>
> Instruments capable of detecting prehistoric sounds have recently made this remarkable discovery.
>
> The Thesaurus Rex originated in Great Britain. During the Rococo period it migrated to the South where it quickly became Italicized.
>
> Scientists believe its diet was rich in pronouns and probably included phrase fruit and synonym. Perhaps its most satisfying meals consisted of Grammar's Cookies and Mother Tongue.
>
> Equipped with only a semicolon, Thesaurus Rex experienced severe difficulty with its vowels and ate itself into extinction.
>
> Animals with large vocabularies visit the American Museum of Natural History every day. They come to see dinosaurs, minerals, and a variety of exciting exhibits, 79th Street and Central Park West.

The perfect fit.   While a unique treatment is essential in devising creative concepts, it is also important to find a "Big Idea" that fits the product, the audience, and the situation. Sometimes the best idea is the obvious one. You can scratch around and try to create something that is unexpected and find all your effort is going into the search for novelty. In fact, you may be looking at the idea, but it was so obvious you couldn't see it.

Ogilvy and Mather distributes a little book to its employees titled, *Obvious Adams*. The book is written in turn-of-the-century literary style and it recounts the career of an early (mythical) advertising genius whose one great gift was the ability to see the obvious solution.

The point is that there is a certain elegance in an idea that fits perfectly and solves the problem neatly. Mathematicians speak of a formula as being both elegant and parsimonious. What this means is that it is a solution that fits perfectly and has no wasted effort. This doesn't mean the idea is dull or bland, it just communicates its message perfectly and economically.

An example of student work that uses the elegance and parsimony of the obvious solution is one created by a team of Michigan State students that won the national student advertising competition sponsored by the American Advertising Federation. The assignment was to develop a campaign for Coors Beer to use with the college student market. The students went round and round with dozens, even hundreds, of ideas—many of them fancy, contrived, and convoluted.

Finally, against deadline, they decided to use the idea of "college life." It seemed so obvious they almost didn't use it. The slogan, "Coors, the taste of college life," positioned Coors as *the beer* of the college market and the executions focused on the crazy, zany side of college, all the things college memories are built on.

In an earlier AAF competition, where the product was Rold Gold pretzels, the San Jose State University team won with the theme: "The only pretzel worth its salt." Once again, the simplest and most obvious idea was clearly the winner. Everyone in the room said to themselves: *Gee, I wish I had thought of that.* That's the kind of response that comes when an idea is both unexpected and fits perfectly.

There's another consideration in looking for the perfect, but obvious, solution. It often is just a little below the surface. You get so involved in trying to come up with something cute and novel, that it is difficult to spot the great idea that is hiding under the contrived situations and fancy phrases. Sometimes just simplifying will expose the Big Idea that you couldn't see because of the verbiage.

Visual and Verbal

An effective creative concept, then, is one that communicates a clear central idea with a unique treatment that is both attention getting and memorable. This clever idea that makes a good advertisement original and distinctive is a perfect package of verbal and visual elements. All media use both words and pictures—including radio, where the visual is created in your mind. Both the visual and verbal are important and in an effective message they will be integrated and interactive—one reinforcing the other. (See Exhibit 1-3.)

One person who brought the verbal and visual together was Bill Bernbach, and it is clear in the work of his agency that art directors and copywriters get equal time. Some of the finest advertising ever done by Doyle Dane Bernbach illustrates the perfect marriage of visual and verbal.

The classic VW advertising campaign includes a stark picture of a lowly VW Beetle with the headline, "Lemon." Another classic is one for the VW bus that shows a group of nuns with the headline, "Mass transit." One of the greatest VW television spots opens with a man climbing into a VW Beetle on a dark snowy morning and, as he drives through the storm, the announcer asks: "Have you ever wondered how the man who drives the snowplow gets to the snowplow?"

Rather than argue the relative merits of visual and verbal, it might be more constructive to follow the Bernbach model and strive for the perfect blend of words and pictures. Obviously, the strategy may dictate a particular type of ad depending upon the objectives. A heavy copy ad with a strong direct response appeal may, in fact, need a verbal emphasis. An arresting visual might even get in the way of the promise. An image campaign may need a strong visual with words used as brand reminder. The Marlboro man can never say anything that speaks as well as his silence.

EXHIBIT 1-3:   "Or buy a Volkswagen" employs an interesting use of closure to involve the reader in the creation of the message concept. (This ad is used with express permission of Volkswagen of America, Inc.)

Or buy a Volkswagen.

Birth of a Concept

We'll close this discussion of creative concepts with two case histories. The first is the story behind the "Little Tramp" concept used by the Lord, Geller, Federico, Einstein agency for the introduction of the IBM personal computer. The second is the story about how BBDO developed the "good things" campaign for General Electric.

The Little Tramp.   In an article in *Advertising Age*, Daniel Burstein describes how the "unlikely IBM–Charlie Chaplin marriage came to be."[46] The IBM personal computer appeared on the market late in 1981, long after Apple and Radio Shack had established strong dominance in this market. There was some skepticism that IBM might not even be competitive.

The Lord, Geller agency assigned the introductory campaign to its creative director, Tom Mabley, and its art director, Bob Tore. Mabley explained how he got started. "I closed my door for a month and read every computer magazine I could find. I was trying to figure out how to tell the history of the computer in a 30- or 60-second spot."

Burstein relates that "Mabley and Tore can't remember exactly how the Chaplin idea first came up, but both are certain that when it did, they knew it was perfect." The team was discussing the problems of big computers and their unfriendliness. They knew they had to break down the public fear of the computer and communicate the simplicity of its operation. Furthermore, they knew the market had changed and that "experienced number-crunchers, tinkerers, and electronics enthusiasts had given way to the ordinary mortal as the chief personality in computer buying's demography."

Tore recalls their initial thinking as visual. "We had the idea of showing the history of the computer shrinking—a big white box in a white, sterile room that would get smaller and smaller. We wanted to have a person reacting to it, and with all that white background, we obviously needed a character in a black suit to stand out."

Mabley recalls that they decided they needed a product figure or character, but Dick Cavett was doing Apple and Bill Cosby was working with Texas Instruments so the market was already a little cluttered. "We knew we wanted a single, friendly person who would represent Everyman. But we didn't really see a need for on-camera dialogue. That pointed to mime."

They considered Marcel Marceau and some other mimes, but the figure in black who doesn't speak was obviously Charlie Chaplin. Mabley explains, "Charlie Chaplin's Little Tramp character is lovable to all kinds of people at all ages. He's vulnerable, but he's clever. He has incredible problems, but he always finds a solution. He's an individual. . . . He's Everyman."

Another little detail is an important part of the concept. There's always a red rose shown against the sterile white environments. According to the creative team, the rose symbolizes the creativity of the human spirit. (See Exhibit 1–4.)

EXHIBIT 1-4: "How to balance the books" is one advertisement of a series used to introduce the IBM personal computer. (Courtesy of IBM)

Good things. General Electric has maintained its own continual, uninterrupted public perception research since the 1950s. In the summer of 1979, both BBDO and Young and Rubicam were asked to develop proposals for a corporate image campaign. At the time both agencies were handling GE business and neither realized that this assignment would turn into a creative shootout. The story is told in a *Madison Avenue* article.[47]

The GE research had found that, while GE products are pervasive and located throughout every home, the public didn't have any coherent perception of the breadth of the corporation's activities. Furthermore, BBDO researchers had found that more and more people looked at GE as old-fashioned and traditional. The image was flat, boring, unexciting—but nice.

Dennis Berger, the BBDO creative director, admitted that it was hard to get excited about this assignment. "We thought this assignment was make-work."

At first the creative team developed two concepts. One was a presenter-style "Do You Believe in Magic?", which endowed the consumer appliances with all manner of attributes. The second was built on the line, "You ain't seen nothing yet." It was criticized because, while intriguing, it was not quite believable and suggested capabilities that GE didn't have at the time.

Their third concept illustrates the idea of thinking through the obvious. Berger explains that it was developed "when we looked at reality." The creative team asked, "What does GE do to make life better?", and that question turned out to be the creative concept and the key to the award-winning campaign. However, it was a long way yet before the idea jelled.

Berger explained, "The one thing we knew was that we were going to use music." He went on, "Any creative person knows that music is a good tool for creating excitement, for changing an image." He added, "We also ruled out humor because it didn't seem appropriate." Len McCaron, vice president and executive art director, said, "We thought of mothers putting their children's pictures up on refrigerator doors with magnets; fathers taping baby's first sounds; kids listening to radios on skateboards."

From such images they began to compose a song starting with lines like, "We make your daughters dance, we wake you to the sun, and so on." They couldn't come up with an ending other than "We make the things that make life good." They brought the pieces of the song to Philip Dusenberry, executive creative director, who thought the ending was the "klunkiest one I ever heard." Dusenberry was haunted by it and, four days later, riding to the office in a cab, he reworded it to "We bring things to life." Still unhappy, he added the word "good" just before "thing." Dusenberry explained that "a good creative director doesn't shove anything down his writers' throats," so he just read it to them and asked what they thought.

This line turned out to be the "magic" that holds the entire campaign together. The executions were developed in vignettes, similar to the original images the crative team used in their brainstorming. When BBDO presented it to

GE executives, the creative team knew by the look on their faces that they had a winner—even before Y&R presented. Furthermore, as it turned out, BBDO got all of the GE business because of the strength of the concept and its ability to be used across all of the GE product lines.

The final campaign uses the vignettes to present the GE product line. Berger explains, "If we featured them, the whole thing would look like a catalogue." The products are portrayed in scenes as true to life as possible and you may see the side of the washer rather than the front, the radio is in the background, and the refrigerator is human scale rather than monumental, like so many appliance ads. But the magic of the GE "good things" concept is that it gives a glimpse of "the sweetest moments in people's lives" and GE is associated with those moments.

NOTES

1. David Mars, "Organizational Climate for Creativity," *Occasional Paper* No. Four (Buffalo, N.Y.: Creative Education Foundation, 1969).

2. J. P. Guilford, "Traits of Personality," in *Creativity and Its Cultivation*, ed. H. H. Anderson (New York: Harper & Brothers, 1959). Also, *The Nature of Human Intelligence* (New York: McGraw-Hill, 1967). Also, "Creativity—Retrospect and Prospect," *Journal of Creative Behavior*, 7:4 (1973), pp. 247–52.

3. James Webb Young, *A Technique for Producing Ideas*, 3rd ed. (Chicago: Crain Books, 1975).

4. S. A. Mednick, "The Associative Basis of the Creative Process," *Psychological Review*, 69 (1962), pp. 220–32.

5. Leonard N. Reid and Herbert Rotfeld, "Toward an Associative Model of Advertising Creative Thinking," *Journal of Advertising*, 5:4 (1976), pp. 24–29.

6. Edward de Bono, *Lateral Thinking: Creativity Step by Step* (New York: Harper and Row, 1970).

7. Bruce G. Vanden Bergh and Keith Adler, "Take This Ten Lesson Course on Managing Creatives Creatively," *Marketing News*, March 18, 1983, sect. 1, p. 22.

8. W. J. J. Gordon, *The Metaphorical Way of Learning and Knowing* (Cambridge: Penguin Books, 1971). Also Jack Fincher, "The New Idea Man," *Human Behavior*, March 1978, pp. 28–32.

9. Betty Edwards, *Drawing on the Right Side of the Brain* (Los Angeles: Tarcher, 1979).

10. Thomas R. Blakeslee, *The Right Brain: A New Understanding of the Unconscious Mind and Its Creative Powers* (New York: Berkley Books, 1983).

11. Harry Reinert, "One Picture Is Worth a Thousand Words? Not Exactly," *Modern Language Journal*, April 1976.

12. John R. Rossiter and Larry Percy, "Attitude Change Through Visual Images in Advertising," *Journal of Advertising*, 9:2 (1980), pp. 10–16.

13. I. A. Taylor, "The Nature of the Creative Process," in *Creativity: An Examination of the Creative Process* (New York: Hastings House, 1959).

14. Young, op. cit.

15. Rollo May, *The Courage to Create* (New York: Norton, 1975).

16. Alex F. Osborn, *Applied Imagination,* 3rd ed. (New York: Scribners, 1963).

17. May, op. cit.

18. Larry Plapler, "Perspectives on Creativity," *Advertising Age,* June 4, 1979, p. S-20.

19. Ron Hoff, "Ron Hoff Talks Corporate Advertising," *Wall Street Journal* house ad that ran in *Advertising Age,* June 27, 1977, pp. 16–17.

20. Joel Raphaelson, "Perspectives in Creativity," *Advertising Age,* June 4, 1979, p. S-19.

21. Leonard N. Reid and Herbert J. Rotfeld, "Toward an Associative Model of Advertising Creativity," *Journal of Advertising,* 5:4 (1976), pp. 24–29.

22. Hal Newsom, "Good Newsom," *Wall Street Journal* house ad that appeared regularly in *Advertising Age.*

23. Reva Korda, "Fond Memories of a Hall of Famer: How Bernice Fitz-Gibbon Trained the Troops," *Advertising Age,* March 29, 1982, p. M-11.

24. Carl Hixon, "Leo," *Advertising Age,* February 8, 1982, p. M-25.

25. Nancy F. Millman, "Don't Shoot Until You Know the Whys of Their Buys," *Advertising Age,* January 16, 1978, p. 36.

26. Joseph H. Winski, "He Swims Against the Tide," *Advertising Age,* April 26, 1982, p. M-6.

27. Shirley Polykoff, "Will You or Won't You Take a Chance," *Advertising Age,* February 1, 1982, p. 45.

28. Millman, op. cit., p. 36.

29. E. E. Norris, "Seek Out the Consumer's Problem," *Advertising Age,* March 17, 1975, pp. 43–44.

30. Polykoff, op. cit.

31. Leo Burnett, "Keep Listening to That Wee, Small Voice," in *Readings in Advertising and Promotion Strategy,* eds. Arnold A. Barban and C. H. Sandage (Homewood, Ill.: Irwin, 1968), p. 155.

32. Alton Ketchum, "Creating Under Pressure," in *Readings in Advertising and Promotion Strategy,* eds. Arnold A. Barban and C. H. Sandage (Homewood, Ill.: Irwin, 1968), p. 149.

33. Hixon, op. cit.

34. Reid and Rotfeld, op. cit.

35. Bruce G. Vanden Bergh, Leonard N. Reid, and Gerald A. Schorin, "How Many Creative Alternatives to Generate," *Journal of Advertising,* 12:4 (1983), pp. 46–49.

36. Guilford, op. cit.

37. Osborn, op. cit.

38. Gordon, op. cit.

39. de Bono, op. cit.

40. Don Koberg and Jim Bagnall, *The Universal Traveler* (Los Altos, Calif.: Kaufmann, 1976).

41. Osborn, op. cit.

42. May, op. cit.

43. John Fiedler, Panel Discussion: "Can a Scorpio Creative Director Find Happiness with a Virgo Researcher?", 1982 AAF Conference, Atlanta.

44. Marybeth Lareau and Wally Olesen, "Is Your Thinking Big Enough to Recognize the Big Idea?", *Madison Avenue*, November 1982, pp. 24–30.

45. Leo Bogart, *Strategy in Advertising* (New York: Harcourt, Brace & World, 1967), p. 83.

46. Daniel Burstein, "Using Yesterday to Sell Tomorrow: How the Unlikely IBM–Charlie Chaplin Marriage Came to Be," *Advertising Age*, April 11, 1983, p. M4–5.

47. Barbara Mehlman, "BBDO Brings 'Good Things' to Client GE," *Madison Avenue*, November 1982, pp. 44–54.

Creative
Strategy

Chapter Two

2.1 MESSAGE STRATEGY

In a guest column in *Adweek*,[1] Malcolm MacDougall, president of SSC&B, emphasized the necessity for strategy and creativity to work together. He said that "advertising people are beginning to realize two simple things: "Brilliant creative execution does not move the consumer unless it is built upon a unique and powerful strategic position and, second, a unique and powerful strategic position will not move the consumer unless it is brought to life with a brilliant creative execution. In advertising, strategy and creative thinking must work hand in hand."

Strategy is a plan of action, a detailed scheme for achieving some goal. A *plan* is a complex, multidimensional document that outlines the procedure to be followed. In it you review important aspects of your situation, identify certain critical decisions that have to be made, evaluate your options, and, finally, choose the best approach. Strategy is based on research—how else can you know what your situation is? And the heart of strategic thinking is an analysis of options.

Developing a creative strategy is like working a jigsaw puzzle, except that there's no guarantee that the pieces will fit. The pieces that you have to work with come from your research findings—your analysis of the marketplace, the product, and the consumer. Your creative strategy develops as you puzzle out the significance of all this information. There are a hundred ways to advertise any product—you have a variety of appeals and selling premises and stratagems to choose from.

These decisions are outlined in a document called a *copy platform* or creative workplan. It begins with the statement of your objectives. Then it usually contains a description of the problem to be solved by the advertising, a summary of the product analysis in terms of its attributes and distinctive features, and a delineation of the targeted audience. Your statement of your creative approach will include a product position statement, the appeal, the selling premise, and a stratagem, which serves as a summary of the creative strategy for this product. You may also include a description of the execution format and a brief outline of the execution details.

The copy platform is a one-page document outlining the essence of your creative strategy. It is a document used within the agency to discuss and agree on an approach. Not all agencies use a document like this, and some use different dimensions or call them by different terms. Some develop a brief statement, others prepare a manuscript complete with discussion and justification. But some kind of document is useful during the planning stage just to make sure everyone agrees on the approach.

Problem Statement

From your preliminary client discussions you should have some general idea of what the problem is to be solved. The *problem statement* should focus on what you hope to accomplish through advertising. In other words, there may be a distribution problem, but that's not something that can be solved with an advertisement. On the other hand, if the consumers see your product as high priced when it really isn't, then that's a problem that can be solved with an advertising message.

You might also remember that the focus is on the product's problem, not your problem. Don't approach this statement in terms of what you have to do, that is, "how can I make this ad exciting and attention getting?" That's your problem as a professional, it's not the product's problem in the marketplace.

Product category. In many cases, the problem can be found by looking at the marketing situation. Different types of product categories in different stages of development require different message strategies. Characteristics of the product category can create communication problems.

Some products are big-ticket items; others are minor purchases. Some require frequent repeat purchases; some require long-term use. Some product categories are dominated by a market leader; others are fragmented and competitive. They can be products with significant high involvement by the consumer—that is, the consumer spends some time in searching, weighing alternatives, and seeking out opinions from family and friends before making a decision. They can also be low-involvement products as described by Herbert E. Krugman, director of research at General Electric—products that are purchased without consideration and frequently on impulse.[2] People have inherent interest in some kinds of products, and little or no interest in others.

Product differentiation is another characteristic that affects the problem situation. When products are differentiated—in other words, when there are major differences between brands, models, or types—then advertising is likely to play a major role in pointing out the differences. The role is informational or educational. With some products there are only minor differences between one brand and another. Advertising's role, then, is to establish a unique image.

Loyalty is another factor that can be determined to some extent by product category. A J. Walter Thompson study, for example, found that personal care products is the product category most shopped for by brand name. Within this category, toothpaste has the highest brand loyalty, followed by deodorants and mouthwashes, then toilet soaps. The product category that has the lowest brand loyalty ratings was shoes.[3]

Advertising directed to brand-loyal categories will utilize more reminder advertising and "inoculation" techniques to reinforce the already persuaded. In categories with a low level of brand loyalty, message strategies focus on developing familiarity with the name and encouraging impulse purchasing.

An analysis of the research findings in terms of creative strategy for big-ticket items suggests that the problem is informational or educational. Reminder advertising for the brand is especially important for big-ticket items. Likewise, strategies that use testimonials or seek to develop interpersonal communication may be useful, given that information is sought from other people.

Life cycle. The advertising problem may also be tied to the product stage in what is called its "life cycle." The message situation involving the fewest problems would be *reminder* advertising. That is a type of advertising where the product is established and the advertising operates on a relatively low level, keeping the product name in front of the consumer, who probably has already purchased the product at least once. The message needs a high level of repetition and is often directed against an inattentive or semiattentive state. The learning is either incidental or associational. Reminder advertising seeks to maintain previous attitudes such as liking, acceptance, desire, and preference. The action desired is repurchase.

New product introduction is much more complex than reminder advertising. These products may be brand new items in the marketplace, such as home computer games, or they may be improvements on old products, such as Sony's Walkman. During the introductory stage, the problem is to develop consumer awareness of the new product and its name. Consumers are in the dark about the product. Information is provided to educate them and to encourage initial trial of the product.

As Leo Bogart said in *Strategy in Advertising*, "There's no place to go but up or out."[4] He said the advertiser's objectives are twofold: to create a sense of awareness or familiarity, which permits the brand to be anchored as a significant reference point in the consumer's mind, and then to create from scratch a favorable positive set of associations that will cause the product to be tried, perhaps even preferred. Bogart emphasizes that simply making the consumer aware of the existence of a new brand is a major accomplishment. It is unlikely that the advertising will register complicated copy points at the same time.

In the case of a new product category, the advertising may be generic in the sense that it promotes a new use of product rather than a specific brand. The Minnetonka advertisements for liquid soap had to explain what liquid soap is and how to use it before the brand name of Softsoap could be registered.

During the rapid *growth* stage, the number of brands competing in the same market tends to increase. Often, prices will fall and the sales base expands rapidly. The emphasis begins to shift from knowledge of the product and category to brand identification. New products taking on established leaders may begin comparative advertising. Consumers may often be confused, particularly if there is a proliferation of brands. Advertising seeks to create a position of distinctiveness in a cluttered market.

The *maturity* stage is a complicated one. With most products there is usually some ceiling on rapid growth, which means that the market passes through a saturation period and then settles down to some clearly defined pattern of leaders and followers. In a stable situation the advertising is largely brand image. It is reminder advertising, in the sense that it keeps the product's name in front of prospects who have already heard of or tried it. Consumers still need reasons and arguments to support their convictions and preferences.

From time to time, during the maturity stage, established brands may introduce line extensions. These new products go through the usual introductory period; however, the effort is simplified because they already have an established "reputation platform." They simply need line identity and trial.

A major problem with the stable maturity stage is that it tends to produce "me-too" advertising. The distinctiveness between brands washes out as everyone tries to look like some stereotyped image of the category. Detroit-style automotive advertising is often criticized for its look-alike nature. With most cigarette advertising, you can remove the name and not be able to tell which brand is being advertised.

The advertising message problem that occurs in the rapid growth stage is product differentiation. Differentiation is used here to mean that the product's salient features are established and emphasized. This situation would exist in the growth stage in a cluttered market. It is a differentiation strategy in the sense that the product stands out with a distinctly recognizable image and position. In the differentiation situation, your primary message problem is to create comprehension of copy claims and some generalization and discrimination.

The maturity stage may also see the development of an intensely competitive situation. Glass Plus took on Windex in what had previously been a one-brand category and made major inroads in share of market simply by broadening the scope of the product's position. Pepsi challenged Coca-Cola in a series of taste tests that shook the giant of the beverage industry to the point that it retaliated with its own taste test and eventual change of formula.

In a state of challenge, your advertising will focus on comparative claims and counterclaims with careful attention to support and justification. The FTC often gets involved in validating or challenging claims in hotly contested markets. It's a message situation where one product not only has differentiation in the market, it has a strong enough position to launch an assault on a competitor that also has an established and distinct position.

In the competitive situation your primary problem is to change existing attitudes, to stimulate switching. That may involve both extinguishing old attitudes and forming new ones. In an intensely competitive situation, the message strategy would try to stimulate some level of emotional excitement in the prospect. ("I'd rather fight than switch.") Recall is even more difficult because now recall involves not just copy points but also arguments and defenses, claims and counterclaims. In order to understand such messages, generalization and discrimination must be operating on a high level.

Comparative advertising is looked upon with favor by consumer groups and the FTC because it is thought to provide useful price and performance information that helps consumers to make rational decisions. Detractors say that comparative advertising is not good strategy because the named competitor benefits as much from the ad as your product does.

Does comparative advertising work as a persuasive tool? Stanley I. Tannenbaum, chairman of Kenyon & Eckhardt, quotes seven years of K&E research that shows "our use of the comparative commercial has been effective simply because when two or more products are designed to do the same thing, the consumer benefits by learning which one does it better."[5]

In the same article Andrew G. Kershaw, chairman of Ogilvy and Mather, recites study after study showing no significant difference in recall or persuasion for comparative television commercials. He concedes that comparative advertising in print may be more effective because the medium lends itself to "full and thoughtful comparisons." He also reported the findings of an O & M study[6] of comparative commercials. The conclusions are:

- Comparative television advertising does not offer any advantage to package goods advertisers
- It does not increase brand identification
- It makes consumers more aware of competitors
- It results in lower belief in claims
- It results in increased miscommunication and confusion
- It is not more persuasive

The biggest criticism of comparative advertising is that it may cause confusion as to which company is the sponsor. Also, it provides free promotional time for the competition. It demands additional legal and research support for claim substantiation. Another problem is that it demands a high level of involved information processing skills by the audience, which might not be available in a tightly competitive, highly cluttered marketplace.

There is only one marketing situation where it may make sense to use comparative advertising, and that is where there is an established market leader and your company is either number two or up and coming. If you decide to use comparative advertising, Tannenbaum has some suggestions from K & E's experience:

- Use comparison only in significant product attribute areas
- Use where there is demonstrable superiority
- Use where the major brand is perceived more positively than your brand
- Identify but never disparage the brand leader
- Whatever advantages you might gain by using comparison, you could lose, if the brand leader is able to counterargue in a more meaningful attribute area where the leader enjoys superiority
- Lean over backward to be fair or you may generate sympathy for the competition
- The consumer must be able to verify the comparison; he or she must be able to prove it

The last stage in the product life cycle is the *decline* stage, where it is assumed the product slowly sinks into gentle oblivion. Sometimes the marketplace changes and the product becomes obsolete; sometimes it just loses its edge. When, and if, the product reaches this stage, then advertising and promotion is usually reduced or eliminated in an attempt to maintain profits as long as possible.

Some, however, say that a product does not necessarily have to reach this last stage. Not only can products be managed to maintain their maturity position, they can also be turned around if they are found to be slipping.

Examples of successful turnarounds include General Foods' Brim decaffeinated coffee, General Mills' Nature Valley granola, and Johnson & Son's Edge shave gel.[7] The key to such turnarounds is spotting some significant change in the marketplace or consumer attitudes and repositioning the brand to take advantage of the change. That can mean finding a different appeal, repackaging, focusing on a different product feature, or identifying a different market segment.

The advertising problem also might be discovered by looking to outside events that influence business economics. For example, in the seventies American subcompact cars were facing challenges from foreign small cars that cost less and consistently rated better on gas mileage. Foreign small cars, on the other hand, were facing increasing import duties, which were forcing their prices up so much that they could no longer be considered "economy" cars. Both categories had to respond to these outside influences. American small cars became more and more economical and the imports began stressing luxury features. In the adaption process, their entire positioning strategy flipflopped.

The importance of developing an insightful statement of the problem was stressed by Joel Raphaelson, executive creative director at Ogilvy and Mather, in a special section of *Advertising Age* on creativity. He said, "The creative process should concentrate on defining the problem accurately and finding a precise solution."[8] There's no sense throwing darts at the wall if the bull's-eye is invisible.

Objectives

Objectives are the heart of any strategy statement. They specify exactly what you hope to accomplish with your plan. You will probably find in the overall marketing plan a set of marketing objectives. These objectives deal with such goals as sales (by unit or dollar value) and share of market.

Advertising objectives *do not* include sales objectives. There are too many other marketing decisions affecting the sales level besides advertising. Advertising objectives *do* focus on communication effects. *Advertising* is defined as marketing communication, and this means the end result of an advertising plan is communication about a marketing promotion. Therefore, advertising objectives stick to results that you can expect to accomplish with a message.

But first the message has to be seen, interpreted, and remembered, and this involves affecting the way people receive messages. Advertising is a form of persuasive communication so advertising objectives will specify how the message is expected to motivate or stimulate the audience. Advertising is also educational in that we often want the audience to learn or know something as a result of the message. So advertising objectives must consider how the audience can best learn the message.

In order, then, to understand how advertising works and to better appreciate what you can and can not accomplish with advertising, it is helpful to understand the basics from the foundation disciplines of psychology and perception, communication and persuasion, and education or learning.

Communication.   The basics begin with a simple communication model developed by Wilbur Schramm.[9] The model is used to illustrate the factors that are important to the process. Schramm's model identifies a *source* that originates the message and a *receiver* that is the destination for the message. The source *encodes* the message by translating personal thoughts into signals such as words, and the receiver *decodes* the message by translating the signals back into some kind of personal meaning. The message may be ink on paper, sound waves in the air, a road sign, a flag, a hand waving, or any other signal capable of being interpreted.

Noise is a term used to describe all possible obstacles that can keep a message from getting through clearly. You identify noise as such things as garbled language, inappropriate terms, clutter, and technical difficulties in reception, as well as psychological problems with either or both the sender or receiver—such as fatigue, anger, excitement, and so on. (See Figures 2–1, 2–2, and 2–3.)

FIGURE 2-1:   Basic communication model

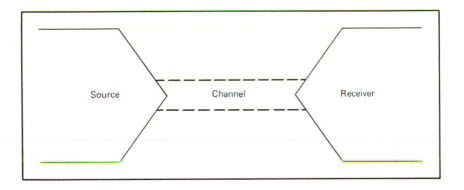

FIGURE 2-2:   Elaborated communication model

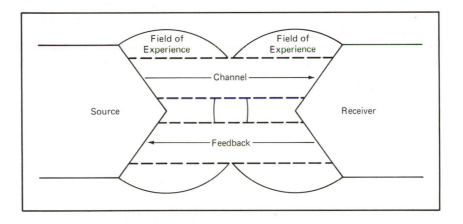

FIGURE 2-3:   Mass media communication model

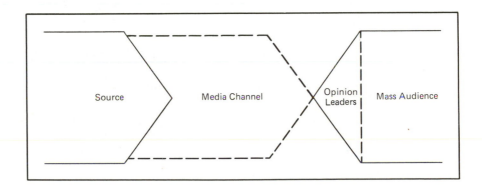

When you develop objectives for advertising messages, you will probably concentrate on the receiver and message parts of the model. Obviously the message can be manipulated in a number of ways to create a number of responses, but the focus of the objective is on the communication effect *on the receiver.*

Noise is a real problem in advertising, particularly from clutter on the channel. You will use feedback in advertising to determine if your message had the expected effect. This feedback is usually structured as some type of research or copytesting.

Perception.   The roots of communication theory, learning theory, and persuasion are in psychology. In order to understand what happens at that point of impact when the receiver "gets the message," you need to understand a little bit about the psychology of perception.

Perception is defined as the process by which the receiver assimilates messages through various senses, interprets the messages, and reorganizes them for the memory system. There are two terms from perceptual psychology that you will use in advertising objectives: attention and memorability. Beginning copywriters are often advised to concentrate on getting attention and making the ad memorable—or "grab" and "stick."

Attention is a mental state indicating some level of arousal. Perception operates on the conscious level by first exciting attention, a state where the receiver is, to a greater or lesser degree, concentrating on the message. Attention operates as a filter screening the amount and types of messages the receiver perceives. The idea behind attention is that far more stimuli come to us than we are able to concentrate on; therefore, we have to sort out the messages on some basis.

The next level of arousal is *interest,* which can be defined as a state of absorption in the message. This is where the interpretation process begins. It differs from attention in that there is an element of curiosity or fascination; it involves a higher level of excitement than attention. There are three types of interest operating in advertising: product interest, self-interest, and interest in the content of the message. An advertisement whose objective is to develop or sustain interest must speak to one or all of these three areas.

A third level of arousal that follows from attention and interest is *excitement.* The mental state of excitement is important to advertising because it is a necessary precondition to the development of emotional responses. Excitement means that the message stimulates or is capable of arousing feelings and emotions in the receiver.

In addition to arousal, there is one other perception-related area that advertising objectives must address, and that is *memory.* Messages are filed according to some personal pattern of organization using slots or files for related information. Messages are seldom retained in their original form; they are usually compressed and restructured to fit the individual's organizational pattern.

Most information is filed as fragments or traces—key words or visuals. These fragments are pulled back to the top-of-the-mind by the use of cues; in other words, certain words or visuals will elicit previously learned information. That is what you hope is happening when you measure the recognition or recall of a message.

Memorability is one of the most commonly stated objectives for advertising. In order to be memorable, the message has to be easy to be compressed for filing. That's why writers are concerned about slogans and television producers worry about "key visuals." They understand that only the essence of the message will remain in memory—assuming it is interesting enough to get filed. Repetition of a message develops this cueing process to establish a solid association.

An example of how memorability is developed in advertising is found in positioning. The idea behind positioning strategy is to understand how consumers sort, select, and slot brand images. There is room only for a limited number. The ones that get filed are the ones that are the most salient. Simple messages are easier to file than complicated ones.

There are two types of memorability of major concern to advertising, and these are recognition and recall. *Recognition* means that the receiver is aware of having seen the ad before. *Recall* is a higher order level of memorability and means that the receiver has the ability to remember specific information.

Learning.   Learning theory has its roots in psychology, just as communication theory and perception do. There are two primary schools of thought: the connectionists, who believe we learn things by making associations, and the cognitive psychologists, who believe we learn by acquiring insight, understanding, or comprehension of the whole picture. As far as advertising is concerned, both schools are right. Advertising seeks to develop *both* association and understanding. They are two different ways to acquire knowledge, and most people use both methods at different times for different learning tasks.

In advertising, we also use *classical conditioning* when we urge consumers to buy a product that will satisfy a need identified by our messages, such as bad breath. The need cues an association with the product. Classical conditioning is used with products that are frequently purchased, usually low priced, and often low in involvement—products such as soap, toothpaste, soft drinks, cigarettes, and beer.

Instrumental conditioning attempts to create an association, using a reward or reinforcement to encourage the development of the association. This kind of learning is most commonly identified with B. F. Skinner and his pigeons. Instrumental conditioning is used whenever the objective in advertising is to make a promise to the prospect: use this product and you will be beautiful, young, macho, or wise. Advertising makes good use of promises and rewards.

Vicarious learning, a type of classical conditioning, is another type of association that is particularly relevant to advertising. In vicarious learning, one person learns by participating as an observer of someone else's experiences. This is a process of learning through imitation. In many advertising situations, particularly with demonstrations and new product introductions, the strategy is to help the audience learn "how-to" information by participating vicariously in an experience with the product.

A lower-level type of learning, described as incidental, occurs when traces of the message are assimilated into memory even though the receiver is basically inattentive. This is why people can remember having heard or seen a brand name when they get to the store, even though they didn't pay attention to the advertisement for that product on the television the night before. Incidental learning uses simple messages and high levels of repetition.

Cognitive learning, derived from Gestalt psychology, suggests that understanding is developed from pieces of information that serve as meaning cues. Cognitive theory focuses on the comprehension of essential relationships and understanding based on insight. A good advertising example of cognitive learning is found in Ogilvy's classic advertisement for Rolls-Royce, which begins with the headline: "At 60 miles an hour, the loudest noise in this new Rolls-Royce comes from the electric clock." Readers understand that the tiny detail of the clock ticking stands for the entire concept of excellence in automotive engineering.

Associated with cognitive theory is a higher-order level of learning focusing on generalization and discrimination. The activity of generalizing and discriminating suggests an ability to see (understand) differences in relationships. This is the basis for higher-order reasoning leading to such activities as synthesizing, concluding, and decision making.

Persuasion.   In the early days, advertising was used to provide news about products. The news might be hyped up with circus poster design and screaming headlines, but the information was basically news announcement. In 1905 Albert Lasker and John E. Kennedy, both giants at the legendary Lord and Thomas agency, coined the phrase "Salesmanship in print." Instead of continuing as a form of reporting, advertising became a persuasive tool focusing on attitude development and change. The strategy and style of the field changed radically from that day on.

Persuasion is defined as "those situations involving conscious intent on the part of one person to influence another."[10] The definition itself states the importance of this concept to the development of advertising objectives since its phrasing includes a goals statement. In general, persuasion affects how we *feel* about something: more specifically, persuasion affects the structure of our beliefs, opinions, attitudes, and behavior, and how they can be influenced by outside agents. In this discussion, we use the word *attitudes* to refer to the entire "affective" structure. (*Affective* refers to how we feel about things; *cognitive* is what we know.)

Attitudes are basically positive, negative, or neutral. Our attitude structure as consumers is organized around opinions about products, the purchasing environment (when to buy, how much to pay), our social environment (what others are buying), and our self-concept or self-image. This provides a rich fabric of feelings, all interwoven and interactive, but held together by certain basic patterns.

We hold this structure together with defense mechanisms. We operate with an internal logic and, when our attitudes are in conflict, we are in a state of mental tension called *dissonance*. In order to reduce the tension, we either have to change how we evaluate something (positive, negative) or change our cognitive structure (what we know about something). In other words, something's got to give. This is important to consider in comparative advertising and loyalty campaigns.

Another area of persuasion that provides insight into advertising objectives is the influence of others on our attitudes. One of the things we know from communication theory is that word-of-mouth communication among peers is more believable than mass communication from an anonymous source. Specifically, in persuasion we look at two types of influence: influence by groups and influence by leaders.

In terms of advertising objectives, there are a number of useful applications of the basics of persuasion theory. The defense structure is important to you when you are developing a message strategy. You may find yourself specifying objectives that attempt to maintain balance by reinforcing brand loyalty or creating dissonance through comparative advertising. Sometimes you may be trying to resolve tension by using two-sided arguments or counterarguments.

An example of the two-sided argument approach is the classic Volkswagen compaign that acknowledged that the Beetle was "ugly," thereby establishing a position of candor for the car, a position that had never been used in automotive advertising before. We could summarize persuasive objectives as creating new attitudes, reinforcing existing attitudes, or changing old attitudes. Most of what happens in persuasive communication can be structured around one of those three objectives.

Our original definition of persuasion included behavior as well as attitude. *Behavior,* or action, is the final test of persuasion. In advertising the behavioral objective is buying, and that is the bottom line for both the advertising and the marketing strategy. The problem is that there is no clear picture of the relationship between attitudes and behavior.

We know that affecting attitudes is easier than affecting behavior. You will find it is easier to get people to believe a copy point (or at least say they do) than it is to get them to buy the product because of that copy point. Furthermore, we know that people often say one thing and do another. Because of the lack of a clear interdependent relationship between the two, it is best to consider action as a separate persuasive objective.

This behavioral objective can take several forms. Probably the easiest form is to get someone to try a product sample or investigate a product using a response card in a magazine. This is a low-level form of action. Coupons are designed to stimulate this type of trial or investigation. A more complex form of action is the deliberate purchase of a product after some consideration.

Formulas.   A number of formulas exist already to help with the task of setting objectives for the advertising message. These formulas attempt to provide a structure to help you think through what it is you want to accomplish with your message. Probably the most famous formula is one known as AIDA. It proposes the following four steps in the buying process: Attention, Interest, Desire, and Action. Colley's DAGMAR (Defining Advertising Goals for Measured Advertising Results) proposes a model of awareness, comprehension, conviction, and action.[11]

A marketing model developed by Lavidge and Steiner[12] identifies the following steps in the buying process: awareness, knowledge, liking, preference, conviction, and purchase. These six levels are grouped into three basic categories: cognitive—the intellectual, mental, or rational state; affective—the emotional or feeling state; and conative—the striving, deciding, or action state. This model is often called the "learn-feel-do" model. The Lavidge–Steiner model has become one of the most widely accepted models in the consumer behavior area.

Another view of how advertising works has been developed at Foote Cone & Belding. The FCB model[13] includes elements of Krugman's low involvement/high involvement theories plus Lavidge and Steiner's "think-feel-do" hierarchy. The resulting matrix splits the consumer response into thinking and feeling across the top and low and high involvement down the side. Within the matrix are implications for relevant objectives, products, media, message strategies, and testing methodologies. A simplified version focusing on message strategy is given below:

THINKING	FEELING
1. INFORMATIVE (thinking) Model: learn-feel-do Products: car, house Creative: specific details, demonstration	2. AFFECTIVE (feeling) Model: feel-learn-do Products: jewelry, cosmetics Creative: executional impact
3. HABIT FORMATION (doing) Model: do-learn-feel Products: food, household items Creative: reminder	4. SELF-SATISFACTION (reacting) Model: do-learn-feel Products: cigarettes, liquor, candy, gum Creative: attention

Another useful model that describes how advertising works in terms of communication effects is one developed by a University of Wisconsin professor, Ivan Preston. Preston's model focuses on the role of association in advertising messages.[14] He explains that "success in obtaining intended sales response occurs fundamentally because of the value of what the advertiser associates with the product." The associations are conveyed in the descriptions, attributes, claims, benefits, people, and lifestyles depicted—in short, whatever associations the message attempts to create.

The reason why Preston's model is useful is that it is built on the communication process and includes all the variables that affect how we perceive and process a message. In particular, it focuses on the very important concept of association, and illustrates how the association process is fundamental to advertising communication.

Low-involvement advertising.   Herbert Krugman, a General Electric scientist, first developed the concept of "low-involvement" advertising.[15] Krugman uses the term to refer to a type of product, message situation, and advertising medium. Low-involvement products are the ones that we buy often without any major search or consideration—such as toothpaste and soap. A low-involvement medium is television, which doesn't put many demands on the viewer.

The situation has implications for message objectives. Krugman's theory is that we don't follow the traditional hierarchy in purchasing these products. In other words we don't move through the attention, interest, desire, and action sequence of steps. In fact, we may not attend to the message, may have little or no interest in the product and the message, and may still buy the product.

Message effects.   The FCB model and Krugman's low-involvement theories acknowledge that not all people move through a purchase sequence in the same way. While the AIDA model is easy to understand and use, it may not be very realistic. Furthermore, as you think about the message effects identified in the various models, it might strike you that in some cases you are dealing with apples and oranges. Some of the lists are dominated by objectives from learning theory; others by objectives stemming from persuasion and attitude change. Others focus on behavior. Most of them pull effects from all these various domains together in some kind of a sequence. However, it seems apparent that all of these various effects can happen at the same time rather than sequentially.

Perhaps it would make more sense to reorganize all of these miscellaneous objectives into some kind of structure related to our underlying foundation theories. We know that advertising follows the information transmission process described in the communication models. We earlier identified three basic areas or domains of effects: perception, learning, and persuasion.

From our review of the three domains, it appears that there are five classes of effects relevant to advertising. From perception are derived the two basic classes of arousal and retention. From the domain of education comes the class of learning. From the domain of persuasion come the two classes of attitude and behavior.

Previous models tried to structure a hierarchy based on the concept of process or time sequence—first you do this, then you do that. The approach proposed here suggests that all of the areas are equally important, interdependent, and operating simultaneously. The effects proceed along parallel lines rather than in sequence.[16] When receivers decode a message they are in some state of arousal, their memory processing system is involved on some level, their learning process is engaged on some level, and their attitudes and behavior are affected on some level. The effect represented by the phrase "on some level" suggests that there is a continuum ranging from no effect to high effect.

Setting objectives involves specifying the specific type of effect and the level desired for each of the domains. The list below summarizes the types of sample objectives that might be generated from this approach. (See Figure 2–4.)

Writing objectives. Writing an objective is fairly easy if you master a simple form. Just remember that an objective is a statement of goals: what message effects you want to accomplish. The "to accomplish" phrase is the key. This tells you the statement is basically a verb form: you want your reader or viewer *to do* something. So begin your statement with some form that starts out, "to . . ." In a speech, Paul C. Harper, president of Needham, Harper, and Steers, developed some sample objectives that provide guidelines for the verb format: to induce trial, to sustain preference, to intensify usage, to confirm imagery, to change habits, to build ambience, and to build line extensions.[17]

Then specify exactly *what* it is you want to accomplish. Don't be vague, don't just say "to create awareness." Specify what you mean by awareness (recognition, recall) and specify of what (name, slogan, logo, theme, copy points, etc.).

Next specify *whom*. We assume it is your target audience, but is there any special group or segment and, more important, *how many* of them do you expect to be affected by your message? Do you expect 90 percent to recognize the package or would you be happy if 10 percent understood the copy point? You need some idea what percentage of the audience is to be affected so that you can measure the success of your effort after the advertising is completed. Generally speaking, the simpler the objective in terms of effects, the more people you can expect to affect. With the high order messages (more complicated, more involved), the fewer the number of people who will be affected.

The only way to know exactly what percentages to use is to compare your objectives with a set of objectives from a similar campaign. You need a benchmark. If your client develops objectives annually, you can base this year's objectives on an analysis of last year's responses in comparison with the strength of the message and the marketplace history. After all, these objectives are basically predictions.

The last piece of information that needs to be contained in an objective statement is *when*. In other words, you need some indication of the length of time the advertisement or campaign will be running.

The complete formula for developing an advertising message objective, then, is as follows:

FIGURE 2-4 Domains of message effects

MESSAGE OBJECTIVES

PERCEPTION

Arousal

- Create awareness of ad, product, brand
- Create interest in product, brand, message
- Create excitement about product, brand, message

Retention

- Recognize ad, image, slogan, logo, position, copy points, etc.
- Recognize brand, product
- Recall image slogan, logo, position, theme, copy points
- Recall brand, product

EDUCATION

Learning

- Register claim, USP, benefit, product attributes
- Comprehend claim, USP, benefit, viewpoint
- Associate product with logo, slogan, theme, key visual, jingle, lifestyle
- Differentiate attributes, claims

PERSUASION

Attitudes

- Register psychological impact (emotional appeals)
- Register positive disposition
- Evaluate attributes, claims, viewpoints positively
- Acceptance of claim, argument (agreement)
- Correct false impression
- Reposition
- Challenge position, claim viewpoint
- Counterargument—position, viewpoint, claim

Behavior

- Increase traffic
- Stimulate inquiries
- Stimulate trial
- Stimulate purchases
- Stimulate repurchase

To do _____   (appropriate verb form) _____

What _____   (specify activity to be measured)_____

To whom ____   (target audience or segment) _____

How many __   (what percentage) _____

When _____   (time frame) _____

If an advertisement is single-minded, and that is thought to be the most effective strategy, then there will probably only be one overriding objective from one of the domains. Advertising campaigns that are built on a planned sequence of messages over an extended period of time may be developed with a set of several objectives. But keep in mind, the simpler and more direct your strategy, the greater the impact and effect of your message. Advertisements that try to do many things frequently accomplish nothing at all. Use a rifle, not a shotgun.

An example of how sets of objectives are packaged, measured, and presented is found in an article on Goodrich's attempt to clarify the name confusion between itself and Goodyear. The *Advertising Age* article[18] reported the results of the campaign as showing consumer awareness of Goodrich as a different company rose 122 percent from 1975 to 1976; perception of the company as innovative was up 232 percent; preference for its radial tires rose 85 percent; and recognition that BFG was the first U.S. manufacturer of radials was up 490 percent. If objectives are carefully spelled out beforehand, then it is easy to measure the effectiveness of the advertising afterward.

Target Audience

The objective of targeting is to identify your most profitable prospects. Not all people use your product or service. Of those who are customers, not all use it to the same degree. There is a rule-of-thumb in advertising—it's called the 80:20 rule. Basically, it means that 20 percent of your market buys 80 percent of your products. The objective of targeting is to draw a circle around that 20 percent. Demographic information sets the boundaries of the group. This information is usually stated as a range: 18–25, $25,000–$35,000, and so on. When you have a range, then you have upper and lower boundaries of a group of people.

Targeting, for creatives, is more complicated than just identifying demographic boundaries. John O'Toole, president of Foote Cone & Belding, wrote an article in the seventies in which he asked if Grace Slick and Tricia Nixon Cox were the same person.[19] He started out with a set of facts: a woman, 25–35, family income over $15,000, urban working, college graduate, 2–3 members of household, white, upper-income family with professional or executive father who belongs to the Republican party.

He observed, "That's more information than you'd normally get, but let's err on the side of the devil. We have the prospect pretty well defined now, right?" He goes on to answer, "Sure. It's Tricia Nixon Cox, married in a beautiful White

House ceremony and exemplifying the straight life." But he continues, "It's also Grace Slick, of Jefferson Airplane, who isn't quite into marriage but gave birth two years ago to a daughter who she originally named god, but whom Miss Slick now refers to as China."

The point? Lots of information you have to work with in your definition of the target audience is really noninformation. Demographics are useful, but only up to a point. To get a fix on a target, you must dig deeper and look into lifestyle and psychographic information. Advertising is most believable when it is written directly to one person—a warm, living, breathing person—preferably someone you know like your mother, brother, or friend. That's the ultimate in targeting—to identify a typical consumer who is someone you know.

Profiles. In order to move to that level of targeting, creatives must be able to translate this data about groups of people into a profile of a typical prospect. Creatives aren't interested in people as groups, only as individuals. Efficiency, for a media planner, means finding the largest possible group of prime prospects. Efficiency, for a creative, means finding the person who represents the *ideal prospect.*

Sometimes there is a tendency to resist targeting because you may see the process as eliminating potential prospects. But this way of thinking misses the point. Targeting is to help you write your message to a real audience. It doesn't reduce the size—potential consumers who are interested can and will see the message—it just aims your creative effort more effectively.

In personal sales it's easy to know a lot about your prospects just by observation—and that lets you tailor your message directly to their needs. By looking at them you can estimate age, race, sex, and so on. Sometimes income can be estimated by looking at clothes or the car they drive. Their level of education may be apparent in their speech. You can make judgments about their personality and their needs by the way they make decisions and ask questions. As they mull over the price and compare product features, you can tell what is most important to them—are they worried about the expense, the maintenance, the ease of use? This information lets you target your sales message directly to the needs of this particular person.

In advertising, we rarely have the luxury of speaking to one person face to face. Advertising is a mass sales tool, and we know the audience is large. But in spite of the fact that we address groups of people through a mass medium, the most effective sales message is still the personal one delivered directly to an individual.

John O'Toole speaks eloquently to the need for fine-tuning the targeting. "What we need is more recognition of that paradoxical truth that guided the great communicators from Homer to Robert Frost—that the way to move millions is to talk to one single person." He concludes, "And when the chord is struck in one, the vibrations reverberate in millions."[20]

When creatives target an audience, they look at all the demographic and psychographic information that was accumulated in the background research and try to see patterns. They separate out the relevant details, trying to identify those characteristics that separate the targeted prospect from the rest of the mass market. Then, concentrating on those critical discriminating variables, they pull together a profile of a person.

Notice that you concentrate on certain variables— not all of the demographics or psychographics are equally important. What you have to do is sort through and identify the relevant characteristics and then build a profile on them. It may be something so simple as "people who shop in malls" or "young music students."

The idea is to move away from the dry details and breathe some life into the important characteristics. John O'Toole expressed it succinctly. "Anyone who still sees the consumer as a passive and static set of demographics is reading these events the way General Custer read his intelligence reports."

Once you have developed a profile, then identify someone you know who fits those characteristics. This step is entirely dependent on the breadth of your own personal background experiences. If you come from a typical middle-class, college-educated WASP home, and you've not made much of an effort to explore the world beyond your own social class, then you may have trouble with the identification. But let's assume that the profile describes someone you know— an aunt, a friend in high school, the guy you worked next to on the line during your summer job. Give your typical prospect a name and a personality.

Now that you have a real, live human being locked into your mind, walk this person through the buying process for your product. What moves the individual? What appeals to him or her? What motivates the person? What does he or she laugh at? Or scorn? How does the person make decisions? What steps does he or she go through in considering your product? Where might this person get off track? What does he or she understand and misunderstand?

Segmenting.   So far we've been discussing targeting in terms of arriving ultimately at the typical prospect, but targeting can be more complicated than that. Within the targeted group of prospects, there may also be individual segments—smaller groups of people with different patterns of needs. It may be that your client asks you to reach a certain segment of the audience. For example, if you were working on a beer account, you might be asked to target specifically at the younger end of the overall market, and develop a strategy aimed at formative drinking patterns. For a retail store, you may be asked to reach the downtown shopper as opposed to the mall shopper.

Carving up the audience into segments leads to the identification of primary and secondary audiences. What you are doing is identifying a hierarchy of prospects. In other cases you may have different segments, with no hierarchy involved. Levi's, for example, sells jeans to young women, men, farmers, and a number of other distinct segments. Each segment is important and demands a different advertising strategy.

Another type of segmentation effort is one developed by Stanford Research Institute (SRI) and used by a number of advertising agencies. Called the Value and Lifestyle System (VALS),[21] the model describes three types of consumer groups: the need driven, the outer directed, and the inner directed. Within the need-driven category are the "survivors" and the "sustainers." Examples of survivors are elderly widows and the sustainers are often single women with families and minimal incomes.

There are three types of people in the outer-directed category: "belongers," "emulators," and "achievers." *Belongers* are traditional, conservative, conventional, and unexperimental. They are a huge stabilizing home-oriented force in our society. The *emulators* are trying to break into the system and are ambitious, upwardly mobile, and status-conscious. *Achievers* are leaders who are affluent and capable. They created the system and defined the American Dream.

There are also three types of people in the inner-directed category: "I-am-mes," "experientials," and "societally conscious." The "I-am-mes" are often the children of the achievers. They are young, exhibitionistic, and inventive. The *experientials* are those who want direct experience and vigorous involvement. They are much involved with inner growth and naturalism, and they are more interested in process than in product. The *societally conscious* have a high sense of social responsibility and support such causes as conservation, environmentalism, and consumerism.

There is a fourth category comprised of a very small number of people that VALS calls "integrateds." These are the rare people who have it all together. They can meld the power of outer-directedness with the sensitivity of the inner directed. They are only 2 percent of the population and not a large market, although important as leaders and influencers.

As an example of how VALS can be applied to advertising, Young and Rubicam used this kind of audience analysis to identify the proper strategy for Merrill Lynch. The previous advertising theme used a herd of bulls as a symbol. Y&R determined that such a strategy was inappropriate because the campaign was directed at achievers, not at belongers. The new campaign with the single bull in a challenging circumstance is thought to be more appropriate for that particular audience.

Targeting an audience, profiling a typical consumer, and segmenting the group into equally important subgroups is a complicated process. It takes lots of information and insight. But if it's done right, it can lead to brilliant message strategy.

An article on psychographics described targeting strategy by the White Stag Women's Sportwear division. Using primarily psychographics, the article reported that the company "was startled to discover a profile of not one, but five different types of women with five different lifestyles. In short, a potential and unsuspected $1.2 billion market."[22]

Distinctive Product Feature

All products have features. Some are more interesting or more complicated than others. Some features are more important to the users. Some are distinctive—in other words, the competition doesn't have the same features. What you have to do now is decide which is the single most important and distinctive feature to emphasize in your advertising.

One way to approach this analysis is to develop an attribute matrix. Down the side begin listing the important features. Rate those features that are both important to the consumer and distinctive in the marketplace. From that analysis you can see which of the highly rated features has the most potential.

Attribute analysis is useful because it lets you analyze the product in terms of two decision variables: distinctiveness and relevance. From this type of analysis, you are able to compile a list of product features arranged in order from the one feature that is most distinctive and most relevant to the features that are least distinctive and least relevant.

Obviously, attribute analysis depends upon your knowledge of the prospects and their likes and dislikes. You may have enough information as a result of your background research so that you can complete the matrix intuitively. In many cases, however, you'll find there simply aren't enough clues to let you make the judgments necessary to rate the features. In that case, there's only one resource—so you'll find yourself headed back out into the field with another series of questions.

It's easy to design a simple study to help you with attribute analysis. You take the list of features and ask a representative sample of your target audience to rate the features. You simply ask them how important the features are to them. For example, if you are trying to sell a car, you might have a list of features that include such items as miles per gallon, styling, maintenance, durability, luxury, roominess, handling, price, and so on.

If your targeted audience is young female buyers, they might rate the items radically different from an audience of older male executives. Depending on what group you are in, you might have a difficult time intuitively rating the list for someone else. Better to ask than to guess.

This initial part of the survey determines how important the features are. The second part asks the consumers to rate your product. You want to know what features are important as well as how high your product is rated on those features. Ideally, your advertising strategy will emphasize some feature that is both important to the target and highly ranked for your product. It wouldn't make sense to push a feature that the audience doesn't care about or, conversely, a feature that your product doesn't rank very well on.

The Competition

If you've done a thorough job of background research, then you probably have a list of potential competitors—both direct and indirect. The next step is to do the same kind of analysis that you did with your list of potential prospects: you target the competition. Not all of the potential competition is equally important. Some are unassailable, others are more vulnerable.

When you targeted the audience, you were trying to identify the most efficient group to reach; when you target the competition, you are trying to identify the competitor who is most likely to give up share of market. Remember, if you are going to grow, then someone else will shrink—unless you can broaden the entire market. But most likely you are trying to increase your share of a relatively static market, and that increase has to come from someone.

To do competitive targeting you will need a version of the product attribute matrix that you developed when you analyzed your own product for its distinctive features. In that analysis you considered "distinctiveness in the marketplace." Now dig into that in more depth. Analyze your product's distinctive features against the competitors' features and then compare all sets of features against the wants and needs of your target. That's how you determine advantage. From this analysis of features and needs, you should be able to see, in fact, who is your most direct competitor.

But that's only part of the targeting process. The direct competition may, in fact, be the strongest marketer in the field. That company or brand may be unassailable. If you look around, you might find another competitor with similar features and target audience that is not so entrenched. It's very difficult to steal market share from an entrenched leader, but much easier to compete with a company that has a fuzzy image, minimal advertising, pricing, or distribution problems, or some other sign of a weak marketing program. You are looking for signs of vulnerability. Then you build your strategy on the features that emphasize your competitive advantage.

An interesting example of a small company that took on the giants and won the successful new product introduction is the Minnetonka Company, makers of a line of soft soaps. Liquid soap has been available for decades—in institutions, gyms, racquet clubs, and so on—but not in homes. Minnetonka believed that liquid soap has a big advantage over ordinary bar soap in that it is not messy—it's squirted into the palm like hand lotion. Softsoap was a phenomenal success during the first year after going national, and the tiny company captured 10 percent of the total soap market from such giants as Procter & Gamble, Colgate, and Lever Brothers.[23]

Position

Positioning is a term for an advertising strategy that became popular during the 1970s. The phrase comes from an article by Jack Trout and Al Ries that appeared in *Advertising Age* in 1972.[24] Trout and Ries describe positioning as how your product is perceived *by your audience* in relationship to the competition. It is a concept melding the competitive situation and your product's uniqueness in that market.

Probably the two best-known positioning examples were described in the Trout and Ries article. Prior to the "Un-Cola" campaign, 7-Up had a rather fuzzy image in the market. There was no term to describe a clear or white soda. "Un-Cola" clearly positioned 7-Up as the alternative to traditional colas. It also struck a responsive chord in a population that was on the edge of social rebellion—a position opposite to the traditional drink was a viable concept and socially acceptable.

The other classic example was the Avis "We Try Harder" campaign, which positioned Avis as "Number 2" but made that position a symbol for drive and hard work. Avis works harder because Avis is the underdog. The position is one that most Americans can easily identify with. It, too, strikes a responsive chord.

The theory behind positioning is that there is limited space in the consumer's memory. In order to occupy a "slot" in the memory bank, your product needs a distinctive position relative to the other products in the category. You may have seven competitors, but most consumers would only be able to identify two or three—and the ones that get identified are the ones that "stick out" in their memory. A clear and coherent position is the key to brand and product recall.

It's easy to check a product's position. Ask yourself (or your target audience) what they think of when they think of your product. "When you think of Avis . . . you think of a company that tries harder because it is Number 2." When you ask yourself or your prospects that simple question, whatever they respond is the position they have in their minds. It may not be the position in your mind or in your advertising or in your client's mind. It may not relate to anything marketing oriented at all. But if that's what they respond, that's what your position is.

Your goal in strategy development is to identify the appropriate *available* position for your product and then to evaluate that ideal position relevant to your current one. If the product is new, then you will be *establishing* a position. If it's been around awhile, then you will either *reinforce* or *change* the existing position. In other words, positioning strategy demands that you know both where you are and where you are headed.

Notice the word "available." Positions aren't lots for sale. They are carefully staked out and seldom moved. If you want to change a position, it can be done, but it's an incredible effort. Miller's Beer was changed from a woman's beer, "the champagne of bottled beer," to a macho beer for truck drivers and lumberjacks. The same change was engineered for Marlboro cigarettes, which originally was seen as a slightly feminine brand. In both cases, it took a tremendous advertising effort to manipulate the position.

Likewise, it takes a tremendous effort to occupy a position already taken. Trout and Ries are adamant in advising against trying to assault a leader on the leader's own position. Their advice is to find a new position and carve that out for yourself.

That's the reason you see so much criticism by advertising professionals of "look-alike" advertising. Thomas Murray, creative director and chairman of an Ohio-based agency, Murray & Chaney, decries the attitude by some clients who seem to believe that, to be associated with the leaders, their advertising needs to look like that of the leaders. He observes "Do not expect advertising or graphics or demeanor in the marketplace that is identical to the market leader's to make you a leader."[25] He explains, "At worst you will come across to the consumer like a cheap imitation to be avoided at all costs. At best, your advertising will be confused with the leader's." He concludes, "Figure out your own niche in the marketplace."

We've mentioned the new product success story of Softsoap. Part of the success lies with the position. Bob Taylor, president of Minnetonka, explains that Softsoap was billed as a "panacea for messy bar soaps." He explains that it was a strategy that wasn't met with a lot of enthusiasm. "Everybody said our position statement was wrong, that we should not be selling 'eliminate messy bar soap' because that's not a proprietary position. Everybody who goes into liquid soap can eliminate messy bar soap." But Taylor knew he had a unique position because, while other liquid soaps *could* claim that statement, no one else *was*.

He recounts that he was advised to talk about the skin-softening benefits of the formula as well as the packaging and other features. But he disagreed. He saw a clear and unclaimed position in eliminating messy bar soap. That position statement helped Minnetonka's sales soar 191% in the first year.[26]

A successful position is not one that can be communicated in a mouthful of marketing jargon. It is short, usually a phrase, and it's expressed in natural language. Remember the test of your position statement is to ask your prospects, after the ad is run, how they see the product. Will they respond with your phrase? At best all they will remember is something simple, something single-minded, something distinctive.

2.2 CREATIVE APPROACH

We've discussed the various types of basic strategy decisions you have to make in the development of the copy platform. Now let's consider how we discuss the various types of message options. First, we will discuss some general approaches that we're calling "stratagems." Then we'll talk about appeals, selling premises, and some common advertising message formats.

Stratagems

A *stratagem* is a scheme for taking advantage of an opponent. We are using this term to talk about different ways to develop creative strategies, given the product's particular attributes, the characteristics of the consumers, and the overall marketing situation. These are broad, general categories of message approaches. They summarize your message strategy.

One of the earliest sets of stratagems can be found in a textbook by Julian Simon.[27] Simon calls these "creative strategies" and lists 10 of them: information, argument, motivation with psychological appeals, repeated assertion, command, brand familiarization, symbolic association, imitation, obligation, and habit starting.

In a study of ads, the authors found that over half used only four of these strategies: information, argument, psychological appeal, and symbolic association.[28] They also found that, of the ads with high "noted" scores—in other words, the readers could remember having seen the ad—68 percent used information, 64 percent used argument, and 56 percent used symbolic association strategies. In terms of the "read most" scores, argument was high with 62 percent, followed by symbolic association with 54 percent, information with 50 percent, and psychological appeals with 46 percent.

Another set of stratagems was developed by Charles Frazer, a University of Colorado advertising professor.[29] His categories are more inclusive, and they are defined in terms of their relevant marketing situation. Frazer's strategy alternatives include:

Generic: No effort at differentiation; claims could be made by any in the market. Used in monopolistic situations.

Preemptive: Uses a common attribute or benefit but gets there first. Forces competition into "me too" positions. Used in categories with little differentiation or in new product categories.

Unique selling proposition: Uses a distinct differentiation in attributes that creates a meaningful consumer benefit. Appropriate in categories with relatively high levels of technological improvements.

Brand image: A claim of superiority or distinction based on extrinsic factors such as a psychological differentiation. Used with homogeneous, low-technology goods with little physical differentiation.

Positioning: Establishes a place in the consumer's mind relative to the competition. Suited to new entries or small brands that want to challenge the market leaders.

Resonance: Uses situations, lifestyles, and emotions that the targeted audience can identify with. Used with highly competitive, nondifferentiated product categories.

Anomalous/affective: Uses an emotional, even ambiguous, message, to break through indifference and charge the product's perception. Used where competitors are playing it straight.

The five alternatives below are recommended to you as a set of basic stratagems based on simplifications of the work of both Simon and Frazer. They are intended to be used as summary statements that describe the general orientation of your creative strategy.

Information: A straightforward statement of fact; uses news announcements and assertions.

Argument: Uses logic to develop a reason why, benefit, or position. A rational approach.

Image: Uses the process of association to establish identification of the brand or identification with a lifestyle.

Emotion: Attempts to influence feelings, to generate affective responses.

Entertainment: Grabs and holds attention by presenting amusing and interesting messages.

Information.   This is a straightforward statement of fact. It uses assertions, claims, and announcements. A news announcement is an effective use of this type of message strategy, while the "brag and boast" style of ad is an example of an ineffective use of an informational statement. You will find information strategies used to announce new products and improved product features, as in a Tylenol ad for its new package design. They can also be used in highly competitive categories to announce results of tests and trials.

Argument.   An argument strategy uses reasoning and logic to develop a rational appeal. These are involved messages that demand that the audience be able to "follow through" the logic to reach a conclusion. They demand a certain level of interest and a moderate level of information processing skills from the audience. They use explanations and comparisons to prove their point. The argument message is used with major purchases and products that have distinct technological differences, whether big ticket or not. They are usually employed in highly competitive situations.

Image.   Advertising that seeks to develop a strong memorable identity for a product or company is called *image advertising*. Image advertising tries to wrap up all the pieces of the perception into a tight, simple concept or symbol. It emphasizes psychological associations rather than physical product differences. Image advertising is indirect and long term. It develops a "reputation platform" for the brand or company rather than immediate sales.

Image advertising can also be said to include such strategies as lifestyle advertising, which try to associate using a product with an attractive environment and a type of person. Rugged men smoke Marlboros, fun-loving teenagers drink Mountain Dew, and the Charlie woman walks tall and takes it all in stride.

Emotional strategies.   Emotional messages intend to excite feelings such as love, anger, hate, joy, poignancy, or sorrow. Humor is also considered an emotional advertising strategy. Bill Bernbach, founder of Doyle Dane Bernbach, was one of the industry's greatest spokesmen for touching feelings. In a speech in Detroit he said, "The only way to get people to remember what you've said is to make them feel."[30]

A classic example of emotional advertising is N. W. Ayer's famous campaign for Bell Telephone long distance, "Reach out and touch someone." Emotional campaigns such as "Reach out" are particularly relevant in times of personal anxiety. Dr. Ruth Ziff, director of research at Doyle Dane Bernbach, conducts studies to identify how people are feeling about their lives.[31] In 1982 she found the reason for the phenomenal success of campaign strategies like "Reach out" is that they stress poignancy. She was surprised to find that "emotional concerns came up as often as they did." She observed that "our society, with its changes, its divorce rate, the singles scene, has definitely heightened concern about loneliness and isolation."

Bob Gage, art director at Doyle Dane Bernbach, describes the effectiveness of emotional strategies in an interview in a *Wall Street Journal* house ad: "You have to hit 'em where their heart is. You can sell far more if you're emotional rather than intellectual." He continues. "Take Polaroid. They don't sell cameras, they sell love. People take pictures of people they love."[32]

Emotion is useful with parity products and products that elicit a low level of involvement or commitment from the prospect. Hal Riney, head of Ogilvy and Mather's west coast office, observes that most products and services don't really have anything to say that distinguishes them from the competition. "Most of the time the facts haven't done me a lot of good." Riney's answer to that dilemma is to use emotion. "Knowing what and how to use an emotion is the most important part of an advertising person's job." He explains, "We're asking advertising to depend too much on the rational, and much less, or not at all, on the effective element of our business, which is emotion. The rational element is often merely what people use to justify their emotional decisons."[33]

Some products are natural for emotional advertising such as perfume, cosmetics, phone calls, and greeting cards. One of the most interesting emotional ads is for Paco Rabanne, a men's cologne. It was written by Roger Proulx, Ogilvy and Mather, and it won numerous awards—and a few uplifted eyebrows for its very open treatment of what Proulx calls "sexuality and sentiment."

Because of the emotionalizing of the American spirit, other product categories are using emotion, categories where one might not think there is a natural link, such as soft drinks and fast food. A number of McDonald's Clio-winning commercials touch the feelings. A classic commercial using poignancy is the "Mean" Joe Green commercial for Coke. It's a story of a little boy who tries to get the attention of his football hero and keeps getting rebuffed. Finally the boy offers his hero a Coke, and the tough football player responds . . . with a smile . . . and the little boy goes away with a treasured prize, a football jersey. It's another spot that hits the "emotional buttons."

A Hallmark Clio winner called "Moving Day" is a real tear jerker. It shows a grandmother in the attic sorting through things as she prepares to move. She comes across a box of old cards and goes through them with her granddaughter. She finds one that goes back to her first wedding anniversary and has to stop to fight back the tears. The spot has a "visceral twang." People respond to it with an intaken breath, a response "from the gut."[34]

Entertainment.   Advertising messages are presented in highly competitive and cluttered media environments. As was discussed in the section on message objectives, getting and keeping attention is extremely difficult. One of the techniques used to combat the clutter is entertainment. Entertaining messages are interesting; they captivate and mesmerize. Their function is to hold attention. You will hear criticism of this entertainment strategy. Some people in advertising feel that entertainment is irrelevant and gets in the way of the commercial message. While entertainment can overpower the selling message, it is still essential in certain situations.

Television advertising, for example, is particularly concerned with entertainment because the medium is essentially an entertainment medium. In order to compete with the programming, the commercial has to be equally amusing and interesting. In fact, some of the best entertainment on television is found in the commercials.

An entertaining message is amusing; it leaves people feeling good about the ad and the product—but only if the product is remembered. The secret is to tie the product tightly to the entertainment dimension. Don't just tell a funny story and stick the product in as an afterthought. The product has to be an integral part of the message or it will get lost in the entertainment.

Entertainment is used primarily with parity products where there is little differentiation—products that are frequently purchased, low in involvement, low in loyalty, and relatively inexpensive. The entertainment is used as a reward to the reader or viewer for paying attention to the message, even though this is not a product that normally generates much information attention.

These stratagems are just ways to communicate the essence of your message strategy. They help you focus your efforts and refine what it is you hope to accomplish with words and pictures.

Appeals

One of the most important creative strategy decisions involves the choice of an appropriate appeal. The concept of advertising appeals comes directly from psychology. Advertising messages speak to human needs. One way to analyze needs is to use Abraham Maslow's famous hierarchy of needs.[35] Maslow's hierarchy begins at the bottom with basic needs called physiological and safety. Moving up the ladder, next come love and affection, called the "belonging needs." Then come esteem, self-actualization, and the need to know and understand. Finally, at the top of the hierarchy are the aesthetic needs.

With Maslow's hierarchy, the most basic needs are at the bottom and must be satisfied before needs at the higher levels can be addressed. This is useful to understand in advertising. There is no sense promoting tennis shoes as a jogger's luxury when the target audience is a mother with six kids who can barely afford to buy one pair of shoes per child.

In advertising strategy we tend to speak more of appeals than needs. We take the basic human need and translate it into a motivational structure.

Advertising appeals are strategies that speak to particular human needs. An appeal is a message about a need that has the power to arouse innate or latent desire.

Hundreds of appeals can be used in advertising; however, some are more basic and more frequently used than others. Advertising professionals intuitively refer to the ad's basic appeal when they present an idea. They will say something like: "We're using an economy appeal here" or "This is an appeal to convenience." The following list contains most of the basic appeals used by advertising:

- Acquisitiveness: money, possessions
- Affiliation and belonging
- Aspiration: achievement, accomplishment
- Comfort
- Convenience: save time, effort
- Economy: save time, money
- Egoism: recognition, approval, pride, status
- Emotional appeals:
  - Fear: safety and security, personal embarrassment
  - Family: affection, protection
  - Love and sex
  - Nostalgia
  - Humor: happiness and joy, laughter
  - Poignancy
  - Relief
  - Sorrow: grief, suffering
- Health
- Respect: heros and role models
- Luxury
- Mental stimulation: curiosity, challenge, involvement
- Pleasure: amusement, entertainment, excitement
- Sensory pleasure: touch, taste, smell

You can see how these appeals are used in advertising if you watch an evening's worth of commercials or page through one issue of a magazine. Watch for such lines as "Bake someone happy" (family affection) and "Be a Pepper" (affiliation, pleasure).

A psychologist, Dr. Melvin Hattwick, has analyzed psychological appeals and condensed the list into eight basic wants. In his book, *How to Use Psychology for Better Advertising,*[36] he identifies the following needs as most basic to advertising strategy:

1. Food and drink
2. Comfort
3. Freedom from fear and danger
4. To be superior
5. Companionship of the opposite sex
6. Welfare of loved ones
7. Social approval
8. To live longer

Hattwick considers these eight basic wants to be of the greatest importance to advertising because they are easily aroused, they are strong, and they are practically universal.

The goal of creative strategy is to identify the one appeal that is the strongest and that will trigger the buying action. Some of the appeals are low in motivation; some are high. The intensity of the appeal needed is based on the advertising problem.

Security.   Security is one of the most pervasive appeals because it includes money, health, shelter, food, and clothing—most of our basic needs. Some products have natural security appeals such as medicine, health care products, and insurance.

A security appeal is best handled in a straightforward approach although emotion can be used successfully. New England Life has even used soft humor to sell insurance. The use of an authority figure may be appropriate for some security appeals.

Fear.   Fear is the opposite of security because it focuses on threats to well-being and family. The threats could be major, such as tornados and fires, or personal, such as acne and bad breath. Regardless of scale, the threat is a motivator if the copy can speak believably to the reduction of the threat.

The copy tactic is simple: pose the threat and explain how your product eliminates it. A simple problem–solution. But both the threat and the solution have to be believable. Fear appeals have been studied to determine what level of intensity is appropriate. Most research has found that a mild level of fear advertising is more effective than intense fear appeals. Some prospects will retreat from an intense message; others will feel that they have been unnecessarily manipulated.

In a study of fear and humorous appeals, the author discovered that "mild forms of humor were found to be more persuasive than mild forms of fear."[37] He explained that this is apparently due to the negative effects created by fear appeals: "even when compared with straightforward appeals, fear effects were essentially negative." This negative halo may do more damage to your brand than the attention-getting aspect of fear appeals warrants.

Humor.   Humor is an effective emotional appeal in that it can create warm feelings about the product. If you can get your prospects to smile, then they will approach your message from a positive point of view. Perhaps some of that goodwill will be associated with the product. Humor is a strong attention-getting device, and it is also effective at maintaining interest.

Humor can be successful because people like to be amused. The problem with humor is that the idea has to be universally funny and that's very hard to accomplish. There is another problem with humor in advertising. The funny idea may go off on its own and leave the product behind. The audience can remember the joke, but forget the product. That's called "vampire creativity."

Sex.   Sex can be a strong appeal because most people want to be seen as attractive to the opposite sex. If your product enhances the attraction, then a sex appeal may be relevant. If that link is missing, then sex may be inappropriate. There's no logical reason to use a half-clad woman to sell tires.

Esteem.   Esteem is the need for recognition, respect, and status. We all want to be admired. That's fairly universal. An appeal to esteem is relevant for either nonessential items or major purchases that have high visibility. Status can sell sunglasses as well as cars and homes.

For a status appeal to be successful, it must relate both to the product and the prospect. Is it really a status item? That has to be believable. Does the audience care? Young people in the late sixties and early seventies were retreating to the country, communes, and other self-sufficient lifestyles. They could not be moved much with status appeals. There are times and places where acquisitiveness is not seen as a virtue.

Price/value.   Economy is an appeal to save money and, in most cases for most products, there is always an economy angle. However, economy is more complicated than just saving a few pennies. Most people understand the price/value tradeoff—the more you pay, the better the quality; the less you pay, the lower the quality. When you use an economy appeal, consider the implications for quality. The objective is to establish the economy concept without undercutting the perceived quality.

Sometimes economy is not a factor at all. Your client may be top of the line and want to maintain the image of the "most expensive" product. In that case you would have little reason to use an economy appeal. In some cases you may want to admit that your product costs more as a way of signaling that fact that it must, therefore, be better quality.

Convenience.   Convenience is an appeal to people who are concerned with saving time and effort. That's most of us, most of the time. But you do have to match the product, user, and situation. How easy is easy-to-use? Does it matter in this situation? If you are trying to kill time, then convenience may not be a virtue. If your product lends itself to a convenience appeal, then make it informational. Consider demonstrating what the result of the convenience might be.

Sensory pleasure.   Sensory pleasure can be overpowering when used with the right product. This appeal is used to demonstrate the sensory benefit of using a product. Appetite appeal is commonly used for food and restaurants. Cold beverages, hand lotions, and ointments are all sold for sensory reasons. "Take the Nestea plunge" with the tea drinker falling into a swimming pool is a good example of a strong sensory creative tactic. The D'Arcy agency is a master at using mouthwatering visuals on television—as with the Red Lobster commercials—to develop the appetite appeal of food.

Selling Premises

Selling premises identify the principle being used to motivate the target audience to respond. Some can be classified in terms of their logical or emotional orientations. Others have been grouped in terms of their focus on either the product or the consumer. This discussion will present five different types of selling premises and describe them in terms of both orientation and focus.

Claims.   Early advertising was almost exclusively product oriented. A manufacturer came up with a great idea, produced the product, and offered it to the public. The advertising reflected the manufacturer's enthusiasm about the product. A claim is a simple statement about what the product can do or has done, supported in the body copy with proof. It's usually straightforward.
A campaign for Chevrolet developed around the simple claim: "Nobody's bigger in small cars than Chevrolet." The idea is that if Chevrolet dominates this category, then the product must be good. An ad for Canon cameras starts off with this headline: "Nobody has been able to make fine photography this simple." The ad announces the introduction of a new automatic 35mm camera, a type of camera many people consider to be difficult to operate.
Both of these headlines are simple assertions. The body copy in each ad explains the point. Most copy that is built around a strong claim in the headline is followed up by body copy that amplifies, explains, substantiates, or proves the claim. An unsubstantiated claim is considered ineffective advertising because the response it usually elicits from the reader or viewer is: Prove it! If there is no proof, the claim is dismissed.
Another problem with claim copy is that it is easy to fall into a category of advertising called "brag and boast." Take a simple claim, add a little puffery, focus on the company rather than the user, and you have copy that strains credulity.
Basic claim copy is a straightforward statement about a strong product feature. It can be effective advertising. It is especially useful when you have a news announcement to make—something that's honestly newsworthy. It is a

logical approach and demands that the consumer have some latent interest in the product or product category. It can get attention; but it may not be very persuasive (for reasons that will be apparent when we discuss other types of selling premises). If you elect to use a claim approach, remember to avoid brag-and-boast statements and unsubstantiated claims.

Benefits.   Benefit advertising is another rational message strategy but this type of message focuses on the prospect. While the claim focuses on product features, benefit advertising focuses on what the product's features can do for the prospect. It takes the basic claim and reinterprets it in terms of what the product feature means *to me*, the typical consumer.

Benefits are the buying motives behind the features. These buying motives may be obvious or buried but they rarely stop with the product's feature. For example, some stereo tape recorders have a feature called "Dolby"—but what does Dolby sound really mean? Why should I care about that feature? Why should I care about rack and pinion steering, disc brakes, overhead cam engine? What do all those features mean to me? Translate those features and explain how they benefit me.

A good exercise to use to sharpen your ability to spot benefits is to take any common item, list its features, and then reinterpret each feature in terms of a buying motive. Shoes—what are the physical attributes of the shoes you are wearing? What are you really buying—besides just foot protection? Now go through the list of attributes for that pair of shoes and beside each attribute write a benefit. What does each attribute mean to you? That's benefit analysis, and you can practice it daily.

Benefit advertising uses carefully crafted explanations. An example from a Texas Boot advertisement illustrates how a product feature is first identified and then interpreted in terms of consumer needs. "Texas Boots have a unique double pegged shank so my feet will never again suffer from fallen arches." The product attribute is the "double pegged shank"; the benefit is never having to worry about fallen arches. The word *so* is the cue to the reader that a benefit is being provided.

The Texas Boots ad continues with another feature and benefit statement: "Texas Boots also have double lined leather inner soles and leather outer soles. This means my feet can breathe—so they stay dry. And that's important, particularly when I'm hunting." The feature is the leather inner and outer soles; the benefit is to stay dry—and, to make sure the reader gets the point, the copywriter reinterprets the benefit, making it come alive in a realistic situation. That's a double-layered benefit statement.

Benefit advertising is rational. It is used with products that have strong selling features that need explanation. It is also used with a targeted audience that has some inherent interest in the product. Low-involvement products, like chewing gum, would seldom use benefit advertising. (See Figure 2–5.)

FIGURE 2-5:   Identification of a benefit

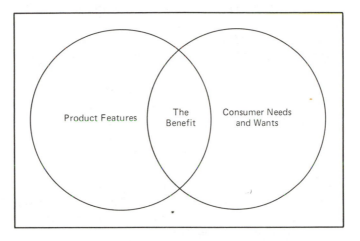

Reason-why.   The phrase "reason-why" advertising comes from the legendary Lord and Thomas advertising agency. Albert Lasker, the president, John Kennedy, the strategist, and Claude Hopkins, often called the "world's greatest copywriter", established the concept of reason-why advertising in the early 1900s. *Reason-why* is a type of benefit statement. It can be a strong rational stimulant to an otherwise indifferent prospect.

Reason-why advertising is based on a very tight logic. The structure behind a reason-why statement is a syllogism that states a fact and then follows with support. It is usually connected with a phrase like "because," "that means," or "so that." The formula for planning a reason-why statement is as follows: The fact is __ claim __ and that means __ benefit __ . This statement presents the reason why you should buy this product.

An example of reason-why copy is found in an ad by Wilkinson Knives for its "Sword," a type of self-sharpening knife. The headline says, "Finally, a kitchen knife that sharpens itself." That is a straightforward claim. The reason why the feature is important is developed in the subhead: "Introducing a knife that is sharp every time you use it, year after year."

The subhead states the benefit that is then explained further in the body copy: "The new Wilkinson Sword Self-Sharpening Knife is actually a knife and a sharpener in one." That is the important copy point. The second paragraph explains how the feature works: "Every time the stainless steel knife is inserted or removed from its storage case, it receives a professional sharpening. So it is sharp time after time, year after year." That ending sentence summarized the reason why.

Promise.   Another basic type of selling premise is the use of a promise. This type of advertisement makes a prediction about what will happen to the consumer in the future if he or she uses the product. The logic behind a promise in advertising is: If you buy __product__ , then __promise__ will happen.

An example of a strong bold promise is found in an ad by Scott for its Plus 2 Turf Building. The headline says: "We'll get those dandelions out of your lawn and that's a promise."

An example of another promise-based ad strategy is used by IBM for its Displaywriter Typewriter. The headline not only promises what the product delivers, it demonstrates it. The classic headline is a demonstration in print: "It makes impossibel impossible." The copy explains: "When an error in spelling mars an otherwise perfect piece of work, a strange thing happens: people remember the spelling error more than they remember the otherwise perfect piece of work." That introduction brings a situation to life where the product's feature can deliver its promise. It is a stage-setting device. (See Exhibit 2–1.)·

As you can see from this example, promise advertising is a type of benefit advertising too. If the promise is correctly stated, then inevitably it will turn out to be a benefit to the consumer.

Unique Selling Proposition.   The concept of the Unique Selling Proposition was developed by Rosser Reeves, former head of the Ted Bates agency, and explained in his book, *Reality in Advertising.*[38] It's a type of selling premise that can be described as all-encompassing. (See Figure 2–6.)

The USP interweaves the consumer's perceptions with the competitive situation and a strong claim about the product. The key, however, is differentiation. The more distinct the product in the marketplace, the stronger the advertising message. In his book, Reeves outlines three characteristics of strong USPs:

1. Each advertisement must make a proposition to the consumer. Not just words, not just product puffery, not just show-window advertising. Each advertisement must say to each reader: "Buy this product and you will get this specific benefit."
2. The proposition must be one that the competition either cannot or does not offer. It must be unique either in the brand or the claim.
3. The proposition must be strong enough to move the mass millions, i.e., pull over new customers to your product.

An example of a Unique Selling Proposition is the ad for Xerox based on the idea that the Xerox 5600 can copy both sides of a page. The headline reads: "Now you can copy both sides of this page without . . . turning it over." The first part of the headline was printed at the top of an otherwise blank page. The headline was completed on the back side of the page.

EXHIBIT 2-1: The "impossibel impossible" advertisement is an interesting use of visual communication to demonstrate a product feature. (Courtesy of IBM)

It makes impossibel impossible.

The IBM Displaywriter System.

When an error in spelling mars an otherwise perfect piece of work, a strange thing happens:

People remember the spelling error more than they remember the otherwise perfect piece of work.

The IBM Displaywriter helps stop spelling errors like these from happening.

Because it's more than just a text processor. It's a text processor that lets you check the spelling of up to 50,000 words *electronically.* At up to 1,000 words a minute. In 11 different languages.

The Displaywriter also lets you edit, revise, change your format, do math, merge, and file with electronic speed.

All of which goes toward giving you a flawless finished document.

Which is exactly what you want to stick in people's minds.

As opposed to the alternatove.

I am interested in learning more about the IBM Displaywriter System. Please have your representative get in touch with me.

NAME _____ TITLE _____
COMPANY _____
ADDRESS _____
CITY _____ STATE _____ ZIP _____
BUSINESS PHONE _____

IBM

400 Parson's Pond Drive—Dept. 804
Franklin Lakes, N.J. 07417

2-1-11-82

Call *IBM Direct* 800-631-5582 Ext. 2. In New Jersey 800-352-4960 Ext. 2
In Hawaii/Alaska 800-526-2484 Ext. 2

FIGURE 2-6:   Identification of a unique selling proposition

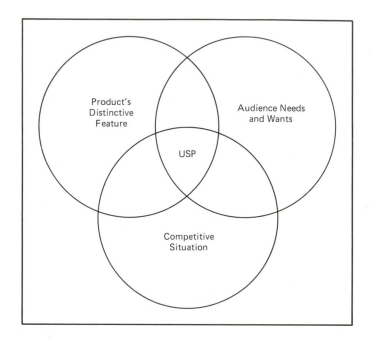

Product's
Distinctive
Feature

Audience Needs
and Wants

USP

Competitive
Situation

2.3 MESSAGE FORMULAS

We've discussed the series of decisions you have to make in the development of creative strategy. The last set of decisions involves the details of the execution, the tactics you want to use to make your creative strategy come to life. In advertising, we use the term *execution* to refer to how we carry out or develop the concept. *Strategy* refers to the plan; *tactics* refers to the execution details.

There are a number of different message formats commonly used in advertising. They summarize different approaches to the execution. These formats will be described here just to give you some of the common terms for message executions. There's no reason to believe that you are locked into using these and there's always room for new approaches.

Straight line.   There's a whole category of commercials that rely on words or the human voice for a persuasive message. The most common format, particularly in print, is the *straight-line* message. It's usually worded as an assertion; it merely states the selling proposition. Such copy lines as the following illustrate straight-line advertising:

* Head and Shoulders is gentle on the hair
* Anacin, the ingredients three out of four doctors recommend

- Excedrin is the extra-strength pain reliever
- Chevrolet Caprice, one of the "Ten Best Cars," foreign or domestic
- Clinique: In just one shave, this man will change his shaving habits

While the content may be image, lifestyle, or emotional, the phrasing is a simple statement or assertion. In some cases the copy is authoritative, even dogmatic.

In television advertising, the commercial equivalent of straight-line copy is the *straight announcer*. This can be an effective approach if the person is interesting, the voice is exceptional, and the message is intriguing. The danger is that it can become a dull "talking head." These spots are used most often in local advertising because they are cheap and fast to produce.

A variation on straight-line copy is the *news* announcement. This strategy is used when you have something newsworthy to tell your prospect. That means it has to be something new and something unknown. If it's honestly news you may have a strong strategy, since most people find it hard to resist a statement announcing something that is new.

Dialogue.   A dialogue format can appear in several different forms. The witty repartee by James Garner and Mariette Hartley has made Polaroid commercials much watched and appreciated by viewers. Another ad that used a conversational style was the Paco Rabanne commercial, where the guy reminisced in a teasing but romantic way about the evening they had the night before.

Another type of dialogue is the *interview*. This approach uses a question-and-answer format, with the announcer doing the asking and someone of significance doing the responding. The person being interviewed may be a celebrity or an authority or a typical person representative of the targeted audience.

The testimonial.   There are three types of testimonials. The product spokesperson can be either an authority figure, a celebrity, or a satisfied product user. The testimony itself can be a monologue, a dialogue (conversational), or woven into a little playlet.

A common testimonial is to use the words of a satisfied product user. This strategy uses someone who is "Mr. or Mrs. Average" and truly represents the *typical user*. This can be a "candid camera" technique where the consumer responds in an unrehearsed manner with spontaneous comments.

The problem with this typical user is that the person may not be attractive or admirable. For example, in the famous Alka Seltzer commercials the husband says, "I can't believe I ate the whole thing," and the wife responds, "You ate it, Ralph." The spots are cute and the phrases became part of the American vernacular. The criticism of the commercial is that most people didn't want to identify themselves with the overindulgent buffoon with the big belly. It was a cute spot, but the characters didn't represent anyone you would want to know—or be.

The other side of this argument is that successfully identifying "Mr. Average" tends to foster dull stereotyped characters who speak in clichés. It's awfully hard to make someone interesting who was created from demographics.

Another type of testimonial is the *authority figure*—a stereotyped character representing a professional category such as doctor, dentist, lawyer, or chemist. Television is filled with well-known personalities who speak with respected voices in certain areas, such as Karl Malden, Robert Young, and Bruce Jenner.

There are also manufactured authority figures such as Mr. Goodwrench for car maintenance. Madge the manicurist is an authority figure for hand care. Some authority figures are real, but relatively unknown to the public until after their advertising campaigns—such as Lee Iacocca for Chrysler and Frank Perdue for chickens.

Obviously, the key to authority figure advertising is to match the person to the product. If there isn't a natural link, then the authority appeal won't work. Joe Namath may have an image as a womanizer, but it still is a little hard to believe that he is an expert on pantyhose.

The same philosophy guides the use of *celebrity spokespersons.* Celebrities are used in advertising because they are glamorous. They are also exciting and attention getting and it is hoped that some of their excitement will transfer to the product. One problem with celebrities is that their image may overpower the product. You can remember Susan Anton and Raquel Welch, but can you remember the products they advertised?

There has to be some natural link between the celebrity and the product, some reason to believe they would actually use and speak in behalf of the product. Hank Aaron is a natural for Wheaties and Orson Welles communicates the concepts of quality and dedication for Paul Masson Wine. The association between Catherine Deneuve and Chanel #5 is obvious.

George Burns, one of our most beloved performers and a natural presenter for many products—including products for denture wearers and cigar smokers, was not very effective when he tried presenting for a catfood. There was no reason to believe that he would be a cat lover, or that he would be personally involved in feeding a cat.[39]

Michael Landon, on the other hand, presents very well for Kodak. First of all, he is actively involved demonstrating how easy the cameras are to use, and he also has that "All-American family man" image that links naturally to the product.

McCollum/Spielman, an advertising research company, has studied the selling power of stars and developed some guidelines for the use of celebrities.[40] One thing they found out is that most of the celebrities used in commercials are men. They came from entertainment and sports, with a few from a miscellaneous category of cooking experts, astronauts, journalists, politicians, and corporate executives.

Women, rightly or wrongly, were primarily starlets chosen for attractiveness. Males have been used for a variety of professions, but women are used primarily for feminine beauty aids. The women presenters, however, were generally more convincing. An interesting use of a woman presenter was found in a Clio-winning commercial for tires that used Joan Rivers. The message format was a straight announcer, but the spot had gentle humor and was highly interesting.

McCollum/Spielman has a number of suggestions to make about the use of stars:

- Set the selling strategy and then find a star who fits, not the other way around
- Make sure your star's image and personality are compatible with the product
- Give your star a logical reason to recommend the product
- Make it clear why the star should be regarded as an authority on this product
- Get the celebrity involved with the product—display, demonstrate, and work with it

They also have some suggestions on what to beware of:

- Stars that have lost their glitter
- Athletes and their ups and downs
- Idiosyncratic styles and personalities of comedians

Dramas.   There is power in a good story to get attention, maintain interest, and be remembered. A good story can come in several forms. It could be a narration, like a storyteller would tell. It can also be acted out, like a play. Since television has all the benefits of cinema, then it makes sense to use dramatic techniques particularly in television advertising.

There are five basic steps to a dramatic form. First is *exposition*, where the stage is set for the upcoming action. Next comes *conflict*, which is a technique for identifying the problem. The middle of the dramatic form is a period of *rising action* where the story builds, the conflict intensifies, the suspense thickens. The fourth step is the *climax*, where the problem is solved. The last part of a drama is the *resolution*, where the wrapup is presented. In advertising that includes product identification and a call to action.

Problem–solution.   If your research identified a major consumer problem, then it might be appropriate to use a problem–solution message format. A common use of the problem–solution format is the *product as hero*, where the consumer is stumped by some situation. The product comes to the rescue and solves the problem. It's a strong approach because the product is front and center, and it's very difficult to remember the ad and not remember the product, too. What makes the problem–solution advertisement different is that it dramatizes a situation. To be effective, this format must use believable situations and the problem must be a common one.

An example of problem–solution advertising is found in an ad by American Express targeted tightly to one segment of the market—in this case, the young businesswoman. The headline asks: "How will you pay for your first business lunch?" The visual shows a young woman with a table of older male executives. This is a situation that will probably trigger an emotional response in the target audience, because it is one experience that many young businesswomen dread facing. The copy answers the question: "With American Express Card, of course—your first business card. Because having the Card says a lot about your understanding of the business world. Even if you're only getting started in it."

Slice-of-life.   The most common problem–solution form is a peculiar format called the *slice-of-life*. This format is used frequently for packaged goods advertising by such advertisers as Colgate-Palmolive, General Foods, and Procter & Gamble.

Procter & Gamble mapped out a strategy for its agencies to use with slice-of-life ads. The memo stated: "All drama is based on two elements: conflict and resolution. Conflict is what 'hooks' the viewer; it is dynamic, out of balance and cries out for something to happen. Resolution is the force that moves dramatic imbalance to a conclusion." P&G's memo also recommended that the conflict should be visual, such as a dirty shirt, rather than some internal state that can't be pictured.[41]

The criticisms of the slice-of-life format haven't been aimed at its dramatic form, but at certain aspects of its execution. Most professionals believe that the problem has to be believable for an ad to work. Many of the packaged goods situations are criticized for being silly.

More specifically, slice commercials are criticized for being verbose and using phony dialogue. Their critics say that "real people would never say something like that." While these spots sell, there is a residue of distaste. Research has found that consumers often feel insulted by what they see as silly in these slice-of-life commercials.

But Hank Seiden, executive VP and director of creative services at Hicks and Greist in New York, makes a point in its defense: "To me 'slice-of-life' is irrelevant—it's just another executional format. It receives more credit—and blame—than it deserves." He continues, "It isn't 'slice-of-life' that makes Procter & Gamble advertising so successful; it's the comparative side-by-side demonstrations that are included with the format.[42]

Others who defend the successful P&G advertising point out that another factor is that you are allowed to listen in on someone else's conversation. Listening to a P&G slice-of-life commercial is like eavesdropping, and many of us are compulsive eavesdroppers.

Another type of slice-of-life message involves vignettes. They use a number of very short stories showing a variety of people trying the product. The award-winning campaign for General Electric that uses the "We bring good things to life" theme is a series of vignettes. Each vignette involves a GE product in some natural setting. The vignette strategy is often used with lifestyle cues.

Demonstrations.   The demonstration is a dramatic form that is a good technique for teaching *how-to* information. It is particularly strong if there is curiosity and suspense. The *torture test* ads are examples of dramatic demonstrations. The FTC (and your competitors) will be watching these very closely to make sure that the demonstration is accurate and relevant. For example, the FTC suggests that dropping a car off a 20-foot cliff to demonstrate durability is not valid. That's just not the same wear as driving a car to work for five years.

Comparisons.   Side-by-side comparisons can also be a dramatic form. Usually there is some problem—a stain, for example, on two similar pieces of clothing. After application of the product, the difference in stain removed is visible and obvious to the viewers. The FTC demands that these be actual tests and that all the variables have to be similar, except for the product application.

Symbols.   In addition to dramatic and word-oriented formats, there are also approaches that try to develop strong symbolic messages. Harry McMahan speaks of the "continuing central character" (CCC), which he identifies as a strong identification and memorability link. [43] Some of these characters are fictional spokespersons such as the Marlboro Man, Mr. Whipple, Cora, and Mrs. Olsen. Others are fantasy characters such as Charlie the Tuna, Tony the Tiger, and the Jolly Green Giant. According to McMahan, the Pillsbury Doughboy is valued at $20 million, which is one creative concept that even the accountants understand.

Fantasy is another type of symbolism used in television commercials. Television is entertainment and most viewers watch it as an escape. That makes fantasy a natural medium. The Herbal Essence shampoo commercials use animated fantasy with exotic and beautiful images that come to life from the artwork on the bottle's label.

A *mood* format is a strategy that makes an attempt, either in print or in broadcast, to establish some kind of evocative imagery. It's a poetic form that relies on word choice, descriptive phrasing, and evocative visual images.

Metaphors and analogies are another type of symbolic message that works well in advertising. With *analogy,* you are telling a story and likening it to something else. For example, the gorilla bellhop for American Tourister is an analogy. The message is that bellhops can beat up a suitcase as badly as a gorilla can.

Using a bull to symbolize an investment firm is a form of metaphor. This approach has worked so well for Merrill Lynch that it has a campaign built around the bull in such situations as a china shop and taking shelter from the rain in a cave. They are all highly symbolic visuals and situations.

The Honeywell ad uses the old lion and the thorn fable, but modernizes it with a graphic that shows a lion constructed of microchips and other electronic wires and gadgets. It's an intriguing visual metaphor. (See Exhibit 2–2.)

Sometimes even hospitals need a little tender loving care.

Honeywell has a computer system that helps hospitals solve those thorny clerical problems.

And that gives the staff more time to concentrate on patient care.

It's called VITAL*, an advanced, computerized hospital information system.

At hospitals like Huntington Memorial Hospital in Pasadena, California, and Deaconess

Hospital in Evansville, Indiana, VITAL processes admissions, discharges, transfers, doctors' orders, pharmacy orders, and test and treatment results. This data is only available to people who have a need to know—whenever and wherever they need it.

Honeywell has been helping progressive hospitals get these kinds of results for years. And

with our new Level 6 family of minicomputers, we have more to offer than ever before.

Maybe that's why organizations of every kind are turning to The Other Computer Company.

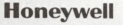
Honeywell

*VITAL system software is licensed by National Data Communications, Inc.   Honeywell Information Systems, 200 Smith St. (MS 487), Waltham, Massachusetts 02154

Spectaculars.   A type of music commercial is the *song-and-dance* spectacular. This type of commercial comes right out of the dance hall routines of the Radio City Rockettes and the Busby Berkeley extravaganzas that dominated movies in the thirties and forties. It is used for its entertainment value.

Spectaculars featuring music, such as all-jingle commercials, are also useful for reaching a young audience. Frequently, they will be combined with a lifestyle appeal.

The Dr. Pepper campaigns by Young and Rubicam have used some great song-and-dance routines. The "Be a Pepper" campaign, starring David McNaughton, was a classic song-and-dance routine. A Clio-winning commercial for Dr. Pepper Lite started off with a woman ordering a Diet Dr. Pepper in a diner and ended up with a fantasy song-and-dance routine on the surface of a pinball machine.

Special effects.   This category uses some production technique so novel that the special effect itself generates attention. On radio, some of Ken Nordine's experiments with multilayering of sounds[44] involves interesting special effects. In print you might see such techniques as embossing, day-glo inks, and scratch-and-sniff inks.

Computerized graphics have created a new world of special effects in both print and televison with images that are manipulated and distorted. These *electronic spectaculars* are incorporating techniques that have been developed for such movies as *Star Wars, 2001,* and *Tron.* These images intensify novelty and visual complexity to create mesmerizing images—a new visual experience that is riveting, something you haven't seen before.

A study of advertising effectiveness by the Mapes and Ross research firm, quoted by David Ogilvy and Joel Raphaelson in an *Adweek* article,[45] found that the following message formats scored above average in terms of their ability to change brand preference. (Remember that preference is a test of persuasion and involves a higher level response than recognition or recall.) The seven formats identified by Ogilvy and Raphaelson include:

- Problem solution
- Humor (if pertinent to the selling proposition)
- Relevant characters (personalities developed by the advertiser who become associated with a brand)
- Slice-of-life (enactments in which a doubter is converted)
- News
- Candid camera testimonials
- Demonstrations

They also noted that celebrity commercials are not particularly successful in changing brand preference. Cartoons and animation are effective with children but below average with adults. Commercials with a lot of very short scenes and many changes of situations are also below average.

2.4 AGENCY PHILOSOPHIES

Some agencies have utilized a distinctive approach to development of their creative strategies. They use the same analysis of appeals and selling premises but package the procedure in different ways. The following are four examples of distinctive stratagems.

Inherent drama.   The term "Inherent Drama" expresses the philosophy of the Leo Burnett agency. Carl Hixon, in his article on Leo Burnett, described it this way: "Somewhere in every product are the seeds of a drama which express that product's value to the consumer."[46] This philosophy is built on a foundation of consumer benefits plus an emphasis on the dramatic element. In expressing the benefit, Burnett people are urged to find the drama in the little things, the little decisions. The dramatic element is highlighted in Hixon's description: "Finding and staging this inherent drama of the product is the creative person's most important task."

Burnett traces his interest in product drama to early readings of de Maupassant and Flaubert and their descriptions of their own literary training. Burnett was not searching for "wild and crazy" ideas. He was more interested in the classical view of drama as theater touching basic emotions.

Story appeal.   David Ogilvy is a proponent of a type of advertising that seeks to develop "Story Appeal," a message strategy similar in some ways to Burnett's Inherent Drama. Ogilvy's theory is that a creative concept that is interesting, perhaps even curiosity provoking, will build attention.[47]

Ogilvy's classic example is the man in the eyepatch used as a continuing figure in Hathaway shirt advertisements. There was always a touch of mystery, an untold story, about this figure, and that made the Hathaway advertising highly attention getting as well as highly memorable. Ambiguity, if it is carefully handled, can be used effectively to create Story Appeal.

Belief dynamics.   Another distinctive selling philosophy that has been developed by a particular agency is "Belief Dynamics," the creative strategy philosophy of D'Arcy-McManus, Masius. Belief Dynamics combines research into consumer attitudes to identify clusters of beliefs that can be either strengthened, reinforced, changed, or modified in some way.

The idea behind Belief Dynamics is that "all behavior is based on beliefs." Therefore, to affect behavior you have to affect beliefs. Walter Armbruster, director of creative services, describes a person as "the Marvelous Mixer"[48] with a structure of some 437,632 beliefs. He says, "Some are rational, some are only feelings. Some are alive, some are dormant. Some are conscious . . . some are unconscious." All of these beliefs can be grouped into identifiable clusters.

The selling premise is based on the idea of understanding these clusters of beliefs and using them as a foundation for identification of appeals. All the analysis is reduced to one sheet of paper that spells out "exactly what we're trying to do to whom . . . what beliefs we must create or alter or intensify.''

Armbruster says that the bottom of the form spells out exactly *why should he/she* . . . He explains that the ''why should he/she'' statement demands that the dynamics of the belief be spelled out. He says it ''keeps us and the client from kidding ourselves. A why-should-he like 'established 1897' or 'quality is our watchword' obviously won't cut it.''

Human contact.   ''Human contact'' is a phrase used to describe the type of advertising associated with the N. W. Ayer advertising agency. One of Ayer's best-known efforts is the ''Reach out'' campaign for the Bell System. The campaign is also the best example of Ayer's use of emotion to touch the common chords in us all. (See Exhibit 2–3.)

But Ayer's brand of human contact involves more than just emotion. Ayer mixes emotion with warmth and soft humor to reach out and touch its audiences. Louis Hagopian, chairman and CEO, explains the chemistry of this delicate mix:[49]

EXHIBIT 2–3:   Ayer's ''human contact'' advertisement expresses the agency's unique advertising philosophy. (Courtesy of N. W. Ayer, Inc.)

Reach out and touch someone.

In New York, a writer from Iowa thought about home.

"When I made the call," he said, "I got this terrific feeling. And the same from the other end."

That's the beauty of a phone call from far away. Wherever you are, you're never too far to reach out and touch someone you love.

It's also the beauty of the new Long Distance advertising for AT&T.

According to research, it's reaching out. And one of the most important, pleasurable and successful advertising assignments we've ever worked on is working better.

Sooner or later, you've got to make human contact.

A phone call can make it.

So can advertising.

Not only for the new clients just coming to us, but for a client who's been around here for a long time. Like seventy years.

Ayer makes human contact

N.W. Ayer ABH International U.S. Offices: New York, Chicago, Los Angeles, San Francisco. Overseas offices throughout the Americas, Europe, Asia.

"In a time when people are uneasy with high tech, advertising can offer them high touch. It's far more efficient to touch people with warmth and an understanding of their concerns than to impose your message on them and hope that your name sticks."

Ayer's philosophy is based on some fundamental values: people respond to friendliness and to facts that help them solve a problem. People smile at gentle humor and warm up to the person (or company) that knows how and when to use it. People like pictures and tunes that are pretty. Given a choice between the silly and the sincere, people will choose the sincere. Given a choice between beauty and ugliness, people will choose beauty. These are the fundamental values that guide Ayer's philosophy.

This chapter outlines the major pieces of a copy platform. First, you identify some *critical problem* that the advertising can solve. Then you develop a statement of your *objectives*, what you hope the message will accomplish. Next target the appropriate *audience*, identify the distinctive *product feature*, target the vulnerable *competition*, and from these decisions identify a distinctive position in the marketplace.

Next comes an outline of the message strategy. The topics you might find in a copy platform include the *appeal*, the *selling premise*, a *stratagem* statement that describes the message approach, and other executional details such as message format information with supporting description of tone, product portrayal, location, and characters. (See Figure 2–7.)

As was mentioned earlier, not all of the terms are used in exactly the same way or order by all agencies, but the concepts are fairly basic and universal. (See Figure 2–8.)

FIGURE 2-7:   Copy platform outline

COPY PLATFORM

1. Advertising problem:
2. Advertising objectives:
3. Product's distinctive feature:
4. Target audience (relevant demographics and psychographics, segment, and profile):
5. Competition:
6. Position:
7. Message strategy (overall stratagem plus relevant appeal, selling premise, message format, and execution details):

FIGURE 2-8: Sample student copy platform

"CARRY-ON" PORTABLE TELEPHONE

Advertising Problem:
This is a high-priced luxury item that is being sold by direct response. Prospects must be taught how it works and where it can be used.

Objectives:
To receive a "noted" score of 90 percent with a coupon return rate of 12 percent.

Distinctive feature:
The distinctive feature is the portability. The cordless phone can be taken anywhere within 500 feet of the radio receiving unit.

Target audience:
Older upper-middle and upper-income businessmen and families. People who see themselves as getting important "can't be missed" phone calls. The family market is secondary.

Target competition:
Extension phones and phone recording units.

Position:
The Carry-On is the best cordless portable telephone available on the market. It goes where extension phones can't go.

Message Strategy:
Appeals: 1. Convenience 2. Status

Selling premise: Benefit strategy and promise

If you buy the "Carry-On," you can use the phone in places where you normally wouldn't have a standard extension phone. You don't have to miss important phone calls.

Execution:
"It goes where you go." Depict unusual, almost inaccessible places around the home with distinguished older man in cardigan and corduroys and pipe answering a phone. Places could include in attic, in basement, in garage, in the yard. Phone is positioned front and center with recognizable setting in background. Headlines vary with setting. Tagline provides continuity: "Carry on with Carry-On."

Supporting copy points:
1. Identification of unusual places where you wouldn't expect to find a phone
2. Explanation of how the radio unit receiving device works
3. Price
4. Purchase information

NOTES

1. Malcom D. MacDougall, "Emerging from the Creative Coma," *Adweek,* November 30, 1981, p. 2.

2. Herbert E. Krugman, "The Measurement of Advertising Involvement," *Journal of Advertising Research,* 11:1 (February 1971), pp. 3–9.

3. "Personal Care Area Has Most Brand Loyalty, JWT Study Says," *Advertising Age,* January 24, 1977, p. 9.

4. Leo Bogart, *Strategy in Advertising* (New York: Harcourt, Brace & World, 1967), pp. 15–16.

5. Stanley I. Tannenbaum, "Comparative Advertising: The Advertising Industry's Own Brand of Consumerism," 1976 Annual Meeting of the American Association of Advertising Agencies, White Sulphur Springs, W. Va., May 1976.

6. Andrew G. Kershaw, "The Mischief of Comparative Advertising," 1976 Annual Meeting of the American Association of Advertising Agencies, White Sulphur Springs, W. Va., May 1976.

7. Nancy Giges and James P. Forkan, "Product Life Cycle Theory Thrown," *Advertising Age,* May 24, 1982, p. 56.

8. Joel Raphaelson, "Creatives Take a Look at the Creative Process," *Advertising Age,* June 4, 1979, pp. 5–19.

9. Adapted from Wilbur Schramm, "How Communication Works," in *The Process and Effects of Communication* (Urbana: University of Illinois Press, 1954).

10. Judee K. Burgoon, Michael Burgoon, and Gerald R. Miller, "Learning Theory Approaches to Persuasion," *Human Communication Research,* 7:2 (Winter 1981), pp. 161–79.

11. Russell Colley, *Defining Advertising Goals for Measured Advertising Results,* Association of National Advertisers, 1961.

12. Robert C. Lavidge and Gary A. Steiner, "A Model for Predictive Measurements of Advertising Effectiveness," *Journal of Marketing,* 25 (October 1961), pp. 59–62.

13. Richard Vaughn, "How Advertising Works: A Planning Model," *Journal of Advertising Research,* 20:5 (October 1980), pp. 27–33.

14. Ivan L. Preston, "The Association Model of the Advertising Communication Process," *Journal of Advertising,* 11:2 (1982), pp. 3–15.

15. Herbert Krugman, "The Impact of Television Advertising: Learning Without Involvement," *Public Opinion Quarterly,* 29 (1965), pp. 349–56.

16. Sandra E. Moriarty, "Beyond the Hierarchy of Effects: A Conceptual Model," in *Current Issues and Research in Advertising,* eds., James H. Leigh and Claude R. Martin, Jr. (Ann Arbor, Mich.: Graduate School of Business Administration, (1983) pp. 45–56.

17. Paul Harper, "What Advertising Can and Cannot Do," Speech to New York Conference of the Conference Board, New York Hilton, October 20, 1976.

18. "Incredible Ads Ignored, Says Goodrich's Ross," *Advertising Age,* May 16, 1977, p. 28.

19. John E. O'Toole, "Are Grace Slick and Tricia Nixon Cox the Same Person?", *Journal of Advertising,* 3:3 (1973), pp. 32–34.

20. Ibid.

21. Philip H. Dougherty, "New Way to Classify Consumers," *New York Times*, February 25, 1981.

22. Patricia Brooks, "Psychographics: Is It the Elusive 'Perfect Marketing Tool'?", *TWA Ambassador*, April 1978, pp. 24–27.

23. Rebecca Fannin, "Hard Sell for Soft Soap," *Marketing and Media Decisions*, October 1980, pp. 66–67.

24. Jack Trout and Al Ries, "The Positioning Era," *Advertising Age*, April 24, May 1, 8, 1972.

25. Thomas Murray, "Make Your Ads Talk to People, Not to Yourself," *Advertising Age*, May 16, 1977, p. 67.

26. Steve Raddock, "Now He Sings in the Shower," *Marketing and Media Decisions*, Spring 1982, pp. 123–31.

27. Julian L. Simon, *The Management of Advertising* (Englewood Cliffs, N.J.: Prentice-Hall, 1971), pp. 174–83.

28. Alan D. Fletcher and Sherilyn K. Zeigler, "Creative Strategy and Magazine Ad Readership," *Journal of Advertising Research*, 18:1 (February 1978), pp. 29–33.

29. Charles F. Frazer, "Creative Strategy: A Management Perspective," *Journal of Advertising*, in press.

30. Stuart Elliott, "His Ads Speak Softly, Carry Big Selling Sticks," *Detroit Free Press*, October 27, 1980, p. 2C.

31. "Who's Worried Now?", *Marketing and Media Decisions*, May 1982, pp. 74–75.

32. "True Gage," *Wall Street Journal*, a house ad that ran in *Advertising Age*, January 5, 1978, p. 17.

33. Joseph M. Winski, "He Swims Against the Tide," *Advertising Age*, April 26, 1982, p. M–3.

34. Sandra E. Moriarty, "Advertising Appeals to Pathos and Poignancy," *Madison Avenue*, April 1983.

35. According to Maslow's 1970 revision of the need hierarchy in Frank Goble, *The Third Force* (New York: Simon & Schuster, 1971).

36. Melvin Hattwick, *How to Use Psychology for Better Advertising*, (Englewood Cliffs, N.J.: Prentice-Hall, 1980).

37. George W. Brooker, "A Comparison of the Persuasive Effects of Mild Humor and Mild Fear Appeals," *Journal of Advertising*, 10:4 (1981), pp. 29–40.

38. Rosser Reeves, *Reality in Advertising* (New York: Knopf, 1963).

39. "Starpower: Will the Force Be with You?", *Topline*, a newsletter published by McCollum/Spielman, August 1980, p. 8.

40. Ibid.

41. Harry McMahan and Mack Kile, "Slice Sells with Drama," *Advertising Age*, September 14, 1982, p. 68.

42. Hank Seiden, *Advertising Pure and Simple* (New York: AMACOM, division of American Management Associations, 1978).

43. Harry McMahan, "The Seven Factors to Creative Successes," *Advertising Age*, December 17, 1979, pp. 41–42.

44. Jeff Lind, "Once upon a Ken Nordine," *Illinois Entertainer*, May 1977.

45. David Ogilvy and Joel Raphaelson, "Agency Boredom with Analysis Cripples Execution," *Adweek,* September 27, 1982, p. 72.

46. Carl Hixon, "Leo," *Advertising Age,* February 8, 1982, p. M-8.

47. David Ogilvy, *Confessions of an Advertising Man* (New York: Dell, 1964).

48. Walter A. Armbruster, "The Dynamics of Belief Dynamics," *Journal of Advertising,* 3:3 (1974), pp. 25–34.

49. Louis T. Hagopian, Speech to the Milwaukee Advertising Club, November 19, 1980.

Advertising Style

Chapter Three

3.1 ADVERTISING AND WORDS

Most people in advertising spend their professional lives in search of the right "magic words." Copywriters, of course, are trying to find the right words to warm up a mood or soften resistance. The creative team struggles together to come up with a concept that expresses an appeal in words and pictures. The account executive tries to express the complexities of a marketing situation in a simple position statement. And—throughout the industry—both agency and industry executives are looking for the magic words to sell, defend, explain, and justify their recommendations and decisions.

Recruiters and interviewers patiently explain to students that what they look for is not so much technical knowledge but communication skills. Writing skill is required in every area of advertising. Ralph Zeuthen, a management supervisor at Compton Advertising, explained the need for good writing skills in an article in *Advertising Age:* "This year Compton people will put literally billions of words down on more than a million pieces of paper. It's a fair guess that, every day, the average word output matches the bulk of a bulky novel. Whatever else we are, we are undeniably people of the written word."[1]

The Right Word

You have to love words to be a copywriter—or even to be in advertising. Advertising is a search for the clever twist, the pun, the powerful description, the punch, the essence of nuance—for words that whip and batter, plead, sob, cajole, and impress. People in advertising get paid good money for playing very skillful word games. But you have to be good at it. You have to be an expert at words or, rather, a student of them. You know their meanings, their derivations, their moods and feelings, their sounds, and the reverberations and vibrations they create in someone else's mind.

John Caples, a legendary copywriter and a member of the Copywriters Hall of Fame, was a master of words. He once made the point that a simple change in a single word can have major impact on the effectiveness of a message. For example, he wrote, "once I changed the word 'repair' to 'fix' and the ad pulled 20 percent more."[2] Caples worked in direct response advertising and he learned to love research because it told him about the power of his words. He "studied" everything he wrote and developed an extraordinary feel for the power of English.

In contrast to Caples is the latest development in computerized copywriting. An article in *Advertising Age* described a program developed to write real estate ads.[3] Designed by a team of a magazine publisher, a copywriter, and a computer programmer, the program is based on some 60 "pools" of interchangeable words and phrases. After the characteristics of the house are fed into the system, the computer selects the most important attributes and then selects up to 10 combinations of word pools that could accurately describe the house. An example of headlines generated for the hypothetical sale of the White House include:

Fabulous Patrician Home with Unique Charm
Executive Estate with Great Flair
Deluxe Home with Distinction
Stately Home with Special Charm
A Baronial Home in a Preferred Area

The creators of the CompuAd service hope to move next to used car advertising, then to recruitment advertising. After that . . . ?

Literal meanings.   Words have exact meanings and writers like Caples are deliberate in their search for the perfect word. A column that ran in *Advertising Age* written by Michael Gartner focused on the use and misuse of words. He quotes this headline from a *Wall Street Journal* ad: "Rid your home or plant permanently of pests and varmit with DeciMate." He wondered if the manufacturers of the product knew that the word "decimate" to the literally minded means to kill only every tenth one. He also notes that "varmit" is a singular and "varmits" is plural; however, he speculates that the ad writer really meant vermin and that this word is both singular and plural.[4] Copywriters not only get chewed out, they get fired for mistakes like that.

In another column, Gartner quoted a classified ad: "Well seasoned mixed firewood. $88 a chord." He observed that while "it struck a responsive *chord,* the wood is stacked in *cords.*"

X **Connotative meanings.** Words have meanings beyond the literal—meanings that are suggested or implied by their usage. These are connotative meanings. Only a sensitive writer like Caples would sense the difference between "fix" and "repair." *Fix* is something common people do; *repair* is what experts do. That's a distinction that is not found in any dictionary, but in tightly targeted advertising a shade of meaning that announced such critical distinctions in the audience could make the difference between advertising that is on target and off target.

Writers and teachers of writing assign personality characteristics to words. In an article in *Writer's Digest* magazine,[5] Gary Provost described what he called "power" words. First, power words are *short*. "Rich" is stronger than "wealthy"; "rape" is stronger than "sexual assault." Power words also are specific. "Doberman" is more powerful than "dog"; "gossip," "prattle," and "chat" all have more power than "talk."

Provost also describes power words as honest. He says that he might tell a friend her child is a little "undisciplined," but in his memoirs he would write that the kid is a "brat." Power also comes from active verbs. A passive compound verb like "was driving" is much weaker than "drove." He also suggests eliminating the "to be" verbs such as *is, am, was,* or *will be.* They are static. "Cigar smoke was in the air" is weaker than "cigar smoke filled the air."

Provost characterizes power words as "sense" and explains that, as you crowd more meaning into a short space, you gain power. The word *bully* is a sense word packed with punch and describes a person better than a phrase like *a mean person. Wrote rapidly* can be changed to *scribbled* and *kissed lightly* to *pecked.* Provost says power words are usually the most familiar; obscure words just get passed by. A dentist may know what a *mandible* is but the rest of us respond better to *jaw.* However, he notes that many familiar words are common to the point of boring. Instead of *wet,* for example, he suggests *moist* or *damp.*

An example of an advertisement that flirts with the unusual, obscure word is found in an ad for the Cayman Islands. The ad tries to break away from the clichés of travel promotion with a headline that says, "The climate of the Caymans is conducive to concinnity." While *concinnity* may be a perfectly good word, since it means "a harmony of fitness" and "studied elegance of design," it is totally unfamiliar. (It took three dictionaries to find one that had a definition.)

On the other hand, a beautifully written ad for cashmere sweaters uses strong distinctive words carefully chosen for their imagery. It begins: "On the slopes of the world's highest mountain range begins a remarkable journey that ends on one of life's lovely miracles." The power words are found in the second graph that continues: "Here the precious, downy fleece of the Kashmir goat is hand-plucked and taken by ox-cart to a railroad, then a coastal steamer and finally a cargo vessel which churns across the ocean to Scotland."

Study the word choices and feel the richness of their imagery: "downy fleece," "hand-plucked," "ox-cart," "coastal steamer," "cargo vessel," and "churns across the ocean." Even though the end product is a delicate sweater, the writing reflects the feel of raw unprocessed fleece in transit. You can almost smell it.

Words also have gender. In an article on "whip words," Charles Ferguson says that men manage the language and have used typically male expressions to express power.[6] He explains that "man words carry the oldest articulated feelings of the role. Those seeking to arouse people to good causes use man words naturally, whether they are appropriate or not." An example is hymns, which he says "resound with battle language."

He also notes that "in periods of national crisis the emotions of the male military tradition" are expressed in words of killing and conquest. These are used openly, he says, "to stimulate the contentious and combative side of our nature." Advertising talks about campaigns, targets, and strategies, obviously a field dominated by male language.

An example of an advertisement that uses strong male language to flag the reader is one by Smirnoff. It is also an example of a repositioning attempt. The ad shows a hunk of pastrami on top of a hunk of swiss cheese with a martini in a glass precariously balanced on top. The ad is clearly trying to associate martinis with such male eating situations as Sunday afternoon football, and this comes through in the phrasing of the headline that states: "Chow down!"

Good writers are verbal hypnotists. As Provost explains in his article on "power" words, "hypnosis is an artificially created sleep-like condition in which an individual is extremely responsive to suggestion."[7] And then he observes, "I can't think of any one more responsive to suggestion than an enthralled reader." How reading hypnotizes is a function of word choice. Provost says, "Some words are absolutely mesmerizing. Some merely induce a mild trance. And some are so poorly chosen that they wenfranckmonckin jar the reader out of his trance." Wenfranckmonckin, of course, is the misfit word that jarred you out of your reading trance. You are reading along hearing the words in the author's tone of voice and then something jars you into waking up and you're conscious of reading. The trance is established by well-chosen words and broken by a bad word.

Well-written advertising copy tries to create this hypnotic, mesmerizing state where reading becomes total concentration. One aspect of this kind of writing is using words to create mood and atmosphere, a verbal spell.

Certain products lend themselves to atmosphere writing—namely perfume, cosmetics, and liquor. Old Grand Dad has been running a "Spirit of America" campaign that features beautiful shots of landscapes, often nostalgic, and a few lines of copy to capture the mood of the illustration. One depicts a riverboat scene through trees from the bank. The illustration caption says "Sundown on the Mississippi." The copy reads, "'Men with imagination as big as the Delta Sky tamed the Mississippi. And at sunset, rivermen still wind down the day sipping America's native whiskey, Kentucky Bourbon." Another ad in the same series shows a cowboy on horseback herding cattle. Titled "Wyoming winter," the copy picks up a famous line from an early Jordan car ad:

"Somewhere west of Laramie, men still ride from dawn til dusk. And settle down to a shot of Bourbon against the chill of the night."

One of the most impressive advertisements ever was written by Bill Marsteller as a house ad for his agency. It ran in the *Wall Street Journal* under the headline "The wonderful world of words." The entire article plays with the connotative meaning of words. It starts out: "Human beings come in all sizes, a variety of colors, in different ages, and with unique, complex and changing personalities. So do words. There are tall, skinny words and short, fat ones, and strong ones and weak ones, and boy words and girl words." The rest of the copy illustrates the sizes, colors, ages, shapes, and personalities of words. (See Exhibit 3–1.)

Associations.   One aspect of connotative meaning is the associated meanings of a word. *Association* is the process of making connections in the mind; the connections may or may not be logical to someone else. It's just what pops into your mind when you hear or think of a word.

Associated meanings are of specific interest in naming things. The National Marine Fisheries Service (NMFS) puts seafood on the American table. Unfortunately these fish have such unappetizing names as pout, pigfish, gag, snook, dogfish, shovelnose, and ratfish. There has been some success in changing the common names or relabeling them by the species name. For example, redfish sells better as ocean perch and pollock sells as Boston bluefish. NMFS found that a name change can overcome this public resistance, not to the fish, but to the name that is perceived as ugly or has an unpleasant association.

Probably the most famous sophisticated research into product names was conducted for a product that wound up with an absolutely unmarketable name, the Edsel. (Of course, some say the design was unmarketable, too.) Over a three-year period the agency came up with and tested, using association and projection techniques, some 2,000 names; then started over again with a new list of 18,000; whittled that down to 6,000, only to have the chairman throw them all out and use a family name, Edsel.

Some of the names considered included Mars, Jupiter, Rover, Arrow, Dart, Ovation, Altair, Phoenix, Drof (Ford backward), Zoom, Zip, Corsair, Citation, Pacer, Ranger. You might note that some of these rejects have since appeared as successful car models. Marianne Moore, a poet, suggested Intelligent Bullet, Utopian Turtletop, Bullet Cloisonné, Pastelogram, Mongoose Civique, and Andante con Moto.

Sounds of Words

The sound a word makes can be a critical aspect of its choice. The noted columnist, William Safire, once ran a contest in the *New York Times Sunday Magazine* for the most beautiful word. He called it the "Miss Word Contest."[8] The entries were categorized by sounds—meaning didn't count—only words that

EXHIBIT 3-1: "The wonderful world of words" is a house ad by Marsteller Inc. that expresses the power of well-chosen words. (Courtesy of Marsteller Inc.)

Human beings come in all sizes, a variety of colors, in different ages, and with unique, complex and changing personalities.

So do words.

There are tall, skinny words and short, fat ones, and strong ones and weak ones, and boy words and girl words and so on.

For instance, title, lattice, latitude, lily, tattle, Illinois and intellect are all lean and lanky. While these words get their height partly out of "t's" and "l's" and "i's", other words are tall and skinny without a lot of ascenders and descenders. Take, for example, Abraham, peninsula and ellipsis, all tall.

Here are some nice short-fat words: hog, yogurt, bomb, pot, bonbon, acne, plump, sop and slobber.

Sometimes a word gets its size from what it means but sometimes it's just how the word sounds. Acne is a short-fat word even though pimple, with which it is associated, is a puny word.

Puny words are not the same as feminine words. Feminine words are such as tissue, slipper, cute, squeamish, peek, flutter, gauze and cumulus. Masculine words are like bourbon, rupture, oak, cartel, steak and socks. Words can mean the same thing and be of the opposite sex. Naked is masculine, but nude is feminine.

Sex isn't always a clear-cut, yes-or-no thing on upper Madison Avenue or Division Street, and there are words like that, too. On a fencing team, for instance, a man may compete with a sabre and that is definitely a masculine word. Because it is also a sword of sorts, an épée is also a boy word, but you know how it is with épées.

Just as feminine words are not necessarily puny words, masculine words are not necessarily muscular. Muscular words are thrust, earth, girder, ingot, cask, Leo, ale, bulldozer, sledge and thug. Fullback is very muscular; quarterback is masculine but not especially muscular.

Words have colors, too.

Red: fire, passion, explode, smash, murder, rape, lightning, attack.

Green: moss, brook, cool, comfort, meander, solitude, hammock.

Black: glower, agitate, funeral, dictator, anarchy, thunder, tomb, somber, cloak.

Beige: unctuous, abstruse, surrender, clerk, conform, observe, float.

San Francisco is a red city, Cleveland is beige, Asheville is green and Buffalo is black.

Shout is red, persuade is green, rave is black and listen is beige.

Oklahoma is brown, Florida is yellow, Virginia is light blue and Massachusetts is dark green, almost black. Although they were all Red, at one point Khrushchev was red-red, Castro orange, Mao Tse-tung gray and Kadar black as hate.

One of the more useful characteristics of words is their age.

There's youth in go, pancake, hamburger, bat, ball, frog, air, surprise, morning and tickle. Middle age brings abrupt, moderate, agree, shade, stroll and uncertain. Fragile, lavender, astringent, acerbic, fern, velvet, lace, worn and Packard are old. There never was a young Packard, not even the touring car.

Mostly, religion is old. Prayer, vespers, choir, Joshua, Judges, Ruth and cathedral are all old. Once, temple was older than cathedral and it still is in some parts of the world, but in the United States, temple is now fairly young. Rocker is younger than it used to be, too.

Saturday, the seventh day of the week, is young while Sunday, the first day of the week, is old. Night is old, and so, although more old people die in the hours of the morning just before the dawn, we call that part of the morning, incorrectly, night.

Some words are worried and some radiate disgusting self-confidence. Pill, ulcer, twitch, itch, stomach and peek are all worried words. Confident, smug words are like proud, lavish, major, divine, stare, dare, ignore, demand. Suburb used to be a smug word and still is in some parts of the country, but not so much around New York anymore. Brooklyn, by the way, is a confident word and everyone knows the Bronx is a worried word. Joe is confident; Horace is worried.

Now about shapes.

For round products, round companies or round ideas use dot, bob, melon, loquacious, hock, bubble and bald. Square words are, for instance, box, cramp, sunk, block and even ankle. Ohio is round but Iowa, a similar word, is square but not as square as Nebraska. Boston is, too—not as square as Nebraska, but about like Iowa. The roundest city is, of course, Oslo.

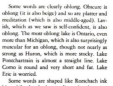

Some words are clearly oblong. Obscure is oblong (it is also beige) and so are platter and meditation (which is also middle-aged). Lavish, which as we saw is self-confident, is also oblong. The most oblong lake is Ontario, even more than Michigan, which is also surprisingly muscular for an oblong, though not nearly as strong as Huron, which is more stocky. Lake Pontchartrain is almost a straight line. Lake Como is round and very short and fat. Lake Erie is worried.

Some words are shaped like Rorschach ink blots. Like drool, plot, mediocre, involvement, liquid, amoeba and phlegm.

At first blush (which is young), fast words seem to come from a common stem (which is puny). For example, dash, flash, bash and brash are all fast words. However, ash, hash and gnash are all slow. Flush is changing. It used to be slow, somewhat like sluice, but it is getting faster. Both are wet words, as is Flushing, which is really quite dry compared to New Canaan, which sounds drier but is much wetter. Wilkinsburg, as you would expect, is dry, square, old and light gray. But back to motion.

Raid, rocket, piccolo, hound, bee and rob are fast words. Guard, drizzle, lard, cow, sloth, muck and damp are slow words. Fast words are often young and slow words old, but not always. Hamburger is young but slow, especially when uncooked. Astringent is old but fast. Black is old, and yellow—nearly opposite on the spectrum—is young, but orange and brown are nearly next to each other and orange is just as young as yellow while brown is only middle-aged. Further, purple, though darker than lavender, is not as old; however, it is much slower than violet, which is extremely fast.

Because it's darker, purple is often softer than lavender, even though it is younger. Lavender is actually a rather hard word. Not as hard as rock, edge, point, corner, jaw, trooper, frigid or trumpet, but hard nevertheless. Lamb, lip, thud, sofa, fuzz, stuff, froth and madam are soft. Although they are the same thing, timpani are harder than kettle drums, partly because drum is a soft word (it is also fat and slow) and as pots and pans go, kettle is one of the softer.

There is a point to all of this.

Ours is a business of imagination. We are employed to make corporations personable, to make useful products desirable, to clarify ideas, to create friendships in the mass for our employers.

We have great power to do these things. We have power through art and photography and graphics and typography and all the visual elements that are part of the finished advertisement or the published publicity release.

And these are great powers. Often it is true that one picture is worth ten thousand words.

But not necessarily worth one word.

The *right* word.

The Wonderful World of Words

the ear of the hearer would find beautiful. The winners in some of the most "beautiful" sound categories are as follows:

zh: *illusion and mirage*
s: *quintessence, celestial, crystalline, with russet and sunset as runners-up*
sh: *ravish*
w: *wherewithal, wonderland, windward, dawning, and waterfall*
m: *mom followed by madrigal, meander, and mesmerize*
v: *lovely, evanescent, suave, gravel*
f: *dolphin, effervescent, taffeta, daffodil*
l: *lilacs, lullaby, laurel, lavender, lanolin, soliloquy, cellar, hollow*
m & l: *marshmallow, marmalade, melancholy, llama, lemonade, salamander, pell mell*

And the winner of the Miss Word Contest was from the *l* & *m* lexicographic category—"mellifluous." Incidentally, Safire also determined that the leader in the "Ugly Word Contest" was "glut."

Consonants. Advertising is particularly enamored of a sound linguists call the "plosives." These are *k, p, b, c, d,* and *g.* A Michigan State advertising professor, Bruce Vanden Bergh, described the effect of these letters: "When the sound is actually made, a small explosion is created by the sudden rush of air out of the mouth almost creating a popping noise."[9]

Vanden Bergh noted that of the top 200 brand names on the 1981 *Marketing and Media Decisions* list, 172 contained at least one "plosive." Some examples are Bic, Buick, Burger King, Cadillac, Coca-Cola, Colgate, Datsun, Delta, K-Mart, Kodak, Kraft, Pabst, Pampers, Pepsi-Cola, Pizza Hut, Tab, and Tide. He comments that "given the intent of brand names to be easily recognized (and remembered) amid the clutter of names in the marketplace (350,000 or more), it makes sense to get the greatest impact possible from the first sound you hear in the name." Nasals like *m* and *n,* for example, are much weaker and less attention-getting consonants.

The s sound has a number of interesting effects. In advertising, it is used to create a mood than can range from soft and sultry to sophisticated or siren. In a marvelous piece of writing for Rolls-Royce, the copywriter used the s sound in a heavy paragraph of product attribute description. Notice how the repetition of the s ties the otherwise hard mechanical functions into a soft, easy flowing, well-oiled piece of machine art:

To cite but three examples, a unique automatic air-conditioning system maintains any temperature you desire at two levels of the interior: a sophisticated rack-and-pinion system turns the humble steering wheel into a thing of ease and precision; a self-leveling suspension system lets you forgive and forget the rudest of uneven roads.

(7) In terms of strong sounds, advertising copywriters have long known that consonants give the distinctive color to a word. Scotty Sawyer, one of Marsteller's all-time great copywriters, wrote a column recommending the use of short words—four-letter words, to be exact—because they are heavy with consonants.

He explained how it occurred to him that four-letter words are so effective: "They have such a high percentage of consonants. Now consonants are what give words definition. Vowels are just connectives between consonants." He cited "scratch" as a word he considers a beautiful example of consonant vowel ratio: "Seven letters, only one vowel. It even has an onomatopoetic effect: 'scratch' sounds like a scratch."

Onomatopoeia.   Certain words have been created as an echo of a sound: clatter, clang, clink, ping, rat-a-tat, ding-dong, tick-tock, hum, whir, buzz, gurgle, and splash are a few examples. (Notice the consonant/vowel ratio in the preceding list of words.) These words are rich in audio imagery, and their associations reverberate in the mind of the reader or hearer.

A wonderful example of the use of *onomatopoeia* in advertising was in the classic "Head for the mountains" campaign for Busch beer. The campaign broke with an ad that showed a close up of a can of Busch being opened and the word "BUSCHHHHHHHHH!" sprayed across the double-page spread. The copy by Jim Kochevar read, "Introducing a new beer with a bright new taste. And even a sound all its own."

Another example of elegant copywriting using word sounds is found in the "Sounds of Silence" tourism campaign for Ontario. In one, the illustration shows two fishermen on a foggy lake. Onomatopoeia is carefully worked into the first sentence, which reads: "The dip and pull and ripple of the paddle, the whistle whirring of the reel, the echo of the loon." The scene comes alive by its sounds because the copywriter has crafted an indelible audio image.

Another type of sound-alike is the word play behind puns. One of the curiosities of the English language is that a word sound can be spelled in a number of different ways. When spoken, "white shoes" sounds like "why choose?" This sound-alike phenomenon was the basis for a Hazel Luggage ad that showed a variety of attractively arranged briefcases and the headline, "Which Hazel?"

Alliteration.   Another dimension of word sounds is repetition. *Alliteration* is the repetition of the same sound—usually the initial sound, although it can be in other parts of the word. Words with high internal alliteration include *bobble, dawdle, bumblebee, orangutang,* and *tintinnabulation.* The last word, defined as the noisy ringing of bells, is also onomatopoetic.

Usually, however, alliteration occurs within a phrase or sentence with multiple words beginning with or repeating the same sound. A poetic piece of copy for Cabriole perfume ends with this description of the fragrance.

A melding of flowers
and more flowers

mingled with a fresh flourish
of spices.
We call it Cabriole

Parallel construction. Repetition of sounds can also be constructed from one phrase or sentence to another. This is a literary device called *parallel construction*. It is used for emphasis and accent. With heavy bold words, it is like pounding on the table with your first. With softer words it is a gentle form of insistence. An ad by Nationwide Insurance targeted to young career women used parallel construction in the headline: "Your own car. Your own phone. Your own place. Your dad's insurance?"

An advertisement for Thunderbird used parallel construction for effect in the headline and the body copy. The headline states: "Pure form. Pure function." The two primary subheads are: "The observer's perspective," and "The driver's perspective." The closing body copy reads: "If you have not yet driven one, we strongly urge that you do. It's pure form. Pure function. Pure Thunderbird."

In addition to emphasis, it is also used to develop a cadence or flow and to control the pace of the reading. An example of a well-constructed parallel sentence is found in a paragraph from the Rolls-Royce ad for the Silver Wraith II. The preceding sentence talks about the engineers and artisans who build Rolls-Royce. The copy continues with this sentence:

> *It is in their marrow to revere the past, relish the present and welcome the future all at once, because the driving force behind a Rolls is not merely to come and go, but to go on and on.*

That passage is an inspiring example of parallel construction, alliteration, and sensitive word choice.

Rhyme. The most common type of sound repetition used in advertising is *rhyme*, where the ending sounds of the words are repeated. Early advertisements around the turn of the century and up until 1930 or so used full rhyme in the body copy. More recent advertising style uses copy that speaks directly to the audience in natural language, so that these old "poetic" ads now sound quaint. Occasionally, full rhyme is used deliberately for effect. Primarily, rhyme is used in radio copy for jingles.

An example of rhyme used in body copy is found in an ad for TraveLodge. It used a series of six photos in a panel layout with the following string of subheads.

"Wine" (bar scene)	*"Dine" (restaurant)*
"Plan" (meeting rooms)	*"If you can" (swimming pool)*
"Save" (typical room)	*"Rave" (driving away in car)*

A Beefeater Gin advertisement uses full rhyme for body copy in a parody of the famous poem, *The Children's Hour*. (See Exhibit 3–2).

Rhythm.   Rhythm is the musical sound of words. The pattern of words with their stressed and unstressed syllables can be used to create a cadence and the cadence can be soft and gentle, sprightly marching, or even foot stomping.

Poetry is scanned in terms of certain conventional patterns of stress, and this scanning system is useful for anyone writing copy where the beat or meter is important. Jingle writers, in particular, need to be able to use this notational system to analyze the metrical structure of their phrases.

The symbol / is used to indicate a stress and the symbol v is used to indicate unstressed or weak stress. A common pattern of two or three beats is called a ''foot,'' and there are four common types of metrical feet. These four patterns are as follows:

> Iambic: v /
> Trochee: / v
> Dactylic: / v v
> Anapestic: v v /

Iambic is the beat of the march: *dactylic* is the beat of the waltz. Generally, two beats are stronger than three, and the stressed last syllable is stronger than the stressed first syllable. The old literary stereotype calls trochee and dactylic passive or feminine meters (fashion and passion). The unstressed first syllable is considered aggressive or masculine (inventive, perform, assure, iconoclast). The Beefeater hour, obviously targeted to males, is written with an anapestic foot.

> v   /   v v / v v / v v /
> *The Beefeater hour: it usually comes*

The anapestic foot is also the meter behind limericks.

The most famous advertisements to use rhythm and rhyme were the Burma Shave roadsigns—perhaps the most famous and best liked advertising campaign ever. Each of the four lines was on a successive sign and created a moving billboard effect. The folksy down-home rhymes captivated road-weary readers.

> *He played the sax*
> *had no B.O.*
> *But his whiskers scratched*
> *so she let him go.*
> *Burma Shave*

Most advertising copy is not written to a beat, although cadence can be important when you are trying to develop a well-crafted parallel construc-

EXHIBIT 3-2: The "Beefeater Hour" is an unusual use of a poetic
form in advertising copy. (Reprinted with permission
of James Burrough and Kobrand Corporation)

tion. Where metrical scanning is more useful is in the writing of slogans and jingles. Both use meter and cadence and since jingles are set to music, the beat may, in some cases, be more important than the words.

Slogans are short and catchy. Their memorability is enhanced by the use of rhythm and sometimes rhyme. They should be easy to slide off the tongue. Notice the cadence in the following slogans:

When you care enough to send the very best
We bring good things to life
You deserve a break today
The pause that refreshes
99 and 44/100 percent pure
When it rains, it pours
When it positively, absolutely, has to be there overnight
The wings of man

Jingle writing demands a good ear for rhythm. All songs are written to an underlying beat pattern. It is the repetition of the words to a beat that makes jingles so memorable. An example of a slogan that has been adapted to a jingle format is "Look for the union label" and "When you've said Bud, you've said it all." Once you've heard the jingle, it's almost impossible to say the slogan without hearing the beat and melody in your mind.

A campaign jingle that uses effective alliteration as well as a strong beat and memorable melody is the Doublemint "double doubling" theme. The "Be a Pepper" song-and-dance spectaculars along with the "Catch that Pepsi spirit, drink it in," jingles are strong rhythmic songs.

McDonald's has had success with rhythmic chants, including the famous "two all-beef patties," which had all the kids in town competing to see who could say it. Another McDonald's television commercial called "Double Dutch" has a team of four girls doing intricate fancy footwork to the old double dutch jump-roping game. The rhythmic chant the jumpers used to coordinate their split-second footwork is nothing other than a recital of the McDonald's menu: "Big Mac, Filet of Fish, Quarter Pounder, French Fries, Icy Coke, Thick Shakes, Sundaes, Apple Pies." It's interesting to see that you can impose a strong beat pattern on something as variable as a list of menu items.

Word order.   Word order is another important consideration in the analysis of cadence. You may break the natural cadence deliberately to add an attention-getting discordant beat. In addition to calling attention, word order can add emphasis and change meaning. An example cited by William Safire in a *New York Times* column[10] illustrates the difference in wording between the following variations on the famous song:

I only have eyes for you
I have only eyes for you

I have eyes for you only
Only I have eyes for you

The power of word order to affect meaning was illustrated in the same Safire column by a quote from John Glenn about his meeting with Reagan. Glenn described himself as "sitting down with the most powerful single man in the free world." As Safire pointed out, "Who is the most powerful married man?" Obviously, what Glenn had intended to say was: "The single most powerful man."

Euphony. "Euphonious" is a 50-cent word that means everything fits well together and the resulting sound is pleasant, agreeable, and harmonious. It is used here to summarize all the intricacies of phrasing—the exact literal meaning, the connotations and nuances, the sounds including onomatopoeia, alliteration, parallel construction, rhyme, and rhythm—in short, all the aesthetic considerations of any literary work. Advertising copy, when it is concerned with using the right words, is as much of an art form as any other literary effort.

An example of advertising that can be described as "euphonious"— and also poetic—is a long-running campaign by Waterford Crystal. A typical ad from the series will feature one goblet or bowl, and the copy will try to develop the essence of this piece of crystal. Notice the cadence, alliteration, and parallel construction in the following Waterford example:

Light a Crystal Fire.
The light of
the stars.
The light of
the sun.
The light of
Waterford Crystal.
A legend
blown by mouth,
cut wholly by hand,
with heart.

This is the copy for an ad used to introduce a book inspired by the campaign. (See Exhibit 3–3.)

Waterford pours forth memories.
It conjures up fantasies,
evokes poetic imagery,
provokes the creative spirit,
celebrates life's mysteries.
It is never too early nor too late
to assume the title:
Waterford Collector.

EXHIBIT 3-3: Waterford Crystal is an elegant product whose image is reflected in the elegant phrasing of its copy.
(Courtesy of Waterford Crystal)

Some begin at birth.
Others as nonagenarians.
To the collector,
a piece of Waterford crystal
is more than a drinking vessel,
more than a vase,
a decanter, a lamp, a chandelier;
more than a family heirloom,
more than an object d'art;
It is an incentive to lose weight,
to win forgiveness,
a way to attract a lover,
to distract a patient,
to symbolize hope,
to crystallize a dream,
to bid adieu,
to hail the seasons,
to raise spirits,
to diminish melancholy,
to mark events,
to start traditions,
to end a day;
It is a noble rite of passage.
Born of the breath of man,
Waterford is life's child.

3.2 WRITING STYLE

Literary style and advertising style are entirely different. In literary style, writers display their unique way of looking at the world. A writer's style is personal, like facial features and fingerprints. The writer's unique viewpoint colors and shades all his or her messages so, regardless of the content, you can tell by the style of the writing who the author is.

In advertising writing the author is anonymous—no byline, no ego trip. There is no personal style. The good copywriter, like a good actor, can shift to reflect the product and the message strategy. The copywriter may work on an ad for tissues one day and trucks the next. The writer must be endlessly adaptable.

Rather than uniqueness of style, versatility of style is valued in advertising. The writer still uses literary style to express nuances and personalities, it is just that the personality expressed is the product's, not the writer's. Advertising copywriting demands the same high level of writing talent. Some might even say it is harder to master many styles than it is to develop one.

If the writer—or, in many cases, the agency—seems to be developing a personal style, it is probably because the products are in the same or a related category. David Ogilvy's urbane, sophisticated style was mirrored in the products his agency handled, such as Rolls-Royce, Steuben Glass, and Hathaway Shirts.

Idiomatic language.   Advertising writing does have some general style characteristics. Ad copy is written the way people talk, and it recognizes that different people talk different ways in different situations. That's called *idiomatic language*. A well-targeted message will mirror the natural language used by the target audience in normal situations where they would encounter a discussion of the product. For status products, like Mercedes-Benz, you might find yourself using formal sentence constructions, but for most of our everyday products we use everyday language.

One aspect of idiomatic language is that it is contemporary. Key phrases from the vernacular are used to establish this contemporary cue. There are phrases that peg speech as "in" or, if you are not careful, dated. Dated expressions include such phrases as "cool," "neat," "with it," "to be sure," or "spaced out." These trendy phrases were current at one time, and they now sound as old as last year's leisure suit looks.

Contemporary phrases are used in advertising deliberately to identify the product with a trend, particularly in fashion or in any area related to design. Advertising is transitory. Such phrases can be used as long as they are still current. If the campaign is a long-running one, it is wise to avoid this aspect of vernacular language.

An analysis of this use of trendy language was developed by William Safire in a *New York Times Sunday Magazine* column.[11] He analyzed a popular electrical metaphor:

> To turn on, as in turning on a light, was originally drug culture lingo, later gained sexual overtones, and now means "to excite, interest or titillate"; one who is "turned on" or "switched on" is hip, with it, an avant-gardian.

He continued, "The latest version of this electrical connection is 'plugged in.' If you are still saying 'turned on,' you are not plugged in." He found this metaphor in a Macy's ad for Gloria Vanderbilt corduroy jeans. The ad was head-lined: "Gloria Vanderbilt switches to plugged-in cords." Safire observed that "with corduroy clipped to 'cords,' the word gains an allusion to an electrical cord, which plugs in to a neat fit."

Safire also noted that this same ad used "punched up" to describe a color labeled "grape." The Macy's creative director explained that "punched up" went well with "plugged in" and that "punched up is fashionese for 'made brighter'—cobalt rather than navy, grape rather than burgundy."

Idiomatic language doesn't sound (or look) like the formal English used to write essays. It is conversational; it sounds like the natural language you would use talking to a friend or writing a letter to your mother. Reva Korda, a creative head at Ogilvy and Mather and a member of the agency's board of directors, advises writers not to labor too long on a writing assignment because the naturalness of the writing will wither.[12]

She explains that "an advertisement is not an intellectual exercise, and the longer you take to write it, the further away you will get from the person you are talking to. Because that's all advertising is—talking to a friend, and telling him, or more likely her, about a service or product."

Brevity.   Some specific characteristics of conversational language that are used in advertising writing include the use of short sentences, even sentence fragments. Conversational language is spoken in thoughts and "thought" expressions are usually very simple sentence constructions—and short. Thoughts don't always come out constructed in full-blown sentences, particularly if they are run-on thoughts. For that reason you will see lots of sentences in advertising writing that begin with *and* and *but.*

Short paragraphs are another characteristic of advertising writing. Most paragraphs in advertising are rarely longer than a couple of sentences, and some are only one sentence long. There's a visual reason for that. Copy that is written in short packages looks easier to read than the long, gray, forbidding paragraphs you find in textbooks.

Personal.   Advertising copy is also written in personal language with lots of "yous." Avoid the corporate "we," which sounds pompous, but use the other personal pronouns. "I" is used in testimonials. The reason for emphasizing "you" is that it forces you to think in terms of your consumer's interest and benefits. It also overcomes some of the distance and anonymity that plagues most forms of mass communication.

Another characteristic of advertising copy is the use of present tense and active voice. *Past tense* may be found in corporate "we" copy where there is a tendency to list what has been accomplished or to explain why something was done the way it was. *Present tense* develops the feeling of immediacy, of a conversation that is happening as you read. *Active voice* is a more powerful form than passive and advertising values dynamic, assertive language. Contractions are okay also. They're a natural part of natural speech.

Simple.   Advertising writing is simple. Simplicity is valued for clarity of meaning and ease of reading. Use simple words; use simple sentence constructions. Caples was a believer in the power of simplicity. He said, "Simple words are powerful words. Even the best educated people don't resent simple words."[13] He continued, "They're the only words many people understand. Write to your barber, or mechanic or elevator operator." The ad called "Keep it simple" is an institutional ad by United Technologies. (See Exhibit 3–4.)

Rathbun in an article in *Writer's Digest* made the point that long, fancy words are often just masquerading for learning.[14] These pompous words are pre-

EXHIBIT 3-4: **"Keep it simple," with its emphasis on clarity of communication, is one advertisement from a corporate campaign for United Technologies.** (Courtesy of United Technologies Corp.)

Keep It Simple

Strike three.
Get your hand off my knee.
You're overdrawn.
Your horse won.
Yes.
No.
You have the account.
Walk.
Don't walk.
Mother's dead.
Basic events
require simple language.
Idiosyncratically euphuistic
eccentricities are the
promulgators of
triturable obfuscation.
What did you do last night?
Enter into a meaningful
romantic involvement
or
fall in love?
What did you have for
breakfast this morning?
The upper part of a hog's
hind leg with two oval
bodies encased in a shell
laid by a female bird
or
ham and eggs?
David Belasco, the great
American theatrical producer,
once said, "If you can't
write your idea on the
back of my calling
card,
you don't have a clear idea."

tenders, just "pretentious words and phrases that express ordinary thoughts." The list below includes some of Rathbun's pretenders as well as some compiled by Marsteller's Scotty Sawyer. The list contains the pretentious word followed by its simpler synonym:

attempt (try)	*inaugurate (begin)*
purchase (buy)	*incarcerate (jail)*
purloin (steal)	*employ (use, hire)*
antagonist (enemy)	*obtain (get)*
veracity (truth)	*maintenance (care)*
prevaricate (lie)	*produce (make)*
terminate (end)	*facilitate (help)*
peruse (read)	*eliminate (save, get rid of)*

The tendency to use pompous words creeps into advertising copy. William Safire, in his *New York Times* column, noted that ad copy has moved from simple nouns to elegant nouns that require elaborate adjectives.[15] He quoted the following Pentax ad:

> Sixty years of research and human engineering have given rise to a remarkable photographic instrument. The Pentax LX is a photographic instrument of such quality that it will exhilarate you.

Note the use of such phrases as "human engineering," whatever that means, and "photographic instrument" instead of camera. He also observed that Chrysler is now calling its product "America's personal driving machine" instead of a car.

Natural. These are the primary characteristics of advertising writing: idiomatic language, short sentences and paragraphs, sentence fragments, personal pronouns, and direct address, present, tense, and active voice. It's natural writing using simple language—not affected, not cute, not pedantic or preachy. It's a conversation about the product, service, or idea. If you can't imagine yourself saying what you've written to someone you know who fits the profile of the target audience, then you haven't written natural language.

An example of advertising style is found in an ad for Bayer aspirin. It is targeted to a businessman and shows an executive at his desk with his hand to his head and a pained expression on his face. The headline says, "Even for this headache . . . all you need is Bayer." The copy, using short sentence fragments and direct address, says:

> Too much to do. Not enough time to do it. Result? That "business" headache. Even for one that bad, all you need is Bayer aspirin.

Advertising style sounds simple—it *is* simple. But it is not simple to *write.* Few people write as they talk. The minute you pick up a pencil or strike a typewriter key, all those years of English composition will bubble to the surface and you'll find yourself writing formal English using complete sentences with multiple levels of phrases and bigger, more impressive words. Writing simple is more difficult than writing formal.

Reva Korda has some suggestions on how to write natural.[16] She observes that "if you've got a pretty good idea of what you want to say, and you haven't complicated the whole thing so disastrously that you've wound up terrifying yourself, the advertisement will write itself."

The most common complication is strategy hypnosis. You can study the M.B.A. jargon and worry about positions and objectives until all your powers of imagination have been turned off. It's like throwing a blanket over the whole creative process. There's nothing wrong with studying the research and the strategy as background—you have to know the background before you know *what* to write—but don't get hypnotized by the marketing lingo.

Put all the formal documents in your bottom drawer and forget all the pompous phrasing in the creative platform. A lot of the bad writing we see in advertising comes from lifting the copy platform or strategy statement and turning it into the ad copy. It will never read like natural language.

Strategy hypnosis often creates "writer's blocks." You know you're not doing something right because you can't write. Korda explains it this way. "If you have a lot of misery writing it, if it isn't coming naturally, something is probably wrong. Maybe what you're trying to say is too complicated. Maybe it isn't worth saying at all. You don't agonize over talking to a friend, and you shouldn't have to agonize over writing to a friend."

There's a little book called *Zen and the Art of Archery,* which Professor Ed Stephens at Syracuse University uses to teach his copywriting students how to write naturally. The author, Eugen Herrigel,[17] describes agonizing over the right moment to release the arrow and finally comes to the point of understanding that, when the arrow is ready to fly, it releases itself. In the same way natural copy writes itself. It's a beautiful metaphor to explain the concept of "naturalness" in any creative area.

The Right Tone

The word *tone* is used to describe a general atmosphere or a manner of expression. We say that "John speaks in an angry tone of voice." It is an elusive general word that implies shades of coloring, nuances, emotion, or personality. When a creative director or a client says, "It just doesn't feel right," he or she is probably referring to the tone.

Perhaps the best metaphor is tone of voice. We modulate and inflect our words to express emotions. The same thing happens with the choice of words (and visuals) for an advertisement. Some ads speak with authority and confidence. Some are bold, brash, loud, and screaming. Others are meek, reserved, and understated. Some have fun; some are angry. Identifying the right tone for an ad is just as important as choosing the right words for the headline.

The tone is determined by the product and its message objectives. The problem is to match all the elements to create a harmonious, perhaps even euphonious, tone. A circus barker style of delivery would be inappropriate for flowers, diamond rings, or a funeral home.

One way to analyze advertising tone is to develop a personality sketch of the product and the targeted audience. Robert H. Bloom, president of the Bloom Advertising Agency, has developed a concept he calls the "Personality Description Model" that his agency uses to create consistent, effective messages.[18] PDM is a description of the product as if it were a person. Bloom gave an example in an article in *Advertising Age* of a PDM he created for Southwest Airlines:

> She is probably somewhere between 20 and 25 years old and looks somewhat younger, perhaps 18 to 20. She is charming and goes through life with great flair and exuberance.
>
> The first thing you notice about her is her exciting smile, her friendly air, her wit. In reality, she is quite efficient, and approaches all her tasks with care and attention. However, because of her dynamic personality, her efficiency is not obvious, and is generally taken for granted.
>
> She is friendly and warm. Her hobbies are most likely horseback riding, swimming, and metal sculpture.

Another way to control the tone is to work with a photo file. Keep a file of photos of people—just clippings from newspapers and magazines. Pick out a photo that looks like a typical member of your audience. What kind of language would you use to talk to this person?

A variation on this technique is to ask yourself how the target would most likely hear about the product. Would he or she hear from a friend, from a relative, from a doctor, from a co-worker? Pick out a second photo that looks like the ideal source. Put the two photos on your desk in front of you and imagine these two people having a conversation about your product. What kind of language would they use between themselves? Would they be happy, excited, enthusiastic, sarcastic, logical, joking, sincere, relaxed, assertive? These adjectives all describe tone of voice. Let the tone of that imaginary conversation determine the tone of your copy.

The Chrysler turnaround ads featured Lee Iacocca, the president, using a mildly pugnacious tone of voice. After all this man was begging the government to save his company, fighting off creditors and critics, cajoling the unions, and trying to build back the confidence of his employees and dealers. You wouldn't expect him to be meek and humble.

An ad that ran in the middle of the debate over federal loan guarantees was headlined: "Would America be better off without Chrysler?" The copy is signed by Iacocca and John Riccardo, chairman of Chrysler. It's tough and blunt in tone:

> It's a fair question.
> You've heard from all the pundits, the instant experts, and the vested interests. They all have their favorite version of what's wrong with Chrysler.
> Now we'd like to set the record straight.
> We've made our share of mistakes in a tough competitive business. And we're willing to accept responsibility for them.
> But to turn our back on 140 thousand of our own employees would be irresponsibility.
> To close the doors in 52 American communities in which Chrysler is a major factor of the local economy would be irresponsibility.
> To deny employment to the 150 thousand people who work for the dealers who sell Chrysler products would be irresponsibility.
> To curtail the income of the hundreds of thousands who supply goods and services to Chrysler would be irresponsibility.

Another ad in an entirely different tone tries to sell Parker Brothers game of Sorry® to parents. The tone is one of a sympathetic friend who understands that parents have to play dumb kids' games whether they want to or not. The copy reads:

> Your seven-year-old asks you to play a game with her. You feel bad if you say no. You feel worse if you say yes and have to play a boring kids' game for an hour.
> Avoid this dilemma. Play Sorry.® It's a very amazing game. There's enough skill involved to keep you interested, and even excited.
> And there's enough luck to give your kids a real chance to beat you fair and square.

An appropriate tone of voice usually adds power to the advertising message. There are some tones, however, that can be relatively ineffective in advertising. Pedantic, preachy advertising that sounds like the stereotyped "schoolmarm" shaking her finger at you is rarely effective. No one likes to be lectured at or to.

The corporate "we" is a type of announcement advertising that consistently gets the lowest possible readership scores. Advertising should speak to the reader's interest rather than to the corporate interest. Similar in tone is the "brag-and-boast" style of advertising. It is "we" copy full of pompous, puffed statements of self-importance. Besides being irritating, there is nothing in it for the reader that makes it worth reading.

A negative tone sometimes comes across in copy. In your haste to control a competitive corner, you may sometimes find yourself taking potshots at the competition. Be very careful of negative blasts; they have a tendency to back-fire. If you have a positive statement to make about your product, then stick to the positive. Even strong comparative advertising can be written from a positive stance. There's something self-defeating about potshots. They smear your own product or client with a negative pallor at the same time they undermine anything you might have to say that is positive.

There's another type of negative that creeps into copy. Sometimes you will find copy that takes potshots at the reader. It's subtly patronizing. This is often inadvertent and the copywriter doesn't even realize the tone is there, but it is there and the reader recognizes it on some subconscious level. Usually, the copywriter is trying to write to a target that he or she can't identify with and it comes off as a putdown.

Along the same lines, be careful of threatening copy. Fear appeals have to be very carefully handled. Threatening copy is usually repelling rather than selling. If you have too much of an emphasis on cancer, you may be turning off the very person you are trying to reach.

If advertising works at all, it does so because it generally makes people feel good about themselves, their lifestyles, their decision making. A negative or threatening tone of voice rarely leaves people feeling good.

Another tone problem encountered in advertising is boredom. Yawn. The writer is bored, the creative director is bored, the artist is bored, and, as seen through their eyes, the product can never be anything but boring. Unfortunately, this malaise strikes the pseudosophisticated types who sometimes get jobs in advertising and then try to impress everyone with their urbane *savior-faire*. It's phony. It's boring. It reverberates through their writing and it doesn't sell. You've got to be able to get excited about a product to write exciting copy that sells.

Adese

The first section described what advertising writing *is:* this section describes what it is *not*—or at least what it's not supposed to be, since there are probably more examples of bad writing than there are of good writing. *Adese* is formula copy. It uses pat phrases, clichés, puffery and hype, generalizations and empty phrases, frayed out-of-date language, and stock promises.

Adese is a form of copywriting that is stilted, artificial, and hackneyed. It's the kind of copy that we all remember as "ad copy." We remember it for its style and for its quaint form—not for its message or for the product. It's the kind of advertising that gets laughs for comedians; the kind that gets parodied on TV.

Adese causes a problem in copytesting since most people carry a bundle of adese in their heads as typical of the genre. When you ask them which one they like best, they will often choose the version that comes closest to stereotyped ad writing.[19] After all, "that's what an ad is supposed to sound like." An ad, in other words, is supposed to fit their stereotyped concept of adness, which means it has to be high in adese.

Formula phrases.   So what do we mean by adese? The first category is the formula phrase. Often, this is a stock opening and closing. It is the "red flag" of adese because it signals that stereotyped ad writing is coming. Some typical formula phrases identified by advertising students are:

Introducing, announcing, presenting
Special introductory offer
Something we discovered
Doctors recommend
Your opportunity to
Congratulations, you have just
Welcome to the world of
You can't go wrong
Quick. Send one dollar and get
Yours from America's finest company
Brought to you from the workshops of
Don't wait any longer
Buy one today
Replace free of charge
For as long as you own
Don't settle for anything less
Backed by our unconditional guarantee
Fly/buy now, pay later
Last chance at these low prices
Avoid the last-minute rush

Puffery and hype.   Another highly visible form of adese is puffery, characterized by those exaggerated superlatives underscored with anonymous subjective opinions. Rotzoll and Rotfeld, two advertising professors, describe puffery as different from other advertised claims in that it uses exaggerations and inflated claims that the consumers are presumed not to believe.[20] In other words, it is thought that consumers see a statement like "the most beautiful" as just "seller's talk." Rotzoll and Rotfeld found in a study of puffery that many consumers do, in fact, believe such statements, even if they are puffery.

Puffery is not illegal in advertising, but it is unnatural in writing. When *Saturday Night Live* skits make fun of advertising, they are usually parodying the puffery. It's hype, and it robs copy of believability. Some examples of puffery found by advertising students include:

The most exciting, brilliant, effective, reliable, unique, perfect, important, romantic, talked about
The only, the latest, the most, the finest, the best

As close to perfection as you'll ever get
An exceptional opportunity
The best-kept secret in 50 years
Better than any other
Sheer elegance
The finest ingredients
An engineering triumph
The best the world has to offer
One of a kind
Perfect for every occasion
The ultimate experience
Incredible, exclusive, tremendous, amazing

Clichés.   Clichés are statements that were originally unique, strong attention getters. The first time a distinctive statement is used, it can stop the audience because of its novelty or unexpected imagery. When it gets borrowed and used over and over, it becomes a *cliché*. Clichés often use unexpected juxtapositions and metaphors. A statement becomes a cliché, not because of its phrasing, but because of its overuse. You tire of it easily because of its lack of novelty. Some familiar ones identfied by copywriting students are:

Talk of the town
Out of this world
Ripe old age
Everything but the kitchen sink
Broad daylight
Cold, hard cash
Night owls, early birds
Bottom line
High time
Mint condition
Quick as a flash

Frayed phrases.   A variation on the cliché is a phrase that comes to life on a television show, in a song, or as a slogan for a character actor. Sometimes it is a catchy phrase from another ad. The phrase gets attention and comes into popular usage as a fad phrase, but usually only for a short time. During that period you hear it everywhere. After the phrase wears out, it sounds terribly dated. Some examples are:

Where's the beef?
I can't believe I ate the whole thing
Believe it
Wild and crazy

Nothing ventured, nothing gained
The real thing
The new you
Love me, love my _____
Never on Sunday
Nobody does it better
It's happening/what's happening
Get truckin' keep truckin'
Would you believe
Don't look now, but . . .
If you like _____ , *you'll love* _____

Empty phrases and generalities.   The largest category of adese is one the scholars call "glittering generalities." These are empty phrases, space fillers. They may hint at some vague benefit, but without any substantiation, they carry little meaning. Some examples found by ad students are:

Fresh, luxury, quality, powerful
New, distinctive collection
A sign/symbol of quality
Choice beyond the traditional
An enchanting preview
You have never experienced anything like it
Intimately fresh
Deliciously different, totally different
Delightfully refreshing
Our reputation has been proven
Years ahead of its time
Age-old secret
An honored gift
The preferred taste
Names that are synonymous with quality
So much for so little
Made with you in mind

Stock promises.   Many advertising messages are benefit oriented; this means that the copy focuses on the user's benefits rather than the product's features. It describes what the product or service will do for the prospect. In some cases, it makes a promise to the prospect about what good things will happen to the person if he or she uses the product or service. But even this strategy has its stock phrases—both reasons why and promises. These phrases are used as codes to shortcut or signal the benefit. Here are some common stock promises uncovered by ad students:

You can't go wrong
Special protection
Assembles in a jiffy
Easy twistoff cap
Free with any purchase of _____
Convenient locations near you
Fits all sizes
Fun for the entire family
Last chance to buy at these low prices
One week from today you'll look more beautiful
Look years younger
Light, pure, natural, dependability, reliability, performance

Adese is easy to spot when you know what to look for. The formula phrases, puffery, clichés, frayed phrases, empty phrases, and stock promises are the working tools of a lazy copywriter. To improve the quality of advertising writing, everyone in the field needs to be sensitized to such stereotyped writing. Recognizing adese is a form of aesthetic judgment that anyone can develop.

NOTES

1. Ralph Zeuthen, "Top Notch Writing Offers Your Product or Idea a Better Chance," *Advertising Age*, April 21, 1975, p. 65.
2. John Caples, "Caples on Copy," *Wall Street Journal*, house ad series.
3. Jacques Nehr, "Computers as Ad Writer? Realtors Claim It Works," *Advertising Age*, August 11, 1980, p. 3.
4. Michael Gartner, "Words from Gartner," *Advertising Age*, April 11, 1982.
5. Gary Provost, "Pack Every Word with Power," *Writer's Digest*, February 1983, pp. 21–23.
6. Charles W. Ferguson, "How Whip Words Show America to Be Male Dominated," *National Observer*, April 17, 1967.
7. Provost, op. cit.
8. William Safire, "Miss Word of 1982," *New York Times Magazine*, June 27, 1982, pp. 9–10
9. Bruce G. Vanden Bergh, "More Chickens and Pickles," *Journal of Advertising Research*, March 1982.
10. William Safire, "Sleazy Does It," *New York Times Magazine*, December 27, 1981, pp. 7–8.
11. William Safire, "Effectificity," *New York Times Magazine*, January 10, 1982.
12. Reva Korda, "How to Break the Rules: Heresies About Writing copy," *Advertising Age*, March 5, 1979, p. 47.
13. John Caples, "Caples on Copy," house ad by *Wall Street Journal* that ran in *Advertising Age*.

14. Frank Rathbun, "Conciseness in F Major," *Writer's Digest,* August 1977, pp. 45–47.

15. William Safire, "By Any Other Name," *New York Times Magazine,* December 6, 1981, p. 22.

16. Korda, op. cit.

17. Eugen Herrigel, *Zen and the Art of Archery* (New York: Vantage Books, 1971).

18. "Product Personality Will Help Ads," *Advertising Age,* October 11, 1976, p. 89.

19. Sandra E. Moriarty, "E-Z Copy," *Industrial Marketing,* January 1983.

20. Herbert J. Rotfeld and Kim B. Rotzoll, "Is Advertising Puffery Believed?", *Journal of Advertising,* 9:3 (1980), pp. 16–20.

The Copy
Package

Chapter Four

The pieces that make up the copy package can be pulled apart and analyzed separately, but they are all woven together to create a total effect. We may talk about these pieces separately but remember that the impact of the advertising message is a function of synergism—all the pieces working together. The creative concept is the thread that runs throughout and ties everything together, including the visual elements.

The major pieces of the copy package include the headline, other display copy including overlines, underlines, captions and subheads, the lead, the body copy, transitions, the wrapup, and the signature. All of the display elements work to accomplish one of two overriding functions: to get attention and to stimulate interest.

4.1 HEADLINES

The headline is the most important part of the copy package. It works together with the visual to establish the creative concept or theme, the "Big Idea" that makes the advertisement interesting and original. This is called the integration of copy and art. The synergistic effect created when both the verbal and the visual are linked with a strong concept separates the outstanding ads from the mediocre.

117

Attention.   Headlines have several objectives, but the primary function of the head is to get the reader's attention. It is a red flag; its job is to make the reader stop. It has to be arresting enough *to be seen* when the reader is concentrating on other matters, such as the editorial content and other competing advertisements. It also has to be arresting enough *to stop* the scanning process. Many people "read" newspapers and magazines in a rhythmic fashion that involves briefly scanning the headline and visual and then turning the page. The rhythm has to be broken before an ad can be attended to or read. It takes verbal dynamite to break through either the editorial concentration or the almost mindless scanning.

Self-interest.   The next function of the headline is to capture the reader's self-interest. That's how an "arresting" headline works—it breaks through the wall of indifference by speaking to the reader's interest. Techniques employed to accomplish this include headlines that promise something or arouse curiosity. A claim can be arresting if it is unexpected or surprising. When you write a head, put yourself in the reader's place and ask, "What's in it for me?", or "Why should I stop and read this?"

An example of an arresting head is an old one for Fiat; it used type easily half the page in size with a headline that screamed "$400 back." This is verbal (and visual) dynamite. A more restrained example is found in a trade ad for General Electric that used both curiosity and a promise. It stated: "Changing the lamps in their office saved $23,000 a year."

Strong, arresting claims make good flags. An example is a headline for Peugeot that states: "Every Peugeot goes through hell to get to America." The supporting copy explains all the tests the car goes through at the factory.

Segment and target.   Another function of headlines is to sort out the audience and select the targeted prospects. It should be immediately clear from the headline whom you are addressing. You can segment by using questions and direct address, such as: "Are you a woman who . . . ?" or "A car for those who . . . ?" The targeting can also be a function of stylistics and word choice. An ad for Smirnoff discussed in a previous chapter used the headline, "Chow down," to specify a macho audience.

Another example of a clearly targeted headline is in an ad for Allstate Insurance that asks: "Do you own a small business?" There's no doubt whom the ad is speaking to and, furthermore, because of the compelling question, it is unlikely that an owner of a small business could avoid reading at least the headline, and probably the rest of the ad as well.

Product Identification.   Identifying the product or at least the product category is another function of the headline. The reader should be able to tell at a glance whether the ad is about raincoats or automobiles.

If it takes too long getting to the point, either in print or in broadcast, you may find your impatient consumer tuning the message out entirely, and turning the page. There sometimes is a valid reason for using ambiguity; but that technique will always override product identification. You have to decide if it's worth the sacrifice. The ads that most successfully meet this objective will not only identify the product category, but also the brand. Wise old heads in advertising usually recommend that the brand name be in the headline if at all possible. Two examples of headlines that have strong brand identification are:

> *Old Volvos never die. They pass on.*
> *With so many fine gins around why choose Bombay?*

Sell.   The final function of a headline is to start the selling message. If a head speaks to a reader's self-interest as an attention-getting device, it has already accomplished this objective. The essence of the selling premise should be clear in the headline. The Mobil One oil ad that promises "Get up to 10 extra miles out of a tankful of gas" is a good example. Strong benefit headlines are especially good at this. Lipton's ad explaining how to make solar tea—"Let the Sun brew your iced tea"—is a good example of a benefit head.

Automotive advertising is often feature or product oriented. An advertisement by Mercedes-Benz breaks that mold. It promises this appealing benefit: "It is reassuring to know that the Mercedes-Benz 240D can take you farther on a tank of fuel that any other car sold in America." That's an extremely long headline, but somehow it fits the Mercedes-Benz personality. Another strong benefit head that uses an interesting visual demonstration is found in the ad for the IBM Displaywriter highlighting its self-correction feature: "It makes impossibel impossible."

Types of Heads

This discussion of headline objectives has introduced several common types of headlines. Most headlines can be categorized as either focusing on the product or focusing on the user. A third category would include those heads that play word games as an attention-getting technique. Of the headlines discussed so far, claim, demonstration, and news announcement tend to be product oriented. These can be strong heads, but intrinsically they are less powerful than heads that speak to the self-interest of the audience. Benefit and curiosity heads tend to be user oriented.

News.   News is attention getting if it is a subject of interest. Americans have a compulsive need for news and find it hard to resist reading a news announcement. That's why so many ads use the word "new" in the headline or in an overline. The word has been run into the ground, but it is still a powerful attention getter.

An example of an entire campaign, and a highly successful one against all odds, is the Merit cigarette campaign. Merit cigarettes were introduced after cigarette advertising was banned from television. The industry predicted that there could never be another major brand introduction nationally. Knowing that the brand identity would be limited to print messages, the Merit strategy was to adopt all of the stylistics of newspaper stories—a strong typographical layout, a newspaper typeface, a news announcement headline, and a long news story. An example of one of the headlines demonstrates the use of the newspaper treatment. It reads: "Twelve-year effort ends with unprecedented flavor in low-tar smoke."

Emotion.   A headline with a strong emotional appeal is user oriented. A seasonal ad appealing to the sense of pride of an achiever is one used by Johnnie Walker Black that reads: "For those of you whose success cannot be measured by an Oscar, Emmy, or Tony."

A Phillips Petroleum ad explaining the company's contributions to medical emergency care used this head above a picture of an automobile accident. "How to save hours when there isn't a second to waste," a good example of an alarming head with a mild appeal to fear.

Headlines for DeBeers diamonds use a touching romantic appeal: "For all the times I worked late and never gave you a ring—Happy Anniversary." Headlines like these try to punch the emotional buttons using such appeals as pride, alarm, fear, love, nostalgia, and anger.

Curiosity.   Heads that stimulate curiosity are generally user oriented. A headline that uses a question can be intriguing. An example of a campaign that uses questions as an audience involvement technique is one by Philips Oil. Over a picture of a forest, the headline asks: "Can you find the oil well in this picture?" Canadian Club has been running a campaign where readers are invited to look for cases of Canadian Club that have been hidden at various places around the country. It's a curiosity technique that is also high in involvement.

How-to.   Another major category of user-oriented headlines features the "how-tos." Advertisements that teach consumers how to do or to use something are strong in both attention and self-interest. An example of an arresting "how-to" headline is found in an ad for American Savings Bonds. It says: "How a minus on your paycheck can be a plus in your future." The word play between minus and plus adds to the interest. Another example of a how-to head, also with a twist, is one for Republic Travelers Checks that reads: "How to pay a Czech in Prague."

Word play.   These last two headlines also are examples of the third category—headlines that play with words. The verbal twists are used as attention-getting devices, and they can be effective at stopping the scanning. They have problems, however, in that they may fail to identify the product category or to state a selling premise. If they aren't strong enough to pull the reader into the body copy, then there is very little residual effect in terms of advertising power.

One that does effectively identify the product category is a cartoon ad by Talon that shows a father and son out on a dark night looking at the stars. The father says, "And that, son, that's the Big Zipper." The stars in the sky, of course, spell out "Talon." (See Exhibit 4–1.) Another successful word play is a headline for a Christmas season ad that artfully incorporates the brand name: "Dewar's unto others."

Heads with Problems

Headlines can fail for a number of reasons, usually because they don't accomplish the previously stated objectives: get attention, speak to self-interest, segment the audience, identify the product or product category, or state the selling premise. They can also fail because they are poorly written and unclear.

Garbled.   A classic example of a garbled head is one for a short-lived cigarette named Tall. In addition to creating much confusion in the market, this particular ad got rave (rabid) reviews in the letters-to-the-editor column in the trade press. The headline for the introductory ad read: "Why is this cigarette selling with no advertising and it's hard to come by?" In addition to several serious syntax problems, it also defies logic. If there's no advertising, then what are we reading?

An equally obscure headline appeared on an ad for Cuervo Especial. The illustration is of a woman in tennis clothes. The head reads: "I always drink Cuervo Gold. Now and then." Always—now and then? Such an ad is a classic example of headline hash.

Labels.   The most unarresting headlines are labels, particularly if the label is just the product name. Labels are static; they have no verbs and they have no action or impact. A liquor store in a small community ran a series of newspaper service ads on how to buy wines. The idea was good but the headlines were weak labels. One ad, for example, was headlined "Generic wines." There's just not enough content in a static phrase like that to pull anyone into the body copy. So what about generic wines?

Another example was pointed out by Fred Messner in his column in *Adweek.* He quoted the copy for a trade advertisement that described the five steps used by the company to insure quality control. The copy was fine but the headline was "Heiser quality." Messner commented that it was "a static label type of headline that doesn't manage to say much—yet manages to sound smug while saying it."

Verbless.   A problem related to label headlines is the use of verbless heads. A headline without a verb is an idea with its guts cut out. The verb adds life, action, motion, excitement, vigor, and power to thoughts. Without a verb, it just sits. A classic example of the power of a verb is the previously quoted Smirnoff headline: "Chow down." The verb, or really verb phrase, is commanding, as well as arresting.

EXHIBIT 4-1: **The Talon "big zipper" ad uses a play on words that is reinforced in the graphics. Chester Gore/Eric Mower and Associates, Inc. was the agency.** (Courtesy of Talon, Inc.)

Ads without verbs often lack attention power as well as vigor. A trade ad for Triangle Engineering's ventilators demonstrates this lack of power. The headline reads: "Energy free comfort cooling." There may be a real benefit here, but it's hiding behind punchless phrasing. The response is, typically, "So what?"

Hanging heads.   A hanging head is an incomplete thought—you have to read the body copy to get the point. It's a great device for pulling readers into the copy. Unfortunately, someone who gets impatient and turns the page after reading the head may have no usable information at all, and no product identification. We know from decades of copytesting research by the Starch Company that 80 percent of the people who read a head will not read the copy.[1] A hanging head with its incomplete thought is a real gamble.

The Heublein and Air New Zealand advertisements illustrate the problem of hanging heads that don't clearly identify the product category. Both ads use the same identical head—"Paradise found"—which is a twist on Milton's famous *Paradise Lost*. It's an interesting phrase and an arresting twist, but there is not enough direct link to the product category for the headline to fulfill its identification function.

Questions.   Be careful of question headlines. They are used to develop curiosity and reader involvement, but they can backfire. A question that seems obvious to you (because you have the answer in your mind) can be obscure to everyone else. The opposite problem is more common. Most question heads tend to be too obvious. "Would you like to double your income? Would you like to live to be 100?" These obvious heads turn off the audience and invite "smart ass" responses. A common response to many of these heads is to mutter to yourself, "Dumb question." A negative reaction like that isn't particularly conducive to a positive product association.

Long heads.   Some of the direct response research indicates that long heads work—at least for direct response ads. David Ogilvy and John Caples believe heads should be long enough to tell the story. Most copywriting books, however, recommend short, succinct, to-the-point headlines. They know that the reading public spends a very brief period with any ad, and that short heads are more likely to break and stop the scanning process. Most copywriters feel that a head has a better chance of being read if it's brief and quick.

The disagreement might lie with the nature of the message. Certain products, particularly big-ticket, high-involvement ones, speak to an audience with an already developed high level of interest. They will not only tolerate, they will welcome, long heads and long copy. Direct response ads, where the prospects have to sell themselves, also need lots of information in the headline. Other products, such as package goods with frequent repeat purchases, have low reader interest. In these situations, short succinct headlines may be more appropriate.

It may also be a function of the message. If you have an involving story to tell, then the headline can demand more time from the reader. If the message is primarily reminder, then the reader doesn't expect to make a major time commitment.

Automotive advertising is one category where you may find both short and long heads, depending upon whether the ad uses an image theme or an attribute approach with its need for explanation. For example, an ad for Datsun 20-SX is selling the image of a sporty car and lifestyle. The short head says: "Step on the exhilarator!" An opposite approach is found in an ad by Mercedes-Benz. The long headline asks: "The Mercedes-Benz 240 Diesel—is it the world finest economy car, or is it the world's most economical fine car?"

The best advice probably is to watch out for long heads. They do tax the reader. If you use them, make them inescapably intriguing and make them fit the tone and style of both the product and the targeted audience.

Cute and contrived.   Headlines can try too hard to be attention getting, and the result may strain credulity. Often they just sound sophomoric, like something you would find in a high school yearbook.

An example of a head that tries too hard to make its point is by West Virginia Brand Hams. Apparently, according to the picture, there are three varieties of hams offered. The head tries to pick up on that by stating: "There is only one West Virginia Brand Ham. This are it." That's the kind of headline that makes you wince.

An example of another headline that is too contrived is one written for Stouffer's Side Dishes. It reads: "What a diamond ring does for your finger, Stouffer's Side Dishes do for dinner." It's an attempt to stretch a metaphor, but it's stretched so far it falls apart.

Borrowed interest.   One definition of a creative idea is the juxtaposition of two previously unrelated thoughts. Often, in advertising, a characteristic of the product is associated or juxtaposed with some unexpected situation to create a new way to look at the attribute or benefit. It's a technique used to add an unexpected twist. It also can be another form of a contrived head. A dull idea will hitchhike on a well-known concept, or even on a cliché, and attempt to create some excitement for the product by mere association with something else exciting. This is called "borrowed interest." Sometimes it works; more often, it backfires.

An example of borrowed interest that seemed to work is a trade ad for the electronics industry that used an Alice in Wonderland theme. This ad was evaluated by the Copy Chasers in their *Industrial Marketing* column as an extreme example of "borrowed interest."[2] A storm of protest arose with the company's president, as well as others in the industry, citing the results of the advertisement. Apparently, it was both a strong attention getter and had a very high memorability. The Copy Chasers concluded that Lewis Carroll, a famous mathematician, understood the intellectual affinity between mathematics (and electronics) and fantasy—perhaps better than the Copy Chasers did.

Another Copy Chasers example of borrowed interest that didn't work very well is an ad by EMC Controls. The picture shows Frankenstein-like characters. The head is a quote from the plant manager of USS Chemicals: "We avoided a chamber of horrors when we contacted EMC Controls." The horrible creatures might get attention but they also steal the essence of the message—even if the promise were spelled out a little more clearly.

Hype.   Headline hype is found in brag-and-boast statements and puffed-up phrases. A number of ads critiqued in the Copy Chasers column suffer from this form of adese. An example of pure hype is the headline for Consolidated Freightways: "The greatest thing since the wheel." The Copy Chasers chided Consolidated for overstatement and exaggeration.

Another hype head featured in the Copy Chasers column came from an ad for Micro-Plate company. It reads: "Innovative technology that improves productivity, quality, and economy." The vague, general, pompous words tell you nothing about Micro-Plate's business, or about what the company has to offer its customers in terms of specific services.

Other Display Copy

The word *display* is used here to mean copy that is set in larger or bolder type than the body copy (text) of the advertisement. The headline is the most important element of the display copy. Related elements include overlines and underlines, captions and subheads. The function of these secondary display elements is to establish a logical progression of attention-getting pieces of copy.

A carefully written advertisement will structure the reading process so the reader moves from initial interest to involvement and eventually to concentration on the body copy. The headline establishes the initial interest and these other display elements create the pattern of progressive involvement until the decision is finally made to settle in and read the body copy.

Overlines and underlines.   These short pieces of copy serve as appetizers—they lead to the head or from the head to some other element. In most cases, their function is to establish and reinforce the progression. They may also be used to break a long or complicated headline into shorter, more easy-to-read segments.

FTD Florist uses this lead-in overline: "Wherever you are . . . the man from FTD will find you." The picture shows a woman traffic officer with a bouquet of flowers. The headline says: "I got it in traffic, the FTD Birthday Party Bouquet." There are lots of things going on in this overline/headline combination. They introduce the idea of personal delivery of flowers anytime, anywhere, and dramatize it with a testimonial from someone receiving flowers in a most unlikely situation. The complexity necessitates the use of the lead-in line.

Underlines are more common than overlines in advertising. Their primary purpose is to pull the reader from the head down into the body copy. They also fulfill the function of segmenting long complicated thoughts.

A succinct use of the headline/underline combination is found in an ad by Harrah's Casino. The head is a hanging head, but the underline is used to provide the missing identification. The headline says: "The truth about slot payouts." The underline follows: "In 1982, Harrah's paid out more money than any other casino in the world." Curiosity is developed in the headline and a strong claim is stated in the underline.

Captions.   Next to the headline, with its attendant overlines and underlines, captions have the second highest readership. Starch data shows that the reading pattern is established first with the headline and then drawn immediately to the captions under the illustrations.[3] Unfortunately, captions are rarely used in advertising. Most copywriters seem to feel the body copy of the ad, in a simple layout, acts as the caption. They are missing a good bet, however, since a caption is an irresistible hook into the reader's interest.

In addition to their pull, captions also serve an information function. In spite of the use of carefully contrived visuals in most advertising, there is still a need for explanation of illustrations. Journalists are aware that a photo can mean different things to different people. You'll rarely see a photo in a newspaper or a magazine that isn't accompanied by an explanatory caption.

Most advertising illustrations could benefit from additional explanation in the caption. But the real value of a caption is that it is one more chance to try to capture the attention and stimulate the interest of the reader. It's a shame to leave out a piece of copy with such intrinsically high readership.

An example of an ad that makes good use of captions is the Peugeot ad discussed earlier. Each of the six little photos that frame the body of the ad shows a car on a different part of a test track. The headline reads: "Every Peugeot goes through hell to get to America." Under the pictures are these short but graphic captions: "fiendish ribs," "nasty cobblestones," "wicked curves," "cruel bumps," "twisting stairs," and "mean moguls."

Call outs.   Johnson and Johnson baby products used the caption treatment to package the main pieces of the body copy. The head reads: "How to bathe a mommy." Positioned around a picture of a woman are short paragraphs with arrows pointing to various parts of her body. These "call outs" describe the good things Johnson and Johnson does for feet, hands, makeup removal, moisture absorption, and skin softening. Starch research has also shown that call outs have extremely high readership.

Subheads.   Display lines embedded in the body serve two purposes. First, they break up long, forbidding blocks of copy and make it appear more inviting to read. The primary purpose, however, is to stimulate interest. Most people, before they decide to read the body copy, will scan the subheads first to see if the copy sounds interesting. These little subheads provide your last chance to move your target from scanning to reading. They don't just summarize the copy that follows; they package the copy to maximize its enticing features.

An example of a subhead that is carefully crafted to entice as well as to extend the thematic concept can be found in a Toyota ad. The headline reads: "The right shape for right now." The first subhead says: "Engineers say it's right." The second subhead uses parallel construction to heighten the force of the message: "Experts say it's right." The final subhead associates the product with the theme as a wrapup technique: "Celica GT-S: the right stuff, plus . . . "

4.2 BODY COPY

If the display copy is successful, then it pulls the reader right into the body copy, which serves to explain and further describe the product. As we have mentioned before, the Starch research indicates that only about 20 percent of those who read the headline will continue to read the body copy. That means 80 percent stop after the headline. That's a depressing statistic for copywriters but it certainly establishes the challenge.

Disinterest.   We know that our audience for advertising messages is largely indifferent. Only a very small part of the audience is in the market at the time they see the advertisement. The disinterest level, particularly for low-involvement product categories, is very high. If we win a reader and he or she continues on into the body copy, it's like making a religious conversion—truly a major accomplishment.

Poor writing.   In addition to feeling disinterest, a lot of readers may turn away from ad copy because it is poorly written. It may not be targeted to the right audience. It may be confusing and unclear. It may be dull and full of artificial adese. Why would anyone want to read an advertisement if the editorial copy in the magazine or newspaper surrounding the ad is more interesting? Advertising copy needs to be just as interesting as the surrounding editorial matter and, given the built-in problem of audience disinterest, it needs to be more interesting.

The truth is that a lot of advertising writing is dreadful. It's full of clichés, adese, puffery, pompous phrases, and boring lists of product features. So those are the challenges—and the obstacles faced by every copywriter—to overcome the disinterest and to write lively, interesting, and personal copy.

Function.   The purpose of the headline is to flag attention; the other pieces of the display copy help stimulate interest. They throw out hooks and dangle interesting bait to entice the reader into reading the body copy.

The body copy's function is to expand on the selling premise, which should have been introduced in the headline or in the attendant overlines and underlines. The body copy elaborates, compares, explains, instructs, and persuades. It uses all the established literary techniques of definition, description, narrative, dialogue, and argument to flesh out the message.

The Lead

The lead is the first sentence of the body copy. It marks the transition point where the reader's involvement changes from skimming to reading. The interest has been stimulated by the display copy, but it is up to the lead to establish the mood of concentration. This is a point of critical transition.

In addition to establishing this critical change of mood, the lead has several other functions. The headline and visual introduced the creative theme, and most good leads will feature the theme and carry it into the body copy. The selling premise often gets traded off. It takes over as the primary concern of the remainder of the body copy, which continues from the second paragraph on to the end.

Leads may often be "hangers." Here curiosity and ambiguity are used deliberately to force continued reading. In order to understand the point, the reader has to keep reading. Magazine articles are written this way. Interesting magazine leads are called "zingers," and certain magazines such as *Time* and *Newsweek* have turned the writing of compelling leads into a fine art. Donald Hall, in his book on writing, described zingers as "constructed to grab the reader by the hair."[4] Zingers use such techniques as questions, jarring quotes, controversies, anecdotes, and startling statements.

One example of an interesting head and lead is found in an ad by IBM that describes the company's robotics systems. It uses a curiosity angle for a headline, "obotics," and the lead that follows is a hanger. It reads: "This story begins with the period at the end of this sentence." The second paragraph explains that the robotic arm pictured in the ad can locate a hole that size and accurately insert a pin. The robotic arm is actually holding the missing "R" from the headline. It's a strong curiosity provoking lead that makes sense only if you read on into the copy. (See Exhibit 4-2.)

A good example of a strong tie between the headline and the lead is found in an ad by Buccellati silverware. The ad shows a fork with tongs down and the back of the fork facing you. The headline reads: "Only Buccellati has the nerve to turn his back on you." The lead continues the thought: "Because he has nothing to hide." The copy explains that Buccellati feels both sides of the silverware are important. The creative concept, which focuses on the back side of the silverware, is the link between the headline and the lead. (See Exhibit 4-3).

The Closing

Thematic wrapup. We will come back and discuss the middle of the copy, but first let's talk about the closing. The *closing* copy is part of the thematic package and works hand in hand with the headline and lead to establish the creative concept. Usually, these three pieces are written together. The headline introduces the idea, the lead builds on it to entice the reader into the copy, and the wrapup refers back to it.

A good example of the relationship between these three can be seen in the previously discussed Buccellati ad. After the headline and lead duo established the concept of the back side of the silverware as an important sign of quality, the body copy continues with a discussion of silverware craftsmanship. The closing paragraph refers back to the original theme and uses a little twist to an-

EXHIBIT 4-2:   The IBM ad, "obotics," uses visual demonstration to
make the point that its robotics arm can handle high-precision work.
(Courtesy of IBM)

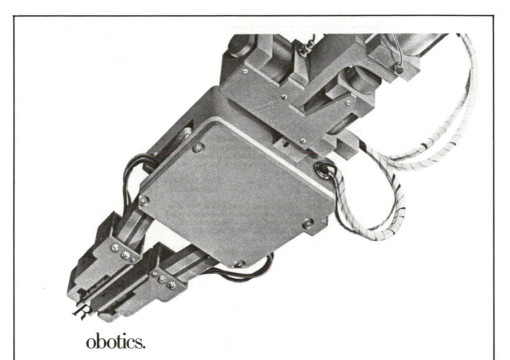

obotics.

This story begins with the period at the end of this sentence.
The robotic arm above can locate a hole that size and
accurately insert a pin, once or thousands of times.

Today, IBM robotic systems controlled by computers are doing
precision work on complex, tedious or even hazardous tasks. Using
special sensors in the "gripper," they are assembling complicated
mechanisms, rejecting defective parts, testing completed units and
keeping inventories.

Communication between the system and its computer is made
possible by the most advanced robotic programming language yet
reported. The language and the robotic systems it controls are
part of our continuing commitment to research and development —
a commitment funded with more than $8 billion over the past
seven years.

IBM robotic systems can improve productivity, worker safety
and product quality.

And that's precisely why we're in business. **IBM**®

EXHIBIT 4-3: **The concept of handcrafted silver is expressed in the headline, visual, and body copy of the Buccellati advertisements.** (Courtesy of Buccellati Inc.)

chor it in the memory: "So when you're ready to choose fine silverware, be sure to get both sides of the story."

Call to action.   Another function of the wrapup is to state a call to action. The importance of the call to action varies with the nature of the ad. If it's direct response, then the call is extremely important. It's also important in

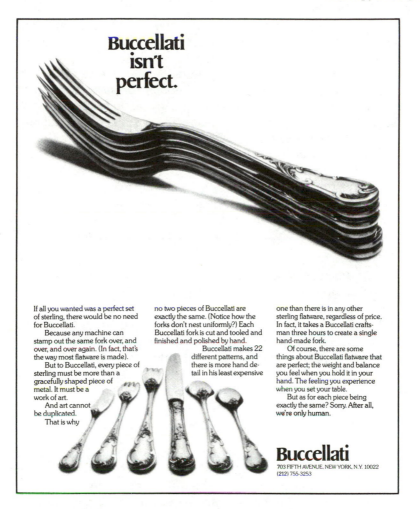

Buccellati isn't perfect.

If all you wanted was a perfect set of sterling, there would be no need for Buccellati.

Because any machine can stamp out the same fork over, and over, and over again. (In fact, that's the way most flatware is made).

But to Buccellati, every piece of sterling must be more than a gracefully shaped piece of metal. It must be a work of art.

And art cannot be duplicated. That is why no two pieces of Buccellati are exactly the same. (Notice how the forks don't nest uniformly?) Each Buccellati fork is cut and tooled and finished and polished by hand.

Buccellati makes 22 different patterns, and there is more hand detail in his least expensive one than there is in any other sterling flatware, regardless of price. In fact, it takes a Buccellati craftsman three hours to create a single hand-made fork.

Of course, there are some things about Buccellati flatware that are perfect; the weight and balance you feel when you hold it in your hand. The feeling you experience when you set your table.

But as for each piece being exactly the same? Sorry. After all, we're only human.

Buccellati

703 FIFTH AVENUE, NEW YORK, N.Y. 10022
(212) 755-3253

---

local or retail advertising. Reminder and image advertising are less dependent upon an immediate response so the call may be deemphasized.

One example of a call is the Buccellati ad, which encourages readers to look at both the front and back of silverware. That's a form of decision instruction. Other ads will give specific information on where to find the product or how to buy it. Local advertising has a set of critical information that accompanies the call to action. This includes store address, location cues such as "corner of 15th and Baker," or "across from Safeway," phone number, store hours, and credit card acceptances.

Facilitators. Another aspect of the closing is a category of information called *facilitators*. These are devices used to make the inquiry or purchase easier. An 800 number is a common example. Any incentive offers, such as a cents-off coupon or special premium offer, are considered facilitators. An order blank and a coupon for additional information are common direct response facilitators.

Some of advertising's greatest names are strong believers in coupons. David Ogilvy, for example, used coupons for very classy products. A recent O & M campaign for Saab used long copy, ended with a coupon to get more information about the car, and generated a tremendous number of responses.

An absolute master of coupons and contests was Howard Gossage. Gossage was a rather eccentric west coast adman who injected advertising with sophisticated humor and just plain fun. He devised contests for Quantas to give away kangaroos; he offered free Oregon fir trees for Blitz Brewing; he offered Beethoven and Bach sweatshirts for Rainier Ale ("A brewer's idea of culture"). In one campaign he offered samples of shirt materials for Eagle shirts. The Eagle shirt ad, incidentally, had 11,342 replies and set an all-time record for a *New Yorker* ad.[5]

Identification.   The final function of the closing is to provide the corporate or store signature. This can be a distinctive logo or simply the name of the store in plain type. Store or product names are expected to be at the bottom of the advertisement, and usually they are found either in the center or the right corner. The right corner is the point of exit and the idea is to leave the reader with a solid product or store identification as he or she turns the page. The signature may also include a slogan or a campaign theme tagline. These are reminder devices used to anchor the identification securely in the mind.

The Body of the Body Copy

Elaboration.   The middle section of the body copy elaborates on the selling premise. If the head was a claim, then the body provides the support or proof. If the head is a benefit, the body explains how and why the benefit is derived. The elaboration is built point by point, usually beginning with the most important feature or benefit. There should be a logical progression through this sequence of points. The points can be arranged moving from the most important to the less important, from a series of different viewpoints or uses, from one feature to another, or from one reason to another.

Unity.   The logic of the sequence of thoughts is an important aspect of the total coherence of the copy. Typically body copy discusses a number of details, attributes, substantiation points, or benefits. In spite of the variety of information presented, there is a need for interpretation or unity. All of the parts should be pieces of an overall picture. This conceptual unity, the perspective, is difficult to achieve but essential if the copy is to hold together.

With any product in advertising, there are a variety of approaches and a multitude of features. For any one ad you choose one approach from many and feature a few of the many possible attributes. The creative concept determines how the attributes relate to one another. The objective is to provide lots of variety in the support and documentation and still have a single-minded concept. This is much harder than it seems.

A good example of this conceptual unity is in an advertisement for the Volvo station wagon. The concept that holds it all together refers to the safety features necessary for a family car. The headline says: "A wagon built to carry cargo more precious than groceries." The body copy features a number of attributes:

A WAGON BUILT TO CARRY CARGO MORE PRECIOUS THAN GROCERIES

Any station wagon can take a load of stuff from one place to another.

The Volvo wagon, on the other hand, was designed to take a load off your mind as a parent.

Volvo realizes, for example, that it's impossible to keep both eyes on the road if you have to keep one eye on the back seat.

So to keep the kids in place, we provide you with things like child-proof door locks on all the rear doors. Including the back one.

And to virtually guarantee that you can focus your attention on the road at all times, we give you defrosters for the front side windows, and the rear window comes with its own wiper, washer, and defroster.

On the road, the first thing you'll notice is how quickly our overhead cam engine can put trouble behind you. Should trouble appear ahead, you'll appreciate the way our rack and pinion steering can help you steer clear of it. And the way our four-wheel power disc brakes can stop short of it.

In spite of all these precautions, we realize that accidents do happen. So we've planned for the unplanned.

Where many wagons may feature a front end designed to impress the neighbors, the Volvo wagon features a front end designed to help absorb the impact of a collision.

Our passenger compartment is surrounded by a protective steel cage.

Our doors have steel tubes running through their insides for added protection, instead of imitation wood running down their outsides for frivolous decoration.

There's also a padded dashboard. A collapsible steering wheel. A gas tank designed not to rupture in a rear end collision.

Look at it this way.

There's finally a wagon that shows as much concern for your children as you do.

Transitions. Conceptual integration is an important aspect of unity; a careful use of transitions is another. *Transitions* perform two functions. First, they keep the logic on track. They serve as signposts that mark the progression from one idea to another and establish the relationship between the ideas. Second, they tell the readers where they've been and where they are headed—the overall view or perspective.

Transitions are important because without them it may be hard to follow the discussion from one point to another. Copy with poor or missing transitions appears to have jumps, breaks, or leaps in the logic.

You've been in conversation where someone is talking about something and then all of a sudden switches to an entirely different topic. It leaves you confused. Even worse, your mind tends to wander away from the discussion and tries to figure out the connection—what could possibly have led the speaker to such a jump? It short-circuits the conversation and often leads to termination of the discussion. When you are writing ad copy, you desperately want your reader to stay with you so any diversion, intended or not, is unwelcome. Attention to transitions can avoid these leaps and left turns in logic.

There are a number of devices used for transitions. Remember the objective of a transition is to link ideas and establish the relationship between them. The most basic form of transition is linking words such as "so," "and," "but," "therefore," "however." Other transitional words establish sequential relationships, such as "at the beginning," "first," "second," "then," "furthermore."

Repetition of key words is another form of transition. It establishes, or maintains, a relationship between a thought and something that preceded it. Repetition is a reminder function. (Repetition can also be annoying if the same word is used too close and too frequently.) Parallelism is another aspect of repetition that strengthens transitions. Parallel construction repeats the structure of the sentence, sometimes repeating key phrases. It is a good technique to carry over and emphasize a connection.

Short form references to something previously discussed is another type of transition. Pronouns are a common example of this type of linkage. On first reference you speak about a person by name, sometimes by title. The next reference is to *he* or *she*. The connecting link between the person and the personal pronoun is understood in context. Abbreviations perform the same function. If you refer to the American Association of Advertising Agencies in the first mention, then you can just say 4As in the subsequent references and the identity is still understood.

Study the Volvo wagon ad we just analyzed for body copy development. Notice how many transitions are used to cue point of view, location, and the logical progression from one idea to another. The copy uses a number of specific transitional phrases. In the first five short paragraphs, you will find "on the other hand," "for example," "so," "and" all used to establish relationship between thoughts. Another major transitional phrase is used at the end to indicate transition to a summarizing activity: "Look at it this way."

Transitions are also used to cue the addresser and the addressee and indicate who is speaking. In the Volvo ad the lead two sentences address the reader in personal language as "you, a parent." The third sentence refers first to the Volvo viewpoint in the abstract. The second reference in the following paragraph changes to a personal pronoun: "we." All further references to the speaker are through this personal pronoun.

Point of view is also expressed in the transitions. The first third of the Volvo copy takes a general look at the car's features as seen through the eyes of someone sitting behind the wheel. The use of phrases like "eyes on the road" and "eyes on the back seat" establish the relationship of the visual contact points through the rearview mirror and the windshield.

Those phrases also use parallel construction to emphasize the rhythmic transition from looking ahead to looking behind. Using the "eyes on the back seat" as a mental reference point, the copy then moves around the inside of the car— side doors, rear doors—and then back to the side front where it talks about side window defrosters. The circular scanning is completed as the attention swings back to the rear window where the wiper/defroster feature is introduced.

In the copy you've just sat in the car, looked forward and back, and then once around the inside. All of that scanning is done by transitions that serve as directional signposts. The next major directional cue announces a major change of location.

The sixth paragraph starts out with a bold transition: "On the road . . ." The rest of the copy goes through a test drive experience pointing to the features you notice as you drive. The transitional cues include such situational phrases as "the first thing" and "should trouble appear." The signposts cue not only what you notice but also the typical worries that come to mind when you drive a new car. Such phrases as the rather vague "trouble" and the more specific "collision" establish those hypothetical situations.

The Volvo copy is an example of good body copy development and masterful transitions. The reader's attention proceeds through a variety of features from several different situations and viewpoints, and yet the relationships are clear throughout. There are no surprising unexplained jumps. The logic is sound and the points lead from one to another as clearly as if arrows were pointing the way. And yet the transitions are subtle and unobtrusive. The only obvious one is used, and properly so, to signal a major change in viewpoint. It's really a fine piece of copywriting.

Those are the basic pieces of the body copy package. They work together to support a concept or theme, and yet they all have individual functions to perform. The lead has to turn the reader from scanning into reading. The body of the body copy elaborates on the concept and provides explanation, justification, or proof of the claim or benefit used in the headline. The body copy is carefully crafted with transitions that lead from point to point with no unexpected jumps that might lose the reader.

The closing wraps up the argument by referring back to the idea and creative concept introduced in the headline. It provides the call to action and any facilitators necessary to spur the action. It is also responsible for leaving the reader with a clear identification of the product, service, or store.

4.3 WRITING TECHNIQUES

There are a number of ways to approach any message. You can focus on a news-worthy feature and make an announcement of it; you can define important aspects; you can describe the features, moods, or lifestyles associated with it; you can tell a story about it; you can develop a logical argument explaining what its benefits are; or you can explain how to use it. These are just a few of the types of copy you will find used in advertising.

Some ads use one approach; others will use several different techniques. Most of the messages can be grouped under a set of basic categories of writing styles. These are common literary styles but they are used in advertising too. The basic categories are announcement, description, narration, and explanation. A good copywriter needs to master all four writing techniques and must know when and why each approach is used.

Announcement

Copy that states a fact about a product or service uses an *announcement* style, sometimes called a straight-line style of writing. It's basically a journalistic approach, and it is used primarily for news announcements.

Straight-line style. This style uses assertions, or statements of fact, to establish that something exists or has been reported or found. The Merit cigarette campaign is one that uses a strong news peg. The Merit ads report some new fact that has been discovered by research and treat the announcement as a straight news story. Any of the ad copy approaches that use the "now you can buy" formula tend to be announcement messages.

An interesting use of the announcement technique is found in an ad by Crest that states: "On April 6, 1976, the official publication of the American Chemical Society listed the great discoveries of the last 100 years. We're proud to be one of them." The double-page ad then lists column after column of break-throughs in chemistry, some 80 in all. The development of stannous fluoride by Crest is the first entry under 1955.

Definition

A variation of straight-line copy is a style of writing that focuses on defining terms. A definitional advertisement is often used with a new product or with a new ingredient. The early Crest ads, for example, used definitional strategies to explain stannous fluoride. The ads announcing major additives in gas and engineering breakthroughs in product design are often definitional. A *definition* is a statement of the meaning of a word or phrase, a distillation of the essence of the concept. It explains the most essential and the most typical features of the word being defined.

Synonyms.   One way to define is to list *synonyms* and explain the differences among them in terms of their shades of meaning. You are substituting the unfamiliar word with one of similar meaning that you think the audience might know. Another way to define is to list the pieces or components. In other words, what is included in the concept or what is it composed of? This is the *inclusiveness* dimension of definition, the significant features of the category represented by that word. Product advertising often defines what a product means in terms of its significant features or attributes.

A third technique of definition is to explain in terms of *exclusiveness*. In other words, what are the discriminating features that separate this concept from all others? In advertising, exclusiveness is used to identify points of distinctiveness.

Functional.   A fourth type of definition is *functional*—a statement of what the concept does. Often, in advertising, a product or service will be defined in terms of what it does for the user or how it is used. Descriptive detail also is used in many of the definitions as a technique for elaborating on how the features work.

Definition is a type of writing used in combination with other techniques. One advertisement that focuses almost exclusively, however, on definition is a service ad by General Foods explaining nutritional terms found on package labels. The headline says: "Dear General Foods. All this talk about nutrition gives me 100 percent of my daily requirements of confusion." The copy begins: "There's a tendency for people's eyes to glaze over when reading things like 25 percent U.S. RDA Thiamin. You'll find mysterious-sounding terms like this on the nutritional labels on any General Foods products." Under the subhead, "What's a U.S. RDA?", the copy reads: "It stands for United States Recommended Daily Allowance, and it tells you the amounts of various nutrients considered adequate for maintenance of good nutrition in most healthy persons in the United States."

Most definitions in this advertisement are functional; they explain what the nutrients do for you. For example, notice how the copy explains such concepts as thiamin, niacin, and riboflavin. This is an unusual piece of copy in that you normally don't see an entire advertisement that uses definition for copy development.

Description

Descriptive writing develops images that stick in the mind. We know from psychological research that images are easier to remember than words. Things we've seen as images we code directly into memory. Print is most often recorded in the form of the visual, which then cues the concept. Television is remembered as a key visual. Radio spots, other than jingles, are also retained as a picture-in-the-mind. The goal in using strong descriptive copy, then, is to stimulate the images to help record the visual.

Experiences.   Descriptions bridge experience. In some cases, you may be writing about something entirely new. You have seen it but your audience hasn't. With your words, you make the experience of seeing it come to life for them.

In some cases, you may simply be cuing their memory processes. They have had similar experiences, so your well-chosen words bring their experiences back to mind. The more experiences you have in common with the audience, the easier it is to describe the object. You can tell someone that a buffalo looks like a bull with a shaggy hump. If they have seen a bull, then the gap in experience is easier to bridge. But how do you describe an umbrella to someone who has never seen one before? Or a claw hammer? Some gaps in experience are very difficult to bridge.

Description is a manifestation of your personal research. Writing demands a constant process of data gathering. Writers make mental notes of every new experience. They observe details that others miss; they note their feelings and responses; they associate details with other related situations. Good writers define meanings in the minor minutiae of daily life. And they use all their senses.

Sensory details.   Description is the reporting of sensory details. You have seen something you want to tell your audience about so you describe for them what it looks like, as well as how it feels, smells, tastes, and sounds. These are the five senses that writers use to describe their experiences.

If you want to develop your sensitivities, make a habit of describing to yourself any new experience—riding a roller coaster, eating a new food, wearing a new suit. What is it like to eat a melting ice cream cone on a hot summer day? What does the sting of a mosquito feel like? The smell of a liniment, the sound of an amusement park? Tune in to these experiences and relive the sensations in your words. Describe them for an imaginery friend who is unfamiliar with the experience.

Explicit.   Description that records details explicitly is analytical in tone. There are two dimensions to this type of writing: order and point of view. *Order* is the sequence we use to report the sensory impressions. When we look at a picture, we scan it so quickly that we record a number of details almost simultaneously. But we can't write details simultaneously; they have to be recorded one at a time in a sequence of some sort. As Donald Hall says in his book on writing: "The order is not critical; but it is critical that there be an order."[6] In other words, it doesn't matter how the details are arranged as long as there is some logic to the order.

In visual description the order is usually spatial. The details may be recorded in standard western scanning patterns such as left to right and top to bottom, or perhaps from the center to the periphery or from the periphery to the center. The order for other types of situations may be temporal, recording the first thing you observed and the next and the next and so on. The sensations may move from visual to sound, to smell and back again to visual. The logic is based on the pattern of decreasing impact—a temporal sequence of impressions.

The second aspect of explicit description is the *point of view* of the observer. If you record the details as you experience something, then maintain that orientation as you put the experience in words. Be careful of shifting to someone else's viewpoint or to an impossible angle. If you are writing from an imagined viewpoint, constancy is even more important.

Often in advertising, therefore, the copy will be written from the viewpoint of the user. To write this you have to imagine yourself, or remember yourself, in the role of a user experiencing the product or service for the first time. What did you see/hear/smell/taste/feel first? What was the most indelible sensation? How did you move through the sequence of experiences? What caught your attention next and next and next? How did you proceed to build a layer of sensations into a total impression? Is it a coherent picture?

A good example of an advertisement that uses explicit description is a truck driver ad for Raleigh cigarettes. The headline says, "The road to Raleigh is," and the body copy continues with a description of what it is like to be a truck driver. The first section is a view from the driver's seat. The order is from close to distant:

> *Yellow lines and just laid asphalt.*
> *Endless stretches of black ribbon that*
> *run all the way to where the sun disappears.*
> *It's telephone poles and fence posts,*
> *you keep passin' 'em one by one.*
> *It's those rows of corn, that sea of wheat.*
> *Tall trees blockin' out the sun.*

Then the view shifts from the scenery outside the window to the objects noticed inside the cab:

> *It's 13 speeds in an overdrive gearbox.*
> *And a CB handle*
> *when you've got the country music turned off.*

Then it moves to internal reflections by the driver himself:

> *The road to Raleigh is a man*
> *who gets up when he wants to . . .*
> *goes to bed when he says.*
> *Pushes himself to the limit*
> *and then relaxes with gusto.*
> *He doesn't give a damn what you think.*

For the conclusion, the writer puts it all together as a total sensory description of what it's like on the road—in all weather, on all roads, at all times of the day.

> *The road to Raleigh has*
> *the feel of hard rain*
> *and blowin' snow.*
> *The light of a rising sun,*
> *The pale of a pea soup fog.*
> *It's got the smell of hot coffee.*
> *And the stench of diesel fuel.*

And finally it all wraps up with the theme and a product identification.

> *It's got men.*
> *It's got freedom.*
> *It's got the flavor you can only get*
> *When you're on the road to Raleigh.*
> *Take the road to flavor.—Raleigh Lights.*

It's unusual to see description used in such a poetic form throughout an advertisement—particularly for cigarettes—and particularly for macho truck drivers. Description is usually found in occasional paragraphs mixed in with other styles of writing. The Raleigh ad manages to romanticize the road without using syrupy words. That's the power of description used as a stylistic form. (See Exhibit 4–4.)

Evocative.   The Raleigh ad used explicit description but, even with its rather straightforward description of sensory impressions, it still began to move into the second type of description. *Evocative* description moves from recording sensory details to recording feelings associated with them. It is used to create mood and to tug at the heart strings. It takes description out of the senses and into the emotions.

An example of evocative description is found in a perfume ad for Je Reviens. The headline, "The world's smallest harvest," is clearly an understatement in advertising, but it sets the stage for the description of the harvest of a rare wildflower used in the perfume. The copy describes the flower, the area where it grows, and the camaraderie of its harvest.

> *After the last snow has melted, the children of Lozère go with the town's old people into the mountains to gather a rare wild flower. For on the slopes surrounding this tiny hamlet the wild narcissus grows. And because it grows one here, one there, in crevices and on the steepest of slopes, to pick these fragile yellow and white flowers requires the patience of the old and the agility of the young.*

EXHIBIT 4-4: "The road to Raleigh" is an interesting use of prose aimed at a traditionally "macho" audience. The ad was developed by **Cunningham and Walsh.** (Copyright Brown & Williamson Tobacco Corporation—all rights reserved)

The story of old folks and kids working together is supported by a touching photo of an older gentleman and a cute curly-headed little boy with a basket of flowers. The second paragraph describes the scarcity of the flowers and also introduces several other rare flowers used in the production of the perfume.

Metaphoric.   A third type of description uses the power of metaphor to create a total sensory impression. A *metaphor* takes the identity of characteristics of one thing and associates it with something entirely different: for example, "a barn of a house," "the hand is a leaf fluttering in the wind," and "God is a mighty fortress." Similes are more obvious metaphors. A *simile* states that something *is like* something else. Earlier, a zebra was described as *like* a horse, but with stripes. The word "like" cues the use of a simile.

Metaphorical description is powerful because it impresses like a picture does—all the sensory details come flooding across your mind from the depths of your imagination and memory. A metaphor is a summarizing device—it can synthesize and provide perspective because it stimulates the total experience, the whole picture.

Technical.   Another type of description is found in *technical* writing. It uses literal descriptions with the details given in exact dimensions—the quantification dimension is critical to develop an accurate representation of the object.

Technical descriptions may be useful in research reports, but they don't communicate very well. For example, "two circular plates 3 inches in diameter attached to a curved cylinder approximately 2½ inches in diameter" is hard to recognize as a description of the hand piece of a telephone. A metaphor described it better: "A banana-like handle squashed flat at each end."

A second type of technical description is functional—telling how something works. A *functional* description can be hard to follow if you describe how it works before you tell readers what it is or what it is like. You can describe the telephone as an object that comes in two pieces—one you hear from and talk into, the other you dial. This describes the primary functions of a phone, but it leaves your audience ignorant in terms of what a phone is or what it looks like.

While accuracy is an important factor in literal description, it may not provide the cues needed to develop a picture in the mind. A hamburger can be described metaphorically as "big as a bass drum." That's not accurate, it's an exaggeration, but it describes the bigness of the hamburger better than saying that it is 2⅞ inches high. Better yet is the description used by McDonald's in the famous "two all-beef patties" chant. The jingle simply listed the ingredients included in a Big Mac, and the point was made dramatically that this is a *big* hamburger.

Narrative

Narrative writing tells a story. Stories are little plays, anecdotes, or dramas that describe an experience, happening, or event. The description is more elaborate than recording sensory impressions. A story brings to life a setting, characters with their distinctive expressions, voices, and gestures, dialogue between the characters, mood, and the action as the story develops. The Je Reviens perfume ad, which we discussed earlier for its descriptive techniques, is also a good example of a story.

Anecdotes.   There are several types of narrative techniques used in advertising. The most common is the anecdote with an anonymous voice describing some little happening. An example is an advertisement by Apple Computers that described a bizarre home disaster where an Apple got baked at Thanksgiving. The copy says:

> Last Thanksgiving, a designer from Lynn/Ohio Corporation took one of the company's Apple Personal Computers home for the holidays.
> While he was out eating turkey, it got baked.
> His cat, perhaps miffed at being left alone, knocked over a lamp which started a fire which, among other unpleasantries, melted his TV set all over his computer. He thought his goose was cooked.
> But when he took the Apple to Cincinnati Computer Store, mirabile dictu, it still worked.
> A new case and keyboard made it as good as new.

The point of the ad is the durability if the machine.

Storytelling.   Another type of narrative is the *storyteller* format; it reads like a piece of good fiction. The scene is set, characters introduced, a point of suspense established, the action rolls, and finally some kind of happy ending is achieved—usually because of the product.

An example of the storyteller technique is an ad for After Eight Chocolate Mints that reads like a mystery novel. The headline reads: "*Lord Horace calls in the police*" and the underline is "*Chapter 1 of 'The Last Mint,' a baffling story of low doings in high places.*" This is a long copy ad. It parodies a mystery novel but a bit of the copy will give you a feel for the piece:

> Welcome to Blodstoke, the modest country home of Lord Horace and Lady Penelope Blodgett-Stokes, known to their friends as Chuff and Binky. Forty-eight bedrooms, two bathrooms.
> In this four-century-old house, where the dining table is a bit too long for a decent game of ping-pong, a major crisis has arisen: there is a mysterious shortage of After Eight Chocolate Mints.

Process.   Narrative copy can also be used to describe processes such as the invention, use, or production of a product. This kind of narrative may rely less on dramatic techniques, but it may be more effective at relating product features. An example of *process* narrative is found in an advertisement by Jack Daniel's. Under a photograph of two oldtimers in overalls standing next to a row of wood kegs is the following copy:

> These men can tell exactly what's happening inside every barrel in a Jack Daniel's warehouse.
> In the heat of summer the whiskey is expanding into the charred inner wood of the barrel. Come Halloween, it's starting to cool. And inching its way back toward the center. Over the aging period, this gentle circulation of whiskey is going on constantly. Of course, it can't be perceived by the human eye. But after a sip of Jack Daniel's, we believe you'll recognize its importance.

Plot.   The concept of action and a developing story is more commonly known as plot. Plots are constructed with a beginning, middle, and end. A plot is a summary of a sequence of events over time leading up to some conclusion. A story is usually told from a viewpoint, often the viewpoint of an anonymous observer, and it is constructed around some focus of interest. In advertising writing the focus of interest is often a problem, a problem that the product can solve. In a typical format the problem is posed, suspense develops while a search is under way for the solution, and finally the product is introduced as the hero to solve the problem.

The dramatic value of the narrative can vary from a little anecdote used as an attention-getting device to a full-blown play or fiction format. Print uses the visual to establish setting, mood, and sometimes character. Development of those dimensions continues in the words. Since print is a flat dimension, it's more of a challenge to introduce plot and action.

In television advertising, however, the audio and video not only set the stage, they also provide vehicles for action and plot development. Radio uses the audio cues to establish setting and create characters, but the pictures are created in the mind of the hearer. Because of the power of imagination, radio dramas are particularly involving.

Dialogue.   This is a technique used in narrative writing, and examples of dialogue are found in the After Eight Chocolate Mint ad. The writer, from an anonymous viewpoint, is recording conversations between Lord Horace, McPhee the butler, Lady Penelope, and the Chief Constable. This is standard fiction style.

The award-winning ad for Paco Rabanne, which was discussed in the chapter on message strategies, uses a different style of dialogue. This is straight dialogue, raw and without any anonymous author's commentary. It reads like a script or the transcript of a conversation. It gives you the feeling of overhearing a personal, intimate conversation that you weren't supposed to hear between two literate, worldly, loving, teasing people. The dialogue records both sides of what is clearly a phone conversation. You can tell that because of the initial word cue. The personality of the characters comes through only in their words; there are no scripting cues to tell you if they are angry, happy, or sad. But the copy is so well written that the euphoria of a new love shines through the sophisticated repartee. The photo shows a young man in shorts on a porch sitting at a typewriter. He's talking on a phone:

Hello?

—How's the Great American Novel going?

So far it reads more like the turgid insights of a lonely Albanian date-plucker.

—Did I hear the word "lonely"?

There's a fog rolling in.

—You're in Pawgansett, dear. It holds the world record for fog.

The t in my typewriter is sticking. I have 17 cans of lentil soup. And my Paco Rabanne cologne, which I use to lure shy maidens out of the woods, is gone, all gone.

—You're going to have to do better than that.

All right, I'm lonely. I miss you. I miss your cute little broken nose. I miss the sight of you in the morning, all pink and pearly and surly.

—And you want me to catch the train up?

Hurry! This thing they call love is threatening to disturb the peace. And darling . . .

—Yes?

Bring a bottle of Paco Rabanne, would you?

The maidens are getting restless.

—Swine!

Occasionally, you'll see *monologue* used in advertising copy. Testimonials are the most common examples of the monologue form, particularly for television. The leading character reports his or her experiences with the product.

Story appeal is used in advertising because it builds interest. Storytellers have been mesmerizing minds for thousands of years, and a well-told story can be the most captivating form of copy. Earl Nightingale, of all people, did one of his radio programs on an advertisement for Cruse Wine.[7] He read the following copy over the air straight from the ad:

Long, long ago, when knights were bold and kingdoms were personal property, a 15-year-old girl named Eleanor was married to Louis VII, King of France. What she lacked in maturity she made up in her dowry. She was heiress to Aquitaine, an area equal to almost one quarter of modern France.

(The copy then goes on to detail Eleanor's life and the wars fought over this property, which includes Chateau D'Issan, the home of the Cruse family and its famous wines.)

After reading the copy, he commented that "my point in reading the ad is to show how well ad copy can be done; how interesting and educational it can be." He explained that he never knew that one woman had been queen of both France and England. He said, "It captured and held my interest until I had read every word and it ended with an intelligent suggestion that I buy the product advertised."

He concluded with some suggestions to all aspiring copywriters: "There is an interesting story to tell about practically all products and services and it is the job of the advertising copywriter to find that story and tell it in such a way that it will capture the attention of the person for whom it is intended. A good product, well advertised, will never offend the reader, listener, or viewer." He signed off by saying, "The one cardinal sin of selling is to be uninteresting."

Writing tips.   Here are some suggestions on how to write narrative copy. First, set up the scene or scenes in your mind—better yet, find a real setting similar to what you imagine. Know your way around the set and what it looks like from every angle.

Develop the characters as individuals before you start writing. Colleen Reece, an instructor of fiction writing, explains her system for character development in an article in *Writer's Digest.*[8] She uses a 38-point "character chart." It is a list of characteristics, looks, special qualities, opinions, demographics, and so on for each major character. If you have a photo file developing, then find a picture of the character you envision and set it up on the desk in front of you.

The photo file technique is recommended by another fiction writer, Roy Sorrells.[9] He also suggests that you close the door and "act out" the story, taking the role of each of the characters. Don't write the words, let them come naturally out of the mouth of the characters as you walk through the scene in their shoes. Get it all down on a tape recorder.

Don't be self-conscious—it doesn't matter if you can act or not. It's just a prewriting exercise—calisthenics for the imagination. But projecting yourself into the scene and into the shoes of your characters will give you more natural and more believable copy. The dialogue, in particular, will flow more smoothly. Plot the action in scenes and move yourself from one scene to another. See the action through the eyes of your characters.

Then go back to the typewriter and transcribe and revise from the tape-recorded "live" copy. If you are writing a simple story without complicated plot lines and action, then just talk it into the tape recorder. Storytelling is a verbal art form. The spirit of the story will come through more honestly if you talk it rather than write it.

Explanation

Explanation is a form of expository writing that assumes the subject of the message is unknown to the audience. You use explanation to translate the topic so that it will be as familiar to your audience as it is to you. Explanation uses all of the previously discussed techniques. Sometimes unfamiliar terms are used in an explanation and they have to be defined. Before you can explain something you often have to describe it first, and sometimes in explaining something you may use narrative techniques to develop a picture of a process. So definition, description, and narration can all be used in explanation, as well as straight-line assertion.

Unfamiliarity.   The need for explanation occurs whenever we try to communicate a new idea or experience to an audience that has not confronted the idea or experience before. The newness may be just in a way of seeing the idea or experience. But whatever it is, you have a mental picture that they don't. You use explanation to get your mental picture to look as much like your audience's as possible.

You can't simply transmit the picture. As C. S. Osgood has said, there are no wires strung from one mind to another.[10] You can't *transmit* meanings; instead, you have to use words to generate a mental picture from the audience's repertoire or previous experiences. Their picture will never be identical with yours, because your experiences are different than everyone else's. The best you can hope for is similarity in the essential dimensions.

These islands of experience may represent a product engineer talking about a new breakthrough, or someone who is mechanically inept trying to explain to the mechanic what's wrong with the car. The islands shift and merge like sand at low tide, but the explanatory problems are basically the same whatever the situation.

The first problem is a gap of some sort—a gap in knowledge or in experience. Most communication operates with a basic assumption of commonality of background between source and receiver. The more common the experiences and the shared meanings, the greater the probability of success in communication. Explanation, by definition, violates this assumption. If both source and receiver shared a common meaning, there would be no need for explanation.

A second problem is that people are afraid to try something new. Adults, in particular, resist new information and new experiences. Advertising copy has to overcome this barrier by providing the initial experience of trial within the ad itself. Let them experience it vicariously, painlessly, through your words and they will be more likely to buy the product. The objective, then, is to make the strange familiar.

The third problem is determining where the audience stands in relation to the experience. This is called *communication distance*. If your audience has absolutely no experience with the product or with anything like it, then you will have more of an explanatory problem than if the product is a line extension of a familiar brand. Gauging this distance is critical to knowing how much of a bridge is needed to get across the experience gap.

The question.   Explanation is built on *inquiry*. Before explanation can be used to bridge gaps, the critical questions have to be aroused in the mind of your audience. Questioning cues the existence of a knowledge gap. That's the signal, for example, to a teacher to stop and explain a concept one more time or in a different way. But, without the question, there's no reason for the explanation.

In order for an explanation to be successful, you need to stimulate the questioning process in your audience's mind. An effective explanation operates in a state of inquiry—a curious mind seeking answers. Much of what passes for instruction is a dull presentation of answers to students who have no questions—at least not on the topic under discussion. Like a car in neutral rolling downhill, there may be some motion but it will never make it back up the other side. Ad copy that's written to a mind in neutral will never make it anywhere either.

Explanation is a very important tool in advertising. Every time we have a new product to announce it has to be described, and people have to be taught how to use it, how to say the name, how to recognize the package and logo, and where to buy it. As we said in the chapter on objectives, much of the research, literature, and theory behind the field of advertising comes from educational psychology, specifically learning theory. Admitting that advertising is often teaching makes the copywriter's job much easier.

Any question can lead to explanation, but there are certain key questions that cue different types of responses. Basically, the key questions seem to be *what, why, how,* and *so what.* The *what* question is really preliminary to explanation. It calls for definition and description. The relevant question can be expanded to "What is this like?", and that, of course, calls for a description of sensory details and impressions. Most writers find themselves describing what the subject is like before they move on to the higher order questions of why, how and so what.

One technique is to define terms. An ad by TWA is a good example of this. The headline reads: "TWA redefines First Class." Then it gets serious about defining what makes first class different.

A better class of seat.

Our seats are more comfortable than ever. (Not surprising. They were redesigned with that in mind.)
   In our 747s, our Sleeper Seats℠ recline a full 60 degrees. Which, apart from being extraordinarily comfortable, makes falling asleep in one extraordinarily easy.

An appeal to one's good taste.

The food will come as a rather pleasant surprise. On international flights, there's domestic caviar. Chateaubriand with sauce Perigueux. Lobster Ther-

midor. Vintage wines from California and France. Liquors, cognacs, cordials, and more.

A *why* question leads to reasons, causes, and results. In advertising we talk about a type of message strategy called *reason-why* copy. This message format translates information about the product into a use or benefit to the consumer. It states the "reason why" the consumer should buy the product. Reason-why copy can be identified by certain key phrases that are used to cue this type of explanation: *because, in order that, the reason why, the answer is, the causes are, that's why, the advantages are, and here's proof.* The following headlines cue the use of the why question in advertising:

> *Why do 28 of the Fortune Directory's top 100 manufacturers use NCR shop-floor systems?*
> *— Because NCR provides fail-safe, custom-tailored systems.*
> *Why do women need the American Express Card?*
> *— For the same reasons men do.*
> *We can't tell you who banks at Morgan.*
> *— But we can tell you why.*
> *Aside from its having the Herman's label, here are 13 more reasons why you should buy this down parka.*
> *Why you should open your IRA Retirement program with a company deeply involved in retirement planning.*

How questions call for an explanation of a process. They ask, "How does this work?" or "How do I do it?" "How-to" ads are very common in advertising, and they are used principally to explain how to use a new product. Any time you see suggestions, tips, recipes and menus, a demonstration, or any other kind of process instruction, you are working with a *how* question. Word cues for how explanations include: *the process is, how it works, how to do, a way to, here's what you do, hints, tips,* and so on. Some headlines from sample *how* ads include:

> *Sitting pretty at the sofa factory*
> *How we helped a sofa manufacturer build a cushion of profit*
> *How to fire someone you like*
> *How we're making the incubator safer for babies*
> *How to be sure your business makes the most of the new tax laws*

When you write a process explanation, you have to take an entire experience and break it into small parts. The copy needs to be written in direct address (that forces you to think in terms of the steps your reader will be going through), and it proceeds step by step. The secret is to go back to your first experience in this area and relive it through the mind of someone who is totally inexperienced. What did it feel like? What were your first doubts? What didn't you understand? Where did you start first? Where did you get off track? Remember the learning procedure may not be the same procedure you use now that you are experienced.

A good example of an ad that walks someone through a process is one by Smith-Corona headlined "How to buy a typewriter." The copy has 10 subheads identifying key things to look at when you try out a typewriter. Here are some excerpts:

> Choosing a portable typewriter isn't hard if you know what to look for. This brief guide will help you make the best choice.
>
> Test the feel. Check the slope and height of the keyboard. Check the size and shape of the keys. Make sure the controls are uncrowded and easy to reach. . . .
>
> Try the touch. A responsive touch makes for better, easier typing. Look for a touch that is prompt, easy, and dependable. . . .
>
> Listen to the sound. The typewriter is trying to tell you something. If it sounds tinny, beware. This may indicate that the construction is too light.
>
> Note the look of the type. Lines and individual letters should be straight. The impression should be crisp, clean, and even. The print quality should not vary over the page. . . .
>
> Look at the carrying case. Does it have double walls for air-cushioned protection? Does it have sturdy latches and hinges?

A *so what* question asks for an analysis of significance, synthesis, and perspective. It answers the underlying question, "What does this mean?" This is the highest order of explanation since it calls for interpretation. Words used to cue *so what* explanations include: *this means that, what happened, don't you know, the results mean,* and so on. This type of explanation is not used as often as how or why. Some ads that use *so what* strategies in their copy have the following headlines and copy points:

> "Good news for bad knees." (Converse has developed a new feature for running shoes called a Stabilizer Bar. The copy explains what it does and why it's important.)
>
> "How the simplest business principle of all turns competitors into customers." (Motorola is selling to Japanese companies because of a high level of product quality.)
>
> "Why is Tareyton better?
>
> Others remove. Tareyton improves." (Tareyton uses a two-part filter with activated charcoal which doesn't remove taste while it removes tar and nicotine.)

"Life insurance? What for? I'm still single."
(New York Life explains that you should get insurance while you're young because of better rates and because something might happen that would throw you into the high-risk category.)

Explanatory techniques.   The primary technique basic to explanation is *example* or illustration. Using an example is a way to cite an instance in order to explain the whole. It is a sample that illustrates the points being made, a concrete application of a concept that, in many cases, may be abstract. Most people learn and understand more easily from the concrete and particular. Learning theorists recommend that you use several examples with one representing the typical and one or two others to illustrate unusual applications. A good example functions to make the central point more clear to the reader.

Advertising copy that uses examples often will cue the reader by saying "for example." But sometimes the illustration isn't overt. An ad for American Express says, "A day can seem like a long time. . . .Let's say you're in a strange country and you lose your wallet. . . ." In this case, the content is clearly setting up a situation that illustrates the case in point.

Another technique is *comparison and contrast*, which points out resemblances and differences. As Archer and Schwartz explain in their book on composition,[11] both comparison and contrast "depend upon man's ability to see a pattern in existence, a pattern made up of likenesses and differences." They continue, "Comparison and contrast aims at making the unknown known to the readers by calling their attention to the connection that exists between the two.

In advertising, a simple comparison of two products as to features or uses is an effective way to make a strong claim of distinctiveness. Simple comparisons are usually signaled by such phrases as "things like" and "like . . . as" statements. An example of a simple comparison from a Panasonic ad is "You can use a 60-minute cassette (not 30, like other microrecorders)."

Another technique of explanation is the use of analogies. *Analogies* are extended metaphors. Where a metaphor compares two things in terms of a common characteristic, an analogy compares on the basis of several points of resemblance. For this reason, analogies are often used to explain processes, rather than single objects. The comparison is based on a set of dimensions or characteristics. The Korean Air Line used an extensive analogy in an ad to develop the concept of excellence and pride. The analogy was expressed in a story that began: "In 1593 Korean shipbuilders developed the first iron clad vessel." The craftsmanship and inventiveness of these early ships was then compared with the quality of the modern airline.

Analogies are particularly good techniques for reinterpreting a new experience in terms of an old one. They are experience extenders. You are using your reader's experience as a foundation for building a new concept.

Effective explanations.   Rudolph Flesch, a well-known author of principles of good writing, says that "explanation is an art—a difficult art. . . . But the art can be learned."[12] Even sophisticated, complicated, and technical concepts can be explained to laymen as well as to experts. He has eight points or ground rules for effective explanation. They are as follows:

1. *Nothing is self-explanatory.* Nothing explains itself. There has to be a will and an eagerness to learn. They won't learn anything from an enclosed "self-explanatory" brochure.
2. *Translate technical terms.* Technical terms are a sort of shorthand used by experts. The words are familiar to the experts, but not to a lay audience. Replace every unfamiliar word with a translation.
3. *Go step by step.* This is particularly important if you are giving instructions. Analyze the job from the point of view of someone totally ignorant. Break it down into the smallest possible steps. Describe each step carefully.
4. *Don't say too little.* Don't be afraid of being too elementary. Always assume that the other person doesn't understand things too well.
5. *Don't say too much.* Don't answer questions they didn't ask; don't give them information they don't need.
6. *Illustrate!* The way to explain a general rule is to show how it applies to a specific case.
7. *Answer expected questions.* You're not through with an explanation when you're through. Every explanation should be followed by specific answers to questions likely to be raised. The questions people usually ask are self-centered and immensely practical.
8. *Warn against common mistakes.* No matter how well you explain things, some people will misunderstand. Telling them isn't enough. You have to repeat and emphasize what's right and point out strongly and loudly what's wrong.

Most of the problems with explanations are of four kinds: accuracy, clarity or readability, logic, and word choice. Flesch's Eight Rules touch on these problems. *Accuracy* simply means that the information you have to present has to be correct. People assume that because something is set in type, that it has to be the truth. Not so. Develop a journalist's skepticism about all information you've been given. Test it out. Recheck it with another source. Your explanation can never be any better than the information it is built on.

Clarity is the second basic problem. The information has to be clear to the audience and different audiences have different reading skills and levels. You don't write the same way for children that you do for stockbrokers. Adjust the level of the writing to your audience. There are a number of "readability" tests available to check the level of your writing. The two most common are Gunning's "Fog Index"[13] and Flesch's "Readability."[14] Both of these methods test such factors as sentence length, number of syllables in the words, and the use of personal words.

Logic is another aspect of clarity. Most explanations have to be well ordered in order to be understood. If your conclusions don't follow the steps or are out of order, then you've lost your readers. One of the biggest problems with explanations is holes—big jumps in logic. You know the process, so it may be easy for you to move from one major point to another without the intermediate steps, but for someone trying to follow an argument or a procedure through unfamiliar territory, your little jump may be a big chasm. If they can't make the jump, you've lost them.

The fourth problem is *word choice*. Flesch mentioned the problem with technical terms. It's very difficult for a specialist to spot words that need to be explained. To a specialist all the terms are familiar, to a layman they may be obscure and intimidating. You either have to make the jump back to the lay point of view (and that is not easy) or get someone less familiar with the area to be your pilot test. Check your word choice against their reading of your copy. Do they understand the words as used in context? If not, find a new word, or define the word as you use it.

Copy Problems

Copy hash is a phrase applied to advertising writing that is unclear, inaccurate, illogical, and/or poorly worded. It may sound well phrased when you read it, but when you think about it you realize that it is gibberish. An example of an advertisement that doesn't follow logically is from Sears. The rather obscure headline says: "You can count on Sears to look at a new product from every angle." The underline continues with this quote:

> *"The first thing we did was test 16 of the top-rated running shoes," says the Sears buyer, "as well as the bare foot." Not many companies have the luxury of starting from scratch, but Sears spent nearly two painstaking years developing the 440. Here's why they spent the time:*

(At this point, you are probably wondering what the product is. It's not clear from the headline. Since the 440 was mentioned at the end of the underline, one might expect that this new shoe is the product. The body copy uses a long narrative to explain the development of the 440.)

> *Sears knew it took more than a good factory to make a good running shoe— one that would fit comfortably and help reduce the foot, ankle, and knee problems that runners sometimes encounter.*
> *They went to experts: Northwestern University Medical School Center for Sports Medicine. The doctors kept a sharp eye on stress points*

and suggested possible ways the 440 Running Shoe could aid in helping to prevent the problems that plague runners.

The buyers and Sears' own lab worked closely with this team of nationally known orthopedic surgeons and the manufacturer. Prototype after prototype was discarded as not good enough.

Not good enough because Sears wanted to go further than a shoe that would fit comfortably and minimize problems—they also wanted a shoe that would look attractive, wear well, and sell at a fair price.

The 440 Running Shoe pleased all concerned with its innovative features. Like a cushiony insole you can remove so it will dry out between wearings. A nicety whether you wear the shoe to run the Boston Marathon or go get the groceries.

(A little wordy perhaps, but still the narrative approach is an interesting way to sell a well-designed shoe. The copy continues.)

Finding a better way of doing things is virtually a policy at Sears. Each year, Sears lab tests over ten thousand products and, along with the buyers, keeps up a running dialogue with manufacturers with this aim: How can we make it better?

(What are we selling now?)

Sometimes innovation means portability: the Bionic TV set has a two-inch diagonal measure black-and-white picture and weighs a spanking two pounds. It can hang around your neck like binoculars, and it's only at Sears.

(Now we are selling televisions?)

Often, innovation means a unique feature thought up by Sears first and then patented. Like the Corrector™ key on many Sears portable electric typewriters. This clever key lets you correct mistakes without moving your hands from the keyboard.

(And now we are into typewriters?)

These are a few in a string of product innovations and improvements from Sears. But there is one thing Sears hasn't had to improve upon in over half a century: Its famous promise:
Satisfaction guaranteed
or your money back

And that's it, friends—an ad that starts out with a long explanation of a new running shoe, and then without so much as a transition moves to the company lab, the portability feature of a TV set, and the correcting key on a typewriter. Finally, in the last paragraph, you find out that the thread that holds this mélange together is the company's emphasis on innovation. But no, the innovation wrapup can't even stand alone—it has to take second seat to the company's policy on guarantees. There you have a classic example of an advertisement that suffers from wandering logic and large leaps.

For another example of copy hash, let's turn to a strange advertisement by Kodak. It starts off with this headline:

> The only people who are generous enough to read English themes are English teachers.
> —from You and Aunt Arie, by Pamela Wood, an English teacher

If the headline doesn't leave you shaking your head, then plow on into the body copy and see if you can make any sense of it.

> Foxfire was the first of them. As you can see, the idea has now spread far and wide—high school magazines where students picture the older ways of the community, and never mind teenage fantasy. Pamela Wood's book* telling how to do this advises down to the last detail of film processing, subscription list maintenance, and courteous interviewing technique how ordinary high school kids become chroniclers of lives, joys, place, reality, skills, and culture before and beyond the shopping malls that homogenize the continent. We are interested because photography and today's printing methods based on the photographic process are essential for these marvelous magazines, but anybody of the generations that stand between the chroniclers and their peppery interviewees can admire the professionalism in writing, editing, layout, and management skills that deliver such fascinating and instructive reading for the buyer's dollar. If you were going to say something about inarticulate, uppity modern youth, forget it. Could your own high school teach English this way?

Did the copywriter's high school teach English that way? You might wonder. Where do you begin critiquing something like this? First and most obvious, there isn't a single paragraph break. Given the lack of transitions, the juxtaposition of seemingly unrelated ideas makes for incomprehensible copy.

The headline, of course, was an obscure quote and the lead sentence had nothing whatsoever to do with the head. The lead also contained a reference to "them"—whoever "them" might be. "As you can see" is a ludicrous transition since nothing that came before relates to anything that follows.

There are two serious syntax problems in the second sentence, including a botched parallel construction and a tacked-on, unrelated editorial comment about today's teenagers. By chasing the asterisk, you can find out that Pamela Wood wrote a book entitled *You and Aunt Arie*, but that piece of information tells you nothing.

Then follow the two longest sentences ever to see the stroke of typesetting in an American advertisement. The sentence beginning with Pamela Wood is an unheard-of 49 words. The one beginning with "we are interested" is an even more incredible 56 words. It isn't just the length that offends, it's the circuitous phrasing that wanders undirected through a forest of kids and old folks and shopping malls, and homogenized continents and undefined "we's" plus tours of photography and printing and magazines and interviewing and instructive reading. It all leads to the final non sequitur—the almighty "buying dollar."

The part of the last sentence that contains the clause, "but anybody of the generations that stand between the chronicler and their interviewees," is copied directly from the ad—it's not a typo, nothing has been left out—except meaning and syntax. If you were going to say something about inarticulate copywriters, forget it. This ad is, without doubt, the ultimate example of copy hash.

NOTES

1. Philip Ward Burton, *Which Ad Pulled Best?* (Chicago: Crain, 1981).
2. The Copy Chasers column runs every month in *Industrial Marketing*. The ads discussed in this section were analyzed at a Copy Chasers seminar, Advertising Creative Workshop, Chicago, July 1982.
3. Burton, op. cit.
4. Donald Hall, *Writing Well* (Boston: Little, Brown, 1973), p. 210.
5. Kim B. Rotzoll, "Gossage Revisited: Reflections of Advertising's Legendary Iconoclast," *Journal of Advertising*, 9:4 (1980), pp. 6–14.
6. Hall, op. cit.
7. Earl Nightingale, "Our Changing World," Script #2029: "How to Sell Wine," 1973.
8. Colleen Reece, "Just a Bunch of Words: How to Develop Believable Characters," *Writer's Digest*, November 1981, pp. 28–31.
9. Roy Sorrells, "Ham on Bond: Using Acting Techniques to Improve Your Writing," *Writer's Digest*, July 1980, pp. 39–40.
10. Charles S. Osgood, George J. Suci, Percy H. Tannenbaum, *The Measurement of Meaning*, (Urbana: University of Illinois Press, 1971).
11. Jerome Archer and Joseph Schwartz, "Why, Whence, What: Ends and Results," in *A Reader for Writers*, 2nd ed. (New York: McGraw-Hill, 1966), pp. 252–55.
12. Rudolph Flesch, "Explain," Chapter 9 in *Say What You Mean*, (New York: Harper & Row, 1972), pp. 113–26.
13. Robert Gunning, *How to Take the Fog Out of Your Writing* (Chicago: Dartness Press, 1951).
14. Rudolph Flesch, "A New Readability Yardstick," *Journal of Applied Psychology*, 32 (June 1948), pp. 221–33.

Graphics

Chapter Five

5.1 VISUAL COMMUNICATION

Advertising is a field that exists on images—significant visuals that command attention, symbolize a brand, establish a personality for a product, and anchor the corporate identity in the audience's mind. Communication by visual image is easily the most important dimension of the advertising message. Even in an audio medium like radio, the images produced in the listener's mind carry an important part of the communication function.

In order to understand how visual communication works in advertising, we need to review some of the basics of perception. *Perception* can be defined as the process by which we become *aware* through our senses. Of the five senses, researchers have found that the visual sense is dominant. Some educators theorize that as much as 80 percent of the information we receive comes through sight.[1] Sound contributes another 14 percent, while the remaining senses provide only 6 percent of our information.

One of the interesting anomalies in our culture is the fact that our entire educational system is built around talking and lecturing, which is contrary to the way our perceptual system is designed to work. That also explains why, in some ways, advertising messages are more effective than educational messages—advertisers usually resist the temptation to "lecture" or "preach," and most advertising professionals intuitively know how to use sight for more effective presentation of information.

Perception

Attention.   Advertisements are more or less persuasive depending upon their ability to get attention. Starch research[2] has shown that ads with illustrations are seen more than ads without (recognition), and the more compelling the visual, the more readers will note the ad and the more they will attend to further development of the message. This shows up in the Starch "read most" scores. There is a definite carry-over effect for compelling visuals. High "noted" scores tend to generate high "read most" scores.

What makes a visual arresting? We know that bold graphics, big and bold type, bright colors, novelty, and surprise are strong attention-getting devices. Research in newspaper advertising has proven that size is a factor—the bigger the ad, the more attention it receives. Color is important, too. In a black-and-white environment, spot color or full color is attention getting. In a cluttered environment, simplicity stands out. The principle here is contrast or novelty.

Interest is still the crux of the attention dimension. For someone who is hungry, a platter of steaming fried chicken can be arresting. Appetite appeal has been demonstrated over and over as a strong attention-getting device. It is difficult to describe the taste of a pizza in words, but most of us will salivate when we see a steaming pizza coming out of the oven in a commercial.

The most successful advertising is voluntarily attended to—what a former advertising professor, Charles Mauldin, used to call the "Hey, Martha" phenomenon. This is the kind of ad that finds the viewer or reader calling out: "Hey, Martha, come and see this."

Organization.   We begin to "see" meaning when the information that has confronted our senses begins to "make sense" to us. That happens through a process that psychologists call "organization."

One aspect of organizing that is important to advertising is the psychological concept of figure and ground. We see visuals in a flat field and, as we select various details to attend to, these details become an important "figure" to us and the other details become background. Since we can only attend to one thing at a time, that means everything else automatically has to become background.

As our attention shifts, the relationship between foreground and background will change, and some element that previously was secondary now moves to the foreground and becomes "figure." In the design of messages, contrast is used to establish dominant details and separate them from subordinate elements. Establishing an easy-to-perceive figure is a very important part of visual communication in advertising.

Another way to make sense of what we see is through the process of sorting information into familiar categories and labeling them. You see a small furry animal with whiskers, you compare that little animal with others you have seen, and you come up with the category "cat." The psychologists call that "pattern" or figure recognition. You take a few details, extract the essence of the object from these cues, and assign a label to the whole figure.

Memorability.   We file away memories as traces of visuals, indelible images that are locked into the mind. Advertising research has found that people attend more to the visuals than to the words, and they tend to remember the pictures longer than the words.[3]

You can test this by scanning magazines. Turn the pages in a slow rhythmic fashion and note your own patterns of observation. The first thing you will probably note is that you tend to see the picture first. If you move out of scanning and study the ad, then the words will begin to register. Now close the magazine and try to remember the ads you just scanned. In most cases, you will probably find you are remembering either the visual or the way the ad looked on the page.

The body of research findings generated by Starch has consistently shown that people are more likely to remember a print advertisement if it contains a photo.[4] Other researchers have found that recall of a brand name is significantly higher if the name is integrated with an illustration. Lutz and Lutz have found that pictorial elements are stronger at changing or affecting attitudes than are words.[5]

The memory system works like a filing cabinet. When you put a file away in a file cabinet, you write a little code word on the tab so you can organize it in the system. That tab is a "cue." When you see something new, you will use this cue to bring up familiar categories to use in comparing this new information.

The cueing function is particularly important in advertising. We want our messages not only to be seen and remembered but also recalled and, to recall them, there have to be strong cues. Advertising uses all kinds of sensory information—audio as well as visual—to cue products, labels, associations, and brand names.

Slogans, logos, product characters, colors, and packaging stimulate this triggering process. These details are reminders of a message that, if it was successful, established a positive feeling about the product. You may not remember details of the message, but you remember seeing it and associating it with a brand name and image depending upon the strength of these cues.

Advertising is a very efficient form of communication and must convey complicated messages in very limited time and space. One of the reasons it is so successful in delivering these compressed messages is because the message designers use the cueing process to signal complicated messages and trigger recall.

Because our minds dislike ambivalence, we don't operate very well with information that doesn't fit into any of our categories. We manipulate and distort information in the process of organizing it to fit into our memory systems. Furthermore, a total impression is only filed on the basis of a few salient details. Memory is fragmentary, elusive, and sometimes "creative." If you are designing an advertising message, you might as well accept the fact that viewers and readers will only remember fragments, if they remember anything at all.

The visual image plays an important role in retention. Obviously you can remember words, but you have to work at it. Anyone who has memorized a poem or lines in a play knows the tremendous amount of repetition necessary to lock a sequence of words into long-term memory. We can help verbal memory by using alliteration, rhyme, and rhythm in addition to repetition, but it is still a difficult process. Visual images, however, are easy to scan, identify, file, and recall. For long-term recall, visual information has a distinct advantage.

Visual Learning

We are all visually literate to one degree or another, even though few of us have been taught how to understand the images we confront daily. "Seeing meaning" is analogous in common language to understanding. Such phrases as "I see what you mean" and "I got the picture" mean you comprehend something and therefore you have learned it.

How does advertising use visual literacy? Advertising uses demonstrations to show how products are to be used. "How-to" information is usually presented visually. A cake mix ad may include a recipe, but the dominant visual is usually the finished product showing how it is supposed to turn out. Food advertising visuals include serving suggestions as a form of unobtrusive instruction. Likewise, furniture and home improvement ads inevitably include decorating suggestions.

Advertising is used by consumers to gain information about products and point of view as well as to learn mastery of skills. All of these are educational objectives. Advertisements are read, studied, filed, and recalled by consumers who want information about certain products and issues. And all of that happens without assignments, teachers, grades, or threats of tests. It's a natural form of self-motivated learning that relies heavily upon visual communication.

Realism and symbolism.   Realism is used in advertising to present a literal, accurate depiction of something—a product, an event. Conviction and belief are the objectives of persuasion and they can be addressed most effectively with a realistic image. You believe what you see and in advertising you see it in color, you see the size and shape and the package, you see it performing in tests, you see it compared against the competition.

Symbols are used to express abstract concepts that can't be easily communicated literally. Quality, value, durability, and friendliness are all abstract concepts used in advertising. They can be symbolized but they can't be depicted. There is no literal representation for quality.

Symbols are also used to develop associations. Most symbols are visual. Symbols are often used for identification information, although they can express emotional meanings as well as factual ones. Rossiter and Percy, in their *Journal of Advertising* article on visual imagery,[6] note that visual images can lead to favorable attitudes without words. Images, in other words, can affect attitudes. They point to the Marlboro man as a symbolic statement that says this cigarette is for rugged individuals. A picture of a kitten with toilet paper can very effectively communicate softness, perhaps better than words.

Symbolism works only to the extent that the association is clear, so that there can be no problem with comprehension. A picture of a person in a wheelchair is relatively easy to understand as a symbol for handicapped people. But a peacock has to be learned as the symbol for a television network—there's no inherent visual link.

If the symbol works, it provides a shortcut form of communication. The symbol expresses the essence of the idea, but not the details. It simplifies and because of that it can convey meaning faster than a literal depiction with all its many details. Symbolism is used in advertising for this reason. It is another technique for compressing information and presenting complex messages in short time frames.

Little kids, kittens, and puppy dogs appeal to the sentimental spirit in most of us. As clichéd as these visuals may be, they consistently stop readers, according to the Starch scores. Many of these psychological appeals are best expressed in symbolic visuals—love is a mother and child, childhood is a boy and a puppy, fear is a fire in your home or an auto accident or a burglar. We can put these emotions in words, but a picture dramatizes it more powerfully and strikes at the core of our feelings. The emotional "button" or "trigger" is often a picture.

Most of advertising's persuasiveness comes from its strong visual images. We discussed previously the power of realistic images to "prove" a claim. The "reason-why" is often best demonstrated in the visual; words can support, of course, but the strongest claim will be made visually using words as a reinforcement. Appeals to emotion are also best expressed in images. If you want to express fear or fun or love or status or pride, you can show it with greater impact than you can say it.

5.2 ART

Art, or graphics, is a generic term used in advertising to apply to the visual expression of the creative concept. It includes photography as well as illustration. The creative concept, the big idea around which the ad is built, is a blend of words and pictures. A successful creative concept works like a stew. The flavors blend so that you can't distinguish them individually.

Likewise, in a successful creative concept the pictures and the words are mutually reinforcing. Sometimes a creative concept may be essentially words, at which point the layout speaks as an expressive graphic—as in the Merit announcement style cigarette ads. Sometimes the concept is essentially graphic as in the Marlboro ads.

Most often, however, an advertisement uses both the pictures and the words to tell the story, and one is incomplete without the other. An example is the classic VW ad that shows a lowly beetle in an expanse of white space with the simple headline, "Think small." The picture wouldn't make sense without the headline, and the head wouldn't make sense without the picture.

One of the most difficult problems faced by those who work on the creative side is how to communicate a concept that exists only as a loose picture in the mind. In order to move into the "execution" decisions and make a rough idea materialize on paper, there are some basic decisions that have to be made. Generally, every visual demands decisions in the following areas: illustration or photography, literal or symbolic meaning, use of color, product depiction and execution tone.

Basic Decisions

Photo or illustration.   Illustrations and photographs have an entirely different feeling. In general, an illustration is more unreal, more fanciful; a photograph can be more literal and realistic. These distinctions are inherent in the way we perceive the two forms. Artwork is always a metaphor, an abstraction, a manipulated and constructed image. It can look like reality, but it is never real. It abstracts, it eliminates details, it focuses attention. Because it abstracts, it can communicate faster and more pointedly. It can also intensify meanings and moods. It is an ideal medium for fantasy and escape.

Photography has reality, an authenticity, that makes it powerful. Most people believe their eyes, and when you show them a photograph it appears to be reality. Most people feel that pictures don't lie. For credibility, photography is a good medium. Photographs, of course, can also create evocative, abstract, and fanciful images. But, generally, photography is used in advertising because of its realism.

Literal or symbolic meaning.   While there is a natural tendency to see illustrations as abstractions and photographs as reality, in fact, literal and symbolic messages can be communicated in both forms. A technical drawing of the parts of a tire is a literal illustration; a photograph of an expensively dressed couple in front of a mansion can be symbolic. In addition to deciding whether you want to use an illustration or a photograph, you also need to decide the level of symbolism of the message.

A *literal* picture is realistic, obvious, and gives all the details. A *symbolic* picture is abstract, analogous, ambiguous, and demands that the reader or viewer get involved in translating or creating the meaning. The Taster's Choice ad uses a tie-in with an old radio program, "The Shadow." The product in the foreground and the pot in the shadows symbolize the connection with perked coffee. (See Exhibit 5-1).

The type of picture depends upon the creative strategy. A news announcement or a demonstration of a new use is best presented literally. Any time you need to teach someone how to do something, you will probably need a realistic view. A product that seeks to develop some less tangible psychological appeal may need a more symbolic presentation.

The message determines the nature of the symbolism. Some concepts demand a literal treatment; others are more symbolic. Food advertising, for ex-

EXHIBIT 5-1: **The Taster's Choice "Shadow" ad uses a play on an old radio show. The concept is developed both visually and verbally.** (Created by Leo Burnett U.S.A. and used with permission of the Nestlé Foods Corporation)

ample, tries to develop appetite appeal and uses very realistic images of mouth-watering products to "show it like it is." Abstractions like justice, freedom, quality, economy, and value can never be expressed literally because they aren't literal concepts. They have to be treated symbolically. The best associations are universal and learned early. They are also the ones most prone to be clichéd. Some associations are easy to make—wealth can be expressed through such visuals as caviar, sports cars, mansions, and fur coats. But how would you express gusto and effervescence?

Some simple literal concepts may, in fact, be difficult to communicate too. Roominess in a car is hard to picture. No matter how you shoot it, the inside of a car is still a tight, cramped space. How do you show the ease of handling, the thrill of speed? There's no way in a still picture to show actual motion, so you are forced into symbols and graphic conventions such as blurred tires and hair blowing in the wind. The Maxell ad shown in the chapter on creative thinking is a good example of the exaggeration necessary to depict a "blast" of sound.

Color.   Another basic decision is the use of color. Print advertisements can be produced in black and white, full color, or spot color. The advertising medium has some effect on this decision. Most magazines provide quality full color, while most newspapers are limited in their ability to reproduce quality color images. In addition, full color is more expensive in most advertising media. Spot color, the addition of a second or third accent color, is used to create attention-getting effects in what essentially is a black-and-white format. Television commercials, of course, are generally filmed in color.

There are creative reasons behind the color decision too. Black and white is dramatic and more abstract, since the world is created in color. It is used to create drama and documentary effects. Sometimes it is used just to be different, as in a magazine where all the other ads are in full color. The early VW Beetle ads used black and white in an era when American car advertising was bombastic and colorful. It was a technique of deliberate understatement.

Color, however, is more realistic and it is essential in literal messages. It is very difficult to create a mouth-watering effect for a pizza advertisement when it is depicted in black and white.

Product depiction.   Another critical decision is the depiction of the concept and the product. What will the *content* of the visual be? How does it express your big idea? You may think that describing the content is the easiest part of the proposal process. In fact, it's the hardest.

It is easy in advertising to get carried away with a great idea and forget about the product. For that reason it's important in this part of the decision making to include some thought about how the product is to be treated. The product may be pictured alone or against some dramatic background. The product alone is frequently used with new product introduction when name and product recognition is the primary objective. It is also used in the maturity stage for reminder of the stature and image of the product.

Another technique is to show the product in use. The setting becomes very important here in terms of whatever props are necessary to make the situation credible. People are also important because they become role models, and we must be able to identify with them in that situation. A specific type of product-in-use setting is the demonstration, where the art focuses on the environment and the procedure for using the product.

A variation on the product-alone treatment is the use of a product in a monumental setting. The objective is to create some kind of emotive response to the background situation that will carry over to the product. Cars, for example, are frequently shown against mountains, beaches, and setting sun scenes. Perfume ads show the bottle against exotic locales and elegant, romantic settings. The setting is being used to create an association, to express symbolically the type of psychological appeal identified in the creative strategy.

Another treatment is to depict the benefit associated with the product—especially as it is observed at the point of "the moment after." For example, what does relief look like after the headache or the thirst goes away? The reverse of that approach is to depict "what happens if" you don't use the product—the accident, the pain, and so on.

Execution tone.   The last basic decision reflects the tone of the design to be used in the execution. This also derives from the creative strategy. An illustration, for example, can be executed in a rough, loose, primitive, or tight style. Photographs can depict images that are formal or informal, casual or uptight. Execution style is particularly important for illustrations. If the artist works very tightly, then the art will be more formal, restrained, or even technical. If you ask for a loose style, the art will be more playful and free. Decisions about execution style relate directly to the previous decisions about medium, color, and symbolism.

These, then, are the basic decisions that need to be made in your initial discussion of the graphics. You need to decide, explain, and justify why you are using photographs or illustrations, literal or symbolic images, black and white or full color or spot color. Also, explain how you are depicting the product and visualizing the creative concept. Finally, what kind of artistic style do you envision?

Artistic Medium

If you decide to use art, there are still a number of other specific decisions to be made. An illustration can be rendered (executed) in a number of different mediums.* A black-and-white pencil sketch is the simplest form of line art. A sketch can also be done in color. For fine details a pen-and-ink illustration is good, particularly with cross-hatching details to create shadows.

---

*In art, when you speak of the various graphic techniques, the plural is *mediums.* In advertising, when you speak of various media vehicles, the plural is *media.*

Color can be achieved by using watercolor, tempera, pastels, and felt tip markers. Watercolor and pastels give a soft feeling. Tempera can be both soft and hard. Felt tip markers give a feeling of casualness, although they can provide edge and detail.

Other mediums include wash drawings using gray watercolors over pen and ink drawings to soften the edge and add shadows. Air brush techniques are used to soften edges or to delete entire sections of an illustration or photograph. A scratchboard gives a rough feeling to an illustration. Both scratchboard and cross-hatching are stylized and can create feelings of age and antiquity. Cartooning is another type of line drawing that can be executed either in black and white or flat colors.

Sources of art.   Primitive types of art are appropriate for nostalgia or historical effects. These include woodcuts, engravings, and rubbings. These can be original works or they can be reproduced from antique sources. A source of inexpensive historical art is the Dover Pictorial Archives, which reproduces illustrations that appeared in publications where the copyright has run out.

There are other sources of inexpensive commercial art besides original art done by an artist. A number of commercial art houses provide "clip art." You can buy a book of art or a series of small volumes of art on special topics that can be used anywhere without paying a royalty or needing permission. Of course, anyone can use the same art. There is nothing exclusive about clip art.

The Volk series is one example of this clip art. Newspapers subscribe to mat services such as Clipper, which provides a monthly book of theme- and season-oriented art. They usually contain art related to upcoming holidays and special events.

Photography.   There are photographers who specialize in just about everything from fashion and food to architecture and underwater. Each specialty has its own techniques and effects. Food photography, for example, demands an understanding of cooking and food presentation, and shots are taken under incredibly difficult circumstances. Naturalness in food presentation is sometimes extremely difficult to achieve under the hot lights of a set. Shots of ice cream and beer in ice-covered mugs demands ingenuity and a knowledge of look-alike substances. In fashion photography it can take hours to "pin" a model so that the fit is exact, the creases fall perfectly, and the wrinkles don't show.

In addition to hiring photographers, you can also go to photo houses that will supply stock photos—like clip art. You buy the photo and you can use it without paying any additional royalty. Of course, everyone else can buy and use the same photo.

Photomechanicals.   You can create even more unusual photographic effects as part of the production process. A *line conversion* is a photograph that has been shot for printing, using high-contrast-line art film. It reproduces the image as if it were line art and drops out all the grays. You are left with a dramatic high-contrast, black-and-white image that looks as if it had been drawn.

A number of different graphic effects can be created by changing the screen used when negatives and plates are made for printing. All photographs have to be shot through a screen that breaks the image into little dot patterns. The bigger the dots, the darker the image. The smaller the dots, the lighter the image. That's how the illustration of gray can be created in printing when all you have available is one shade of black ink. (More about this in the section that follows on production.) This dot pattern can be overblown to create an unusual effect.

Other *screen patterns* such as wavy lines, circles, steel etching marks, and linen textures are also available. These special effect screens are used in place of the standard dot pattern and they create a visible texture. All of these special photomechanical effects are available either through your photographer or the printer. They are useful to create different moods and effects and to enliven a photograph that might otherwise be mundane.

A type of art that crosses the line between illustration and photography is *constructed art*. The artist will create an almost sculptural piece from torn paper, fabric, clay, or some other substance creating a surface with texture. This piece of art is then photograhed for reproduction. Often, the technique will involve a montage or collage art form.

This discussion of the critical decisions should provide you with an outline for the type of thinking that goes on intuitively in the minds of most creatives. Taking the concept apart and spelling out the decisions may make it easier to communicate the idea while it is still in the conceptual stage. It also provides the words and outline to be used both in presentation and in justification.

Composition

The way elements are arranged within a picture is called *composition*. Composition is based on both psychology and aesthetics. You are trying to compose an image that directs the eye to the significant elements, while at the same time creating an image that is aesthetically pleasing.

Planes. The first consideration is to define the plane in your visual. A standard magazine page is two dimensional and consists of a vertical and a horizontal dimension. Most layouts are designed to work with this vertical plane and these dimensions. In television, however, the plane is horizontal. The vertical and horizontal are imaginary axis lines that define the orientation of the plane. Occasionally, a print layout will use the visual techniques of illusion to create the feeling of depth. Vanishing lines, creating perspective, are used to establish this illusion of a third dimension in the Passport Scotch advertisement. (See Exhibit 5-2.)

Rule of thirds. One of the first suggestions you will read in any discussion of composition is to avoid dividing things in half. In other words, if you are photographing or drawing a scene, try to position the horizon so that it is

EXHIBIT 5-2:   **The Passport ad uses composition to create a feeling of perspective.** (Courtesy of the Perennial Sales Company, a division of the House of Seagram)

either above or below the halfway mark. An axis line that divides a visual into two equal size pieces is considered to be dysfunctional because there is no dominance between two equal pieces. If one is larger than the other, the relationships become more interesting.

Likewise, you will hear that you should avoid putting your center of interest directly in the middle of a composition. The middle is considered a dead spot, a position of minimal visual interest. It is better to locate the center of interest above, below, or to the side of dead center.

These two principles regarding equal parts and dead center are addressed in a concept developed by Kodak called "the rule of thirds." The principle is that if you divide the horizontal and vertical dimensions of any composition into thirds, you will create an arrangement of nine sections. The four points where the lines intersect are the points of maximum visual impact, and the natural location in a composition for the element you feel should be the center of interest. If you scan through a magazine and check the photographs, you will see that many of them are using the rule of thirds and that the major elements are located on these intersections. Notice where the foremost label is positioned in the Passport Scotch ad. (See Figure 5–1.)

FIGURE 5-1:   Rule of thirds

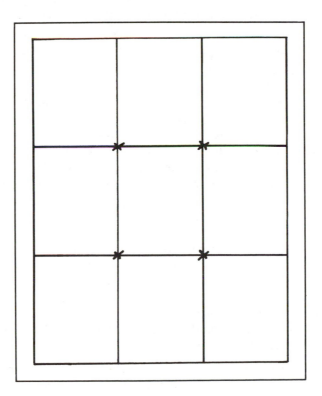

Framing.   Another compositional technique that is used in advertising visuals is the idea of *framing*. In photography, a long-distance scene will be shot using a tree and its limbs in the foreground as a frame that extends across the top and down one side. Sometimes the scene will be framed by a window or by the lines of a door, porch, or column. What this technique does is to establish a more visible distinction between foreground and background intensifying the feeling of depth.

Scale.   A person, tree, car, or other identifiable figure can be used in a composition to establish *scale*. In other words, size is relative and sometimes we can't tell how large or small something is unless we see it next to something else that serves as a visual reference. We know how tall a man generally stands, and therefore a figure of a man next to a rock makes it clear just how large the rock really is. Otherwise, the rock could be tiny or huge and there would be no way to know from the visual.

Leading lines.   Elements within a composition can create a visual pattern of lines, and these lines can be used to direct the eye. A shot of a skeleton of a building under construction may contain a pattern created by the lines of the girders. These lines may converge and pull the eye to the center of attention, or they may move across a space creating a horizontal or vertical sweep that guides the eye just like yellow lines painted on the highway guide the motion of the car. A skilled photographer or artist has a good eye for these internal patterns that can be manipulated to direct the viewer's attention.

Lighting and shadows.   The play of light and shadows creates both psychological and aesthetic effects. Bright lighting creates highlights that suggest openness, happiness, carefree moments, and freedom. The glistening image of reflected light suggests sunlight, ice, or a light shining on a wet pavement.

Colors that are saturated with light, or overexposed, can give a washed-out effect that creates the feeling of softness. A field of wildflowers, for example, might be overexposed to create this effect.

Shadows are dramatic amd mysterious. "Rembrandt" lighting is a technique that lights the center of interest and lets the surrounding details fall into dark shadows. "Rim light" is a technique used to separate a subject from the background. The light is coming from behind the subject and serves as a visual outline of the figure.

There are other techniques for using lighting to create meaning. A single light from the direction of the camera or the viewer will flatten and wash out details. Light from the side, however, will emphasize texture. A diffused light on the face will soften features; however, a harsh light from above will create deep shadows on the face and create sinister effects. High-contrast lighting is harsh and creates dramatic effects. A light colored background is softer than a dark background. Dark backgrounds are often used for dramatic effects.

Camera angle.   Every visual is seen through the eye of a viewer and replicated by the artist or photographer. Every visual is looked at from some specific angle. The most common angle is direct and straight on, as if you were looking at a set on a stage or in a display window from the street. This is the least obtrusive angle.

If you shoot or draw the image from below, looking up at it, you intensify its height. It appears to be taller, more monumental. You look up to something you respect. This technique is used with people who are to be respected, and also for important buildings. In advertising, you will see this camera angle used to create a monumental image for the product. The Mobil One automobile oil can is usually shot from below looking up at it. The can becomes a monumental figure. Liquor bottles are also often shot from this angle.

The reverse is also true. A viewing angle from above looking down tends to reduce the significance of the image—making the viewer feel superior. You look down on things that are beneath you. This angle is used to convey a sense of smallness for pictures of children and pets.

Another viewing angle you may hear mentioned is the "subjective camera," where the camera is in the position of the participant or user. This technique makes the viewer an actor in the visual. An ad for the title of a movie may be shot from below to create the effect that you are in the audience. A writing pen or a watch may be shot from above at the exact distance the pen or watch would occupy if you were looking at it as you use it. An ad for speakers shows them positioned on the floor. The camera is positioned where you would be if you were standing above them looking down.

The "worm's-eye view" is an angle that takes you right down on the surface and dramatizes the size and the perspective of the visual. This is a technique used to dramatize scale. A shot from the plate on a baby's highchair looking up at the baby would be an example of a worm's-eye view.

Images that are shot tilted are seen as dynamic. These angles suggest movement and excitement. The image is seen as unstable or off balance and that involves the viewer or reader. There is a compulsion to right the object and stabilize it, to bring it to a position of rest. It's like a picture hanging crooked on the wall. It attracts your attention by reaching out to you. There is a compulsion to get involved.

The scene. The definition of a scene is another aspect of the viewing eye that creates meaning. A scene can be shot or drawn from a long distance off—a *long shot,* in cinema terms, or even a panoramic shot. A shot can also be close up, so close you see the texture in the paper or the pores on the skin. A long shot is used in cinema and video as an "establishing" shot; it sets the scene by showing the entire location. A close up magnifies and intensifies the significance of the image. It is a more emotional shot. It can also suggest a close, intimate relationship. You are only this close to something you own or care about a lot.

The graphic images used in advertising, whether they are photographs, illustrations, or video shots, are carefully composed to create a variety of different kinds of effects. The photographer, for example, will compose an image by framing the scene within the viewfinder and moving around from one vantage point to another, searching for that elusive image that perfectly combines proportion of elements, leading lines, framing, scale, lighting, and camera angle to create an attention-getting, evocative, and highly memorable image. That's the difference between a picture that has been composed and a simple snapshot. It takes a perceptive and well-trained eye to compose a visual—as well as to critique it.

Print Production Considerations

There are a number of good books available as references for the various production processes.* The following is a very brief explanation of some aspects of print production that have to be considered in the design process. (Broadcast production is discussed in the chapters on radio and television advertising.) Most designers find that their effectiveness as designers is limited by their understanding of the production method and its strengths and limitations.

Halftones and line art.   Art can be either line art or halftone—or a combination of both. Line art is created when you draw on white paper with a solid line. Everything is solid on a plain background. Halftones, in contrast, imply shades of gray. The most common use for a halftone is to reproduce a photograph. When you look at a photographic print, you are able to see a range of images from faint gray to deep black. Photographs are referred to as "continuous tone" because of these middle values. It is these middle tones that cause problems in printing.

In order to create halftones for printing, the image is shot through a screen, using a pattern of tiny dots. These dots break the image into light and dark areas; otherwise, there would be no way to create the gray areas in a photograph. Black ink, after all, is black. It doesn't come in shades of gray. The gray that you see when you look at a printed halftone is really just smaller dots of black with a lot more white area around them. It is an optical illusion.

Line art is an image that is created from a solid black line. There are no shades of gray as you find with photographs. Line art can be shot directly, since there is no reason to screen it. However, if you are using watercolor or wash techniques, then the art does have shades of gray and it has to be screened.

When we speak of fine line screens, we are talking about how many lines of dots there are per inch. The more dots there are, the finer the details that can be reproduced. Newspapers use a relatively coarse screen, usually 65 to 110 lines, while most magazines use 110 lines or finer. Fine printing will go as high as 300 lines. Because of the better quality paper and the more controlled

The Design of Advertising by Roy Paul Nelson, *Art and Reproduction* by Raymond Ballinger, *Advertising Agency and Studio Skills* by Tom Cardamone, *Production for the Graphic Designer* by James Craig, *Graphic Design and Production Techniques* by Peter Croy, *Studio Tips for Artists and Graphic Designers* by Bill Gray.

printing processes, magazines can use a finer line screen than newspapers and reproduce a much better image, although many newspapers are moving toward more quality reproduction—similar to *USA Today*.

Color and registration.   A one-color printing job means that there is only one color of ink printed, whether black, blue, green, or some other color you might specify. Two-color printing usually means you have black plus a "second" color.

If you want full color, printers call that "process color" or "four-color process." The reason they say four colors is because the full-color effect is created by using four specific process colors: cyan (a shade of blue), magenta (a shade of red), yellow, and black. Printing inks are transparent, and all the other colors can be created by mixing and overlapping these inks.

For every color, a separate negative and printing plate is made. The inks may be printed on separate runs through the press (on small presses), or they may be printed by different rollers on the same press. Either way there is a problem getting these colors to align perfectly. This is called *registration*. Color registration is particularly difficult for process color, where there are four separate images that have to align perfectly.

Printing processes.   A word is needed here about printing processes. Historically, newspapers were printed with a process called *letterpress*. With letterpress printing, you have a raised surface that gets inked. When it strikes the surface of the paper, the image is transferred. Type is set in metal and the art and photographs are all engraved (etched) in metal.

In the last 20 years, most printers have switched over to *offset lithography,* a type of printing that uses a smooth surfaced but chemically treated plate to transfer the image. The offset plates are produced photographically. The original art is called "camera-ready." This means it is ready to be shot in the process, or graphic arts, camera. Everything on the "mechanical," (the pasteup) is pasted in place and anything that can be photographed can be printed. There is no heavy metal type, no engravings. It's simpler, cleaner, and faster.

Gravure is a type of printing that uses an incised surface. The images are engraved into the plate and ink collects in these little wells. When the plate strikes the surface of the paper, ink is transferred from the wells to the paper. In order to create this grid of wells, the entire image is screened. It's a fine screen, 150 lines or finer, but that means it is perfect for photographic reproduction. It is also good for long runs, since there is no wear on the printing surface. The limitation of gravure is that the type is screened, too, and that creates fuzzy letters. Gravure is used for fine magazine printing and for newspaper inserts that use color photography.

Another type of printing used frequently in advertising is *screen* printing. Sometimes called "silk screen," the process uses a porous screen of silk, nylon, or stainless steel mounted on a frame. A stencil image is made either by hand or using a photographic process and the stencil is applied to the screen.

The nonprinting areas are blocked by the stencil and the areas to be printed are left open. Using a squeegee, ink is forced through the screen onto the printing surface.

Screen printing is useful because it is versatile. Any surface can be printed on—metal, cloth, glass, wood, and so on. And the surface can be in any shape—round, curved, flat, or irregular. In advertising screen printing is used for containers, packaging, decals, transit cards, table and counter displays, point-of-purchase displays, posters, even billboards.

5.3 TYPOGRAPHY

At first glance, a print ad appears to be mostly just words and pictures. In reality, an ad is much more complex than that, with a number of elements carefully arranged in a layout. As an example of the complexity, let's just look at the words.

Words do more than carry content. In our discussion of copywriting, we looked at the meaning of the words. In this section, we will look at the impression created by the graphic techniques used to display the words. There is meaning, not only in the content of the message, but also in the appearance of the type. Typography is a study of how letterforms are used to create effects from bold to elegant to delicate to brash. (See Exhibit 5–3.)

Letter Characteristics

In order to understand the differences in type, we need to look first at letterforms and notice some of the details that typographers refer to in their discussions of distinctive features.

Serifs.   One of the most important details is the *serif*. This is a little detail at the end of a stroke. If you imagine lettering the capital A, like the one shown here, you would probably start with the diagonal stroke down to the right, then make the stroke to the left and finally make the crossbar. The serif is the finishing detail on the end of the stroke.

It is a slight widening of the stroke, providing a sort of platform for the stroke to stand on. It is thought that the serif detail is left over from medieval calligraphy done by pen or brush. The inevitable blob of ink at the end of the stroke was "finished" with this little tail. In more recent times, block letters have become popular and they are designed without serifs. Hence we have the primary distinction in type between serif and sans serif letters. "Sans" means without. (See Figure 5–2.)

There are some type designs that fit between these two categories, but primarily you will be choosing one or the other. Serif letters are traditional and considered easy to read. Your early reading books were printed in serif letters and most newspapers still are, so you are comfortable with this letter.

EXHIBIT 5-3:   **Lauder's uses an elegant typeface that communicates
the message as much as the words.** (Courtesy of
Hiram Walker Incorporated, Farmington Hills, Mich.)

FIGURE 5-2:   Serif and sans serif letters

Serif:

AM

Sans Serif:

AM

Sans serif letters are considered more modern in appearance. They are clean and free from ornament. They may be considered mechanistic because of their simple, even lines. They reproduce well in newspapers, given their printing limitations, and on cheap paper such as you find in telephone books. Reference materials are often printed in sans serif letters but you don't tend to find long masses of copy, such as a book or the text of a magazine, in sans serif. Sans serif letters are also considered highly visible or easy to read from a distance. That's why you see stop signs in sans serif, as well as billboards and signs.

Most studies of type have not found any real difference in legibility between serif and sans serif but they have found that readers prefer serif letters. That is probably because we have grown up on serif letters and that's what we are used to reading.

X-Height, ascenders, and descenders.   Some other terms that you may hear advertising designers use to describe type include the x-height, and the ascenders and descenders. The *x-height* is the body of the letter, the space occupied by a lower case *x*. Ascenders and descenders are the tails that either stick above the x-height or hang below it. You will find *ascenders* on such letters as *t, h, l, b,*and *d. Descenders* are found on *p, q, y,* and *g.* (See Figure 5-3.)

The relationship between the x-height and the ascenders and descenders is an important factor in both the aesthetics of the type and its legibility. Letters with small x-heights and long ascenders and descenders are delicate. They are also hard to reproduce in printing, particularly in the fast, imprecise printing used by newspapers. Large-bodied letters, however, are bold and more visible. They are thought to be easier to read.

Bowls and counters.   The interaction of thick and thin strokes can be seen in a serif "O." The curved or rounded part of a letter such as is seen in

FIGURE 5-3:   x-height, ascenders,
and descenders

x-height:

cemnorsuvwz

ascenders:

bdfhklt

descenders:

gjpqy

a c, d, or e is called the *bowl.* Another term related to the bowl is a feature called the *counter.* This is the empty space located inside the bowl of a letter like an o or an e. It is of concern because, with poor printing control, the counters will tend to fill with ink. The heavy blobs of ink are unpleasant and blur the letterforms.

Letterform Variations

Case.   One of the most familiar variations is found in the distinction between upper and lower case or capitals and small letters. The phrase, upper and lower case, comes from the old typecases used in hand-setting type. The capitals were above and the smaller letters were below.

There are four ways to handle case: all capital letters (all caps), all lower case, upper and lower case (U&lc), and small caps. All capitals are used to create a blocky look and give a hard edge to the line of type. All lower case is a fashion that comes and goes. The most common treatment is upper and lower case, with the first letter in the sentence and first letter in proper nouns being capitalized. This is designated "U&lc."

Small caps are more unusual. This variation has a special group of capital letters that are designed slightly larger than a normal X-height. They are usually used with regular capitals. Small caps create a very formal look.

Italics.   Most letters have an italic form that slants to the right. This is a design style that picks up the slanted characteristics of running script. It is similar to, but not the same as, cursive or script type. *Cursive* is a typeface category of its own. It leans to the right, but the letters are designed to connect and actually look like handwriting. (See Figure 5-4.)

FIGURE 5-4: Normal and italic letter shapes

Helvetica
Helvetica Italic

The *italic* version is identical to the typeface in design; the only difference is that the strokes are tilted to the right. Italics are used when you want variation while still maintaining the continuity of the same type family.

For example, you might want a caption under a picture to be visually separate from the main body of the text, and therefore you would use italics. It maintains the feeling and the design details of the basic style. In some cases it may appear to be more delicate because of the slant, but it is never bolder. When using italics, remember you are creating variation, not accent.

Weight.   A second letterform variation is found in the weight of letters. A letter can be designed to look light or heavy in comparison to its regular weight. This is done by manipulating the width of the strokes. A bold letter is one that has wider strokes and a light letter is one with very fine strokes. (See Figure 5–5.)

Width.   Width can also be varied in the design of a typeface. Here we mean the width of the space occupied by the letter, not the width of the strokes.

FIGURE 5-5: Variations in a type family by both weight and width

This is Triumvirate Light

This is Triumvirate Heavy

This is Triumvirate Black

Triumvirate Bold Condensed

Triumvirate Bold Expanded

The letter can be condensed or squeezed to occupy less space. It can also be extended horizontally. It is still the same basic design; it is just that this basic horizontal dimension has been manipulated.

When you put all these variations together and start to combine them, you can see how complex typography becomes. A single letter, for example, can be used in its upright form in a normal (or medium) weight and width. However, it can also be italic, bold and condensed, or light and extended—or any other combination. Just the two posture variations and the three weight and width variations give you a total of some 500 variations to choose from for any typeface. And when you add in case, you have another four sets of variations. For one typeface you can choose from some 12,000 possible variations.

Typefaces and Races

You probably wonder how something so simple as a letter can become so complicated. The truth is we have just begun to scratch the surface of the variations available to the designer. Even though an *A* is an *a*, there are thousands of typefaces and each one lends a different appearance to the *a*. Typefaces have distinctive personalities. Even though the effect is subtle, they do add mood and feeling to a message. Some forms are big and blocky; others are delicate and refined. Some are elegant, some are casual. The mood of the message is enchanced by the careful choice of typeface.

Each typeface has a name, such as Century or Bookman or Bodoni or Caledonia. In addition, these individual faces can be assigned to categories of similar "races." In design sessions, typefaces are often referred to by these category labels as well as by typeface name. Most of these regular categories of typefaces come in a complete set of variations. The set is called a "type family." A typesetter may have a complete range of sizes of any one typeface and a complete range of variations, including italics, and all of the weight and width variations. (See Figure 5–6.)

Few people can remember what all these variations look like in the various faces. People who specify type work with reference materials called type spec (specimen) books. If you work regularly with typesetters, you will probably be given a book that contains all of their typefaces in various sizes.

Printers' Measures

In order to specify type, you will need some skill working with printers' measures. Most measurements in the graphic arts industry are calculated in *points* and *picas*. There are six picas in an inch and 12 points in a pica.

The vertical size of type, or type height, is measured in points, a very small measure. There are 72 points in an inch. Standard type sizes of body copy include 5 or 6, 8, 10, 11, 12, and 14 points. The display copy ranges from 18

FIGURE 5-6:   Common categories of typefaces

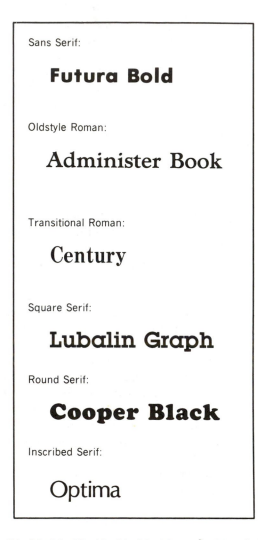

Sans Serif:

Futura Bold

Oldstyle Roman:

Administer Book

Transitional Roman:

Century

Square Serif:

Lubalin Graph

Round Serif:

Cooper Black

Inscribed Serif:

Optima

points through 20, 24, 30, 36, 42, 48, 60, 72, 96, and 120 points. For comparison, a 72-point headline would be one inch in height.

The length and width of columns is measured in picas. A 12-pica column width, for example, would be two inches wide.

The width between lines of type in body copy is also indicated when you specify type. This space is called *leading*. In the days of hot metal type, this space was created by inserting strips of lead between the lines; hence the name leading. Leading is measured in points, and you will normally be specifying one or two points of leading. The larger the body type, the more space you need between the lines. Likewise, the longer the line, the more leading you need.

Letterspacing

The amount of air or space around letters is both a design decision for effect and a legibility consideration. Let's talk first about the design aspects. In the forties it was popular to space everything wide, to allow lots of room around the letters. Contemporary design since that period has consistently moved tighter. Letters are now set so close they touch; sometimes they even overlap. There are sound psychological reasons for this trend. We know that things that belong together need to be close together to be perceived as a unit. Close-set type does, in fact, make it easier to perceive word groups. Mostly, however, the close-set trend is simply fashion.

The real issue in spacing is to consider how much "air" is needed in relation to the surrounding spaces and shapes. You may, for example, have short lines of type and lots of space between words and the type appears to fall apart because of the gaps. On the other hand, if you have long lines of type and small amounts of space between words, the words may appear to be running together. Spacing is always proportional and relative to such things as line length and size of the letters.

In letterspacing we are talking about the amount of space between letters in a word. As mentioned earlier, the fashion is to set the type as close as possible and still keep the letters distinct. But the finesse of letterspacing also considers the shape of the adjoining letters. The amount of space between letters is adjusted to even out the mass and gaps created by letterforms.

A capital T, for example, has lots of unused air under its bars. A capital L has lots of air above the base. An L next to a T would create an unusual mass of white space, more space perhaps than you might find between words, and that white space could destroy the word as a unit. To compensate for these shapes, you would pull the letters close together and let the baseline of the L move under the bars of the T. This is called *kerning*. That means one element of a letter is tucked over or under an element of the adjoining letter.

But there is more to optical spacing than just kerning. Mechanical spacing means that the amount of space between the letters is equal regardless of their shapes. Optical spacing adjusts the amount of spacing to compensate for the density of the letter. Some letters are relatively skinny, like i, l, and t, while others are fat, like M and W. Optical spacing considers both mass and width. The principle is to add space around the skinny letters and tighten the space around the fat, massed letters. What you are trying to do is even out the tone of the letters by compensating for their mass, shape, and openness. (See Figure 5-7.)

Legibility

We have been talking about the effects you can create through the choice of typeface and variation. These are design or aesthetic considerations. Now let's

FIGURE 5-7:   Mechanically set spacing compared to letterspacing that adjusts for the shape of the letters. Below is normal spacing compared to kerned spacing where the letters are "tucked."

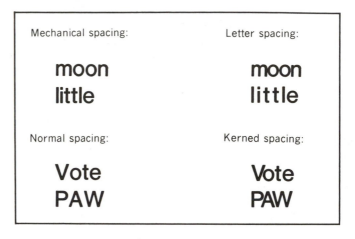

look at the practical side of typography and discuss the principles of legibility. By *legibility* we mean the visibility of the letters, the ease with which they may be perceived.

Another word, *readability,* is often used interchangeably with legibility. For the record, readability refers to how easy it is to understand the message. Studies of readability look at such problems as sentence length and word choice. When we talk about type, legibility is a more appropriate term.

Line length.   One major consideration in legibility, particularly for text copy, is the length of the line. If a line is too long, then you can't find your way back to the beginning of the next line. You may see that problem sometimes with headlines that run across a two-page spread in a magazine. In body copy you will see the same problem when a block of copy is set one column wide to fill the whole page. A line length the width of a normal page is too long to read. Your eye gets lost trying to find its way back to the beginning of the next sentence. A two-column or three-column format works better.

Acceptable line length is really a function of the size of type. Large type can be set on a wider column than can small type; the smaller the type size, the shorter the line length should be. Likewise, the spacing between the lines is a factor. Long lines in bigger type need more space between the lines than do short lines in smaller type.

A general rule-of-thumb for finding the optimum line length is to use 1½ times the length of the lower case alphabet in your chosen type. If you have a type specimen book and it shows the lower case alphabet, simply measure it and calculate the ideal line length from that. For example, if the lower case alphabet measures two inches, then an optimum line length would be three inches. An acceptable range would probably be from about 2½ to 3½ inches.

All caps.   Another problem noted by most legibility researchers is copy set in all capitals. The problem here is that we read by scanning and in the scanning process we identify words by their shapes. An upper and lower case word has distinctive "coastlines" created by the pattern of ascenders, descenders, and x-height. All-caps obliterates the coastline and forces you to slow down and scan for individual letters. The slower your reading, the less efficient it is. If you are using just a couple of words in a headline, then all caps is probably not much of a problem. If you are setting several lines in capitals, then you will probably drive your reader away.

Reverse.   When letters are set "in reverse," that means the letter image appears to be white against a dark background. Reverse is used a lot in advertising because the black is dramatic and attention getting. The only problem is that reverse letters are hard to read. We learn to read little black squiggles on a white background and identify them as letters. When we ask someone to make little white squiggles into letters, then they have to go through a fast, mental transformation changing the letters back into their more familiar shape. We do it all the time, but it does slow down reading and it gets real tiresome if there is a lot of copy.

The same rule-of-thumb applies to reverse that we used with all capitals: if it is just a little bit of copy, it doesn't matter much. If it is a lot, then you may lose your reader. The smaller the letter and the longer the copy block, the more difficult it is to read in reverse.

Contrast.   Maximum contrast between foreground and background is another legibility principle. This is a problem with the choice of color. Yellow or white on black, for example, is strong in contrast. Color combinations become a problem when you use two similar colors for foreground and background. Yellow on white is difficult to read and so is black on blue, brown, or purple. The rule-of-thumb is to maximize the contrast between the foreground and the background.

Surprinting.   Art directors like to print type over a picture because that pulls the type and the art together and makes the layout less cluttered. In terms of simplicity, that may be a good idea. In terms of legibility it is deadly. When you surprint type over a picture, make sure there is no conflicting background detail. Type is made up of small details like ascenders, descenders, serifs, bowls, and counters. When you superimpose that typographic pattern over some other pattern, then the type begins to fall apart. The letters become indistinct.

Occasionally you will see type surprinted over a picture that has an expanse of pavement, a wooden wall, or even clouds. Within the wall or the pavement, however, there is pattern and it will conflict with the pattern of the type. Only surprint type when the area of the picture you want to use is completely empty, such as a clear sky or a white wall. Don't make the type any more difficult to read than it already is.

Type design.   The typeface design, itself, can be a factor in legibility. Highly ornamented or fanciful typefaces are often difficult to decipher. Old English letters are hard to read. Upper case cursive letters are very hard to puzzle out.

Certain typefaces interact with the printing process to create legibility problems. Newspapers are printed fast on soft paper. Any typefaces that have tiny delicate details will have a hard time surviving the newspaper production process. Bold, blocky letters work best in newspapers. The same thing is true with visibility on billboards. The little details fade. It's better to use big and relatively bold typefaces.

Special optical effects can also creat legibility problems. Given the advances in photographic and computerized typesetting, it is possible to manipulate shape, size, and even plane of the type image. Type can lean forward, backward, or to any side. It can be elongated and squished. It can squirm snake-like across the page or it can vibrate like air waves. And it is all done electronically. Just remember, the more games you play with the type, the harder it is to read.

Projected visuals.   Most legibility principles also apply to type that is projected onto a screen such as video, computer, and slide images. There is one difference and that is in the area of reverse letters. A slide projector, for example, projects raw white light that can be very glaring if it is used as a background for type. Background typically occupies more space than foreground and should be neutral or unobtrusive. However, if the letters are projected and the background is black or colored, then the glare is reduced. For that reason, slide and screen graphics will typically use reverse letters out of a solid nonglare background.

Copyfitting

There is one other problem with type: it has to fit the space. It is expensive to reset the type because it didn't fit the layout. It is possible, with some typesetters, to tell them to "set to fit." They will play with the specifications until they get a piece of copy that fits exactly into the shape available on the layout. That's fine, but you lose control over the type specification—and it is expensive.

The solution is to estimate how much type in a certain size will fit in a given space before the type is set. If you can tell from your estimate that you have twice as much copy as you do space, then you can rewrite the copy, adjust the specifications, or redesign the layout. This is a problem with retail and catalogue advertising as well as with brochures and flyers.

Both writers and artists have to know a little something about copyfitting. It all depends upon which gets done first, the layout or the copy. If the layout is done first, then the copywriter will need to write the copy to fit the space allowed. This is how most catalogue copy is prepared and a lot of retail copy, too.

If the copy is written first, then it's up to the artist to estimate how much copy there is in order to know how much space it will occupy on the layout.

Writing to fit.   If you are a writer and you have to produce copy to fit a layout, there are two critical pieces of information you need to estimate before you can begin. First, you have to know how many lines to write, and then you have to know how many characters there will be in each line. Both of these estimates are derived by measuring the copy block and doing some basic calculations using the type specifications.

First, measure the copy block and write down both its width and depth *in picas.* Convert the depth to points (multiply by 12). From your type specs you should know the size of the type and the amount of leading. Add those together and you have the height *in points* that you need to allow for a line. Now divide that line height into the total points available and you will have an estimate of how many lines you need.

For example, suppose your copy block is 7 picas deep. That is equal to 84 total points. If you are using 12-point type with 2 pts. of leading, then your line height is 14 points. When you divide 14 into 84, you get 7 lines. This is a neat example with everything coming out even. However, in most cases it won't be so nice. Always remember to round down. You want the number of lines that will fit *within* the copy block.

Now to figure the character count, you will need to look up or calculate a figure called the character per pica (CPP). This is a simple estimate of how many characters will fit in a pica. It varies with every typeface and every size. Some printers include the CPP in their type spec books. If not, it is easy to calculate. You will need a sample piece of body copy set in the size and face you want to use. Measure a 10-pica length on the lines of type. Count the number of characters in 10 picas and divide by 10. (To be more accurate, you might want to estimate across several lines and then use the average.)

For example, if you have 35 characters, on the average, in the 10-pica line, then your CPP for this typeface in this size is 3.5. In other words, there are 3.5 characters in one pica.

Once you know the CPP, you simply multiply that times the line length for your copy block and that tells you how many characters there will be, on the average, in a line. If you are using a typeface with 3.5 as its CPP and the copy block is 12 picas wide, then you will type a 42-character line. Just set your margins on your typewriter for that character count, and start typing the number of lines you need.

Designing to fit.   The designer goes through a similar process, only in reverse. What you need to know to lay out the copy block is how many lines the manuscript copy will set in your chosen type. Once you know that, you can just rule in the lines, to the specified line height, and you are done.

To estimate the number of lines, you first will need to estimate how many total characters there are in the manuscript copy. Eyeball a point at the right edge of the typewritten lines that seems to represent the average line length.

(Some will be longer, some will be shorter.) You can actually count the number of characters in three or four lines to find out mathematically what the average line length is, but the eyeball technique seems to work for estimating.

Count the number of characters to that point and you will have the average character count used by the writer. Multiply that times the number of manuscript lines, and you will have an estimate of the total characters in the manuscript.

Now turn to your type specifications and find or calculate the CPP for the typeface you are using. Multiply this times the line length you have decided on for the copy block and you will know approximately how many characters of typeset copy will fit in a typeset line. Divide the line count into the total manuscript characters to find the number of lines that your typeset copy will fill.

For example, suppose you estimate that the manuscript line length averages 34 characters and the typed copy is 10 lines long. That gives you a total of 340 manuscript characters. Your specified typeface has a CPP of 2.5 and the line length you want to use on the layout is 16 picas. This means the typeset line will be 40 characters. When you divide the 40 characters into 340 total characters, you come up with 8.5 lines. Now take out your chisel point pencil and rule 8½ lines to size.

If you are interested in reading further* about typography, there are several good books that you might consult. This is only a very brief introduction to a complicated but interesting area in advertising design.

As you work with type, just remember that it has to be beautiful as well as functional. It doesn't do any good to design a fantastic typographic effect if no one can read the type. Keep in mind the principles of legibility, but remember you have so many faces and variations to choose from that your creativity should never feel constrained.

5.4 LAYOUT

We've talked about the pieces of an advertisement—the illustration or photo, the headline, the body copy, perhaps a caption for the picture or pictures, the subheads, as well as the product identification information such as product picture, logotype, and slogan. A print advertisement is a complex piece of multielement design. In television the same pieces can be used, only the images are even more complex because of the addition of sound and motion.

In advertising, art directors are the specialists who make visual sense of all these elements. There are art directors for both print and broadcast. They arrange all the elements through a process called *layout,* creating a visual plan called a *comprehensive* in print and a *storyboard* in video. This chapter will introduce the concept of layout primarily as it applies to print advertising. The additional complexities of video will be discussed in the chapter on television advertising.

Designing with Type by James Craig and *The ABC's of Typography* by Sandra Ernst.

Layout is the process of organizing things. If all the pieces of an advertisement were simply dropped onto a page at random, it would be extremely difficult to make any sense of the message. It would be hard to know what is most important in the message, and where you are to start and end in your scanning or reading. Just like dropping words at random on a page, it would be impossible to find any meaning without sentences and paragraphs and subheads.

Layout structures the arrangement of the pieces so that the visual is easy to read. It provides a visual sentence structure or syntax, a guide to how the message is to be perceived.

Layout always deals with relationships; that's how order is created. When you put a mark or a shape on a piece of paper, there is a relationship between that mark and the page. There is now foreground and background; there is a point of attention, an element that "stands out." The page itself has some basic relationships you need to consider. There are relationships between top and bottom, left to right, horizontal and vertical.

These relationships contribute to organization, emphasis, stability, and movement. The more lines and shapes you add to the page, the more complicated these relationships become. The various pieces can be separate, touching, overlapping, or aligning, converging or dispersing. They can group together or they can separate. They can form and create patterns or they can fragment and exist as discrete units. Every time you construct a layout, you are manipulating the relationships of one element to another and the individual elements to the whole.

Design Principles

There are a number of different ways to discuss the visual principles used to construct a layout. Some of the principles are primarily functional, and they give order to the perceptual process. Others are primarily aesthetic, and they create arrangements that are pleasing or interesting to the eye. The practical principles that will be discussed here are unity, contrast, balance, and movement. The aesthetic principles are proportion, harmony, and tension.

Unity and grouping. We have defined layout as a process of organizing visual elements, so it makes sense that the most important aspect of layout is the organizing function. That is discussed in design literature as unity or grouping. The idea is that figures and patterns take on meaning only if they are grouped so the elements that belong together are seen together. Likewise, we use space to force things apart that don't belong together. Joining and disassociating are the two basic tools of organization.

Disassociating elements is done by separating things that don't belong together. For example, four separate photos can be arranged around a page so that there is no visible relationship between them. White space can be used to create "alleys" of space that push the photos apart. Rules and boxes can be used to separate one element from another. Rules and alleys of white space are barriers. Likewise, boxes enclose some pieces while excluding others. (See Figures 5–8 and 5–9.)

More commonly, in layout, the problem is one of joining things together that belong together. *White space* is an important element in creating unity. The white space is the area between and around the elements—the background, in other words. But white space is more than just background. It can be massed or used as a frame, at which point it becomes an element too.

By decreasing white space, you visually pull elements closer together. The less white space, the closer the fit. That's how we manipulate letter spacing and word spacing to group letters into recognizable words.

In terms of unity, if you want to make the most effective use of white space, then push it to the outside. Ineffective use of white space creates pockets and alleys of trapped space that inadvertently push elements apart that you intended to group together. The rule-of-thumb is: Push the white space to the edge.

Joining is also done by creating *alignments*. If the four pictures mentioned above are dispersed with no visual relationships, they are seen as separate elements. If they are grouped so that there are obvious alignments along their edges, then they create a pattern. If they are aligned and pulled together, then they create a group. Four separate elements can become one group. That's how you create visual cohesion.

FIGURE 5-8:   Alleys and pockets of uncontrolled white space

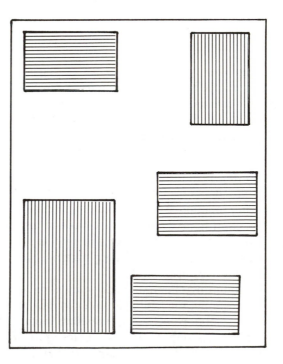

FIGURE 5-9:   Group the elements pushing white space to outside

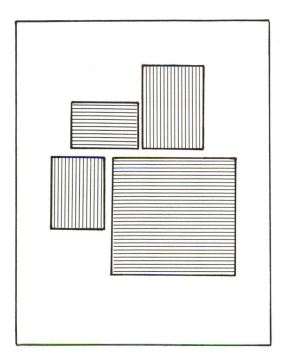

Rules and boxes.   We discussed these earlier as separation tools, but they can also be used for organizing. Rules frame and contain. Rules across the bottom or top, or even along an edge, provide a plane to hang or stack the elements on or against. In this sense, a rule can be an important organizing tool.

Simplicity and clutter.   These are two other terms related to unity that you will hear in critiques of layouts. Simplicity means you use the least possible number of elements, thereby making the arrangement easier to read as well as more dramatic. An old architectural maxim is: Less is more. The idea is that the fewer the elements, the greater the impact.

If you have four separate photos, then the viewer's attention is divided, and there is automatic conflict in terms of where to look first. If you group the four, then you can create one element, although it is more complex. If you use only one photo, then you have the sole attention of the viewer directed at that one element. The more elements you use, the more fragmented the impact. Any time you can group elements, you will be simplifying the layout.

A cluttered design has a thousand elements all fighting for attention. The elements aren't grouped to make perception easier; there are no obvious alignments, and every element seems to be separate and fighting for attention. There is no visual coherence. Discount store advertising will sometimes use clutter deliberately to convey the idea of diversity and of a confusion of products to choose from. But even with deliberate clutter, there is usually some sense of organization to help readers make their way through the design.

Contrast and dominance.   Whenever you construct a layout, you are making a series of decisions. The most important one is how things should be grouped to create a unified impression. The second most important decision is what element should be emphasized. Emphasis in visual communication is created by contrast.

We know from our discussion of the psychology of perception that people can't see everything at once. Most people scan a visual rapidly, but still look at only one thing at a time. Certain important details get *studied* with the eye returning to that detail over and over. When you construct a visual, keep in mind that people can't see everything at once. Therefore, you have to help the selection process by arranging the elements in some order of importance.

As a designer, you must study the elements and decide what *one* element is the most important element, and then what element is next in importance, then next, and so on. Every designer rank orders the elements in his or her mind intuitively. This is the editorial or decision-making side of the visual design process. Just like journalists order facts in a news story, you have to order the elements in your layout in terms of their importance.

Once you have decided what one element you want to emphasize, then you manipulate the layout so this pattern of stress becomes obvious. You do this by creating contrast. If one element is to stand out, then the other elements have to defer. What you are doing is creating a pattern of dominance.

Visual dominance is created by contrasting size, shape, color, tone, or position. The biggest element will stand out. So will the one at the top or the most colorful element or the one with the most unusual shape. (See Figures 5–10 and 5–11.)

If you create patterns of conflicting contrast, you create visual confusion. For example, a large element at the bottom of the page will fight with a smaller element that controls the top. There is a conflict between size and position.

Contrast is a form of visual logic. One and only one item can dominate because if there is more than one big item or an unusual item, then there is no clear pattern of contrast. The rule-of-thumb is: If everything is bold, then nothing is bold. Likewise if everything is big, nothing is big. The other elements have to be reduced in significance in order for one element to dominate. If several items are competing equally for attention, then all you have is confusion.

The decision on what to emphasize should be based on the execution strategy. For example, if this is a heavy copy message, then the headline will probably dominate. But if there is art, then extraordinary contrast has to be used to make the head dominate over the visual. Illustrations consistently overpower headlines unless something is done in the layout to give additional visual weight to the words. Being at the top of the page isn't enough because it is still easy for the eye to be drawn to the art. The head will need an extremely large size to hold its own against the art.

FIGURE 5-10:   Size and position can create dominance

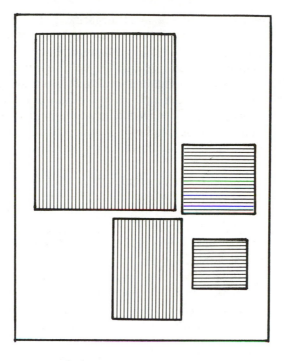

FIGURE 5-11:   Novelty and tone can create dominance

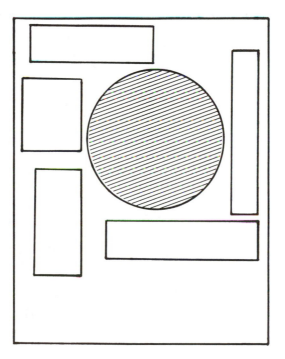

Balance.   When things are organized, they are usually grouped around a focal point. This is the fulcrum of the layout and elements are positioned around this fulcrum to maintain a feeling of visual balance.

When we analyze a layout for balance, we are looking at the optical weights of the various elements and noting how they are balanced or counterbalanced one against another. Optical weights are derived from the same factors that create contrast. A large element is visually "heavier" than a small one, color is heavier than black and white, unusual shapes are heavier than regular ones, and so on. A mass of white space can even be a heavy element. (See Figure 5–12).

These weights are positioned around the focal point, or fulcrum, of the arrangement using the old teeter-totter principle for counterbalancing: lighter weights to the outside and heavier weights to the inside. It's the same technique used when a father sits close to the fulcrum on a teeter-totter to counterbalance his child who sits way out on the far end of the board.

Sometimes this fulcrum is positioned on the center of the page, although it doesn't have to be. There is a natural focal point of a layout, called the *optical center,* that is located slightly above mathematical center. (Mathematical center is found by drawing diagonals from the corners. The mathematical center is the point where the diagonals cross.) (See Figure 5–13.)

FIGURE 5-12:   **In asymmetrical balance, counterbalance the weights around the optical center**

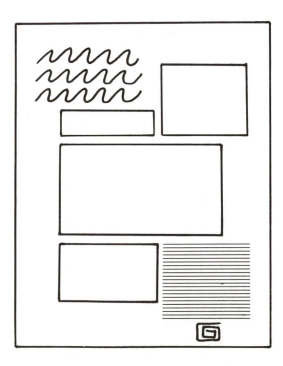

FIGURE 5-13:   Locating the optical center

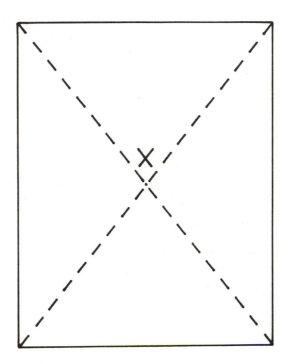

Research has found that when you ask someone to put his or her finger on the exact center of a sheet of paper, the individual will place it slightly above this mathematical center. That's the natural optical center, and the position best used as a point of balance for most layouts. Psychologists speculate that the optical center is positioned higher than the mathematical center because of the natural dominance of the top half of the page.

The focal point in advertising layout usually contains some element that serves as a visual center—in many cases it will be a product. Not all layouts use an obvious focal point, but even if the position is not accented with some critical element, there is still an underlying point of balance, an unstated or imaginary focal point, around which the elements are arranged.

It takes a good sense of visual organization to be able to see how this position functions, something like the unseen anchor that holds the boat stable in the open sea. If a layout is in balance, then you should be able to imagine suspending the sheet of paper on a thread that runs through the optical center. If, in your mind, the layout hangs flat, then it is in balance. If there are too many heavy elements on any one edge, then you should be able to imagine that the layout is starting to tilt.

A layout that is out of balance is one that has the heavy weights on one side without any attempt to counterbalance them on the opposite side. We talk about the elements appearing to "fall off the edge" when a layout is out of balance.

There are two primary strategies for formatting balance in a layout. A *symmetrical* layout is one where all the elements are centered around a vertical, and sometimes horizontal, axis. You could fold it in half and the edges of the elements would form a mirror image. The other type of balance is *asymmetrical.* Here the elements are informally grouped around the optical center, carefully using the techniques of counterbalancing. (See Figures 5–14 and 5–15.)

A symmetrical layout is considered formal, conservative, stable, and sometimes a little dull. An asymmetrical layout is considered more visually interesting, more active, more dynamic. It's more difficult to create asymmetrical balance, but the visual excitement is usually worth the effort.

The type of balance used in the layout should depend upon the execution strategy. If you have described the style as formal, then a symmetrical layout may be appropriate. If you are using a casual or informal tone, then an asymmetrical layout might work better.

Movement and direction. Balance deals with the stability of a layout; movement is concerned with the visual path created for the eye to follow. A layout is like a road map. It tells you where to begin, where to go next, and where to

FIGURE 5-14:   Symmetrical (formal) balance

FIGURE 5-15:   Asymmetrical (informal) balance

end. A layout is always dynamic because the eye is never at rest when looking at (reading) a visual. Successful layout controls the motion and visual signposts are used to direct the eye through the course. The design principle of movement is also referred to as direction in some textbooks. If the layout is successful, then the direction of the eye's movement through the arrangement should be obvious.

The visual paths used in advertising are based on natural scan sequences used by Westerners when they read. The two primary scan patterns are top to bottom and left to right. In addition, the power of contrast can be used to direct the eye to read from big to little, dark to light, color to noncolor, and unusual to usual.

The top to bottom, left to right scan pattern has been called the "Gutenberg diagonal."[7] It summarizes the fact that we normally enter a visual in the upper left corner and exit from the lower right. Most horizontal movement in a layout, then, is to the right and most vertical movement is toward the bottom. Research into reading habits has found that most people will look first at the upper left quadrant.[8] It is the natural entry point for a visual. (See Figure 5-16.)

The *diagonal* is the simplest scan pattern. A more complex variation on that is the *Z pattern*, where the eye enters in the upper left, moves across the layout in the left to right pattern, then drops down diagonally to the lower left, and scans once again from left to right. In essence, that's the standard reading

FIGURE 5-16:   Natural entry points by quadrant

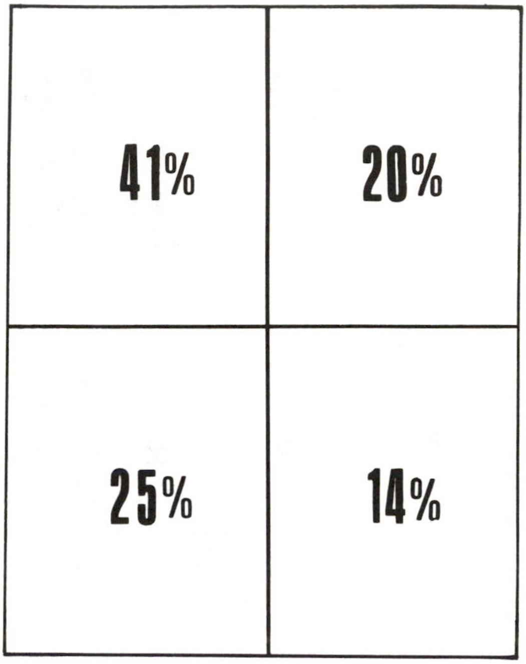

41%	**20**%
25%	**14**%

pattern for lines of type. The Z pattern can be made even more complicated by adding an additional set of zigzag patterns.

Sometimes the focal points will serve as the beginning point. In that case a common pattern is a *spiral* movement with the eye beginning at the center, then circling up to the right, back across to the left, and then down the left edge and across the bottom. The same pattern can spiral to the right. The spiral to the left reverses the normal movement in the sweep across the top of the page, so it is not a good design to use with a long headline, or any headline, at the top. The right spiral ends in the left corner, which is also an unusual ending spot. (See Figure 5-17.)

Another simple pattern is a straight *vertical* line beginning at the top and dropping to the bottom. A formal, symmetrical layout will often use this sequence. The problem here is that the structure of the emphasis has to match the downward sweep. For example, in most layouts like this the most important element is at the top, then comes the next most important element, and so on down to the product signature at the bottom. Usually that means a dominant piece of art, then the headline, then the body copy.

Where there is trouble is when the headline is above the art, but not clearly dominant. Then you are tempted to look first at the art, then up to the headline, then turn the page. Generally speaking, it is usually a good idea to keep

FIGURE 5-17:   **Four common visual paths**

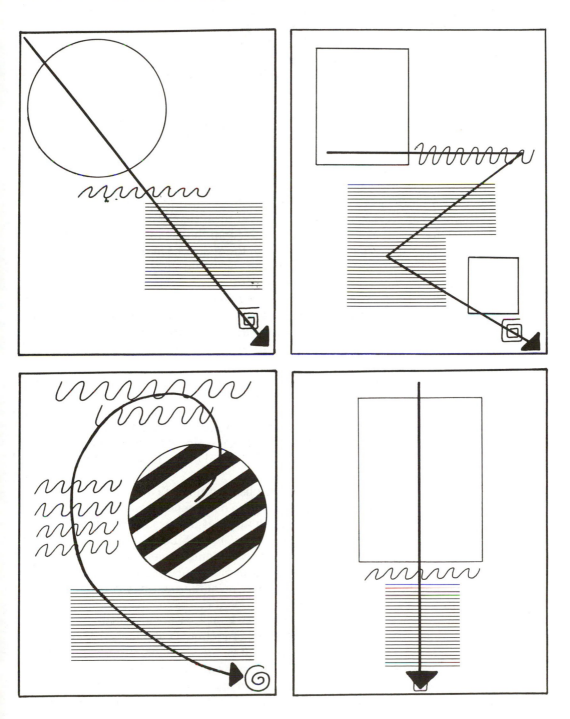

the headline directly above the body copy; that way it can serve its function of enticing the reader into the body copy. If the art separates the head and the body copy, it is easy to read the head and stop.

If the layout is effective, the scan pattern should be obvious. A good exercise to use in evaluating your sense of movement in layout is to take a magazine and some sheets of tracing paper, and try to draw the scan sequence of the advertisements. You will soon see that some are easy to follow and others are confusing.

The chief cause of confusion is having two or more dominant elements fighting for attention. You don't know where to begin—one element may be big or have an eye-catching graphic, the other may be in the normally dominant upper left corner. The message is unclear and the eye is confused. Most people will simply turn the page rather than fight through the confusion.

The diagonal, the vertical, the Z, and spiral patterns are all common but there are more. Some even violate the natural scan sequences. Airplane advertising, for example, will often use a diagonal that scans upward. That's the natural pattern of movement for planes so the sequence makes sense in context. But in order for the sweep to work, all the rest of the elements have to be carefully positioned to reinforce that movement.

Other times, you may want to force an unnatural pattern in order to make the message work or to create some psychological effect. This can be done but, remember, you are going counter to natural scan sequences, so the pattern has to be strong and inescapably clear in order to overcome these natural patterns.

Direction can be built into a layout in other ways. Rules are often used to indicate movement. They can serve as pointers. Such an obvious illustration as the woodcut "pointing finger" is another unmistakable way to establish direction. Signs of all kinds can reinforce the pattern. Alignment of the elements can be used to create movement. For example, a series of illustrations and masses of type all aligned on a strong invisible horizontal line will create an undeniable horizontal sweep. (See Figure 5–18.)

Sometimes there are direction cues within the composition of the art. For example, a football being kicked creates a tremendous movement message. Likewise, the position of an elbow or the angle of the legs in midstride can also direct the eye. A pointing arm in the art may, in fact, be pointing directly at the headline and serving as the leading line from one element to another.

An old rule-of-thumb in layout is to make sure you don't have the eyes looking out of the layout, because the direction of the gaze may cause the reader to look away. It's also considered a directional cue to turn the page. It's a subconscious response, but these cues do work on a preaware level.

These four principles are the basic functional guidelines for layout. Use unity to organize the arrangement, use contrast to signal points of emphasis, use balance to create visual stability, and use movement to establish a strong visual path for the eyes. There are other principles that are best described as aesthetic; their function is to create layouts that are pleasing or interesting to the eye.

FIGURE 5-18:   Two examples of directional cues used in layouts

Proportion.   Proportion is a mathematical concept; it states relationships of size in terms of mathematical proportions. When you analyze proportion, you are looking at the relative size of one element to another and of each of the elements to the whole. The idea is that there are certain relationships that fit together better for no reason other than that they look good together. This is not a functional concept; it is totally subjective, and it is the basis of the set of aesthetic standards used by someone with a well-trained sense of design.

The concept of "perfect" or "divine" proportion goes back to the early Greeks. Classical archaeology is a masterpiece of proportion. The Greek designer knew that columns would appear wider when nearer to the eye and narrower when at a distance. They also knew that shapes would appear wider against a white background and narrower against a dark background. In order to maintain the illusion of symmetry and scale, they varied the construction to consider the viewpoint of the observer.

The Greeks also knew that in nature certain dimensions or ratios occur frequently; others seldom. They tested these ratios and developed such concepts as "The Golden Mean" to express these aesthetic ideals. This ratio is *one to the square root of two* or 1:1.41. For practical use, this is standardized at 3:5.

These classical designers discovered that most of the proportions in nature are based on the 3:5 ratio. You will rarely find a perfect square in nature, for example. A square is considered too perfect, too mechanistic, and, because it is based on a 1:1 ratio, it is predictable visually. If a relationship is predictable, it is not as visually interesting as a relationship that is more distinctive. The 3:5 ratio is not one the eye can predict at a glance. The 1:1 or 1:2 relationships are obvious, and therefore not as interesting.

Most books and magazines use page sizes that are close to a 3:5 ratio. The amount of type on the page relative to the overall page size is roughly 3:5. The proportions of the page margins are also 3:5.

In fine bookmaking, the most generous depth is established at the bottom margin of the page and then moves to smaller margins around the page from the outside to the top and then to the gutter. The proportions are decided relative to the overall size of the page. For example, on an 8½-by-11 sheet the bottom margin may be 2½ inches while the top is 1½ inches. That means the margins occupy approximately 40 percent of the vertical depth, which is right in keeping with the 3:5 proportion.

Edmund Arnold, in his book *Ink on Paper*, gives a technique to use for establishing page margins.[9] You start by establishing the outside margin, then use half that width for the inside margin (the gutter). Now draw a diagonal line through your sheet. Where the diagonal crosses the two lines identifies the top and bottom margins. It's a simple way to develop a well-proportioned set of margins for your layout.

In more recent times, given the cost of paper and printing, you will probably note a decrease in the amount of space allotted to margins. Modern books and magazines have moved a long way from the dimensions respected in "fine" bookmaking. But when you see a page layout using the "Golden Mean," you automatically associate the proportions with "classy" design, even if you know nothing about design.

In layouts based upon an underlying structure of grids, the size of the grid is usually based on the 3:5 ratio. If you cut a page in half horizontally, then you have created two equal spaces—a monotonous arrangement. But if you cut the page at the 3/5th point, you will have created two distinctive rectangles. Cut both these rectangles at their 3/5th point, and you will have four rectangles, all perfectly in proportion to one another. A layout grid for page design is developed with all possible combinations of the 3:5 rectangles.

This does not mean that a square, for example, is forbidden in layout. Other proportions can be used effectively, depending upon the creative strategy. A square will be used for brochures and annual reports because the shape is rarely used and that makes it distinctive—even if the basic proportion is considered uninteresting by itself.

Harmony and tension.   The term *harmony* is used in discussion of design to mean that all the design decisions fit together—in style, in concept, in tone, in effect. For example, you might ask yourself if the style of type fits the content of the headline. Does the basic layout approach match the style of art, the concept, the product? Thus, a formal symmetrical layout might not match a warehouse sales ad for a department store. Does it make sense to use a circus banner style of design for a funeral home?

Generally speaking, your objective as a designer is to make all the design decisions work together, to create a unified and coherent visual statement. Ideally, all the design decisions are mutually supportive. There is one problem, however, in that some design principles have different objectives leading to a type of creative tension.

We know that people like messages that are familiar and comfortable. We also know that most people find these messages a little dull. In order to get their attention, then, it is necessary to use the strange and unfamiliar. So there is a constant tradeoff in advertising design between the familiar, which is easy to understand and perceive, and the unfamiliar, which is more attention getting. For example, in the seventies it was popular to design layouts that slanted. The slanted type was a little hard to read, but the visual interest of the angular design was considered to be of more importance.

You may find that it is necessary to sacrifice one principle in favor of another. For example, you may need to deemphasize contrast in order to strengthen unity. These decisions are made very carefully by a designer who is intuitively sensitive to these questions of design interaction.

Layout Formats

The discussion of layout principles gives you an understanding of the decision making that lies behind different arrangements. There are in advertising, however, some fairly common layout patterns. These are arrangements that have been used over and over again and have been found to be highly successful in handling all the different elements in an advertisement.

Picture window. The most basic layout style of all is a form called the *picture window* or the "Ayer #1" layout because of its successful use by the Ayer Advertising Agency.

Basically the layout uses a large dominant piece of art, followed by a headline, then the body copy, and finally the product signature information. It is a vertical sweep and fairly symmetrical. It is the most simple layout to do as well as to read. A large proportion of the ads you see in most magazines will use the picture window format.

Copy heavy. Another common layout style is the *copy-heavy* format. It begins with a strong dominant headline and is followed by a large block of copy usually set in two columns. This is basically a news announcement style, and it takes its appearance from the editorial side of a newspaper or magazine. If art is used, it is small and often inserted into the copy. Art is used to illustrate points being made in the copy rather than as an attention-getting element. The Phillips Petroleum advertisements are classic examples of this layout style. (See Exhibit 5–4.)

Frame. A variation on the copy-heavy format is a *frame* layout. This is a highly disciplined layout style that encloses the copy with some kind of artistic border or frame. It can be just rules, but often the frame will be a product-

related illustration. Sometimes a photo will serve as a frame with the copy dropped inside the photo. But essentially a frame layout is a way to provide ornamentation or attention-getting graphics to what is, otherwise, a heavy-copy layout.

Grid.   Another layout style is the *grid*. With this format there is an underlying grid that structures the placement of all elements. It is used to organize ads that have a lot of elements, particularly many pieces of art. You may see grid-based design used for department store and discount store advertisements where a multitude of products are featured. It can also be used to standardize a layout format, so that various ads in a campaign or across a variety of product lines will all look the same.

A Mondrian layout style is a variation of grid-based design. Mondrian was an early twentieth-century painter who experimented with perfectly proportioned shapes as an art form. The various sized rectangles in a Mondrian layout are fitted together like a puzzle. Occasionally, a Mondrian-based design will be used in ads where there is a need for a structure to bring order to a variety of elements.

Panel.   A panel is another variation on the grid design. *Panel* designs use strips of similar size blocks running either horizontally or vertically. A horizontal version would be a format that looks like a comic strip panel. This format is good for process explanations when you need to show things in steps. It is also good for showing several views of the same product or a variety of product styles.

Silhouette.   There is another common layout style best described by Roy Paul Nelson in his book on advertising design as a *silhouette* layout.[10] What Nelson is referring to is an informal layout, where the art and copy together create a shape other than the more common rectangle imposed by the margins. The elements are grouped internally to create some irregular shape. The key to a silhouette layout is asymmetrical balance and the careful alignment of the edges of art and copy. White space is also very carefully controlled, usually by pushing it to the outside and letting it serve as a frame.

Jumble.   A casual, busy, layout style is one called a *jumble,* or circus, format. This style of layout is playful and uses a lot of elements in something like a maze effect. There is a visual path but it wanders through lots of pieces of art and copy blocks. This is a very difficult style to design because the whimsical effect can easily turn to clutter and the visual path can get lost in the confusion.

These formats are common in advertising, but in no way depict the tremendous variety of layout possibilities available. There are highly successful layouts that violate basic design principles and turn these formats upside down. Once you have developed a sense of design, then the principles and formats are just starting points. New layouts are constantly being created by innovative designers who know that rules can be broken for effect.

FIGURE 5-19: Picture window layout

FIGURE 5-20: Copy-heavy layout

FIGURE 5-21: Frame layout

FIGURE 5-22: Grid layout

FIGURE 5-23: Panel layout   FIGURE 5-24: Silhouette layout

FIGURE 5-25: Jumble layout   FIGURE 5-26: Mondrian layout

Doing a Layout

Thumbnails.   There is a fairly standard visualization process follow-ed in the development of an advertising concept. In the initial conceptual stage, the art director and copywriter will usually kick around ideas using rough sket-ches called *thumbnails*. These are small sketches that are used to depict the basic elements of the idea: key words, a rough sketch of the visual, the approximate size of the copy blocks, the logo or signature, and so on.

During the talking stage, many sheets of paper or newsprint are covered with these miniature sketches—by both the artist and the writer. Many creatives find that making thumbnails tends to stimulate the creative process—it's a func-tional form of doodling.

Semicomps.   Thumbnails are used for getting ideas but, when several approaches begin to sound possible, then you will move to a visualization stage called "roughs" or *semicomps*. These roughs are used to show to other members of the team for critiquing. Sometimes they may be presented to the client repre-sentative if this person operates closely with the creative team in the idea develop-ment stage.

The purpose of roughs is to mock up the idea in enough detail that others can understand the message and critique the approach. Usually, there are several roughs developed so there are approaches to compare. (See figures 5–27 and 5–28.)

Semicomps are executed by lettering in the display type, sketching in the visual, and ruling in the body copy. The idea is to show what the approach looks like without spending a lot of time and money on finished art. There are still a lot of decisions (and changes) to be made at this stage of the game.

Most of the assignments you will be doing in advertising classes will be executed in the semicomp form. Semicomps are called "roughs," but this doesn't mean sloppy. These still need to be executed as carefully and professionally as you can. Money is not spent on typesetting and hiring an artist, but time should be spent to make them look as professional as possible.

Comprehensives.   When the final approach has been decided upon by the creative people and account team, then an artist will develop the *compre-hensives*. These are detailed visualizations of the final approach. Comprehensives look as much like the finished advertisement as possible. The art is carefully prepared, in color, if appropriate. It is usually sketched or painted using felt tips or watercolors.

The type may be "Greeked" in—in other words, you use the same size and type as you have specified but without actually having it set. It may be cut out of some other publication or you may use "nonsense" type available in dif-ferent type styles in transfer type. The idea is to make it look like the actual type without the expense. After all, the copy hasn't received final approval, yet, so undoubtedly there will be changes.

FIGURE 5-27: Thumbnail layouts

FIGURE 5-28: Semicomp or "rough" layout

Most agencies have artists who specialize in doing "comps." It is a peculiar art form. These comps are then used in the official presentations to the agency's review board, if it uses one, and to the client. The comprehensive is the final stage in the visualization process. Corrections and changes are still being made, even at this stage. After the comps are approved, then the planning period is over and production begins. The work of the "keyliners" who turn the comps into "mechanicals" is discussed in the production section of the chapter on art.

Comping type.   Most of the visualization process centers on semicomps, or roughs. Normally, at this stage, the display type will be rough lettered and the body type will be ruled in. The rough lettering should be done as close as possible to the type specifications. If you can't letter at all, it is possible to do credible roughs by tracing letters from transfer type or type spec books. (See Figure 5-29.)

Generally, the body copy only suggests the type size and column width. There are three different ways to comp body types. One way is to use a chisel point pencil or pen and rule in the lines of body copy, using a line that is the approximate width of the x-height. The width of the lead in a chisel point pencil can be adjusted by sandpaper block so that it matches the x-height of the letter.

FIGURE 5-29:   "Comping" display type by tracing

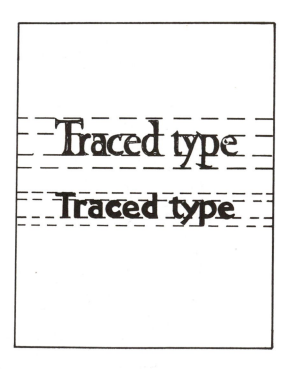

FIGURE 5-30:   "Comping" body copy

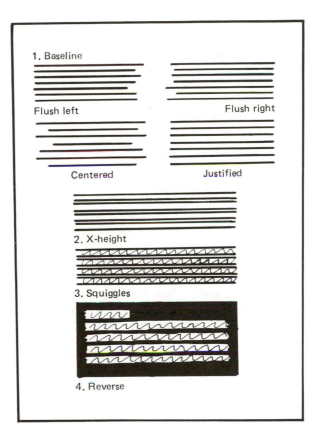

Another technique is to rule the x-height of the type using two lines, one for the upper edge and one for the bottom. A third method is an extension of the x-height ruling. With this technique, you fill in the space between with a squiggly line, which indicates a little more clearly where the type will go. (See Figure 5–30.)

Most writers, as well as designers, can prepare thumbnails and rough comps so it is important to understand how these forms are constructed. These are the thinking and talking pieces used in advertising in the preliminary decision stages. Anyone working on the creative side should be able to develop usable thumbnails and semicomps.

Shlock Design

Another aspect of aesthetics that is important to advertising professionals is a sense of judgment. An aesthetic sense means you can see the difference between "good" design and "not good" design. These are subjective evaluations; there is no way around it. Your ads can be judged on their strategy and their grammar and the skill of their artistic execution but, when the complete package is together, then you have to be able to divorce yourself from your proprietary feelings, step back, and ask yourself if it is "good." That's the hardest thing to do in advertising.

It is difficult to define "good" in an aesthetic sense so perhaps a better way to approach the problem is to discuss what is "not so good." Amateur work is not good—that means poor-quality lettering, writing, and art. Hand-drawn type and illustrations have to be done by skilled artists. Sometimes you may work with well-meaning people who are good but, on the other hand, the level of quality simply isn't there.

Cutesy approaches are usually *shlock*. A too-cute ad is one that tries too hard to be funny or sentimental. It is often sophomoric and more representative of the kinds of trite approaches found in junior high yearbooks.

Clichés are a big contributor to shlock work in advertising. Both verbal and visual clichés are ideas that have been overused. They elicit a response something like: "Oh no, not again." Usually, clichés begin with some interesting or dramatic idea to express a message. They become clichés because they are overused. There is a temptation in advertising to use popular phrases in order to create a feeling of timeliness but, often, by the time the ad has run, the phrase is old and tired.

Adese is another form of shlock work. There are certain formula expressions and settings, both visual and verbal, that scream "advertising" to you. These are hackneyed ways to present messages. They may be appreciated by account executives and timid clients who are afraid to try anything new, but formula work will rarely create positive associations for the product.

Copycat work is another form of shlock advertising. There is a tendency in advertising for the creative work to follow trends. A brilliant idea gets lots of acclaim and emulation from the rest of the advertising community. In order to be "with it," other creatives borrow the technique. Sometimes it is a general trend that reflects a social consciousness, like the use of nostalgia in the seventies but more often it is simply copying the use of a new technique.

The Push Pin Studio during the sixties was copied from one end of the country to another. Guy Bourdin's surrealistic photography for the Bloomingdale's Christmas lingerie catalogue started a new trend in lighting. The fast-talking Federal Express character has look-alikes in all parts of the country.

Layout is used functionally to organize a message and control the way it is presented and perceived. Layout is also an aesthetic activity, and an advertisement should represent certain standards of "goodness" in design. It should be visually pleasing as well as functionally effective. Regardless of what side of advertising you work on, it is necessary that you develop appreciation of good design.

5.5 COLOR

A discussion of color takes you into physics and physiology, as well as aesthetics and graphic production. Color is reflected in and through light. How we respond to it depends upon how it is recorded on the retina of our eyes, as well as how it is modified by light waves from surrounding planes.

There is nothing *red* in an apple; it's all in how we perceive it. If you look at an apple in a dark room, for example, it may seem gray. If you look at it under a blue or green light, it will appear black. However, if you really want to make it look super red, display it against a green background.

Color Theory

Color is light, and we see color only as light is reflected from or passes through some object. If all light is reflected, then we call what we see "white." If all light is absorbed, then we call the object "black." Color is analyzed in terms of three characteristics: hue, saturation, and brightness.

The *hue* is what we call the color: in other words, "red" or "blue" or "green." These colors are created from a spectrum of light, the familiar rainbow with colors that proceed from red through orange, yellow, green, blue, and violet. Approximately 150 separate shades are distinguishable by eye. These colors can be seen by splitting a beam of light through a prism. The position of each color in the spectrum is carefully determined by measuring the reflective properties of its light.

The second way to describe color is in terms of *saturation;* this is the relative strength or purity of the color. For example, we speak of off-white or grayish-blue. This suggests that the saturation of color is not total. In fact, it is possible to alter saturation in two ways: changing the shade or tint. Changing the shade is done by darkening the saturation, while changing the tint is done by lightening the saturation. These modifications are created by adding shades of white or black to the basic hue.

The third way color varies is by *brightness,* and this is a measure of the intensity of the light a color reflects. A bright color reflects lots of light while a dull color will absorb light. A pink, for example, can be bright or dull in terms of its reflective capability.

The color wheel. The color wheel is used to locate the relative position of colors. Primary colors are red, blue, and yellow. The secondary colors lie directly across the color wheel from the primaries. They are orange, green, and violet. (See Figure 5–31.)

In addition to primary and secondary, there is another way to describe these color relationships. The complementary to any color is the color opposite it on the color wheel. The primary, yellow, has the secondary, violet, as its comple-

FIGURE 5-31:   Color wheel indicating primaries and secondaries

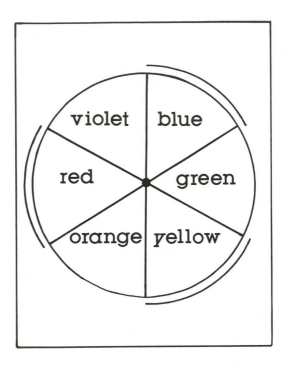

mentary. The primary, red, has green as its secondary. These complementaries are natural pairs of colors. They bring out the best in each other. That is why the red apple looks so much brighter on a green background.

These complementaries used together are also bright and attention getting. They make use of the strongest contrast. For example, you will see yellow and violet, blue and orange, and red and green used to create bold effects. When you use complementaries together, both seem to be emphasized. Neither one is dominant.[11]

Neighboring values are the colors on each side of any given color. These are harmonious combinations of colors. They go together because they share some hue in common. Violet and green are the two neighbors to blue. Either one will be harmonious with blue. The same is true of yellow and green or red and orange.

Clashing or garish colors can be created by working with the relationships that are neither complementary or secondary. For example, red and blue, depending upon the shades used, sometimes appear to vibrate when used together because their hues are in conflict. The clashing effect can be created when two colors are used with shades that move away from the basic hue. For example, red and blue both have violet as a neighbor. If you want to create a clashing effect, use a shade of blue that moves a little toward green or use a shade of red that moves a little toward yellow.

This is the equivalent of a hard-sell use of color. You will occasionally see such clashing effects used in discount store advertising, because it creates this jangling effect. It's the visual equivalent of the fast-talking used car salesman.

Color composition.   Another way to talk about hue is in terms of its light composition. Television uses the *additive* colors of red, green, and blue.[12] They are called additive colors because when you add them together they create white. In color theory terms, white is made up of all colors, the same way a beam of light is. Likewise, when you adjust the color on a color television screen, you can see the dots or lines of color more or less separately. When all three colors come together on the screen, you have white. Projected visuals displayed on a white screen also use additive colors. This is the basis behind color slide and cinema. Stage lights, for example, are modified by "gels" of transparent color.

Printing, on the other hand, uses *subtractive* colors. The primary colors of ink, called "process colors," are yellow, magenta (a shade of red), and cyan (a shade of blue). These are transparent inks and when they are printed one on top of another, they create black. Color prints made photographically are also composed of subtractive colors created and modified through the use of filters.

Color Symbolism

In advertising, color is used for a variety of specific purposes. It creates moods, it draws attention, it emphasizes, it intensifies memorability, and it helps define foreground and background.

Mood.   The primary function of color in advertising is to help create mood and emotional responses. Color tints our language with emotional connotations. We get blue when we are depressed; we see red when we are mad; we're feeling cowardly when we are yellow; we are cheerful when we're in the pink; we're in the dumps when we are in a brown mood or a brown study; and when things aren't going right, we're just generally "off color." These are color labels that our society has attached to certain emotions.

Beyond these labels are definite color associations with moods, and these are used effectively in advertising to create an emotional foundation for a message. Some commonly accepted associations are as follows:[13]

> *Red:* Generally exciting, cheerful, defiant, and powerful. Also associated with heat, anger, passion, war, and blood. Red is stimulating.
>
> *Blue:* Is often considered a happy color. It means peace, calmness, loyalty, security, and tenderness. Also associated with intellectual appeals as opposed to emotional (red). Can be identified with cold, ice, distance, and infinity as well as calm reflection.
>
> *Yellow:* Associated with the sunlight and openness as well as radiance and vividness. Because of its luminosity, it is highly attention getting.

Green: Like blue, also associates with serenity and calmness as well as nature. It is a quiet color. It is used symbolically to suggest hope, meditation, and tranquility.

Black: Associated with distress, despondency, and defiance. Used to suggest hate and death, but also can be used to express power and elegance, especially if it is shiny.

White: In Western cultures, white means purity as well as sanitary and clean. By its lack of apparent color, it also conveys emptiness, infinity, and the inexplicable. White is used visually to express total silence.

A famous advertisement designed by Milton Glaser for Sony tapes used the metaphor, "full color sound," to describe audio richness. Music is described as color, and the colors are then associated with emotions and feelings. It's a multilayered example of metaphor. (See Exhibit 5–5.)

Temperature.   We identify colors in terms of temperature as well as mood. The "warm" colors are those between red and yellow on the color wheel— including orange and gold as well as shades of pink. These are high-energy colors. Cool colors are between and around blue and green, including turquoise and violet. According to color expect Faber Birren, the warm hues generally make the most pleasing shaded colors. Cool hues make the best tinted colors.[14]

Restaurants, particularly fast-food places, use hot colors. They want to convey a feeling of "busyness" and yet friendliness. These colors help to keep people moving; they are less inclined to settle in and dawdle over their meal or coffee. Blues, purples, and silver are used in restaurants that are trying to project an elegant image. Cool colors also are used for sheets and blankets and locations where serenity and reflection are important.

Objectives of Color Use

Attention.   Certain colors are inherently eye-catching. Yellow is powerful because of its luminosity, and it is especially powerful when combined with black. Red is aggressive and a strong attention-getting color. Bright colors, in general, are attention getting—even a hue like pink will stand out when a bright shade is used.

Spot color is a printing technique used in advertising to take advantage of these characteristics of colors. A strong attention-getting color, for example, can be used with the center of interest to make sure the eye is attracted to the most important element.

Emphasis.   Using strong attention-getting colors to attract the eye is another way to emphasize what you believe is the most important element to be seen. Emphasis means contrast, and to make something stand out it has to contrast with everything around it. If the other elements are printed in black or neutral tones and the dominant element is printed in red, then you have assisted the viewer/reader in the process of visually organizing the message.

EXHIBIT: 5-5:   Sony's "full color sound" campaign developed the concept that music is colorful by relating different sounds to different colors. The advertisement was created by **Waring & Larosa, Inc.** (Courtesy of Sony Corporation of America)

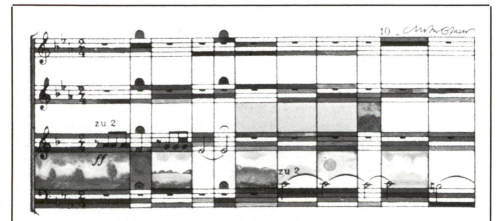

Sony Tape. Full Color Sound.

Music is full of color. Incredibly beautiful color. Color that you can hear...and (if you close your eyes) color you can almost see. From the soft pastel tones of a Mozart to the blinding brilliant flashes of hard rock to the passionately vibrant blues of the Blues.

In fact, one of the most famous tenors in the world described a passage as "brown ...by brown I mean dark...rich and full."

Music does have color. Yet when most people listen to music they don't hear the full rich range of color the instruments are playing. They either hear music in black-and-white, or in a few washed-out colors.

That's a shame. Because they're missing the delicate shading, the elusive tints and tones, the infinite hues and variations of color that make music one of the most expressive, emotional and moving arts of all.

Music has color. All kinds of color. And that is why Sony is introducing audio tape with Full Color Sound.

Sony tape with Full Color Sound can actually record more sound than you can hear.

So that every tint and tone and shade and hue of color that's in the original music will be on the Sony tape. Every single nuance of color, not just the broad strokes.

Sony tape with Full Color Sound is truly different. Full Color Sound means that Sony tape has a greatly expanded dynamic range—probably more expanded than the tape you're using. This gives an extremely high output over the entire frequency range, plus a very high recording sensitivity.

There's even more to Sony tape with Full Color Sound, however. Sony has invented a new, exclusive SP mechanism for smoother running tape, plus a specially developed tape surface treatment that gives a mirror-smooth surface to greatly reduce distortion, hiss and other noise. Each type of tape also has its own exclusive binder formulation, that gives it extra durability.

Any way you look at it—or rather, listen to it, you'll find that Sony tape with Full Color Sound is nothing short of superb.

If you're not hearing the whole rainbow on your audio tape, try recording on Sony tape with Full Color Sound. Then you'll be hearing all the glorious full color that makes every kind of music, music.

Memorability.   Colors are easy to remember and, if you can create an indelible association between a color and a product, then you will be assisting the retention process. Color coding is a process of establishing visual cues.

When you see a green ad in the newspaper with a picture of a cigarette pack, there will probably come to mind the name of the product, Kools. Johnnie Walker Red has a long-running campaign that seeks to establish a link between the warm side of the color red and the product. Color coding can be a very strong tool in brand identity.

Depth definition.   Color can be used to establish the foreground and background relationship signifying the dominant element. A neutral or pastel color is often used as background with a brighter, stronger color used for the foreground elements. In perceiving visuals, we expect to see that relationship.

There are some unusual characteristics of color physics that also contribute to the perception of depth in the background/foreground relationship. Red and orange, for example, have been identified as aggressive colors—they seem to advance toward you. Blue and green, the cool colors, are seen as recessive—they appear to retreat.

There is a physiological explanation for this phenomenon. Red falls on the rear of the retina where the lens grows convex and the result, as explained by vision expert Gerald McVey[15] is that red and orange appear to approach the viewer. Objects in these colors appear larger. Blue and green fall in front of the retina where the lens flattens and, as a result, these colors appear to recede. Objects depicted in blue will appear to be smaller and off in the distance.

For these reasons, it is particularly important to plan your use of background colors carefully. Blue and green are natural colors for background, red isn't. If you use a blue image on a red field, the background may seem to be moving toward the viewer and fights with the image for dominance. The result is that peculiar illusion where the two colors seem to be in motion and changing position back and forth.

Color and Personality

We said earlier that there are different ways of thinking and different learning styles among people. The same thing is true for color responses. Different people respond to different colors in different ways. Color preferences are to some extent a function of personality, but they also reflect social and cultural values. Research has found that extroverts, for example, seem to prefer the more highly saturated colors of blue, red, and green, while introverts prefer pastels.[16]

While preference by sex isn't consistent, some research has found that, in ads and displays, blue brings the highest returns from males while red brings the highest returns from females.

Rorschach tests have found that some people are more responsive to color than to shape. These "color reactors" tend to be more impulsive, open, cheerful, emotional, and easily influenced. People who respond to shape before color tend to be more serious, unemotional, intellectual, logical, and, in some cases, depressed.

Favre and November report a number of experiments with people, products, and color.[17] A group of people were asked to evaluate coffee that had been poured from four different color pots: red, blue, brown, and yellow. The coffee was identical but the perceptions weren't. The coffee from the brown pot was considered too strong, the red pot poured coffee that was perceived as rich and full-bodied, coffee from the blue pot was thought to have a milder aroma, and the coffee in the yellow pot was considered weak.

In another experiment, the researchers reported that housewives given three different packets of washing powder, which varied only in the color of the packet, found significant differences in the product's effectiveness. The soap in the yellow packet was considered too strong, the soap in the blue packet was judged not strong enough, and the packet with a combination of yellow and blue was supposed to contain soap that was "marvelous."

Dr. Max Luscher, a Swiss scientist, first developed his Color Test in 1947 and it has since been used by physicians, psychologists, and other counselors as a diagnostic tool. The Luscher Color Test identifies emotional and psychological troubles that might lead to such problems as heart trouble, strokes, and high blood pressure.[18]

Advertising and Color

Obviously, color reactions are important personality characteristics. Ideally, if our targeting were truly precise, we might be able to design ads using color patterns that would be most motivating for the particular type of personality being targeted by the message.

Color speaks to the emotions rather than to the reason. In some cases, the color and the design of the package are the only real differences between one product and another. Impulse purchases are particularly susceptible to color triggers. Red and yellow are known to be highly effective to stimulate impulse purchases.

In packaging, the first objective of the color is to command the eye. It has to be seen, to jump off the shelf, if it is to survive the intense competition of the self-service environment. Next, the package color is chosen for its ability to associate with certain desired qualities such as elegance, naturalness, softness, and so on.

Brand image is another aspect of advertising that is affected by color characterization. It goes all the way back to school colors—colors chosen to symbolize an entire group of people and all their activities. With the growth of self-service retailing, color is used as a continuity device as well as for identification. The use of a standardized color is an important part of most identity campaigns, as in the Cutty Sark and Kool campaigns. And the color is chosen to reflect the personality of the brand or corporation.

Color communicates. It speaks a language of its own. Successful advertising and successful advertising campaigns will use color as a powerful part of the message design.

NOTES

1. Matthew P. Murgio, *Communication Graphics* New York: Van Nostrand Reinhold, 1969.

2. Philip W. Burton, *Which Ads Pulled Best* (Chicago: Crain, 1981).

3. Julie A. Edell and Richard Staelin, "The Information Processing Pictures in Print Advertising," *Journal of Consumer Research,* 10 (June 1983), pp. 45–61.

4. Daniel Starch, "How Does the Shape of Ads Affect Readership?", *Media/Scope,* 10 (1966), pp. 83–85.

5. Kathy A. Lutz and Richard J. Lutz, "Effects of Interactive Imagery on Learning: Applications to Advertising," *Journal of Applied Psychology,* 62 (August 1977), pp. 493–98.

6. John R. Rossiter and Larry Percy, "Attitude Change Through Visual Images in Advertising," *Journal of Advertising,* 9:2 (1980), pp. 10–16.

7. Edmund Arnold, *Ink on Paper* (New York: Harper and Row, 1963).

8. Robert Heinich, Michael Molenda, and James D. Russell, *Instructional Media and the New Technologies of Instruction* (New York: Wiley, 1982).

9. Arnold, op. cit.

10. Roy Paul Nelson, *The Design of Advertising,* 3rd ed. (Dubuque, Iowa: Brown, 1977).

11. Jean-Paul Favre and Andre November, *Color and Communication* (Zerach: ABC Verlag, 1979), p. 46.

12. Herbert Zettl, *TV Production Handbook,* 3rd ed. (Belmont, Calif.: Wadsworth, 1976).

13. Favre and November, op. cit., pp. 22–24.

14. Faber Birren, *Color: A Survey in Words and Pictures* (New York: University Books, 1963).

15. G. F. McVey, "Putting Color into your Visual Presentation," *Photomethods,* November 1976, pp. 57–59.

16. Birren, op. cit.

17. Favre and November, op. cit.

18. Max Luscher, *The Luscher Color Test* (New York: Pocket Books, 1971).

Print
Advertising

Chapter Six

In previous chapters we have discussed the basics—such topics as creative thinking, strategy, copywriting, and layout and design. These topics are fairly universal in their application across most advertising media.

This chapter, however, will focus on specific types of media and consider the medium in terms of its creative implications. Newspapers and magazines, for example, have entirely different creative needs even though they are both printed publications. Yellow Pages offer an entirely different challenge to creative planning. Brochures, and the various other forms of collateral materials, are also distinctive in how they are created and used in advertising. The final category to be discussed in this section is a group called "out-of-home" media, which include all kinds of signs, posters, and displays.

They are grouped together here because they all, in one way or another, use a printed format. Beyond that, they are all distinctive in terms of how we create messages for them. Every medium has its own needs, and every medium puts a particular type of constraint on the creative process. For that reason, we will briefly review these various types of media in terms of their creative needs.

6.1 MAGAZINES

Magazine advertising is the glitter and gloss of print advertising. Magazine advertising is primarily national, although regional buys are possibly, and primarily, brand oriented. The paper is slick, the color is great, the reproduction is excellent, and many advertisers will usually spend whatever it takes to get the best image they can for their product.

Special interest.   There are certain characteristics of the medium that affect how you will develop messages for magazines. Magazines appeal to special interests. With the exception of a few large general interest publications, most magazines are now highly segmented. They are designed to appeal to groups of people who share some interest such as business, jogging, skiing, auto mechanics, science fiction, hair styling, and gourmet food.

The magazine industry originally focused around a few mass magazines with huge publications such as *Life, Look,* and *Saturday Evening Post.* The development of television with its national networks undercut the mass orientation of magazines. In response to television, magazines found a much healthier orientation serving the special interest market. While the large mass magazines have all about disappeared, the smaller special interest publications are dynamic and growing. Consequently, there are a tremendous number of magazines available and the number is continuing to increase daily. In this age of mass media, the magazine industry has survived and grown on special interest messages.

Periodical.   Magazines operate with a different time frame. They are called periodicals because they are produced infrequently—weekly, monthly, semimonthly (twice a month), bimonthly (every other month), and quarterly. Most of the other major media used by advertisers are offering messages daily, hourly, or by the minute.

Because they are published less frequently, magazines are read at leisure and over time. They are one of the few media available to advertisers where you have some time with your reader and where you can expect readers to come back and review the magazine and possibly your ad.

Custom tailored.   Because the magazine industry is organized by audience interest, there is more opportunity to tailor the message to your target. Not only can you buy a special group, but many magazines will also permit you to specify certain categories of their readership. Regional and demographic editions are available for many of the national publications.

That way you can speak to boat owners (the magazine's special interest group) who live in the Southwest (regional edition). Some publications can also target by demographic data, making it possible for you also to tailor your ad to executives making over $50,000—and who live in the Southwest and are boat owners. Not all publications offer this type of demographic targeting, but more and more are moving in that direction. This is a media buyer's problem, but it can affect the way you address your audience in the copy.

The Audience

Reflective.   The audience mindset is considerably different for magazines. We have already mentioned that magazines are read at leisure and that readers will extend their reading of a magazine over time. What this means is that readers are in a more reflective, less hurried frame of mind when they read magazines. For that reason, they will read longer copy than in newspapers and you can develop more complicated messages than in television or radio.

Personal relationship. They also have a sense of identity with the publication. They have chosen to subscribe to this publication because it speaks to some personal interest they value. Often, people's self-concept is expressed through the publications they read. You may have been in an interview situation where you were asked what magazines you read—that's because magazine reading is a clue to your personality.

Hanley Norins talks about this personal relationship with magazines in his book on copywriting.[1] He says that readers have a sense of confidence in and respect for the publications to which they have subscribed. There is a loyalty factor, too. Some people have been subscribers to their favorite magazines for decades. Magazines are the only media that have this personal relationship.

We subscribe to the local newspaper because it is the local newspaper. In the few communities with multiple papers, there may still be some sense of loyalty, but those cities are few. But regardless, the choice of newspaper is not based on our confidence, respect, or loyalty to the publication. It's simply a practical consideration of availability.

Creative Considerations

Given the special interests of most magazines, obviously magazine ads should be oriented toward the interests of that segment of the market. A soft drink will probably need a different creative strategy for ads that run in *Seventeen* and *Good Housekeeping*. The first thing to remember in writing and designing ads for magazines is to address the audience with a special appeal.

Service. Another characteristic of advertising in magazines is that it is highly service oriented. People read magazines to find out information—and to a lesser degree for entertainment. News is important, but not as much as in newspapers. People read magazines for ideas—new ideas, ways to do things they have never done before, and new ways to think about things. The magazine is an idea medium rather than a news medium.

A successful magazine ad will often speak to this service angle. Readership studies have shown time and again that the highest scores go to ads with tips and recipes and ideas on new uses. That's why people read the editorial side of a magazine and the interest carries over to the ads.

Feature writing. Magazines specialize in a style of writing called "features." These articles tend to be interesting, colorful, anecdotal, and helpful. The writing is good and your ads will have to compete with these articles for the readers' attention. That means your ads have to be just as interesting, colorful, anecdotal, and helpful as the features. If you compare the ads with the articles in most magazines, you will probably notice that the writing is considerably better on the editorial side.

Dominant visual.   Magazines also use dramatic graphics to express the idea of the article and catch the attention of potential readers. In this area, advertisements are just as competitive, perhaps more so. Magazine ads generally do an excellent job of using a dominant visual to capture attention and communicate the essence of the message. If you page through most any magazine, you will notice that most ads use a strong visual. In some cases, like the classic Merit campaign, the ad is designed to be copy-heavy and look like editorial matter. In that case, the all-type layout is being used as a graphic and its message conveys news.

Production Considerations

Reproduction quality.   One of the big advantages of magazine advertising over newspaper is the excellent quality of the reproduction. The quality of the paper is much better. Some magazines use clay-coated paper that is especially good for reproduction of fine details. The printing process is more controlled so there is less of a problem with register of color. Photographic reproduction is particularly good in magazines because they can use a much finer line screen.

Lead time.   Another characteristic of magazine production that affects the design of the message is the long lead time. The deadline for your ad may be six to eight weeks before the publication date. That obviously eliminates anything that is tied to breaking news. You can do seasonal tie-ins but you may be working on a Christmas appeal in September so you have to be mentally flexible to adjust to the mood.

Page domination.   One of the advantages of magazines over newspapers is that the competition is less obvious. There may be just as many ads in proportion to the editorial copy, but the smaller page size of magazines means there aren't as many ads competing with you for attention. You can buy half a page, for example, and not have another ad on the page.

Because of the smaller page, it is more likely that you will be working with a full-page ad. In that case, you are able to totally dominate the space. The only competition might come from an ad on the facing page but that's less serious. Furthermore, you may even be able to buy a spread and control both facing pages, which gives your message maximum impact with no competition.

Total control of the page is achieved with the use of a "bleed." That means the ad is designed to run past the normal margins and right off the edge of the paper. By ignoring the margins, it breaks through the formality of the publication.

Since the environment is less directly competitive, magazine advertising can be a little softer in tone and style than newspaper ads. The display type doesn't have to be as big; the headlines don't have to scream. There is more room for subtlety and ambiguity in magazines. Ads that tell stories have more space to develop the narrative.

Special arrangements.   While most magazines ads are full page, there are some interesting effects that can be created by manipulating the size and placement. A one-column ad in a three-column magazine will give you a highly vertical space that is interesting just because of its extreme shape.

Gatefolds are available in some magazines, usually in conjunction with the inside front cover. This is a way to expand beyond a double-page spread and create a spread equivalent to three or four pages in width.

You can also plan a message that evolves by using successive pages. This is used occasionally with ads that tease, surprise, or in some way develop from page to page. This same technique is used with partial pages. A checkerboard effect is created by using quarter pages in succession. The message can be repeated with variations or it can evolve across the series. These are all techniques used to involve the reader and build memorability.

6.2 NEWSPAPERS

Retail and local.   Newspapers are different from other types of advertising media because they are primarily retail oriented and local. The emphasis in most newspaper ads is on the local store and its merchandise or service as opposed to magazine or television advertising, which is primarily product oriented.

In newspaper advertising, information about the service or merchandise is featured but the store has to be included too—memorability is particularly important for the store identification. So while it is highly product oriented, there is another side of retail advertising that is image oriented but the emphasis is not on the image of the brand, but on the image of the store.

Of course, there are the more traditional product advertisements placed as part of a national buy by the manufacturer. Cigarette advertising by brand is common in newspapers and so are soft drinks. But predominantly you will see local retail advertising in most newspapers. Of course, there are several national newspapers such as the *Wall Street Journal* and *USA Today.*

Not only are they local, they are also affected by their geography. Communities in different parts of the country have different climates, lifestyles, values, and political orientations. Some areas are more conservative than others; some are more outdoors or wilderness oriented. Some areas are more industrial, some are suburban, others are rural. Communities are different and these differences are reflected in the personality of the newspapers that serve them.

The advertising message strategy will reflect the distinctive values of the community. National ads run in local newspapers will often be revised to reflect the personality of the community. A classic campaign by Kent III cigarettes was built on the well-known symbols of various cities. Each city had its own version of the introductory ad, with a headline and graphic that stressed the distinctive feature of that community. (See Exhibit 6–1.)

News.   In addition to local and retail, another characteristic of newspaper advertising is its emphasis on news. News is the medium's reason for existence and advertising that mirrors this function will be the most successful. While some of the national advertising may be image or reminder advertising, most of the local ads announce something or give information about something. The "news peg" is always close to the surface in local advertising.

Newspapers are informative, rather than entertaining. True, there are some entertainment sections in newspapers, but most people read papers for news. Readers *want* information, facts, details. This is one medium where advertising copy can be long because it is in context with the medium.

Timeliness.   Furthermore, newspaper information is fleeting. By definition, news is timely. What happened yesterday is no longer news. That means the information in newspapers is constantly changing and being replaced. Advertising in this milieu is also short-lived. In some cases an ad may be cut out and saved, but generally the objective is to register information about something that is happening *today.* Yesterday's ad, like yesterday's newspaper, is old news. Most newspaper advertisements build their strategies on this factor of timeliness. You will see copy that emphasizes now, today, and immediate action.

Competitive.   Another characteristic of newspaper advertising is its heavy competitive environment. True, there are other commercials on television and other ads in magazines, but none of them occur simultaneously like they do in newspapers. An inside page of a newspaper may have five to 10 ads and if it's the entertainment section you may be staring at 15 to 20. On television and in magazines, the ads follow one another (except for the small space ads in magazines). Few advertising situations are as intensely competitive as those involving newspapers.

Graphic limitations.   Newspapers are printed fast on a soft, spongy, but strong, paper that accepts ink easily and dries quickly. The quality of the image reproduction, given the speed, ink, and paper, is very low. A few papers, like *USA Today,* are using a better grade of paper, but generally you have to design your ads to reflect the production process and the materials used in newspaper printing.

Those are the primary characteristics of newspapers that affect the way the advertising message is created. Newspapers are local and community oriented, most advertising is retail, the emphasis is on news that is timely, the page environment is heavily competitive, and there are serious graphic limitations. We'll refer back to these distinctive features when we discuss message strategies for newspapers.

EXHIBIT 6-1: The Kent III introductory campaign used local tie-ins with major cities. (Courtesy of Lorillard)

The Audience

Newspapers are read by 76 percent of the adult population and, among the well educated, the figure jumps to 88 percent, according to the Newspaper Advertising Bureau.[2] Most newspapers are read by two or more people who will spend approximately 30 minutes with the paper. Most people read their local paper in the morning, and 67 percent say they actually look forward to the advertising in the newspaper.

Receptive.   That last sentence is what makes newspaper advertising different from just about every other medium. In most media, advertising is an intrusion. In newspapers it is just another form of news. People read newspapers to check the ads. Homemakers use it as a shopping guide, a quick way to see what is available and where, and what the going prices are. It's the local marketplace's number one source of comparative shopping information. Newspaper readership studies have shown that most readers do not consider advertising any different than editorial content—it is all news to them. The success of shoppers, tabloid newspapers with nothing but ads, proves that advertising is valued as news, too.

In every other medium you have to worry about catching the attention of an inattentive audience, but in newspapers you have an audience that is interested, searching, reading—an audience that has chosen to read the paper and your ad. That's a tremendous psychological advantage. Newspapers provide the only medium where your ad is not intrusive. This doesn't mean that your ad will automatically get read. As a matter of fact, most people don't really *read* their papers, they just scan them. Given the highly competitive environment, your ad may never even be seen unless it is designed to attract attention.

Heterogeneous.   Another characteristic of the audience is that it is heterogeneous. The only thing that holds this group of people together is that they all live in the same geographical area. The newspaper's readership will include women and men, old and young, black and white, rich and poor, white collar as well as pink and blue collar, and every other demographic range found in any city. That limits the amount of special interest advertising found in most newspapers.

Everyone buys shoes and groceries and keeps their money in a bank or savings and loan. Those kinds of stores and services find it profitable to run big ads in local papers. Fashion ads will be found in the women's or home section of the paper and tire ads will run in the sports pages, which is about all the targeting that newspapers can do. Stores that sell computers and business supplies may also advertise in newspapers, but their ads will probably be smaller because of the inability of newspapers to target by special interest.

The only place where real targeting occurs in the newspaper is in the classified advertising section. There you have people who are interested in looking specifically for a certain product or service. But it is an individual marketplace, rather than a commercial one.

Types of Ads

Display and classified.   The two primary distinctions in newspapers are between display and classified advertising. *Display* ads are boxes of space bought by the advertiser that run on the same pages adjoining the editorial copy. *Classified* ads, the "want" ads, are all-copy notices placed by individuals announcing things they want to sell or buy. Usually, they run in a classified section and there is no concern about having them adjoin editorial copy. Classified ads have a tremendously high readership among the ideal target—people who are actually in the market and ready to buy.

Small space and omnibus.   Two other terms are used to describe types of ads in newspapers. A *small space* ad usually occupies one column. In newspapers, a series of these small ads may be used instead of a large one, but the impact is hoped to be the same because they are repeated often. Size may be sacrificed in favor of repetition.

Omnibus ads are used in department stores and discount store advertising. They are multiple-item ads, and usually they are not related thematically. A discount store, for example, will run a full page ad with 15 items, each representing a different part of the store. They may include what's called "loss leaders," which are used to build traffic by discounting the price. Omnibus ads are complicated to design and can be highly cluttered if there isn't a special effort made to organize them visually.

Creative Considerations

Strategies.   There are two primary kinds of creative strategies used in most local newspaper advertising: image and news. There is also product advertising but that is primarily national advertising by a manufacturer and, in keeping with the newspaper environment, even product advertising is often news oriented.

The first strategy of local newspaper advertising we will discuss is *image* advertising. It is used to develop the store personality. Stores have personalities just like people do, and these distinctive personalities are created by the advertising as well as by the interior design of the store. Macy's is different from Saks Fifth Avenue. K-Mart is different from Gibsons. Stores can be chic, classy, budget, professional, friendly, or haughty and that should be apparent in the design of their ads. This is discussed in more detail in the chapter on retail advertising.

Sometimes ads will be run just to reinforce the image. Merchandise may be depicted, but often it is more general with an emphasis on product categories and brands rather than on specific items. Even in item advertising, the store's personality should be obvious. Every ad is one more chance to build and reinforce that image.

News peg. In keeping with the medium, the primary category of local newspaper advertising is a news strategy. The ad announces some fact that is newsworthy and timely, something people would want to *know*. It may be the introduction of a new product or product line or the availability of a product or service that was not previously available.

Probably the most effective news announcement deals with price. Local newspapers are filled with ads announcing price reductions and special sales. Value advertising may be the number one most common appeal used in local newspaper ads. Price advertising may be supported by copy explaining what the value is. For example, during a period of coffee shortage, Nescafé ran ads explaining that, even though the bottle of instant coffee looked small, there were as many servings in a 10-ounce jar as you get in 2½ pounds of roast coffee.

Another type of news strategy is one that uses a timeliness "peg" such as a season, holiday, or special event. Strohs ran an ad in Detroit celebrating the opening of the baseball season and Alka Seltzer has run ads lamenting national income tax day, April 15.

Breaking news events can also be used as pegs for advertising. During periods of crisis, such as the oil embargo, ads were running in local newspapers on such topics as mass transit, sharing rides, and the virtues of bicycles. Planters peanuts found an election-day peg when Carter was elected president. An award-winning ad was developed when the Christie cookie factory in Canada went on strike. There wasn't an Oreo cookie to be found anywhere in Canada. The agency's creative team solved the crisis by running an ad with a recipe for the vanilla filling that could be used with two chocolate wafers to create a "spare parts Oreo."[3]

Writing style. Advertising writing in newspaper ads reflects news writing. An announcement ad has the responsibilities that a news article has. You have to tell your audience what it is all about. Journalistic writing glorifies the concept of newsworthiness, which is characterized by the elements of timeliness and general interest. Any of the ad copy approaches that use the "now you can buy . . ." formula are announcing a news peg and can be written in news style.

Another characteristic of news style is that it is straightforward. You will rarely find a collection of adjectives and adverbs stacked in one sentence in a news story. It's bare-bones writing and it's powerful because it communicates the essentials quickly and to the point.

Along with the straightforward approach is a concern for brevity. News writing is succinct. Sentences and paragraphs are short. The writing is sparse and no extra words are used. You will see this reflected in advertising in the use of what we call "bulletin" copy. The major points are just listed without the ands and buts. It's very difficult to explain benefits with bulletin items, but it is a good way to give such information as sizes, colors, and other product features.

Straightforward, sparse writing is appropriate in most advertising because of the limited time or space available. It's especially appropriate for newspaper advertising, given the reading orientation of the audience. Newspaper ads should be simple, uncomplicated, and easy to grasp. Remember that the reader is in a methodical scanning pattern and anything complicated will just be ignored.

Design. Given the tremendous competition in newspapers, your ads need to be simple in concept and design just to avoid adding more confusion to the clutter. Newspaper pages are the most cluttered environment in which you will ever place an ad. Any ad that will stand out in this environment has to be either very simple or very well organized.

There are tricks of the trade for designing newspaper ads that get attention. The first is to dominate the page. A full-page ad doesn't have to worry about clutter and a half-page ad has cut down considerably on the ability of any other ad to compete. Another technique is to use spot color. Consistently, those ads with a careful use of color will dominate over their black-and-white competitors. Unusual shapes are also attention getting.

In terms of contrast, either be bold or be simple—depending upon your product and concept. Bold headlines and bold art are attention getting, the visual equivalent of a yell. At the other end of the spectrum, however, is a quiet, simple ad using lots of white space. This approach stands out because it is so different from everything else in the newspaper environment.

With smaller ads on competitive pages, always use a rule around your ad to define your space and then plan internal margins around the ad copy to provide a white space frame. This helps to isolate your ad from the confusion around it.

Incentives. Another characteristic of newspaper advertising is the heavy use of special incentives such as coupons. The function of a local retail ad is to build store traffic and coupons, and special price deals for a limited time are good techniques to bring people in. Coupons are also useful for trial purchases and, since the newspaper ad is frequently announcing something new, it makes sense to use coupons to stimulate trial. Newspapers serve as a shopping guide for local purchases and price-conscious shoppers often search the newspaper specifically for coupons. Of all the coupons used in advertising, approximately 70 percent are in newspapers.[4]

Production

Sizes. A display ad can be a full page, half page, or a smaller size. Display ads are measured horizontally by the number of columns they fill. Most standard newspapers use from six to nine columns. Tabloids (half the size of a standard newspaper page) can be anything from two to five columns. The number of columns and their widths are only now becoming standardized, which makes it extremely difficult to plan an ad for different papers.

The vertical dimension is measured in inches or agate lines. There are 14 lines to an inch so a 42-line ad would be three inches deep. Generally, the larger display ads are measured in inches and agate lines are only used for tiny ads. To specify the size of an ad, then, you would give first the number of columns (width), then the number of inches (depth). For example, you might specify a 2-by-6 ad, which means you will get a display space that is two columns wide by six inches deep.

Design considerations.   Production problems also influence design for newspaper ads. The spongy newsprint soaks up ink and makes it very difficult to reproduce fine details. Photographs can be printed in newspapers, but they lose their crisp image because they can't be reproduced very well. For that reason most newspaper ads use line art. If you do use a photograph, choose a print that is high in contrast.

Another way to solve the problem of poor quality reproduction is to use preprinted inserts. These are usually national ads in a tabloid. They are printed on coated paper using the gravure process, which gives excellent color reproduction.

A national advertiser will produce the insert and then, for a fee, have it inserted in the local newspaper. Sometimes they are mailed directly to the home, but generally it is cheaper to let the newspaper handle the distribution, because the content usually fits the newspaper environment. In other words, they are often announcing special sales and people turn to newspapers for this kind of information.

Color registration is another problem with newspaper printing. The printing process is so imprecise that it is very difficult to guarantee perfect alignment of additional colors. If you use spot color, use a loose application of color so that the registration is not critical.

Mats and proofs.   Once an ad is finished by an agency, it has to be distributed to all of the various newspapers scheduled in the media buy. For those few newspapers that still use letterpress, a "mat" of the finished ad is sent. This is a thick papier-mâché mold into which the printer pours molten metal to make an engraving.

Most newspapers, however, are printed offset, and this simplifies the distribution of the finished ad. These papers are sent "reproduction proofs" that are camera-ready. They are pasted into the paper's page and then shot. For color ads, a set of color separations have to be sent. These are proofs that represent each ink to be used.

6.3 YELLOW PAGES

One of the most underrated local media is the phone book. If you have an ad in the Yellow Pages, then you are advertising every day of the year to every person in the community who owns a phone and who is interested in your product or service. That's a tremendous reach as well as a highly selective one. In effect, you've blanketed the community.

In addition, this is one of the few advertising media that people consult voluntarily and deliberately for commercial information. You have an audience here that is making an effort to search out your store or service. Your ad is not intrusive, it is welcome, and the more information you give, the more they will read. The Yellow Pages are the guide to the special interests of a local community. Whatever the interest, you can isolate ideal customers through their use of certain categories in the Yellow Pages. They select themselves out and the selection is based on the most important variables: interest and readiness to buy.

Uses of Yellow Pages.   The Yellow Pages perform three functions. They serve as a shopping guide, a business reference, and a crisis consultant. The shopping guide role is the most important to the advertiser. For example, many people turn to the Yellow Pages when they want to go out to eat. It's a quick way to refresh their memories on what restaurants are available and nearby. This is a particularly important function for people who are new in town or for visitors. These people have no familiarity with your previous media advertising, so you can't rely on previous ads in other print media, such as the local newspaper.

The business reference function is important to the user. If you want to take a suit to the cleaner, it makes sense to check ahead of time to see if the store is open. In other words, people consult the Yellow Pages for certain types of basic information such as location and hours that they probably can't recall from advertising, no matter how much you might spend in the local paper.

The crisis consultant role is important in times of emergency. If your plumbing fails or you need to call a doctor or your insurance agent, the telephone book becomes your most reliable adviser. The phone book is highly dependable in times of stress.

Creative Considerations

Size.   In terms of the shopping guide function, the primary consideration is the size of the display ad. A simple listing is rarely effective as a shopping guide clue. People tend to evaluate the success or reputation of the business on the size of the display ad. The bigger it is, the more credible the business is.

Regardless of the actual size, it is best to treat the design of a display ad in the Yellow Pages as a small space ad. This kind of ad has certain characteristics. It is simple and straightforward. You don't need any cutesy tricks to catch people's attention because you already have their attention. You can use a strong benefit strategy, however, to separate your store or service from that of your competitors who are all around you.

Message design.   An illustration is useful to depict your product line or to establish the image of your store. Impressions created by the graphics are very important for those people using the Yellow Pages as a shopping guide. Body copy is used to identify the scope of your product line or services. If someone is looking for a particular brand, then you should have the brands you carry in the ad. Credibility statements are also important, such as memberships, citations, or performance achievements.

Reference information.   The most important information, however, is the address, phone number, and hours. This information is run at the bottom in small type in most newspaper ads, but in the Yellow Pages it should be large and bold. In many cases your location information is best expressed through a simple map. People will choose stores on the basis of the one they think is the easiest to find. Having a map in the phone book is sometimes more important than the location itself.

Always give the hours. For those using the phone book as a business reference, that's just as important as the address. The phone number is used by those people who might want to check on special information, like service provided or whether you carry a particular line.

The Yellow Pages display ad is important for any advertiser in any business. The larger it is, the more credible the store or service. Use a graphic to cue the personality of your business. Keep the copy straightforward and simple. Always include the basic business reference information such as address, hours, and phone number—and display this information as largely and as boldly as possible.

6.4 COLLATERAL MATERIALS

In advertising, the term *collateral materials* is used to describe a group of miscellaneous publications including handbills, broadsides, folders, flyers, and brochures. The two characteristics that define this category are that they are all printed and that they are all noncommissionable media. In other words, they are used in advertising as support media and the client is billed for their production costs.

Brochures may be utilized in a variety of ways. Product literature is the primary use. If you intend to make a major purchase, such as a car or a personal computer, you will probably visit stores and dealers and pick up literature on the various lines. This material is used as part of the deliberation and comparison process.

Materials may also be prepared as part of a special campaign or sales promotion. For example, if you are introducing a new product, then you may want a point-of-sale brochure near the product that explains how it works or how it is used. Special promotions may include flyers on contests or premium offers. Direct mail letters often include folders that explain the product, service, or cause in more detail.

Special brochures may also be used in trade advertising campaigns with inside tips or sales suggestions for dealers or retailers. Extremely fancy and costly publications are produced as part of the public relations effort for an institution. These may be corporate story pieces or annual reports.

Types of formats.   There is a wide range of publication formats available in this category. The simplest is probably a *handbill.* It is usually small and often only printed on one side. A *folder* is a single sheet of paper that has been folded in half or in thirds. It is designed to be mailed so it will usually fit in a standard envelope such as a Number 10. Handbills and small folders are also called *flyers.* A *broadside* is a folder that unfolds to be a large sheet of paper and is read either as a poster or as a newspaper page.

Brochure is a general term used to describe more involved pieces that usually have multiple pages assembled and bound as well as folded. A *booklet* is a small brochure, usually less than 8 1/2 by 11, with from 8 to 48 pages. A *book* is a bigger publication, both in size and/or number of pages. A magazine or annual report, for example, may be described as a "book," as well as the hardbound and softbound books you are more familiar with.

Pieces of publications.   There are some other common terms we might want to clarify. A *sheet* of paper is the entire piece of paper, both front and back. A broadside, for example, is one sheet, regardless of how many times it might be folded. Folders are described as having *panels,* rather than pages. A piece of paper folded in the middle will create a four-panel folder; folded in thirds, it will be a six-panel folder.

A booklet, on the other hand, may be made up of four sheets folded together and stapled. The word *page,* is used to refer to one side of a sheet of paper that has been assembled into a brochure, booklet, or book. To create pages in a book, a sheet of paper is folded in half and then in half again, then stapled in the middle and trimmed on the edges. These two folds would give you an eight-page "signature"—four pages on each side of the sheet. Try it and see. Take any piece of blank paper and fold it in half, then fold it again opposite the original fold. You will have created a signature of eight total pages. Staple it in the middle and cut the fold and you will have an eight-page booklet.

Likewise, three folds equals a 16-page signature, four folds equals 32 pages, and five folds equals 64 pages. Obviously, to get 64 total pages, you would be working with a huge sheet of paper. Most long-run magazines are, in fact, printed in 32- or 64-page signatures.

Design Process

The word "dummy" is used a lot in the design of brochures. The "dummying process" is a phrase used to describe how the publication is designed in terms of folding and assembling. The word *dummy* also refers to a particular piece constructed at one step in the process as a mockup of how the final piece will look.

The reason the dummying process is important is that brochures of all types are complicated pieces to design and present. The message is affected by physical decisions relating to size, folding patterns, and binding techniques. The format itself is a message factor, and the design of the format is as important as writing the copy or preparing the art.

The first decision in dummying involves the major decisions on format, size, and folding. Do you want a handbill, broadside, or booklet? You can see the tremendous range in formats available to you. Then what size will the final piece need to be? Will it be mailed? Does it need to go in an envelope? Will it be placed in a pocket as part of a display? Finally, what kind of folding pattern is appropriate and how will it be assembled?

Reading patterns. If you are designing a book or a booklet, then the reading pattern is fairly simple, just page by page. If you are designing a handbill, then it's a question of one side or two, and if it is two-sided then how do you get them to turn it over? But if you are working with a folder or broadside or a brochure that uses folds, then the reading pattern can become complicated. The objective in brochure design is to control that reading pattern and make sure it is obvious from your design where the reader is to go next.

To demonstrate the problem, take another piece of blank paper and fold it in thirds. (You have to do this physically or you won't understand the point.) Now you have created a simple six-panel folder. The side facing you is the cover—*but* either side can be the cover. Do you want it to open from the right or the left? Or are you using it horizontally? Let's assume you follow normal reading patterns and open the folder on the right (fold on left).

Now, which panel is read next as you open it up? The panel on the left or the panel on the right? You would probably assume that the normal reading pattern is to start on the left and read to the right. However, with folders, that panel on the right is the first one you see as you open the folder and it will get first attention. Furthermore, if you read from left to right on the inside three panels, how will you ever get back to this flap?

There is nothing easy about planning the reading pattern in folder design, and it only gets more complicated as you add more folds. The message design has to convey reading cues if you want any folder to make sense as it is unfolded.

Production Process

Thumbnails. The first step in designing a brochure is to fold up little pieces of paper and create a number of roughs. You can go through a pad of scratch paper during this early design stage when you are working through alternative formats. This is the stage when you decide the folding pattern, reading pattern, and location of the basic message elements.

Dummies. As these critical physical decisions are made, then you will move to a semicomp dummy. This is a dummy to size of the actual brochure that is produced using semicomp techniques. The art is sketched in place, the display type is lettered, and the body copy is ruled in. Semicomp dummies are used for approvals and for making the final specifications for typesetting and art sizing.

If the approval process is more formal and elaborate, then you may move to a full comp. Here the art is done as finished as possible, the display type is set, and the body copy is "Greeked." "Greeking" body copy means you use letterforms that look the same size and weight as the type you will be using. It is available as "nonsense" type from various transfer letter companies. It looks *like* the type you want to use, and yet you have not gone to the expense of typesetting. This is particularly important if the copy is still being approved.

A *pasteup dummy* is used when you will not be doing the actual pasteup for production. This dummy is made by pasting in place a copy of the type you received in galleys for proofreading. This lets the printer or pasteup artist, called a "keyliner," know exactly where every piece of type goes.

Mechanical. Keylining is another name for the final step in the production process where the actual mechanical is prepared. A mechanical is a finished pasteup with every element perfectly positioned that is photographed for offset printing. The printing plates are made from the negatives. A mechanical is not a presentation piece and should not be shown to the client. It is strictly for production.

Production Specifications

Bids and estimates. You will need to draw up a formal set of specifications for your brochure in order to get estimates and bids and to guide the final printing process. Sometimes it is hard to get the specs ready at the estimate stage because some of the critical decisions haven't been made. That doesn't help printers any because they have to have answers to certain key factors before they can give you an estimate on the price.

An estimate is a rough guess of the cost. Most printers will eyeball a figure for you, but you have to remember that it is nonbinding. A bid is binding on both you and the printer. All of the specifications have to be nailed down and, if you change anything, then you pay the price for change orders. Likewise, if the costs are higher than the printer bid, then the printer has to absorb the difference.

Quantity. The most important element in writing up a set of specifications for a brochure is quantity. In some cases, this may be the hardest specification to determine because you may want to vary the quantity with the cost. In other words, you may want to print as many copies as the budget will let you. Unfortunately, that is exactly the opposite of how printers think. They start with quantity and all the other decisions vary around that factor.

The number one principle in printing is that the cost per unit decreases as the total quantity increases. In other words, the more you print the cheaper the cost is per unit. That's because most of the cost in printing is in the initial step—typesetting, negatives, and plates—and those costs are a lot if you are only printing 100 copies but they may be insignificant if you print 100,000.

If you have a hard time nailing down the estimated number at the time you are getting estimates, then guess. Your printer has to have something to start with, and there is a lot of difference in cost between 100 and 100,000. Eyeball a number to get it started. You can get an estimate based on 5,000 and then ask your printer to tell you what the cost will be if you increase the run to 10,000. That's easy to figure, and you can see the difference in cost per unit. Chances are the cost will not be double, even though the quantity did.

Size.   This is the second most important piece of information the printer needs. When you give size, it is normally the size of the finished piece. Let the printer figure what the sheet sizes might be that will arrive at that finished size.

You might remember, also, that paper comes in standardized sheet sizes. Your printer will figure how best to cut the sheet so it can be folded and trimmed down to the size you need. In some cases, you may have created a format that is extremely expensive just because there is no way to cut it out of the sheet efficiently. In other words, there is a lot of waste. Ask your printer about that; it may be you can save yourself lots of money just by redesigning it to change one of the dimensions.

Colors.   As discussed in the explanation of color, one color printing means that there is only one color of ink printed, whether it be black, blue, brown, or some other color. A two-color job usually means you have black plus one spot color. Two colors, however, can be any two colors you might want to use. Full color, of course, is process color or the four standard process inks: cyan, magenta, yellow, and black.

On the smaller presses used for short runs, each time a color is added, that means a separate run through the press. Obviously, the number of colors becomes a cost factor. On these presses, four-color printing may demand four passes through the press. The larger presses used for long runs can print four colors of ink at one time. For extremely high-quality printing, you may even specify six-color printing, and there are six-color presses capable of laying down that many inks at one time.

When a printer estimates costs, the choice of press is one of the factors, and that is determined by the quantity and the number of colors you specify. If you are running 100,000 copies and your job is being printed on a press capable of handling four colors at once, then there is no reason to design for one color. The cost of additional colors is insignificant. Ask your printer about that when you get the estimate.

Paper.   Another big factor in printing is paper. You will need to have some kind of paper in mind when you talk to your printer about estimates. Often an art director will specify a particular type of paper, knowing that the paper is a critical factor in the impression being created by the piece. If not, then you may want to ask to see the printer's books of paper samples. You may even see some other publication printed on a paper you like and take that in to your printer as a sample. They may not carry exactly the same paper, but there are often other brands that are close. You will need to specify texture, weight, and color.

Folding and binding.   We discussed folding patterns earlier in this chapter as an important part of the basic design decision. Obviously, it is important to the printer to know the format of the piece and how it folds or is assembled. The best way to make sure the printer understands what you want is to provide a dummy. This dummy should include the folding pattern as well as the layout of the pieces. One of the common mistakes in printing is to print one side of the sheet opposite the direction needed by the design. Then, after the piece is printed and folded, you find the inside is upside down. If you have provided the printer with a dummy, then this mistake is on the printer.

Special effects.   There are a number of techniques available to create special effects in publications. The *die cut* process is a way to cut unusual shapes. The tabs on file folders, for example, are cut using a die. Dies are thin, sharp pieces of metal. The paper is placed on the metal, pressure is applied, and the die cuts the shape out of the paper. That's how holes are cut in the covers of report forms.

The same technique is used for *embossing*. Embossing creates a raised design on the surface of the paper. *Debossing* creates an indention. In both cases a die is made, although this is usually produced through an engraving process. The die has a softer edge than the one used for cutting. The paper is placed over the die (or under, for debossing), pressure and heat are applied, and the paper is stretched and molded to take on the shape.

Foil stamping is a technique used to apply metallic leaf to designs. These thin sheets of metallic leaf may be silver, gold, or bronze. These leaves of metal are placed on the paper and then a die is applied with heat. The leaf transfers to the surface of the paper and bonds to it because of the heat.

Creative Considerations

It should be apparent from this discussion that much of the creative challenge in designing brochures lies in the understanding of production variables. While this discussion emphasizes production creativity, it is well to remember that all of the basic writing and design standards still apply. Messages have to be readable, type has to be legible, and art is still needed to attract attention, explain concepts, and establish mood.

All of the other message design factors are still important; however, the overall design process is complicated by the need to maintain concern for that critical factor of reading pattern. Brochures are more complicated to design—and more complicated to read. Don't lose sight of your reader in the complexity of the folds and special effects.

6.5 OUT-OF-HOME ADVERTISING

Outdoor

Outdoor advertising is the primary way to reach consumers out of home and on the road. Outdoor advertising goes back to the ancient Egyptians, and probably beyond that. It includes any form of posted notice. Billboards came into being in the late 1800s when companies started leasing wooden panels on which printed "bills" or notices could be posted. With the development of paved streets, highways, and interstates, the importance of outdoor advertising has increased.

The car is an important part of American life, and that has made the street and highway a convenient vehicle for commercial messages. Furthermore, people who travel are often looking for information about such necessities as gas stations, motels, and restaurants. Even if they are not actively searching, they may still be interested in advertising along the highways, because it may help break up the monotony of driving. In cities, outdoor advertising can also be used as signposts, giving travel information and location of certain services.

In addition to giving information about services, outdoor is also used for reminder advertising. It is particularly good for product or brand image advertising where there is a simple association to make.

Types of outdoor.   Throughout the cities and all along the highways, you will see homemade signs posted by people who own property, usually advertising their store. These are called "mavericks" and are uncontrolled and unstandardized.

Billboards prepared by recognized companies that are members of the Outdoor Advertising Association come in standardized sizes. The poster panel billboards, which use preprinted strips of posters, are identified by the number of "sheets" or strips needed to paper the board. There are three sizes for the preprinted posters:

> *24 sheet: 8'8" × 19'6"*
> *30 sheet: 9'7" × 21'7"*
> *Bleed: 10'5" × 22'8"*

The 30-sheet poster panel is the most common size. The dimensions given above are the image areas. The 30-sheet poster, for example, has an overall size of 12 feet by 25 feet. The difference allows for a border of white space around the image area. The bleed poster is bigger because it eliminates most of the border area. The 30-sheet poster has approximately 200 square feet of image area. The proportion is roughly 1:2¼.

Preprinted posters are used for national advertising where it makes sense to print thousands of copies. For local advertising, however, printing on this scale is too expensive for one or a few billboards. These boards are all painted by hand by skilled artists who work for the outdoor companies. The original is designed on a piece of layout paper and then projected onto larger sheets of paper the size of the boards. The projected image is transferred in outline form using "pounce patterns" onto the panels and then the artists fill in the color, shading, and lettering. (A "pounce pattern" is a perforated sheet through which the image is transferred onto the panel.)

The standard size of painted billboards is 14 feet by 48 feet. That's a proportion of 1:3½ and it looks extremely horizontal when you work with a painted billboard layout sheet. The overall image area is approximately 600 square feet.

Design Considerations

There are two characteristics of billboards that influence the way they are designed. First, they are seen by people who are moving. Second, they are seen at a distance. Some billboards may be located at intersections where traffic stops and there might be a little time to study the message, but generally they are on the street or highway and they are seen by people moving past in a hurry.

Few words. Whenever readers are moving, you know they don't have time to study a complicated message. They can only glance, they can't read. Therefore, most people who work in outdoor advertising advise to keep the copy short—very few words—only a short message that can be seen in a quick glance. These messages are designed to give a quick impression, not details. All copy is display. There really isn't such a thing as "body" copy on a billboard. The concepts have to be simple to understand at a glance—one single strong idea. There are no frills, no extra verbiage in outdoor copy. It has to get right to the heart of the message immediately.

Bold art. The art is usually super graphic and dramatic. It has to catch the attention of an audience that may not be deliberately looking for that particular message. Since people are reading the message at a glance, there needs to be a strong integration of art and copy—that is, they work together to create the message quickly. The layout needs to be simple, with a visual path that can be scanned at a glance. There's no time to go back up and start over again. The art, as well as the type, is executed in heroic proportions—huge, in other words. (See Exhibit 6–2.)

EXHIBIT 6–2: **The "Buschhhh" campaign tied the name of the product to the sound of a can of beer being opened, an ingenious use of audio imagery.** (Courtesy of Anheuser-Busch, Inc.)

You have to rethink your whole approach to size and scale when you design billboards. They are designed to be read at distances from 100 feet to 300 feet. The greater the distance, obviously, the smaller the message will appear to be. You can test your own response to this distance/size relationship. If you design a layout that is roughly 4 inches by 9 inches and view it from four feet away, you will have the same viewing relationship as looking at a 24-sheet poster at 300 feet. Art that may have looked big on the 4-by-9 layout, up close, shrinks to a postage stamp at 300 feet. That's why we talk about heroic art and type. (See Exhibit 6–3.)

Legible type. Legibility is absolutely critical for billboards. Use type that is big and bold. Sans serif faces are particularly legible for outdoor. Avoid delicate details and letters with extreme contrasts in thick and thin. Be careful of faces that are ultra light or ultra fat in weight. Heavy faces become blobs and fine strokes fade. Ornamental faces are often hard to read under the best of circumstances, but impossible at 55 mph. Use normal letterspacing. Close-set letters will blur together and wide-set letters will fall apart. Avoid all capitals. Your fast-moving audience needs all the help it can get to scan those words and the coastlines are essential in fast scanning.

EXHIBIT 6–3: The Gas Company's "55" billboard campaign used short headlines and interesting visuals to express the concept of turning down the thermostat. (Courtesy of the Institute of Outdoor Advertising)

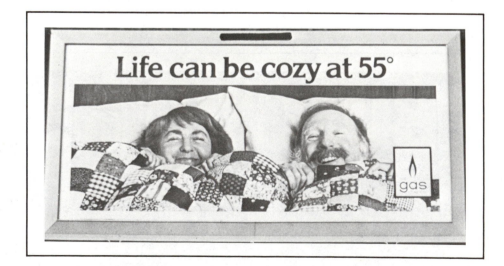

Color.   Color is important for its attention-getting power as well as for establishing associations. In using color combinations, think about the contrast you are creating. If you have type over color or colored art over a colored background, then maximize the contrast. Yellow and black provide the greatest contrast: white and yellow create the least contrast.

Innovations.   Outdoor is a very creative area, and there are a number of experiments going on in the industry. One interesting approach is to create a figure that extends beyond the conventional frame of the billboard. The Marlboro man, for example, extends above the frame on many of the Marlboro boards. Breaking the border is a technique used to create an attention-getting visual. It is unexpected. It also adds impact to the already heroic figure. The industry has standardized the sizes allowed for these extensions. You can go 5½ feet above the board and 2 feet to either side or below.

"Geometrics," a technique developed by Fred Farrari, creative director at Pacific Outdoor Advertising, creates the illusion of 3D. Even though the image is painted on a flat board, the use of perspective and shading creates the image of objects that appear to be three-dimensional. In some cases they appear to be moving toward you. Once again, this is a strong attention-getting device.

Revolving panels have been around for awhile. It is possible to create a board with panels that move and change. This is used in some cases to get multiple messages in the same space. It can also be used as an intriguing device to show change or growth with a figure in the illustration getting bigger or smaller or moving from one side to another. The Corvette board has motor driven extensions that show the trunk, hood and doors being opened. Motion in a message, particularly in a static form like billboards, is very hard to ignore. (See Exhibit 6–4.)

Panagraphic billboards are prepared on a translucent material that is lit from behind. This creates an image that is brighter and more intense. It looks like the projected image that you might see in a movie house.

Spectacolor is a company that specializes in computerized electronic display boards. The most famous one is located in Times Square in downtown Manhattan. These boards can flash color animation as well as logos and headlines.

Inflatables are a form of outdoor display. Winston has a 70-foot pack of cigarettes that floats over major events like golf tournaments. They can even be combined with more conventional billboards to create some eerie effects. Golden Lights cigarettes used a huge inflated hand that appeared to be taking a cigarette from a pack that was painted on a regular billboard.

The term *spectacular* is used to describe billboards that do everything. They have extensions, they may be designed in 3D, they have moving parts and sometimes electronic messages. They are custom designed and custom built for a particular advertiser and left up for a much longer time than the usual 30 days.

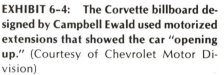

EXHIBIT 6–4:   The Corvette billboard designed by Campbell Ewald used motorized extensions that showed the car "opening up." (Courtesy of Chevrolet Motor Division)

Moving Billboards

External transit.   Moving billboards is a phrase used to describe a type of poster or billboard that is mounted on some vehicle. The *exterior* panels on buses and cabs could be considered moving billboards. You will also see poster panels on delivery trucks that can be rented for a commercial message. On buses you can usually rent space on the top and rear. Delivery trucks provide space on the side. In transit advertising, these exterior posters are sometimes called "dash cards."

Buses follow scheduled routes, usually on main thoroughfares. Their message can be targeted somewhat by buying a certain route. Taxis and delivery trucks travel randomly through the city and targeting, of course, is impossible.

These messages are designed to be seen by people on the outside—pedestrians and drivers of other vehicles. Like billboards, they are seen in a flash. There is no time to study the message unless the vehicle happens to be stopped at a stoplight. The idea has to be simple and clear and the copy has to be short and sweet.

Painted bus. An innovation in exterior transit advertising is the "painted bus." In some cities, the local bus company will let a company rent the message space on an entire bus—the exterior as well as the interior. This bus travels a regular route, and also can be used by the advertiser for appearance at and transportation to special events. Some transit companies will even let you paint the entire bus. Your message is not just limited to standard panels on the front, side, rear, and top of the bus. That's a real creative challenge to a designer.

Trucks. A new concept called "Truck 'n Display" has been developed by a Phoenix firm. This company has a fleet of independent truckers who will rent the side panels of their trucks for commercial messages. These messages can be planned according to the truckers' regular routes—east coast, west coast, cross country, and so on. They are seen by highway drivers as well as by residents in the cities they pass through.

Interior Transit

We've described the exterior transit signs under the heading of moving billboards. Now let's talk about the interior signs, or "car cards." In buses you can rent space in racks above people's heads and down the side of the doors. The space above is generally standardized at 11 inches by 28 inches, although you may see cards as long as 84 inches.

Interior transit is entirely different in concept and use from exterior. Car cards are viewed by a captive, and often bored, audience. They will read these messages as a relief from the tedium of the trip. The messages don't have to be short; they do have to be read at a distance, so legibility is important.

Car cards reach an unusual audience—people who aren't traveling in personal cars. They are usually the young (students riding to school), the elderly, and the poor. In major metropolitan areas, particularly those with subways like New York and Boston, the audience makeup may shift radically. These commuters are often white- and pink-collar workers, as well as executives—a much more upscale audience.

Posters

Almost any kind of posted notice can be called a poster, including several types of media that we have just described—such as transit advertising. The reason for a separate section here is to call your attention to the poster, itself, as an advertising medium—in all its various sizes and shapes.

Poster space can be rented at the point where you catch most forms of mass transit, such as bus stops and shelters, taxi stands and subway platforms. Posters also enliven the walls in bus depots, train stations, and airports. You'll even find them on rented space on trash cans and grocery carts. In addition to rented spaces, posters will also be seen on bulletin boards, kiosks, fences and walls, telephone poles, and even free-standing on their own stakes—campaign yardsigns are an example.

Poster design has always been a highly creative area of graphic design. In the late 1800s, some of the most exciting design of the century was being produced in poster form by people like Aubrey Beardsley, Will Bradley, Eugene Grasset, and Alfons Mucha. These posters advertised products like bicycles, chocolate, books, and special issues of magazines, as well as special events like expositions, theater and opera performances, and the follies. Even today there are poster design competitions, and well-designed posters are sold in galleries as well as in stores.

Posters can be short reminder messages like billboards, and they can be posted in high-traffic areas where people are passing by. These messages just give quick facts—short announcements and reminders. Posters also can present more involved messages and can be posted in places where people wait, like subway stations and bus stops. People at a bus stop are a captive audience and they will read, even study, anything while they wait. The type of design needs to consider the location.

Another characteristic of posters is the use of tearoffs. These are pads of coupons, recipes, or additional information. Readers can take one with them. Most often, the tearoffs stimulate some kind of further response.

Displays

Display advertising includes a variety of categories of media designed to get a message "on display" in some special kind of environment, such as a retail store or a trade show. Displays are not measured media, they are not standardized, and they are as different as creative inventiveness allows.

In a retail store, displays are either merchandise oriented or designed to support a special theme. The theme may be seasonal, like back-to-school, or it may be topical, like fix-up, clean-up. There are generally two categories of display media: product containers and signs.

PoP.   Point-of-purchase displays are the most common form of product displays. Typically, they are provided by the manufacturer to the retailer as a way of getting special treatment for the display and shelving of the manufacturer's product. Typically, they wind up in the back room or dumpster because most retail stores are filled to overcrowding with signs and displays. In order for the local merchant to agree to use point-of-purchase displays, they must be well constructed, easy to maintain, and attractive. In addition, retailers will be more willing to use a PoP if there is some kind of incentive such as a special price deal.

Point-of-purchase displays can be any size, shape, or design. Sometimes you will see "dump bins" where special merchandise is offered on sale. Another variation is the shelf basket, which is frequently used for paired merchandise; thus, a display of crackers might be attached to the cheese section of the cooler.

Display racks and free-standing posters will be found at checkout counters. End aisle displays are large free-standing constructions. Display islands can be set up in the middle of an aisle or open area and also are self contained.

Point-of-purchase displays are unique in that customers are confronted with the message in the store at a moment when they are in a buying mood. It's the last chance for the manufacturer to stimulate the sale.

PoP design is one of the most creative areas available to advertising designers. Companies that specialize in the design and construction of these displays may have a team of artists and sculptors to develop the concept. The sculptors are involved because PoP design is often three-dimensional.

The design involves constructions of cardboard, wood, metal, hardboards, wire, plexiglass, and even fabric. Often, they can be viewed from all sides, which complicates the presentation of the message. Ingenuity is the solution to PoP design problems. They may be designed with cubes and stacks and shelves, with parts that move, and prerecorded audio messages.

Most displays that hold merchandise also have panels for displaying a message. The message can be a simple brand reminder, or it can display product use information. Frequently point-of-purchase displays will include tear-offs with recipes, coupons, or tips for the consumer to take home.

Mobiles. Another type of point-of-purchase is the message that hangs from the ceiling. In most stores there is usually more available space overhead, plus the fact that the mobiles don't have the nuisance value of the free-standing point-of-purchase displays. Mobiles may be provided by manufacturers to hang above their merchandise as another form of point-of-purchase display.

Signs. In retail stores you will find a variety of different signs. As you walk into the store you will probably see window posters announcing special sales. The purpose of these posters is to attract customers into the store and increase store traffic. In many retail stores you will also see window displays, which contain arrangements of merchandise in an attractive setting.

You may confront window posters again if you are in a store that displays its merchandise in glass cabinets—for example, coolers and freezers in grocery stores.

As you walk into the store, you may see large banners overhead; they may even be outside on the face of the building. Banners are often used to provide thematic support for special sales events.

Shelf displays.   "Shelf talkers" are signs attached to the shelf where the merchandise is located. Often, these just give special price information, but they can also be used for thematic messages and merchandising tie-ins. They may be constructed with a simple fold that is tacked or taped to the top of the shelf. In some cases they may be mounted in metal frames. Sometimes they are elaborate forms that even contain prerecorded taped messages.

Packaging

The final impression is generated by the product's package. Some products sell extremely well because the package is eye-catching or particularly involving. Cereal manufacturers have known for years that a flag on the front of the box announcing some special promotion can be the number one incentive for purchasing that particular brand.

Technological change has had a major impact on the packaging industry, and packages are no longer limited to rectangular cardboard boxes. Packages can be clear, shrink-wrapped plastic that reveals the product. They can be made of plastic or styrofoam; they can be round or square or any shape you might want to design.

One of the most innovative packaging success stories is the amazingly successful L'Eggs hosiery package. The combination of the words "legs" and "eggs" stimulated the idea of a small egg-shaped container that protects the hosiery. The free-standing point-of-purchase display center is designed to display these egg-shaped packages and reinforces the egg shape in its design.

The appearance of the product on the shelf is a major factor in its purchase. For this reason, packaging has become part of the advertising design and the strategy of the brand's advertising is reflected in the design of the package.

NOTES

1. Hanley Norins, *The Compleat Copywriter* (New York: McGraw-Hill, 1966), p. 170.
2. "Ten Creative Opportunities in Newspaper Advertising," a slide presentation of the Newspaper Advertising Bureau.
3. Ibid.
4. Ibid.

Radio Advertising

Chapter Seven

Radio is an aural medium. It speaks to your ear and the way it speaks is entirely different from the communication patterns of other advertising media. Which do you think is the most powerful—the printed word or the spoken word? You probably said print since our culture is dominated by printed forms. Al Ries and Jack Trout, chairman and president of the New York–based ad agency, Trout and Ries, disagree. In an article in *Advertising Age,* they claim the "eye is driven by the ear."[1]

After all, spoken language is learned first. Reading and writing are secondary communication forms that only imitate visually what happens in speaking and listening. Most people, when they learn to read, or if they aren't good at reading, will still "mouth" their words. They are falling back on the system they learned first. The same thing happens with "inner speech." We are thinking through things when we talk to ourselves. It's a technique for organizing our thoughts.

Research by a University of Washington psychologist has found that in many ways the ear is superior to the eye. She describes research where you present a list of words both auditorily and visually. People will remember more words if they hear them rather than see them.[2] Furthermore, she found we can communicate faster with audio than with visual messages. We respond to light in 180 milliseconds, but we respond to sound in 140 milliseconds. That's 22 percent faster.

Not only is audio faster and more effective for memory, the images can be more complete. Images generated by audio suggestion will have more cross-sensory details than will visual messages. For example, you can use audio to create a picture in the mind. If I say "mountain" or "beach," you probably think of those words in terms of some image of a mountain or a beach. Unlike visual images, audio creates sensations easily in other sensory channels.

Association studies have found that certain words can generate feelings as well as sensations of smell, taste, touch, and related sounds. For example, you describe a new pair of shoes and mention the smell of leather and most people can respond with a sensation of smelling new leather, maybe even with the feeling in their feet of trying on a new pair of shoes. A picture of a pair of shoes will seldom generate those missing sensations.

Intimate.   Audio suggestion is much more powerful when presented by a live voice than by a printed word. Burt Manning, chairman and CEO at J. Walter Thompson in New York, describes the radio as a friend. He says that radio is "uniquely a communication to friends, to people with the same tastes, the same interests, the same language."[3]

He points out that 99 percent of the homes in the United States have radios and 77 percent have four or more while 95 percent of the cars have radios. We take radio with us everywhere—to the beach, to the bath, to the bedroom. And we listen to it one on one; it's like a conversation between friends.

In the old days of golden radio, the whole family would gather around and listen to radio programs. Now radio listening is strictly an individual activity, something you do alone. It's an intimate relationship just between you and the voice on the radio. The message is personal—someone is speaking directly to you. That's why there is such tremendous suggestive power to these audio messages.

Imaginative.   Dick and Bert, one of the most successful humorous radio advertising teams, described radio as "a theater of the imagination." We mentioned already the power of audio to stimulate multisensory responses, but the greatest power is to create visual images from past experience. That's why radio was so mesmerizing in the old days of "The Shadow" and "The Lone Ranger." It was a very personal type of drama.

The plays you create in your mind as a result of audio suggestion are more real than any print or video image can ever be. They are real because they use your own experience as a platform. Your memories, your experiences provide the settings and the characters. Radio is a listener participation medium. The audience is also the author. No other medium stimulates the imagination in the way radio does, involving the audience in the construction of the message.

As an example of the power of imagination to involve listeners, read the script below. It is from a classic radio spot developed by Stan Freberg for the Radio Advertising Bureau. Admittedly, reading is not as good as hearing, but as you read this try to imagine the produced version. Exercise your skill at audio imagery and actually hear the announcer's voice and the sound effects.

FREBERG:	*Okay people, now when I give the cue, I want the 700-foot mountain of whipped cream to roll into Lake Michigan, which has been drained and filled with hot chocolate. Then the Royal Canadian Air Force will fly overhead towing a ten-ton maraschino cherry which will be dropped into the whipped cream to the cheering of 25,000 extras.*
FREBERG:	*All right, cue the mountain.*
SFX:	*(Creaks, groans, prolonged splash)*
FREBERG:	*Cue the Air Force.*
SFX:	*(Propellers roar into and past mike; wing struts whine)*
FREBERG:	*Cue the maraschino cherry.*
SFX:	*(Screaming, whistling fall, and large plop)*
FREBERG:	*Okay, 25,000 cheering extras.*
SFX:	*(Prolonged and tumultuous ovation)*
FREBERG:	*Now — you want to try that on television?*
SPONSOR:	*Wel-l-l-l —*
FREBERG:	*You see, radio's a very special medium because it stretches the imagination.*
SPONSOR:	*Doesn't television stretch the imagination?*
FREBERG:	*Up to 21 inches — yes.**

Emotion.   The third characteristic of radio that sets it apart from other media is its emotional impact. Because it is intimate and because it uses personal participation and imagination, it has the power to stroke the emotions more effectively than any other medium.

We respond emotionally to the audio channel. When you are moved to tears in a movie, it is rarely because of some emotional image. More likely, you are responding to something that is being said and that is embellished by dramatic use of music and sound effects.[4] The look on a child's face may be "moving," but the tears come when the child speaks. It's the dialogue that tears at the heart. Words, music, and sound effects create mood and mood generates emotion.

In advertising, radio has been downplayed as a creative medium since the advent of television. Radio commercials are assigned to junior copywriters. The radio budget is the first thing to be cut when money is tight since, after all, it is just a support medium.

That kind of attitude is unfortunate because radio in many ways is more creative than television and can create a more powerful impact. There are a few executives in advertising like Burt Manning of J. Walter Thompson and Joel Raphaelson at Ogilvy and Mather who are sympathetic fans of radio. But in agencies, their numbers are few. The bias is for the big-buck medium, television, regardless of creative challenge—and effectiveness.

*Courtesy of the Radio Advertising Bureau.

In spite of the biases, there are some people in agencies who do dynamite work with radio. Copywriter Ginny Redington has a number of hits to her credit, including "Coke is it" and "You, you're the one" for McDonalds. Jim Hartzell at Campbell Ewald wrote that nostalgic classic, "Baseball, hotdogs, apple pie, and Chevrolet."

And the industry is alive with really talented people working in production houses. Chuck Blore is known for his work with K-Mart and AT&T. Steve Karmen is known for all the Budweiser commercials through the years, including "When you say Bud," as well as "Weekends were made for Michelob." "Sooner or later you'll own Generals," Hershey's "Great American chocolate bar," the long-time classic, "You can take Salem out of the country but . . .", and more recently the commercial that became a state song, "I love New York."

Moving away from the music men we find someone like Ken Nordine, who does some of the most creative work in the industry. He has created the phrase, "stare with your ears," to describe his experiments with concepts like interior speech and multilayering of sounds and thoughts. He is well known as a writer and producer, but he is probably best known as the voice on the Levi's commercials.

And then there's Barry Manilow. Who knows where he would be now without his initial work for Kentucky Fried Chicken, State Farm, Dr. Pepper, Pepsi, and McDonald's? You owe such memorable lines as "It's not a cola; it's not a root beer." "It's the Pepsi generation coming through," and "You deserve a break today" to Mr. Manilow.

The Audience

Programming.   A primary characteristic of radio is the configuration of the audience. Radio is a special interest medium rather than a mass medium. It practices something called "narrowcasting" rather than broadcasting. That means various stations reach different types of audience groups, based upon what type of programming interests them. The chart below illustrates the variety of interests served by radio programming:[5]

> *Nonmusic:*
> Religion
> All news
> Talk
> Ethnic and foreign language
> *Predominantly Music:*
> Beautiful music
> Middle of the road
> Rock/Top 40
> Album-oriented rock
> Adult contemporary/soft rock

Country
Big band/nostalgia
Classical
Jazz
Black urban

The typical audience for any of the formats above is clearly definable in terms of demographic and lifestyle characteristics. There is a major difference between people who listen to album rock and those who listen to middle of the road or country.

The fragmented, or rather pinpointed, audience makes it much easier to talk the language of your listeners. Furthermore, you only speak to those you want to talk to. The communication can be more personal, more oriented to their interests, more direct.

Preoccupied. The other characteristic of radio listeners is that they tend to be doing other things while they listen to radio. Maybe they are driving, watching for other traffic and road signs, while they listen. They may be at home working in the shop or the kitchen or studying in their bedrooms. Some people listen to radio while they jog or ski.

Radio functions as a background for our daily lives. We listen with half a mind, partially tuned in but not concentrating. When something catches our interest, then our attention becomes more focused on the message. We constantly move in and out of the attentive state. While radio is turned on and tuned in continuously, attention isn't.

Audio Tools

Music. Because of the peculiar nature of the medium, radio advertising is heavily dependent on the use of music. You will notice in the list of formats that most of them are music oriented. Primarily, we listen to radio for music. Advertising that takes advantage of this special characteristic of the medium will be more appreciated.

You have two basic options with music. You can either write a jingle, which is a music-dominated commercial, or you can write a word-dominated commercial where music is used as a background. This may include the use of a jingle as a distinctive thematic statement that opens and closes the messages. In some cases you may use a straight announcer with no music, but those commercials are rare and demand a legitimate news announcement message. The human voice on radio without music sounds naked.

A "donut" is a particular type of commercial form that opens with standard music; the music then fades and an announcement is dropped in, then the music is up at the end to close. The music is often prerecorded and the local station announcer will drop in the message depending upon current sales and events.

Music has other special benefits for advertising. Words that are written to a hummable melody are more memorable. You can get more repetition in a message when it is sung than when it is spoken. That also aids retention. Jingles are ideal for reminder advertising because of this memorability feature. A catchy tune will stay in the memory longer than a catchy phrase.

Music also creates mood. Listen to the arrangements on radio commercials and you will hear a range of emotions: upbeat, dramatic, weary, nostalgic, happy, soft and low, driving and incessant, to name a few. Music speaks directly to the emotions and in most commercials it is used in the beginning to announce the emotional tone of the spot.

Similar to mood, music can also anchor a setting. The sounds of various instruments cue locations and events. Soft violin music, a calliope, a twangy guitar, an organ—they all speak to images in the mind's eye.

Music can also be used as a form of audio highlighting. In movies, the dramatic moments are always underscored with changes and crescendos in music. Tension builds as speed picks up. Crisis is announced with frenzied arrangements. Quiet, melodious music signifies relief after a problem is resolved. The music speaks its own language and cues a story.

Voices.   Music is the number one characteristic of radio advertising because radio is a music-oriented medium. Voices, however, are still essential as message deliverers. You rarely hear an all-music ad—no words, not even lyrics. Voices carry the message content through the words of singers, announcers, narrators, interviewers, and people in conversations.

The tone and character of the voice is a critical design decision. Little children, old men, teenagers, movie stars, busy executives—they all have distinctive voice characteristics and patterns of speaking—gruff, soft, sexy, tough, sad. Voices are emotional, too. And they all create different mental images in the minds of the listeners.

When you cast a voice, it doesn't matter what the person looks like. The Valentino company records sound effects and production music. They tell a story of needing the sound of a crying baby. They struck out trying to tape real babies and real crying. Finally, they hired a middle-aged actress who executed the finest baby cry the Valentinos had ever heard.[6] The sound is everything; it doesn't matter what is the source.

An example of good voice-casting was reported in a newspaper feature on an early morning announcer for a Boston classical music station. The point is the station wants a voice that won't jar its listeners at that early time in the morning, a voice to wake up to. The announcer is known as "Robert J." and he is well known to his New England fans. Here is how the newspaper reporter described him: "His voice has been described as having the quality of warm fudge. It is indeed dark, warm and rich, and, depending on the taste of the hearer, evocative of fudge, or honeyed whisky, old dressing gowns and slippers, aromatic tobacco or a Persian cat."[7]

That's a well-written description of something as elusive as a voice. It's also a model that you might follow in casting voices for radio commercials. The human voice is varied and rich. There's so much personality that can be communicated in timbre and diction. Voices should be expressive; let them speak.

Little kids' voices have been found to be especially attention getting on radio. K-Mart has been highly successful advertising their photo department with their two "goof-proof" kids. (See Exhibit 7-1.)

Sound effects.   Sound effects (abbreviated SFX) are distinctive to radio. They are used on television, but the sound there is reinforced by a visual referent. In radio the sound effects have to tell their own story.

In fact, you can tell a story with nothing but sound effects. For example, picture this: loud voices arguing, door slams, feet running down the steps, screech of tires, thump. You don't need words to develop a little drama in your mind of someone running away from an emotional argument who isn't watching traffic and gets hit.

Here's a little test of your ability to fill in the blanks in the previous audio drama: Was it a man or a woman? Was he or she hit by a car, a truck, or some other vehicle? What make? What color? What was he or she wearing? What kind of building was he or she leaving? Who was he or she leaving? Why? Most of us add details to the story—maybe not all of the details and maybe not the same ones that our neighbors create. But our imaginations are terribly and compulsively inventive.

Sound effects are the cues we use to create our mental dramas. They signify things. We provide the links and the associations that create stories from these discrete sounds. It's pretty amazing how the whole process works, and yet it does work. Even storytellers use sound effects to stimulate the mental images in their listeners. They know intuitively that some experience-based images are extremely difficult to simulate with words.

Creative Considerations

Attention.   We've discussed the problem of people listening with only half a mind. What this means to you as a message designer is that you have to plan a message that pulls them out of their inattentive state and focuses their attention.

The first three seconds in a radio spot are critical. Chuck Blore, an award-winning radio commercial producer, calls his commercials "cluster busters." The phrase acknowledges the power of skillfully planned and produced commercials to break through the clutter and the disinterest basic to this medium.

You have about three seconds to create this audio "slap in the ear." Words can do it—some powerful phrase or interesting question that compels attention. The voice establishes that interpersonal link. Sound effects are particularly good grabbers. Music can be used either as a mood statement that sep-

EXHIBIT 7-1:   **The "Opposite Sex" script was created and produced for K-Mart by Chuck Blore and Don Richman, Inc. This spot was designed with an announcer "bed" that can be revised to feature various K-Mart camera department merchandise such as cameras, film, prints, and accessories.** (Copyright by Chuck Blore and Don Richman, Inc.)

RADIO copy by

ROSS ROY INC.
2751 EAST JEFFERSON AVENUE
DETROIT, MICHIGAN 48207
TELEPHONE 313-961-6900

CLIENT	K mart	*PROGRAM*	60 Seconds
PRODUCT	"The Opposite Sex" Photo Processing (Xmas Photo Card)	*STATION/NETWORK*	
JOB NO.	23454-2	*SCHEDULE*	KM-678-60
DATE TYPED		*PAGE NO.*	As Produced

DAVID: Okay ... this is gonna be a really good commercial. Are you ready?

JAMIE: Yes.

DAVID: Okay, when I say, "action," you say, "You get a "goof-proof" policy on picture processing at K mart."

JAMIE: I can't say all that. My mouth is too little.

DAVID: Well then, just say, "You only pay for the prints you like ... like those good shots of loved ones or ... members of the opposite sex."

JAMIE: Aw, Jeffrey, (LAUGHS) I can't say all that ... (FADES UNDER)

ANNCR: Show off your loved ones with Christmas photo greeting cards. Take your favorite photo to the K mart Camera Department and order personalized cards that carry a special message to family, friends, and to members of the opposite sex. The price is special, too ... just $6.96 for 25 cards with envelopes.

JAMIE: Jeffrey?

DAVID: What?

JAMIE: Are you the opposite sex ... or am I?

SUNG: (JAMIE & DAVID) K MART IS THE SAVING PLACE.

arates the commercial from the other music being played or as an attention-getting audio theme, as in a clarion call or stage announcement.

Identification. You don't have a visual to show and that can be a real problem for product identification. For that reason audio is used as a theme, a distinctive piece of music that is highly recognizable. Some spots will start and end with this theme as well as use it in the body of the spot. A short piece of music or sound effects that is repeated often is called a "hook." It's used deliberately to create memorability.

Product identification is a problem with radio. You have to introduce the product name as early as possible and then find ways to keep repeating it. A copywriter's rule-of-thumb suggests that five mentions is a minimum. That's the beauty of a jingle; you can repeat it over and over when you sing it. Make sure the pronunciation of the product name is clear; spell it if it is hard to understand. Avoid playing the product name over background music or sound effects that might overpower it.

Location is another aspect of identification that demands careful treatment. Addresses are impossible to remember when heard over radio. It's better to give a location peg such as "across the street from K-Mart" or "on the corner of 13th and Grand." Phone numbers are impossible over radio. If you have to give one, then repeat it several times and allow time during repetitions for your listener to search for a pencil. Remember that a phone number is of no use to someone driving a car so you are losing part of your audience right there.

Radio Commercial Formats

There are a number of standard approaches to radio commercials that you might consider. Jingles or music-oriented commercials make up a high proportion of what we hear on radio daily.

We've already mentioned a straight announcer. That format is used with news announcements. An announcer might also be used as a storyteller in a narrative format. Dialogue involves two people, either as an interview, panel, or participants in a little drama or "playlet."

Dramatic forms include the "slice-of-life," made famous by Procter & Gamble. The slice usually involves overhearing some conversation such as between a woman and her hairdresser, or an executive and a cab driver, and so on. These little dramas can represent mundane daily life, humorous situations, or highly exaggerated fantasies.

Humor seems to work very well over radio and Stan Freberg as well as such teams as Bob and Ray, Dick and Bert, and Stiller and Meara have proven that humor can sell. The problem with comedy is that it can overpower the message. The product has to be an integral part of the routine without becoming an object of derision. The other problem with comedy is that we don't all laugh at the same thing. Humorous presentations need to be tested on a wide variety of people to make sure the joke is touching on a universal theme.

Scripting

A script for radio contains all the auditory descriptions describing source and content of the message.

MUSIC	*(MELODRAMATIC MUSIC UP, THEN UNDER)*
PROF:	*Sometimes a script is written in paragraph form*
	(PAUSE) . . . but most professionals use a format with the source indicated down the left side of the sheet and the content on the right.
STUDENT:	*(SPOKEN REVERENTLY) And aren't scripts also typed double space?*
PROF:	*Right.*
ANNCR:	*And ALL CAPS is used to indicate instructions and descriptions, things that are not to be read. (STAGE WHISPER) Everything in lower case is to be read by someone—the announcer, the characters, the interviewees.*
STUDENT:	*The rule then is: If you don't want it to be read over the mike, then type it in all caps (DRUM ROLL BEHIND THE WORDS "ALL CAPS").*
SFX:	*(CHEERING EXTRAS)*
PROF:	*For music and sound effects the script should include some description of what the voice, sound effects, or music actually sound like (SPOKEN IN A LOUD VOICE THAT GETS QUIETER AS IF SPEAKER HAS FORGOTTEN WHAT HE IS TRYING TO SAY)*
ANNCR:	*Words in music are often indicated in a printed script by italic letters. In a typed manuscript you can underline the words.*
PROF:	*(INTERRUPTING) But underlining is also used to indicate words to emphasize.*

Timing.   Most radio commercials are recorded at certain standard lengths such as 10 seconds (a short ID), 30 seconds, or 60 seconds. When you write a script, you will usually write for a time period that is several seconds shorter than the air time. In other words, a script for a 30-second commercial should time out to 28 seconds; a 60-second spot will time out at 58 seconds. That gives a little time to get the spot on and off air. Radio time is very exact. Above all, you don't want the commercial to run over the allocated length of time. A little under is okay, but never let it go over.

Some scripts are set up with a word estimate down the left edge of the sheet. That gives you some idea how long the script will be in terms of word count. Word counts are only useful if you are writing straight announcer copy or if you allow space on the script for the music and sound effects. The guide below will give you some rough estimate of the length of your writing.

TIME	WORDS
10 sec	20–25
20 sec	40–45
30 sec	60–65
60 sec	120–25
90 sec	185–90
2 min	240–50

Words and sounds.   Listen to the sounds you use when you speak. Even though you are *writing* a script, words are used differently in spoken language than they are in written language. We speak in thoughts and those translate into incomplete sentences. In an English class you would be criticized for that, but it's perfectly okay in radio work. Elaborate sentences with complicated phrases and clauses are only found in written English, rarely in spoken.

Keep your sentences simple. Radio announcers also prefer short sentences but there is one thing to remember about short sentences: they get monotonous if they are stacked together. Vary the length and the construction so you don't set up a pattern of three- and four-word chunks.

Certain combinations of sounds are extremely difficult to pronounce or to understand over air. Some linguistic combinations sound the same even though we spell them differently—"white shoes" and "why choose," for example. With sound-alike phrases, the secret is to use them in a context that makes the meaning clear—and don't focus on that phrase for repetition.

The sibilants sound like hissing over the air, particularly when several of them are grouped together as in "so sensitive it's simply sensational." The stream of s sounds obliterates the other letters in between. It's not only uncomfortable to listen to, it's hard to understand.

The aspirants are sounds created by the expelling of air and they are equally discomforting to listen to when used in a group. The puff sounds like *p* and the barking sounds like *ack* and *ark* are troublesome. The puffs and popping sounds of a phrase like "people pleasing pleasure" are amplified through a mike as are the barks in "back behind the barracks." In print, you would never know there is a problem with such phrasing.

Tongue-twisters are another problem. These are created by repetition of sounds complicated by combinations of sounds that move the tongue up and down or back and forward rapidly. A phrase like "sensitive, sensory experience" will leave an announcer frowning.

How can you know if you have written an unreadable piece of copy? Obviously, the answer is to read it aloud—over and over. Another way is not to *write* the copy in the first place. If you are developing a lot of radio copy, you might find your work improves if you "write" it into a tape recorder. In other words, work out the copy verbally and use a tape recorder rather than a type-writer. Automatically, your copy will be in the form of spoken language and you won't have that artificial problem created by written forms.

Terminology.   Radio production has its own set of terms used to communicate within the industry. If you are writing scripts, you need some familiarity with these production terms.

> *Fade in/fade out:* Fade in is a gradual increase in sound level starting at no sound. Fade out means sounds are gradually reduced until nothing can be heard. Fade in and fade out are used at the beginning and end of most commercials and sometimes in the middle to indicate a passage of time.
>
> *On/off mike:* Sounds and voices that are on mike are spoken directly into the microphone. Sounds that are off mike are spoken at a distance from the mike. They sound off in the distance.
>
> *Segue:* Pronounced "segway," this term is used to indicate a gentle transition from one sound or piece of music to another.
>
> *Cut:* An abrupt and instantaneous change from one piece of music to another.
>
> *Crossfade:* One sound gradually fades into another with the two mixed for a short time in the middle of the fade.
>
> *Up, down, and under:* Used for background music to indicate change in level of music. Up means it gets louder, down means it gets softer, and under means it continues as a soft background.
>
> *Stinger:* A distinctive sound used as an audio punctuation point like the twang of an out-of-tune guitar to indicate indigestion.
>
> *Tag:* An audio logo that is played at the end of a commercial. Sometimes it might be an audio theme, or perhaps just a reminder line "tagged on" the end.

Production.   Radio commercials start on paper as a script. Then they are produced in a rough form as demo, concept, or "scratch" tapes. These are simple versions of the commercial, using maybe just a piano or guitar and one voice. It's the equivalent of a "rough comp" in the layout stage. Enough of the concept is there for the listener to get an idea what the final will sound like, but none of the expenses of the final production have been incurred. Skilled audio producers like Chuck Blore can do demo live, playing the piano and talking through the copy and music. It's quite a performance, and very persuasive.

Most commercials are recorded on 24 tracks, and that means the producer is able to very delicately mix and edit the various voices, instruments, and sound effects. If the soprano is too loud, then she can be toned down. If you don't like the sound of the synthesizer, eliminate it. Recording in the studio is a complicated engineering problem, but much of the real artistry shows up in the post-production editing of the tracks.

Tips

1. Watch out for vampire creativity. If you are too cute, then your listener may remember the spot, but forget the product.
2. Background should be background. Don't let it overpower the message. See Sid Bernstein's comments in his column in *Advertising Age* on this particular problem.[8]
3. Keep it simple. Focus on one idea and build it through repetition.
4. Repeat and repeat. Your audience can't go back and reread. If they tune in halfway through the message, give them another chance to get the point and identify the product.
5. Leave them humming. Steve Karmen, a well-known jingle writer, said it best: "People don't hum the announcer."
6. Don't get bogged down in details.
7. Break up long sections. A long involved sales pitch can lose your listener. Bring in music. Use a doughnut format, or some variation on it.

NOTES

1. Al Ries and Jack Trout, "The Eye vs. the Ear," *Advertising Age,* March 14, 1983, p. M–27.
2. Ibid.
3. Burt Manning, "Friendly Persuasion," *Advertising Age,* September 13, 1982, pp. M8–M9.
4. Sandra Moriarty, "Getting at the Gut with Appeals to Pathos," *Madison Avenue,* April 1983, pp. 26–30.
5. Gary Bond, "Formats for All Seasons, All Tastes," *Advertising Age,* June 7, 1982, pp. M6–M7.
6. N. R. Kleinfield, "The Valentinos Can Supply Sounds of Grunting Gorillas or an A-Bomb, *Wall Street Journal,* October 21, 1974.
7. Dudley Clendinen, "New Englanders Begin the Day Gently to the Music of Robert J.," *New York Times,* January 3, 1981.
8. Sid Bernstein, "We Can't Hear over the Noise," *Advertising Age,* March 5, 1979.

Television
Advertising

Television is a visual medium; however, it is also an audio-visual medium, which means that, with skillful use, you can have all the strengths of audio, plus the impact of visual communication. Good commercials are often written without words or just with words as a reinforcing tool. If a good television commercial is written for maximum visual impact, then it should make sense when you turn off the audio and just look at the video. The audio is a plus—it still gives you the persuasive power of the human voice, the mood of music, and the excitement of sound effects but, with television, these tools are used in support of the visual.

Television has a power because of its use of motion and dramatic imagery. A comparison of print and television advertisements was quoted in a *Journal of Advertising* article on visual imagery.[1] The study found that television commercials were able to produce more favorable product attitudes than comparable print ads. The authors explained that "TV commercials with their succession of visual elements, may provide more opportunities than print for engaging the consumer in product-related visual imagery which may enhance the product attributes."

The key visual. The secret to planning effective visual communication in television advertising is to think in terms of a "key visual." Harry McMahan, a long-term agency producer and developer of many techniques we use today, calls this "The Visual Plus." He describes it as a visual designed to stick in the mind as a memory cue.[2] This one dominant scene is the focus of the entire commercial. It summarizes the whole point of the message.

McDonald's instructs its agencies to plan television commercials around something the company calls the "magic moment."[3] It is a key visual but with an added ingredient. The "magic moment" in McDonald's commercials is the point that creates an emotional response. For example, in a spot titled "Mary Ryan" a young teen girl has a crush on a guy at school. She keeps running in to him in different places and gets flustered and embarrassed. Finally, when she and her friends are at McDonald's, this guy joins them and sits down next to her. That key "magic moment" happens, of course, at McDonald's.

To get the most impact for your money with television advertising, think in terms of these indelible images, the key visual that summarizes the heart of the message. In radio you leave them humming; in television you leave them humming and with a picture in their mind.

Television Tools

The raw pieces of a television commercial can be grouped under the two categories of audio and video. We have already described the use of voices, music, and sound effects in the section on radio advertising. Television uses exactly the same audio materials. The only difference is that these audio materials are used to support a visual rather than to create one. In that respect, television is more exact and makes less demands on the imagination of the viewer. On the other hand, it lacks that wonderful participation that you get when the audio message is jointly created by both the listener and the presenter.

Video.   The video advantage that you get with television that you don't get with any other advertising medium is *motion.* Motion gets attention; motion mesmerizes. The images are not static, as they are in newspapers and magazines. They can walk right off the screen. Television is an offspring of cinema, and that means all of the advantages of "movies" are also available to television.

Some of the other tools of video include *characters.* A television commercial is a very short drama, but within it the writer must develop personalities that are huggable or hateable. The product itself takes a role, becomes a character, and develops a personality. The character of Clara made the "Where's the Beef" commercial for Wendy's so memorable. Without her and her distinctive diction and appearance, the spot would never have been so successful. *Makeup* and *costumes,* are also tools used in the planning of characters. (See Exhibit 8–1.)

Most commercials happen somewhere—on a beach, at a party, in the shop. That means there either has to be a real *location* where the commercial is shot or a studio *set.* Some commercials use both. Like any movie, the setting is extremely important to the development of the message. So are the *props.* Along with the set or location comes *lighting,* which can change the appearance of any environment and make night look like day.

EXHIBIT 8-1. The "father–daughter" television commercial was created by N. W. Ayer for AT&T Long Lines. It is an example of the use of emotion in television advertising. (Courtesy of AT&T)

AT&T Long Lines

Title: "Father/Daughter"
Commercial No.: AXLL 1083
Length 30 Seconds

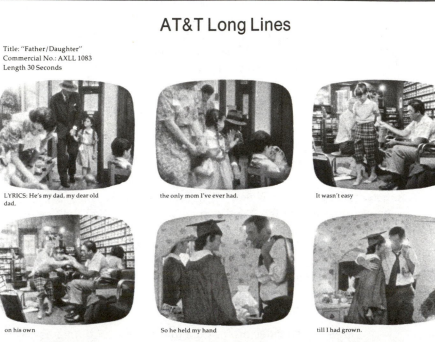

LYRICS: He's my dad, my dear old dad,

the only mom I've ever had.

It wasn't easy

on his own

So he held my hand

till I had grown.

My dear old dad,

I love him so. . .

DAD: I sure hope you're taking good care of my grandchildren.

GIRL: Don't worry, I had a very good teacher.

MUSIC & SINGING: Reach out, reach out

and touch someone.

Even though we're working with a broadcast medium, television still uses graphics. *Letters* on screen can be created electronically in a variety of type-faces using a character generator, or they can "crawl" across the bottom of the screen like a news bulletin. They may even be set in type on a posterboard and shot as a still.

Stills and *stock footage* are two other forms of raw materials used in making a television commercial. Stills would include photographs and artwork mounted on posterboards. Slides and 16mm film are shot through a "film chain." Stock footage is film or tape created for some other use that is being worked into the visual message. Shots of a rocket taking off, for example, are not taken by the agency specifically for a commercial. Instead, it can use stock footage of such scenes from NASA. News footage, obtained from a network or local TV station, is sometimes worked into a commercial.

Filming and Editing

All of these raw materials are assembled into some sort of visual image by recording them on either film or videotape. Film is considered to give better quality than videotape, although recent developments in videotape have made it almost as good as film, at least for advertising purposes. Both film and videotape are shot in color. Rarely will you see black-and-white film used commercially.

Videotape records sound and picture simultaneously on magnetic tape. It's just like an audio tape. You can make a recording and play it back and see what you have recorded. This immediate feedback is useful because you can change lighting, camera angles, action, and so on and then reshoot. Videotape offers a much shorter production and editing time—that makes it faster and cheaper. Videotaped commercials are produced more for local than national use.

Most of the videotape production is done in the 3/4-inch U-Matic format. Some television stations have moved to the 1/2-inch VHS format for their local news filming, but the industry standard still seems to be the 3/4-inch cassette for taping and duping. The 1/2-inch Beta format is rarely found in professional use. Recent developments in miniaturization, however, will probably make all these standards obsolete. As systems become lighter and more portable, the tape also is becoming smaller and better quality. Sony is doing to television production what the Walkman did to stereo sound.

Film is shot in three sizes: 70mm (2 inch), 35mm, and 16mm. You are familiar with 16mm film; that's what your elementary school teacher used to show you movies on rainy days. The 35mm format is larger and equivalent in size to the 35mm film used in 35mm cameras. The 70mm film is twice as large as 35mm film. The principle here is that the larger the film, the better the quality of the recorded image. Movies are produced in 70mm and then shot down to 35mm for commercial distribution. Most commercials are shot in 35mm, although cost-saving efforts are demanding that more and more spots be shot in 16mm. The distribution to local television stations may be either 16mm or a videotape duplicate.

With film, the sound is recorded separately from the picture. The voices, instruments, and sound effects are all recorded on separate tracks and mixed. The film is recorded separately, edited, and then combined with the sound track. It is a much more complicated, time-consuming, and expensive process than videotape.

Lengths.   Most television commercials are produced as 10-, 20-, 30-, or 60-second messages. The 10-second spot is used for a quick reminder. Its only objective is identification. The 60-second spot used to be common but, with the increase in costs, most commercials are now being produced as 30-second spots. Occasionally, a 20-second spot will be produced as a short form of a 30-second spot.

Longer commercials in the 2- and 3-minute range are also being created. They are run on advertiser sponsored programs such as the "Hallmark Hall of Fame" and the "GE Theatre." They are also being used on cable television. The new electronic communication systems with teleconferencing, computers, and satellites are making it possible to create these "infomercials" for home users to access directly.

Some advertisers will buy integrated time blocks where they can stack commercials for several of their products. For example, a packaged goods manufacturer might buy a 60-second block and run three 20-second spots in it. Another variation on this strategy of blocking ads is the "piggyback." Here two products are advertised in the same time frame. A cake mix commercial, for example, might include a short message for the company's icing mix. All of these media buying decisions affect the development of the creative message.

Scenes and shots.   All of the raw materials are recorded on film or videotape according to an organizational system. The underlying structure of television commercials—and movies—is scenes and shots. The shot is what is recorded as a piece of film passes through a camera for a short time. It is the point of view seen by the camera lens as a stand-in for the human eye. As another camera records the action from a different angle, then another shot is being created.

A scene is more complex. It is a series of actions usually occurring in one place. Several different cameras may record different views of various aspects of the action, but it is all built around this one event in this one location. A scene, then, is made up of one or several shots. Most scenes in commercials are four to six seconds long, although they may be shorter or longer to create a special effect. In rare cases, you may see a commercial that is all one shot with no breaks for different views or different scenes.

Editing.   Filming is only the beginning of the production process. In actuality, thousands of feet of film or videotape are shot for every 30-second commercial. That includes multiple angles of every piece of the action as well as different forms of action. When the filming is done, the actual commercial is created through a process called editing.

Individual shots are assembled to create a scene and then the scenes are assembled to create a story. The shots may be taken at different times in different locations in different parts of the world. But it all holds together as a coherent message because of the skill of the editor. The actual footage used is only a tiny part of what was shot. The rest winds up on the floor of the cutting room.

Film is projected at a standardized speed of 24 frames per second, although it can be shot faster or slower to create some special effect. That means a 30-second commercial will have approximately 720 frames. The editor is working with groups of these frames, which are defined as shots and scenes, and can cut them apart or join them anywhere between two frames. Editing, in that sense, is a tangible, physical activity.

But editing involves more than just physically joining two pieces of film. Suppose your script called for a scene of two people sitting at a restaurant having a conversation. They start off happy and end up angry. How does an editor effect the perception of that scene? One thing the editor could do is take the piece of film from the camera that was shooting front and center and use it as a straightforward record of the event.

Another technique would be to assemble various shots of this event to emphasize the essence of the action and its meaning. The editor might start with an "establishing" shot from a distance that shows the table, the people, and enough of the surroundings so that it is recognizable as a restaurant. Then a shot might be used that moves closer and tightly frames the two people on each side of the table. Next, the editor might use a shot of the speaker's face. What we've done here is to progressively focus the attention of the viewer tighter and tighter.

Now the editor might insert a reaction shot of the other person, showing what effect the speaker's words are having. Now back to the speaker who is making a point with his hands. That means the shot has to back off and show most of the upper body. Now another reaction shot, and this can be an extreme closeup that might even be able to catch a tear in the eye. For added dramatic impact, the next shot might be of the listener's hands nervously twisting a napkin. Then back to the speaker who has built up to the emotional climax of the scene. This could be an extreme closeup to focus attention on the anger in the eyes and the taut, thin lips.

The scene ends with a closing shot showing the entire table and both people, but now you can see the change in body positions as the speaker turns away from the table and the other person sits slumped over the table, shoulders bowed and head down.

The point of this scenario is that the editor uses the language of film to create and highlight meaning in the visual message. Skillful editing can make a scene far more powerful than a static shot may be. The editor is constantly asking: How can I show stress or anger or love? What details communicate the essence of those emotions, and how can I use filmic techniques to highlight those details? It's an art form.

Categories of Action

Commercials are shot using living action or some form of animation. On rare occasions, you might create one that is shot "live live." Most of the commercials you see on television are live action. That means you have real people, tangible settings, and real action. Even though the production is shot on film and edited to create the final version, we still describe this as a live action commercial.

In contrast, animation is fiction that has been drawn by an artist (or possibly a computer). The characters are cartoons. The action doesn't exist, you are only seeing the illusion of movement. A character is drawn on acetate, then a series of "cels" are drawn, each one depicting some slight change in arm, leg, or head position. More recently the drawing has been streamlined by the use of computerized images. Only the beginning and the end of the action is drawn and the computer fills in the points in between. That has eliminated much of the costly handwork involved in animation.

When the drawings pass in front of your eyes fast (16–24 frames a second), you think you see movement. Of course, that isn't so very different from live action film. Actually, those 24 frames that pass in a second all are stills. You just think you are seeing movement in "movies." That's because of an optical illusion called the "persistence of vision."

Some types of action cross over between live action and animation. You can shoot live action with kodalith film (an extremely high-constrast film that makes the images look like drawings), play with the color, and come up with something that looks like a drawing even though it started out as real action. A famous commercial for Levi's, called "the stranger," used that technique. (Posterization is discussed later in this chapter.)

Puppets, dolls, and models can be made to move using the same technique that the animators use. If you want the Pillsbury Doughboy to dance, then you shoot him one frame at a time and each time move his arms and legs a little. You have created the illusion of movement from a static object. (Freeze frame is discussed later in this chapter.)

"Live live" is a commercial that is shot live before an audience right on the air. There is no filming, no editing. When Ed McMahon does an Alpo commercial on the Johnny Carson show he is doing a live live-action commercial. If there are bloopers, they are generally unretractable. When Betty Furness couldn't get the refrigerator door open in the famous commercial from the early days of television, she was being filmed live. (On network broadcasts there is a short lag of from 15 to 30 seconds before the videotape is aired, so technically nothing is "live live.")

The Schlitz taste test that aired during the 1981 Super Bowl was produced live live.[4] It took an incredible amount of planning and coordination to bring off a commercial that showed an actual taste test between Schlitz and Michelob using 100 people randomly selected from New Orleans households. The point of doing the commercial live was to stress the believability of the test—no one could question if the results had been doctored. The results, incidentally, gave Schlitz 50 out of the 100 first preferences—which isn't bad for a challenge campaign.

Optical Commands

You need to understand the basics of film language in order to write a script for a television commercial. The terminology can be grouped into four categories: type of shot, camera commands, editing commands, and special effects. All four pieces of information are included in the script.

Distance and angle of shot. This information is needed by the camera operator and the director so that they will know how to set up the shot. It indicates the composition of the visual image. The following are common terms.

Medium shot (MS): The subject fills the screen, but not tightly. You can still see context.

Long shot (LS): A shot used to show the entire setting—all the context. A variation is a *medium long shot* (MLS) or an *extreme long shot* (ELS).

Wide shot (WS): Like a long shot, this shot is used to show the entire setting, but here the emphasis is on the panorama, the wide angle view.

Close up (CU): A shot that comes in close on the subject. It might just show the face or hands. The subject fills the screen. A variation is a *medium close up* (MCU).

Extreme close up (XCU or ECU): This shot is so close it only shows part of the subject, for example—tight on the face, you can't see the rest of the head, or tight on the fingers and you can't see the rest of the hand.

Full shot (FS): This shot shows the full figure, head to toe. Variations on this shot are *shoulder shot* (shoulder and up), *waist shot, bust shot, chest shot, knee shot,* and *hip shot.*

Boom shot: This is a camera angle shot in the studio from above the set with the camera mounted on a boom.

Helicopter shot: A shot from above outdoors. Usually extremely high and shot from a helicopter.

Zero-degree angle: This shot is taken from the angle of the user, as if seen through his or her eyes.

Worm's-eye view: This is a view from a surface. For example, you might shoot a package on the table with the camera sitting right there on that level.

These shots are used to communicate different effects. In the discussion of editing, we introduced the idea that different angles and distances have different meanings. The long shot, for example, is often used as an establishing shot; it identifies the location and context for the action. A close up is dramatic and an ECU is very intense. Close ups are used a lot in advertising because most products are small. Don't be afraid to come in tight on them. A shot from above makes everything you are looking down on look inferior or small. A shot from below makes the figure you are shooting look monumental, larger than life.

The concepts of objective and subjective camera are a result of the angle of view and the distance of the shot. An objective shot is from the point of view of a neutral observer, while a subjective angle is from the viewpoint of a participant. If you use a shot of someone's hands typing on a typewriter and the hands look as if they are your own, that is a subjective camera angle. A "tracking shot" is a type of shot that puts the viewer in the position of someone following something—a trail, for example.

Camera commands.   These commands are also for the camera operator. They explain what action happens to the image as it is filmed. This is very important since television's basic advantage is motion. These commands control the presentation of motion.

> *Pan left or right:* The camera follows the action by swinging the camera head. The tripod or "dolly" (tripod with wheels) is stationary. The head of the camera swings to the left or right with the action.
>
> *Zoom in or out:* The camera follows the action in or out by adjusting the focal plane of the lens. The dolly doesn't move.
>
> *Truck left or right:* Camera follows the action by moving left or right with the action. The dolly itself moves and the head of the camera stays stationary. Camera is in parallel motion to the subject.
>
> *Dolly in or out:* The camera follows the action by moving with the dolly closer or farther back. The lens stays stationary while the whole camera moves.
>
> *Tilt up and down:* The head of the camera swings up toward the ceiling or down toward the floor. This may also be called a "dutched" camera angle.

These basic camera actions create different feelings in the viewer. When the camera stays steady and the action moves past, the pan gives the feeling that you, the observer, are standing still and watching. When the camera moves with the action, the truck or dolly motion makes you feel as if *you* are moving with the aciton.

For example, if you are filming a scene of some action on a motorboat, you can have the camera stay steady and the boat zips past. You have to swing your head to see anything; the pan creates that same kind of view. However, if you were in a second boat traveling alongside the boat with the action, then you would feel that motion and be able to study what was happening in the neighboring boat. They are two entirely different orientations to the observer's point of view—and they create much different effects.

Transitions.   In videotaping, much of the editing happens as the film is shot. A director is controlling the way the images are recorded from several different cameras and, in particular, specifies what kind of transition will be used to move from the image of one camera to the image of another. In film the same kind of transitions are needed, but they are produced as part of the editing process when the two pieces of film, representing shots, are edited together. Some of the common terms used to describe these transitions are as follows:

Cut: An instantaneous switch from one picture to another. It's like an eyeblink, and you hardly notice it because it is largely unobtrusive. Variations include a *match cut,* where the two images are matched in shape and size, and a *flash cut,* where a series of very rapid cuts are stacked together.

Fade in and out: The image begins to appear from a blank screen or it fades to a blank screen.

Dissolve: One image fades to black as a second picture comes up from black. The fades are superimposed so you get the impression one image is fading into another. A variation is a *match dissolve,* where the shapes of the two images are matched—for example, the company's round logo may dissolve into a spinning globe. Dissolves can be fast or slow. A *lap dissolve* is a slow dissolve where the overlap is held for a short time. *Ripple dissolve* creates a shimmering image as one picture replaces the other.

Superimposition: A super is a shot where two images are on the screen at the same time, one over another. It's created by holding a lap dissolve at the midpoint.

Wipe: Like a window shade, one image comes down over the other and replaces it. In addition to top to bottom, wipes can also be right to left, left to right, bottom to top, or corner to corner. Ornamental wipes, such as a diamond, box, circle, or spiral, are also available on most special effects generators. The *flip wipe* shows the new image flipping over and over as it moves toward or away from you. A *clock wipe* shows the image changing as the hand on a clock sweeps around the face.

Swish pan: This transition begins as a fast pan but in the middle the image is completely blurred, then becomes a pan again with a new second image.

Split screen: Two different images are displayed side by side on the screen. With a *quad screen* you can have four images, one in each corner.

These editing commands also create effects. A fade is usually used at the beginning and end of a commercial to separate the spot from what's happening on screen before and after. It's like putting rules around a newspaper ad. Fades are also used to indicate a passage of time or a flashback.

Dissolves give a dreamy feeling, particularly a lap dissolve, and they can also be used for flashbacks. A ripple dissolve is used for cueing before and after scenes, a type of a flashback. A swish pan is used to jump ahead in time. A clock wipe is another way to manipulate time. You will see it in recipes and instructions where the announcer says: "And now, five minutes later . . ." Split screens are often used for before-and-after scenes or product demonstrations.

A typical use of superimpositions is to add the name of the product on screen, either over some key visual or beneath the package. These titles can "pop up" or be "zoomed in" or "zoomed back." They can also "crawl" from left to right across the bottom of the screen.

Special effects.   There are a number of other optical effects available in television production. These either manipulate the image or the motion. Time, in particular, can be speeded up, slowed down, or jumbled. Since this is a highly innovative area, it's hard to keep up with the latest developments. It's also an area that is affected by fads and fashions. Some producer experiments with a new use of an optical effect, and next month a dozen other commercials are using that same technique.

Matting is a mainstay of both television and movie production. The *Star Wars* movies have made excellent use of matte shots to create the appearance of action happening in exotic locations. A matte shot is complicated to produce. It involves shooting both the object and the background in live film, but separately. A special film is then used to shoot the object against a blue background—the film is not sensitive to blue; that film becomes a mask used to combine the two previous images. Using double printing, the object is printed through the mask over the new background, eliminating the original background.

Another way to manipulate the background is to shoot the object against a *rear projection screen*. The background image can be still, like a slide of a mountain or castle, or it can be in motion. It saves shooting at impossible locations or building expensive sets.

Polarity reversal is a technique used to change the image from a positive to a negative form. *Posterization* involves making several exposures of the film, each shot at a different exposure. The long exposure gets all the details, the shorter exposures get fewer details. Then the images are combined and each exposure is assigned a different color or shade. It creates an arty effect from a photographic original.

The image can also be manipulated through lenses. A *fisheye* lens is used to create the appearance of an extreme wide-angle view. In other words, you appear to see the image wrapping around you (if rear projection) or wrapping around a globe in front of you (if front projection).

Soft focus is done by shooting slightly out of focus. *Defocusing* means the image is taken out of focus and then brought back in. *Filters* can be used on lenses to intensify different colors or to desaturate the colors creating overexposed or washed-out images. A *lens prism* creates multiple images from one subject. It can also be used to tilt or slant a horizon line as in a shot of a car turning a corner. A *canted shot* is where the camera itself is on an angle to create an image that is not horizontal.

There are a number of techniques used to manipulate time. *Reverse speed* means the frames run backward. There is something intrinsically funny about reverse motion, and it is used to create absurd, comic images.

Speeded-up motion is another technique that is used to get laughs. This is done by running the film master, shooting at less than 24 frames per second, or editing out every other frame. It gives the effect of old time movies.

Time lapse shoots the action with long periods of time between each frame. It speeds up the action so you can watch something that takes days or years to happen replayed in a short time frame. For example, you might use freeze frame to show a house being built or a caterpillar turning into a butterfly.

Pixilation creates the feeling that you are watching a series of stills. In fact, it may be created from either still or moving images. With movie film, it is achieved by skipping frames and then holding an individual frame longer than normal. It gives a jerky movement to the film.

Slow motion is half speed, and it is created by repeating frames, thus extending the motion. *Freeze frame* or *stop action* appears to have stopped the action in midair. The film may continue to run, but it is simply projecting the same image on successive frames.

Rotoscoping combines live action with animation. When Tony the Tiger appears to be talking to real kids, then you are watching a commercial that was created using rotoscoping. When the product appears to be spinning through the air toward you, the effect was probably created using rotoscoping and freeze frame action.

Hooper White, in his book *How to Produce an Effective TV Commercial,* points out that this is a very expensive technique.[5] In effect, it has to be produced twice: first the live action is shot and edited, then the graphic effects are added frame by frame.

Planning Process

Television ideas are hard to communicate while they are still in the "thinking stage." There are so many things to be covered—the images, the motion, the sound, the sets, colors, acting, and so on. It's very difficult to extract the essence of the idea you see in your mind and put it down on paper so it can be presented, reviewed, debated, and hopefully approved. There are three forms used for expressing the concept before moving to actual production: the key visual, the script, and the storyboard.

We've talked about the key visual before. It is the heart of the concept, the one image that best expresses the message. This is used in initial copytesting when you want to check the concept. It's also used as a planning device. If you have it sketched out, then keep it in front of you while you finish writing or designing the rest of the commercial. It will keep your work more tightly focused on the point of the message.

Script.   The script is an outline of all the critical pieces. It is divided in the middle, and the audio goes in the column on the left and the video goes in the column on the right. The relationship of your typed lines back and forth between the audio and video should give a rough idea of how these two dimensions interact. In other words, if the announcer is describing a product feature, then exactly opposite the lines would be the video instructions identifying how the product feature is to be shot. (See Exhibit 8-2.)

EXHIBIT 8-2.   A working script for a 30-second television commercial.

TV SCRIPT

Client _National Ecology Center_____   Writer _Peising, Grzelewski_____

Length ___:30_____   Title _"America the Beautiful"_____

Video	Audio
ROLL FILM. CRANE IN ON LITTLE GIRL AT WATER'S EDGE. SHE'S PLAYING WITH A PAPER SAILBOAT AND SINGING SOFTLY TO HERSELF..."OH BEAUTIFUL..."	MUSIC: SOFT GUITARS IN AND UNDER ON CUE. LITTLE GIRL: For amber waves of grain...
2. CUT TO CU OF GIRL'S HAND MOVING BOAT THROUGH WATER	2. GIRL: For purple mountain's majesty... above the fruited plain ...
3. TILT UP TO CU OF GIRL'S EYES-- EXPRESSION IS HAPPY	3. GIRL: LOUDER...America, America, God shed his grace on thee (SINGING FADES)
4. MATCH DISSOLVE TO CU OF GIRL'S EYES IN SAME POSITION BUT NOW SHE'S AN ADULT	4. WOMAN'S VOICE: and crown thy good with brotherhood....(LOUDER)
5. TILT DOWN TO CU OF SAILBOAT IN POLLUTED WATER	5. MUSIC COMPLETES LAST BARS OF SONG
6. ZOOM OUT TO LS OF WOMAN AND HER SON STOPPING OVER WATER'S EDGE. SUPER TITLE TO MATCH ANNCR'S CLOSING STATEMENT	6. MUSIC...UNDER AND OUT ANNCR: You can help. Call your local Ecology Center. We need you.

The audio part of the script gives all the audio information—voices, music, and sound effects. The lines to be read are typed in upper and lower case. The instructions and descriptions are typed in all capitals. Every critical detail should be described on the script, such as the type of voice or the type of music.

The video column gives the four categories of optical information: distance, camera action, transitions, and special effects. The distance cue plus the camera action or transition and the subject will be included in most video instructions. For example, you will write something like: "zoom back to a MS of anncr" or "cut to ECU of trembling hands." Use the abbreviations where possible. Script writing is a tight language and uses lots of code to communicate complex information fast.

The purpose of the script is to present the narrative and to describe all other significant aspects of the commercial. It should give you a clear idea of what the relationship is between audio and video, and also how the action tracks across time. What happens in the beginning, the middle, and the end? And how much time do different pieces of action occupy?

Storyboard.   The storyboard emphasizes the visual nature of television. It is a drawing of the key scenes or pieces of action. A storyboard will have a frame for the sketch of the image and under the frame will be a box for the accompanying audio. There is less emphasis in the storyboard on the descriptive elements that you find in the script. The critical role of the storyboard is to help those involved in the approval and production visualize what the creative people saw in their minds when they developed the concept. It should be clear from looking at the frame sketched in the storyboard exactly what the script means when it says "MS of package on table." (See Exhibit 8–3.)

One of the critical decisions in storyboarding is how many frames you need to sketch. If the commercial is a stand-up announcer, then you may need only two or three—the opening shot, the middle with its elaboration of the sales message, and the closing shot. If the commercial, on the other hand, is a fast-paced, flash-cut sequence, then you may need 12 to 15 frames to depict how the action develops.

Generally, the rule for deciding on frames is to use a frame for every scene. If there are six major scenes in the commercial, then there need to be at least six frames in the storyboard. The thing to remember with storyboard frames is that all they do is freeze a sequence of moving action. And a scene is composed of many shots. For example, your script may say "zoom to CU of product in anncr's hands." Does your frame show the beginning, middle, or end of that shot? Is that shot the important one to define the major action of the scene?

Think back on our previous discussion of the "key visual." There should be one visual that comes to mind when the commercial is over. Obviously, that should be one of the frames used in the storyboard. But you can also think in terms of every scene having a key visual—and it will usually be the end of the action, the point of resolution. Those key visuals are what you build your storyboard around. Another consideration is the length of the scene. If it's an

EXHIBIT 8-3. A sample storyboard illustrating the planning of a television message.

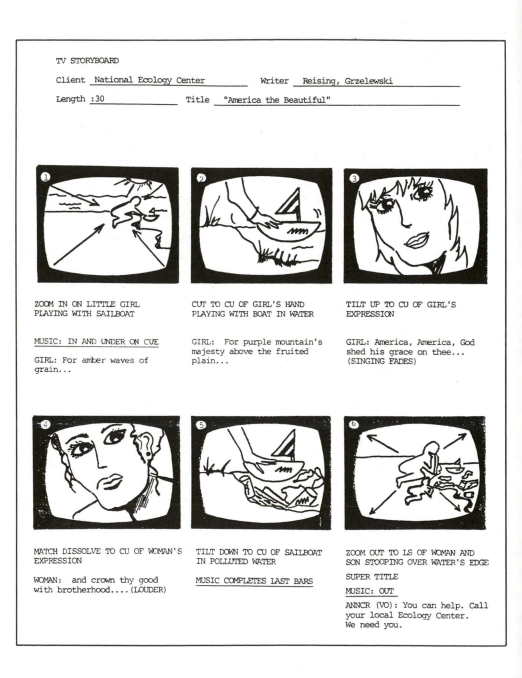

TV STORYBOARD

Client National Ecology Center   Writer   Reising, Grzelewski

Length :30   Title   "America the Beautiful"

ZOOM IN ON LITTLE GIRL
PLAYING WITH SAILBOAT

MUSIC: IN AND UNDER ON CUE

GIRL: For amber waves of
grain...

CUT TO CU OF GIRL'S HAND
PLAYING WITH BOAT IN WATER

GIRL: For purple mountain's
majesty above the fruited
plain...

TILT UP TO CU OF GIRL'S
EXPRESSION

GIRL: America, America, God
shed his grace on thee...
(SINGING FADES)

MATCH DISSOLVE TO CU OF WOMAN'S
EXPRESSION

WOMAN: and crown thy good
with brotherhood....(LOUDER)

TILT DOWN TO CU OF SAILBOAT
IN POLLUTED WATER

MUSIC COMPLETES LAST BARS

ZOOM OUT TO LS OF WOMAN AND
SON STOOPING OVER WATER'S EDGE

SUPER TITLE

MUSIC: OUT

ANNCR (VO): You can help. Call
your local Ecology Center.
We need you.

important scene and relatively long, you may want to use two frames to communicate what's happening.

How long should a storyboard be? Use only what is necessary to communicate the essence of the idea. Don't overstoryboard an idea. You want your instructions to be clear, but leave the producer some room. For example, if you have a clearly defined piece of action, but it can't be filmed in the amount of time allowed, then the producer is going to have to be able to adjust elsewhere. It's a delicate balance; you have to communicate what you want without hamstringing the producer. But do tell the producer what you want. There is wasted effort, time, and money in reshooting scenes simply because they weren't clearly described.

Generally, a 30-second commercial will have four to six scenes that average from four to six seconds apiece. Rarely will you see a 30-second commercial with eight or more frames. A 60-second commercial will have twice that number of scenes and usually no more than 15 frames. These are all rough estimates because the nature of the commercial determines the number of frames needed.

When you make a storyboard, you are usually working with a large horizontal piece of posterboard or newsprint. These sheets should be big enough for presentation to a group of people at a conference table. The frame is usually drawn in a proportion of 4:3 and with rounded corners to represent a TV screen.

A box the same width is ruled underneath the frame and a short version of the audio and video information from the script will be included there (distance, transitions, special effects, music, SFX, dialogue, supers, etc.). Normally, you will have three or four frames across and two rows of frames.

For presentation to a client or a review board, it is advisable to record the audio track on a tape. You may even want to shoot slides of the storyboard, so you can advance the slides in sync with the audio track.

For presentation in a plans book the same format is used, but scaled down to fit on a standard sheet of paper. Sometimes only three or four frames will be shown per page and two pages will be used to reproduce the series. A fold-out page is another way to solve the problem of paper size.

Production notes. In addition to the script and the storyboard, there is a third document developed called "production notes." The primary use of this document is during the bid stage to give the producers and technical suppliers a clear idea of what will be involved in producing the script. All of the details are spelled out—in detail. If you are using a house for the setting, then describe the house, describe the rooms, the decorations, the furniture—whatever is necessary to the feeling and mood.

There are certain categories of information that are included in a set of production notes. Some of these things are always included, while other pieces of information depend upon the special needs of the commercial.

- summary of strategy: target audience, message objective
- creative dimensions: mood, tone, action
- filming technique: live, animation, freeze frame, and so on
- product treatment: package, label, brand name
- casting: voices, parts of body, costumes, makeup
- location and sets: lighting, props
- music and sound effects
- special optical effects
- graphics: art, slides, stock footage, typography

Describe as many details as possible. Will you provide the music. Is it a jingle? Will it have to be composed? Can you use something from a music library? Then describe the kind of music. Describe the beat, the type of sound (rock, country, R&B), singers, instrumentation, and so on. Give every little clue you can. And do this for every category. The production notes may be a 15 to 20-page document by the time you are through.

There are a lot of decisions and a lot of details involved in making a commercial. It is better to think through all of this before you actually start into production, and make sure everyone involved understands the approach and agrees with the decisions. That's one of the roles of the production notes.

Another role is to nail down cost items. The bids are made on the basis of the production notes. If some little detail is forgotten, it may turn out to be a major cost item. Hooper White describes a commercial that was to be filmed in Jamaica. The entire crew was assembled on location, and then the producer found out that the white horse described in the script wasn't available on the island. It had to be air freighted from the States while the crew stood around and waited.[6] If the details are worked out ahead of time, then there will be less opportunity for these little surprises to pop up and break the budget.

Production Sequence

1. *Strategy sessions.* The first step is to get the advertiser, the account management people, and the creative people together to discuss the overall strategy of the commercial. Sometimes this involves two levels of meetings: first, the advertising manager meets with the agency account team, and then the account team meets with the creative people. Most creatives would appreciate being involved with the initial client meetings so they have a better picture of what the client wants.

2. *Creative sessions.* Whatever it takes to get the idea—background research, brainstorming sessions, demonstrations, comparative tests, product focus groups. Usually the creative team, which may involve a creative director, copywriter, art director, and agency producer (depending upon the size of the

agency and the talent it has available in house) will kick around a hundred approaches. Finally, a few possibles begin to surface.

3. *Informal critiques.* At this point, the ideas are still in a "rough" state. Scripts and storyboards are developed and they may be tried out on other staff members, the agency review board (if one exists), top management, the advertising manager, and anyone else who can provide feedback, including a focus group.

These may or may not be subjected to concept testing at this time, but some system is used to decide which one merits further development. Concept testing can be developed at this stage using a sketch of the key visual and a paragraph description of the action. It's rough but it does give you structured feedback on the concept independent of the execution. It can take anywhere from four to eight weeks for this initial idea development stage.

4. *Revisions and finalizing.* A final script and storyboard is developed for official review. This involves final signoff by the agency review board or top executive, legal approvals, and finally the client approvals. Approvals and revisions may add on another two weeks. For copytesting, slides or rough videotapes of the spot may be developed or a film may be made by shooting the frames from the storyboard and using the film with a rough tape.

5. *Production notes.* When the script and storyboard have been officially approved by everyone involved, the production notes are developed. Depending upon the complexity of the concept, the production notes may take from one to two weeks to develop.

6. *Bids.* The script, storyboard, and production notes are sent to producers, studios, production houses, talent agencies, and all supporting vendors. Sometimes particular producers, artists, or musicians are specified because they create distinctive effects. Usually, however, the contracts are awarded on the basis of low bids. Bids often take 10 days to two weeks.

7. *Preproduction arrangements.* Sets have to be built, actors auditioned, music composed, props located, and a thousand other details worked out. Some of this is done by the agency; some by the producer's studio. This can take two to six weeks, depending upon the complexity of the commercial.

8. *Preproduction meeting.* This is usually scheduled three to four days before the actual shoot. The creative people, along with the account management and the advertising manager, meet with the producer and key production staff. Every detail of the script is talked through, every action walked through, every arrangement verified. Of all the hundreds of meetings involved in the development of a commercial, this one is the most important.

9. *The shoot.* The actual production activities are in the hands of the producer, although agency and client are usually represented on the set. Shooting for a 30-second commercial may take from 1,000 to 4,000 feet of film—even though only 45 feet is needed. Sometimes extra footage is shot because the director is trying to get just the right piece of action. In other cases, extra footage

is shot so there are different angles to choose from in the editing process. The "shoot" may take one to two days or as long as a week. This is expensive time since it involves a large and expensive professional crew.

Action is rarely shot in sequence. Some scenes may be shot in the studio, while other bits of action might be shot on location. Also, the film is shot separate from the audio. The two don't come together until the last stages of the postproduction process.

10. *"Dailies" or "rushes."* Direct copies of the footage shot that day. They are available for viewing that evening. The director can decide if the film shot is what is needed or whether it needs to be reshot.

11. *The "rough cut."* The first step in the postproduction editing process. Here the scenes are edited together and the audio is assembled on a separate tape. For initial viewing they can be played simultaneously, even though they are still separate.

12. *The "work print" or "fine cut."* A version that is compiled after all the changes and revisions were made from the rough cut. All editing has been approved and the visual sequence is finalized; however, the special effects are not included yet. The shots are assembled into scenes and the scenes are edited together—the sequence has been assembled but the more complicated transitions are yet to be done.

13. *An "interlock."* Produced after the "work print" is approved. The opticals are added and the audio and video are synchronized together on one piece of sound film. Any changes made in the interlock are presented on a "corrected print."

14. *The "release print."* The final step, a duplicate transferred onto 16mm film or videotape for distribution to television stations. Depending upon the media buy, there may be hundreds of release prints produced.

This postproduction process may take three to four weeks. The entire commercial process will often take 16 to 18 weeks, and maybe as long as six months. It is a complicated, expensive, and time-consuming process.

Cost Considerations

Certain kinds of commercials cost bundles; other approaches are cheaper. If you do a song-and-dance spectacular with a cast of thousands and a complicated set, then you may spend as much as $150,000 on production alone. If you use an announcer in the studio or the product alone you might be able to get by as cheaply as $5,000 to $10,000. Hooper White says the average production cost for a commercial in the 1980s is now running around $65,000.[7] That's a lot of money.

You may think that budgets are strictly the responsibility of the accountants, but the cost factors are derived from the script and that puts the creative people in charge of the bottom line. It is possible to produce a script for $80,000 and a similar and equally effective version for half that amount—just by varying certain aspects of the specifications.

Here are some things to remember:

- It's usually cheaper to film in studio than on location.
- Exotic locations are particularly expensive, no matter how much you might like a trip to New Zealand.
- Sets can be expensive to build (depending upon their complexity).
- Simple locations are sometimes cheaper than sets—such as a real house in the same city (most producers have files on available locations, but you have to be flexible to use something that already exists).
- Every person that appears on camera earns residuals every time the commercial is shown. Do you really need six?
- The less you show of a person, the less you pay. Hands are cheaper than faces.
- Cheap music is available from music libraries and production houses. Do you really need to have original music composed, arranged, and performed?
- Do you need to shoot at night? That means overtime.
- Do you have to fly everyone from New York (or Detroit or Dayton)? Can you shoot here? Or hire them there?
- Can you gang up your productions? If this is one of a series, can you shoot scenes for successive commercials at the same time? You don't have to start over again from scratch each time.
- Do you really need the children? It varies from state to state, but often they have to be accompanied by a welfare worker and you have to allow them time to go to school.
- Do you need the dog? That means a trainer and often a representative from the humane society.
- 16mm and videotape are replacing 35mm. Will the difference in quality be fatal to your production?

The biggest budget buster is lack of planning, according to Hooper White in his *Advertising Age* column.[8] Insufficient time is allowed for every step of the production process and things have to be done in haste. Inevitably, there is waste when you are in a hurry. He points to the problems of insufficient time to work out the production notes and details of the bids. Reproduction planning is critical to the cost efficiency of the commercial.

Likewise, poor communication and explanation is another source of unexpected costs. Having to reshoot because it didn't come out as you wanted usually means that you did a poor job of communicating what you wanted. It's your problem, not the producer's. Production people can't read your mind.

NOTES

1. John R. Rossiter and Larry Percy, "Attitude Change Through Visual Imagery in Advertising," *Journal of Advertising,* 9:2 (1980), pp. 10–16.

2. Harry McMahan and Mack Kile, "In TV Spots, One Picture Worth 10,000 Words," *Advertising Age,* April 27, 1981, p. 50.

3. Marianne Paskowski, "Filmmakers Hear McDonald's Ad Recipes," *Adweek,* December 14, 1981, p. 9.

4. Hooper White, "Countdown to Airtime: How Schlitz Went Live," *Advertising Age,* April 20, 1981.

5. Hooper White, *How to Produce an Effective TV Commercial* (Chicago: Crain Books, 1981).

6. Hooper White, "How to Avoid Foulups Leading to Shopping for Bags and Nags," *Advertising Age,* February 12, 1979, pp. 58–61.

7. Hooper White, "Cheap or Inexpensive?", *Advertising Age,* August 23, 1982, p. M–26.

8. White, "Avoid Foulups."

Advertising Situations

Chapter Nine

We've talked about the basics of creative advertising in discussions of such topics as creative thinking, strategy, copywriting, and design. We also discussed the various media and the implications the medium has for the development of the message. Now we are going to look at various advertising situations and analyze them in terms of the implications for the development of your advertising message.

A number of situations are clearly identified in advertising as specialized areas needing specialized handling. *Retail* advertising is one such area and its opposite, *national* advertising with its emphasis on brand identity, also makes certain demands on the message. *Business-to-business* advertising is another specialized area, and one on which many creative people and agencies concentrate. *Direct* advertising is a huge business and, in some ways, is the most exact and successful of all areas of advertising. *Institutional* advertising deals with such topics as corporate image and public service advertising. *Promotion* includes publicity as well as the merchandising messages created for sales promotion programs.

All of these specialized areas are discussed in most introductory advertising textbooks. They are presented here with an attempt to focus on the creative needs of these areas. The environment in which the advertising is presented affects the development of the message, and this chapter will discuss the implications of the various advertising environments.

9.1 RETAIL ADVERTISING

Retail advertising is primarily local in orientation. Even if the advertising is prepared by a giant national chain, the ads will still be run in local media for an audience that is selected primarily on the basis of its proximity to a local outlet.

Types of stores.   The giants in retail advertising are the large national chains such as Sears, Montgomery Ward, Penney's, Safeway, and K-Mart. These chains include the big three categories of stores: department, discount, and grocery. In any community there will be both national and local stores in all three categories. They account for the greatest percentage of local retail advertising.

Other stores that advertise with frequency are drug stores, men's and women's wear, automotive, hardware, furniture, appliance, shoe, jewelry, music, stationery, florist, and liquor (depending upon state law). In addition to stores like these, retail advertising also includes services such as cleaners, banks, realtors, accountants, restaurants and bars, movies, barber shops, and hair stylists. Newer categories of services, such as doctors and lawyers, are also beginning to advertise under the pressure of consumerism.

In-house.   In many cases, retail advertising is handled in-house. Even the national chains have their own staff to produce the ads and buy the media. On the local level a large department store may have its own staff of copywriters and artists while a smaller store may operate with a staff of one, an advertising manager who does everything. In most retail stores, however, the owner is the advertising manager, and what professional help he or she gets comes as a service from the local media. In fact, most local ads are probably created more by ad sales reps than by officially designated creative types.

Why are agencies not involved? On the local level, most stores are not running enough advertising to justify the cost of using an ad agency—and the agency can't make enough money on the account to justify carrying it. On the national level, the chains are producing a heavy volume of ads at a very hectic pace. Agencies can't work fast enough to keep up with the daily ad diet of a national chain. It takes a specialized staff and production procedure to keep those high-volume advertisers in business.

Media.   Retail advertising is dominated by newspapers. Newspaper advertising is fast to produce, carries a tremendous amount of information, and is relatively inexpensive. It's the ideal medium for most retail marketing.

Direct mail is also used, both for merchandise news and store image advertising. Most major retailers prepare catalogues of their merchandise that are available in stores and mailed to their regular customers. They also mail "stuffers" to their credit card customers. These are image pieces or they announce a special sale or new line. Frequently, they give the regular customer advance information, which helps to build loyalty.

Television may be used—particularly by large retailers. Radio is used by large and small stores and is good for frequent announcements of special events, such as grand openings and major sales. The radio jingle is also useful as an image-building message. It reminds the audience of the store and its distinctive personality, which should be clear from the style of the music.

Television is also good for news announcements describing special promotions. If a store can afford to use television for general merchandise advertising, it is also an excellent medium for depicting the product line. You can show what it looks like in motion and in living color. You can demonstrate how it works and what its benefits are.

Retail advertising may also use outdoor and transit cards on occasion. These media are more enduring than newspaper or television advertising, so they are more appropriate for institutional or image advertising. A large department store, for example, may have an outdoor board on a major freeway or street leading to the store in the hopes of reaching customers who are on a shopping trip. Outdoor does not provide for a long involved message so the purpose is strictly reminder.

Merchandising support materials are also important, such as point-of-purchase displays, shelf talkers, store signs and banners, window posters, and shopping bags.

Objectives

Retail advertising operates directly on purchase behavior as its primary objective. It utilizes immediate action appeals such as price deals and special promotions.

Traffic.   Surprisingly, the number one objective of most retail advertising is to build traffic. Of course, many stores permit ordering by phone or by mail, but that is strictly a secondary objective. The goal is to get as many potential customers in the store as possible. They may come to look at the advertised merchandise, but while they are there they will also see unadvertised specials and products they had forgotten they needed, as well as items that just appeal to spur-of-the-moment purchasing. Retailers use advertising to *get them in the store.*

The strategy underlying this objective of building traffic is to develop reasons why the customer must hurry down to the store. This builds on the news and deadline orientation of local media. An ad may announce fashions for the upcoming season or holiday, using the seasonal peg to stimulate a shopping trip. Sales are the number one draw for most store advertising. A big sale with large markdowns will have a definite effect on store traffic. Special promotions can also draw a crowd. Stores will advertise drawings and free gifts to stimulate traffic.

Store image.   The second major objective of retail advertising is to develop the store's personality. This image advertising may be a general institutional ad describing some key distinctive feature such as selection or quality of the lines carried. It may promote a general product category rather than specific merchandise. But the purpose is to differentiate the store in the competitive marketplace.

This image advertising is not only a function of the special institutional ads. Every ad that runs speaks to the personality of the store. Stores such as Saks Fifth Avenue, Bloomingdale's, Nieman Marcus, Macy's, J. C. Penney's, and K-Mart all have personalities that have been carefully shaped over many years. Every ad looks like the store it represents; they all have a distinctive layout, use of art and type, and phrasing of copy. Even if the signature were covered, you can still recognize the store from the design of the ad. It doesn't matter if the ad contains barbeques or business suits, there is a continuity in the design in print that mirrors the personality of the store, and it continues in the broadcast advertising too.

Stores use news advertising and image advertising, not only to send different messages, but also to select different audiences. Research has found that most loyal customers are more interested in reading specific information about new merchandise available in the store while noncustomers, or people who shop in a different store, may be more interested in reading the image advertising. If the image statement appeals to them, then they might be tempted to investigate. Which type a store uses may depend as much upon the competitive strategy as it does on the merchandise available.

Selling Points

Quality.   Retailers have learned from years of doing business that there are certain pieces of information that consumers look for in retail advertising. Quality of the merchandise is very important because it is used as part of the sort and selection function. The quality of the merchandise determines the respect the store will carry in the consumer's mind. An exclusive women's store is considerably different than a department store.

Price.   Along with quality is price. Most consumers understand the price–quality tradeoff: the higher the quality, the higher the price and vice versa. Stores are positioned on a mental matrix that measures these two dimensions. For example, stores may be categorized as expensive but high quality, affordable, but good value, or low price and either quantity sales or dubious value. The goal of most consumers is to get the best value they can afford, so they use both dimensions.

Selection.   Another big issue with most consumers is selection. Modern consumers are accustomed to having a choice. They expect to be able to choose from large racks showing a variety of styles, fabrics, colors, and sizes. Given the choice between a store with a large selection and one with a small selection, most consumers will opt for the large selection. The exception is with exclusive stores and lines. Someone who is buying a designer dress still wants some choice, but the assumption is that the designer defines fashion for them and the consumer doesn't have to worry about that so selection isn't as important.

Services.   Service is another concern of consumers although probably not as important as quality, price, and selection. Service in the store is still important in most types of stores, although discount centers have eliminated this function as a cost-saving factor. For major purchases, the sales staff still plays an important role in the information gathering process. Since most stores carry a variety of brands, the salesperson is in a position to compare the advantages and disadvantages. While there may be some concern that the salesperson is trying to push the big-ticket item, many customers realize that the store wants to turn over its inventory and that it doesn't matter which brand sells as long as one of them does. For some stores, and particularly for services such as real estate and investment counseling, this consulting role is an extremely important feature to emphasize.

Service is also important in after marketing. If you buy a new car, you want to know that the dealer has a good repair department. For some people, that is a critical part of the decision process. It's a big part of the store's overall image and certainly deserves mention in institutional advertising.

Creative Considerations

Big art.   In designing print ads for retail advertising, the most important thing to remember is to play the art big. If you are selling merchandise, then the consumer wants to see it. Since this form of advertising functions as a respected shopping guide, you don't have to do anything cutesy to get the consumer's attention. The big decision is how best to depict the merchandise.

In retail advertising, the art dominates and the head and copy are supporting. The head should play up the news value. In other words, ask yourself. "What do I need to know or want to know about this product?" The headline points to this information of value. The body copy is for details. Explain the essential points that will affect decision making, such as durability, quality, construction, and style. Keep it factual. Be specific and avoid generalities.

Price.   In retail advertising the price demands special attention. Consumers expect to find the price cited in every merchandise ad. Not only that, there is a whole visual language built on the treatment of the price. If it is printed in a typeface that is the same weight and size as the body copy, then the assumption is that you are trying to downplay the price. In other words, the price is not a selling point—it's high or it hasn't been reduced.

If price is an important angle, then it needs to be bigger and bolder than the rest of the type—the bigger and bolder it is, the more it signals a major savings. With sale prices, you need to give both the regular or suggested retail price as well as the reduced price.

To emphasize further the savings angle, also spell out the amount of the savings, preferably in the headline or in a subhead. Be exact. Don't say just "big savings." Instead say, "save $5.00." Whenever you deal with value as a benefit, specify precisely what the value is. Nobody is impressed if you just use a generality like "good value" or "best values in town."

Pricing can also be employed to move the merchandise faster. Sale prices are a big draw, but multiple pricing is even stronger. For example, if an item is on sale for $3.50, you can put even more punch in the appeal by advertising three for $9.00. Pricing, of course, is a marketing decision, but the advertising needs to recognize the promotion being used and to highlight the strategy. If your store is offering a major price reduction, that information should go in the headline as well as be in bold figures for every item mentioned in the ad. Don't downplay the effect by putting the sale price in small type or by burying it in the body copy.

"Now" copy.   Another characteristic of retail advertising is its urgency. These ads exist in a fleeting environment. That's the nature of news. Given that environment, most retail ads use some kind of immediate call to action. This is direct action advertising, not indirect, like national. The end result of a successful retail ad is store traffic, and that means the ad should conclude with some effort to stimulate a shopping trip. Coupons, special promotions, and deadlines on sale prices are used to make the response as immediate as possible. Don't forget the call to action.

Layout.   The store image is signaled immediately by the style of the layout. If it is busy, crowded, and cramped with lots of items and big bold type, then it is probably a discount or drug store—the kind of store that can discount prices by moving lots of inventory. In contrast, an ad that uses a delicate illustration, oldstyle Roman type, and lots of white space is probably for a store that sells expensive, high-quality merchandise. The layout speaks a language of its own.

Identity.   Store identification is another important part of the creative effort. In retail advertising, it isn't enough just to promote merchandise, you also have to sell the store. It's not good if the audience remembers there is a big shoe sale but can't remember where.

Store identification, however, is not a selling premise. There is a tendency by people untrained in advertising to stick the name of the store up at the top of the ad and let it serve as a headline. That violates what we know about how people read ads. True, they do start at the top and read down, but there has to be something interesting at the top to get them started reading. A store name won't do. The store name can be interwoven with the design and appear in the middle of the layout, but the most common position is at the bottom—for good reasons.

Most stores have distinctive logos called signatures. Like your own signature, the design is intended to reflect your distinctive style. Like all signatures, it is expected to be found at the bottom of a piece of communication. It's your last chance at the end to impress them with the name of the source or sponsor. That's a very valuable position and a very effective strategy. Every retail ad message, whether print or broadcast, should end with the name of the store—even if it was used earlier in the message. In television it is a good idea to superimpose the store name or signature at the very end, so that you have a visual reference to reinforce the name people heard.

Reference information.   In addition to the name of the store, there are certain other critical pieces of information that are part of the ID package. Location is very important, and usually it is better to give a location cue as well as a specific address. For example, you may want to say: "On the corner of 13th across from Safeway." That way your audience can develop a mental picture of the location and file it that way. It's much easier to remember than an actual address.

Store hours are another critical piece of information. How many times have you found yourself on a Saturday morning wondering if a certain store was open yet—or if it is open at all on Sunday. If you want people to come shop at your store, give them all the information they need. You don't want to inadvertently turn away a customer at the door—and have the person go away disgusted.

Credit card acceptance is an important part of the close. Your ad may trigger someone to want to buy that piece of merchandise, but he or she may only be able to purchse it on some kind of credit. If you take the person's credit card, then you've made a sale. Say that in the ad.

And don't forget the phone number.

A Special Relationship

Product involvement.   People who work on the creative side of retail advertising have a special relationship with their products. Usually, the buyer will provide you with a sample. You can use it, feel it, try it on, and get to know the product intimately. The buyer will also provide you with the manufacturer's copy with specifications and photographs. You can walk into the store and watch customers evaluating the product and even talk to them about what they want and don't want.

Feedback.   Furthermore, you have immediate feedback on the success of your ad. You can go back into the store the day it runs and see if there is any increased traffic at the counter. Most retail copywriters have fantasies about milling throngs of people lined up at the counter, all of them holding the clipped-out ad. The moment of truth is usually less exciting as you stand there and wait for someone, anyone, to ask about the product you described in last night's ad.

But still you have the opportunity to see the actual results of your work and to notice the little increase of activity and the smile on the face of the buyer because the action at the counter is faster than normal.

9.2 NATIONAL ADVERTISING

When we speak of national advertising, we really are talking about two factors: geography and subject. First, the advertising is for a branded product and, second, it is advertised in a wider geographical area than a community, city, or even region. The definition only makes sense in comparison to the discussion of retail advertising, which was explained as advertising for a local store or service.

Key differences.   In national advertising the heart of the message is: *Buy our brand of product* (wherever you can find it). In retail advertising the message is: *Come to our store* (we carry all brands). There's a tremendous difference between the two types of advertising and the way they are handled creatively.

We've talked about all the different strategies used in retail advertising, but it can all be summarized as an emphasis on price and immediate action. In contrast, national advertising tends to emphasize image of the product or brand. The price may or may not be given. Most national advertising, particularly for consumer goods, tries to persuade consumers by creating favorable attitudes toward the product. That becomes the foundation for future action.

National advertising is more often indirect rather than direct. In retail advertising you can specify a direct response, "come to our store tomorrow for this special sale," but in national advertising all you can do is build a platform for long-term recognition and acceptance. True, in some cases you may provide a mechanism for immediate purchase, such as a coupon or 800 number, but that is infrequent in brand advertising. We will discuss that approach in more detail in the chapter on direct response advertising.

There also is a difference in the type of media used by the two different forms of advertising. While retail advertising tends to use local newspapers, radio, and television, national advertising relies primarily on network television and magazines. These magazines and programs are more selective than newspapers. In other words, the advertising message can be more tightly targeted toward an audience that matches your target audience for this product or service.

Another critical difference is the attitude of the audience. Consumers tend to use their local newspaper as a shopping guide, and research has shown that they are more inclined to look forward to the ads. They are interested in the ads. In national advertising, however, advertising is an intrusion. Few people pick up a magazine or turn on a television set to scan ads. While magazine ads are relatively easy to ignore if the subject is of no interest, television ads are intrusive and often irritating. Consequently, national advertising has to battle a heavy load of consumer indifference, if not downright resentment.

Branding. National product advertising has developed as it has because of a contemporary marketing phenomenon: products are unique because of the brand—rather than the attributes. Modern technology makes it possible to match the product design and manufacturing standards of almost any product. Therefore, a successful new product is soon followed by scores of imitators. The difference in quality and design may be minimal.

Frigidaire, Kleenex, and Xerox are all brand names of products that at one time totally dominated their categories. The consumer would ask for the product category by the brand name. That's the ultimate in "consumer demand." (see Exhibit 9-1).

Now there are many brands in most categories and, instead of consumer demand, the goal is "consumer acceptance." In general, with branded advertising, the marketing strategy is to get people to believe the brand you are advertising is as good or better than the brand they are using. In many ways, modern marketing strategy has switched to a strategy of brand acceptance rather than brand demand.

The problem of undifferentiated, or parity, products, with their lack of physical differences, is solved by creating a mental difference. The difference between brands, then, is not in the products, but in the minds of the buyers. The difference itself is a construct of the advertising message so the advertising strategy may be more important in the marketing of a product than some of the other marketing considerations.

A national brand for a parity product can fail because of manufacturing, distribution, and pricing problems, but it will rarely succeed because of these factors. Advertising, after all, is where the difference lies.

Objectives

National advertising has three basic objectives: identification, association, and recognition. A particular ad may focus on any one or all three.

Identification. The most important objective is identification of the brand as an entity, establishing the fact in the marketing environment that this brand exists. In order to define existence, the advertising message has to explain what it is and what it isn't. The creative objective, then, is to identify the product and the product category, as well as the brand.

Association. The second objective is association. Once the identification is in place, then there are secondary types of associations to be achieved. Since much national advertising is image building, the bundle of traits that make up that image have to be constructed in the audience's mind. That also is a function of association. If the product is seen as glamorous or exclusive or friendly or durable, then those associations have to be anchored in the message.

Recognition. This is the final objective of national advertising. Recognition is a function of learning, and this means that the audience will remember

EXHIBIT 9-1: **The Xerox ad is an example of corporate advertising that seeks to protect a registered trademark.** (Courtesy of Xerox Corp.)

Just a little reminder from Xerox.

XEROX

You may have heard a phrase like, "I Xeroxed my recipe for you" or "Please Xerox this for me." And they may seem harmless enough.

But they're not. Because they overlook the fact that Xerox is a registered trademark of Xerox Corporation. And trademarks should not be used as verbs.

As a brand name, Xerox should be used as an adjective followed by a word or phrase describing the particular product.

Like the Xerox 1075 Copier. The Xerox 640 Memorywriter. Or the Xerox 9700 Electronic Printing System.

Our brand name is very valuable to us. And to you, too. Because the proper use of our name is the best way to ensure you'll always get a Xerox product when you ask for one.

So, please remember that our trademark starts with an "X."

And ends with an "®."

the basics of the identification and associations created in the message. Most copy research tests recognition in the abstract; in other words, do readers or viewers remember having seen this ad? The real test of recognition, however, is in the store. At the point of decision and selection, do people remember having seen the ad? Do they recognize the product and remember the associations? Do they remember the product's advantages? (See Exhibit 9–2.)

Creative Implications

Anchor the brand.   The most important thing to remember in national advertising is to focus on identification of the brand. The audience has to recognize the brand name, be able to pronounce it, recognize the package and the label, and, if you are lucky, remember the associations created in the ad. It sounds simple; it isn't. Play the brand front and center.

The brand also must be developed as a distinctive personality or image in the market. David Ogilvy built the success of his agency on the idea that advertising's primary goal was to develop a strong brand image. He stated in his book, *Confessions of an Advertising Man,*[1] that "every advertisement should be thought of as a contribution to the complex symbol which is the brand name." Ogilvy defines image as a distinctive and consistent personality. He sees it as a long-term investment. He wrote "The manufacturer who dedicates his advertising to building the most sharply defined personality for his brand will get the largest share of the market at the highest profit."

The "personality" of the brand is a composite of attitudes that the consumers hold about the brand. These attitudes, or mental pictures, have accumulated from past personal experiences with the product, peer comments, and advertising messages. The image may be positive, neutral, or negative. It may represent the product as the advertiser would like to be represented, or it may be radically different from the image the advertiser would like to project.

Leo Burnett was a master of brand images. His agency developed such memorable symbols as the Jolly Green Giant, Tony the Tiger, the Marlboro Man, Morris the Cat, Charlie the Tuna, and dozens of other symbols. Carl Hixon, in his article on Leo Burnett in *Advertising Age,*[2] described Burnett's distinctive kind of advertising as "one that communicated by means of big, nonverbal archetypes." These are some of the most enduring images in advertising. Hixon described them as "ideas that would prove to be their owners' single most valuable property, worth far more than their plants and equipment." Image advertising transcends features and attributes and sells identification with a symbol—the Charlie woman, the Marlboro or Barclay man, or even a lovable tuna who is never quite good enough.

Stand out.   The second thing to remember, and this is what the creatives love to hear, is that the advertising has to stand out. If the only thing that differentiates the products is the advertising, then the advertising has to be different. It has to be more attention getting and more interesting than that of the competi-

EXHIBIT 9–2: **The Penney advertisement positions the Penney "fox" as an alternative to the more expensive "alligator." The ad was created by the J. C. Penney Advertising Department — Rose Baker, copywriter, and Toby Aurilia, art director.** (Courtesy of J. C. Penney)

tion. This isn't just being creative for the sake of creativity. The ad has to be different if the product isn't.

For better or for worse, advertising uses formulas. There are certain strategies that work well for cars and appliances and fashions and cosmetics. We know they work. Advertising managers tend to feel they have to follow the formula in order to be legitimate—and safe. To a certain degree, their instincts are correct. Following the formula is one way to make that critical product category identification.

The thing to remember, however, is that the brand will have a much more difficult time establishing itself as an identity if the advertising is too much like all the others. In order for the advertising to be distinctive, and thus the brand, it has to break with the formula in some way.

This may sound like a license for the creatives to go wild. There is one caveat, however. The advertising message, with all its creativity and distinctiveness, still has to identify the brand and create all those levels of association. It's easy to come up with an interesting and attention-getting message; it's very difficult to associate that message with the product.

Anchor the association.   You've probably heard of "the curse of the Clio" or "vampire creativity." These expressions are used to describe extremely creative ads that don't sell the product. The reason they don't sell is because there is no inescapable linkage between the creative message and the product.

It is difficult to believe, but people have a hard time identifying the product behind such highly creative messages as the gorilla bellhop beating on the luggage (is it Samsonite or American Tourister?) and Mariette Hartley and James Garner's repartee dialogue (is it Kodak or Polaroid?).

The classic ad line, "I can't believe I ate the whole thing," has been attributed to Pepto Bismol as well as to Alka Seltzer. However, no one forgets the product in a line like "Coke is it." Forging an unbreakable link between the story line and the product is extremely difficult, but essential.

The other difficulty for creatives handling national advertising is finding something creative to say. It becomes very difficult to come up with something new and different time after time. While the ad manager may feel comfortable with "me too" advertising, it's the uninspired, perhaps tired, creative people who create tired advertising.

9.3 BUSINESS-TO-BUSINESS ADVERTISING

Business-to-business advertising is a category that includes a variety of different types of activities. The four basic categories included in business-to-business advertising include industrial advertising to manufacturers, trade advertising to the distribution channel, advertising to large-volume institutional purchasers, and advertising to professionals. The characteristic that holds all these different categories together is that the product or service being advertised is used somewhere in the professional area or in the design, manufacturing, or distribution processes.

In earlier days, business advertising was not considered as glamorous as consumer advertising. Frequently, the junior copywriters would get assigned these accounts, giving them a chance to prove their stuff before moving on to the big consumer accounts. Television, in particular, was a big draw for talented people who cut their teeth on business advertising accounts.

Things have changed. There are as many big accounts in business as there are in consumer advertising. The business advertisers are insisting on top-quality production, and they have the money to spend to do it right. You can build a beautiful portfolio faster in business advertising than in consumer work. Another reason for the increased status of business accounts is that in many ways they are simply more interesting. A copywriter working on soap or chewing gum may burn out fast trying to come up with new ways to create excitement for parity goods. Business products are tangible and their selling premises are solid.

The various business categories all have different needs and respond to different appeals, but there is one thing that is common to all of the business advertising strategies: an emphasis on facts. Business purchases are not made as a result of flowery language; they are based on strong reason-why messages.

Most purchases are made as a result of a personal sales call by a knowledgeable sales representative who can provide technical information and explain the intricacies of specifications. The role of advertising is to provide basic facts, to establish a reputation platform for the company, and to open the door for the salesperson. In an article in *Madison Avenue,* William Kinney makes the point that a product gets known, but not sold, through business advertising.[3]

Types of Business Advertising

Industrial.   The heart of business advertising is the heart of the American economy—manufacturing. There are more than 250 business categories served by more than 2,600 industrial publications. That's big business. Every manufactured product that eventually finds its way into the consumer market goes through an extensive process of design, production, and distribution. And at every step of the way there are products and services being used in the production.

Advertising to manufacturers focuses on how your product can help make their product better. They are interested in quality, durability, and design. Price is important because that is a factor in their gross profit margin. Specifications, of course, are critical. The product has to fit.

They are also interested in service and supply. If you are providing an instrument needed in their manufacturing process, how reliable is your service program? Likewise, if you are providing a component, they will want to know how reliable your supply is, particularly if this is an innovative product category where there are limited suppliers. A computer manufacturer, for example, may have to shut down or go out of business if a critical microchip you supply is unavailable. Supply and service are not just code words in industrial advertising. If you let them down, you can cost them millions of dollars.

Trade.   The phrase, "trade advertising," is sometimes used as a generic label for what we are calling business-to-business advertising. We will be using it in a more limited sense. Trade advertising in this discussion is advertising to all the various layers in the distribution channel. Trade advertising is used to push a product through the channel as well as to sell products, services, and supplies to the various levels involved in distribution.

Distribution is complicated. It involves manufacturers that sometimes sell direct and others that sell through sales representatives, brokers, dealers, franchisers, retailers, and discounters. At every layer there may have to be a promotional effort and at every layer there are demands for supplies such as packaging, wrapping, crating, and shipping. Packaging in itself is a big industry.

Trade advertising is easy to summarize: profitability and saleability. Resellers want to know that your product will have a high turnover and not sit on the shelf gathering dust. They also want to know that they will make money selling it. Tell them how fast it will move and how much it will make.

There is a tendency in trade advertising to use profit and turnover as clichés—everyone says the same thing. In order to build a credible message you have to do more than just say it, you have to prove it. Resellers will want facts, testimonies, case histories, and anything else you can find that proves these two points. Build your argument and make it strong.

Institutional.   In another section, we discuss institutional advertising that is image oriented and seeks to sell the reputation of a company or an organization. In this chapter we are talking about advertising to institutions. By institutions we mean high-volume purchasers such as government, military, hospitals, schools, and restaurants. They consume huge amounts of supplies and services as they conduct their businesses but they purchase these goods differently than do conventional consumers. For that reason, they have to be addressed differently in advertising messages.

Most high-volume purchasing is based on one factor: price. Many institutions purchase by bid, and many of them automatically give the contract to the low bidder. You move this market with special price deals and quantity discounts. There is only one other factor that is relevant to this market and that is quality. You can sometimes counter the price factor by using such arguments as durability and long life. If they get more for their money in the long run, then you may be able to override the low-bid decision rule. This is one area where a strong argument can affect the perception of the price/value relationship.

Professional.   Advertising to professionals involves messages to people at work: architects, engineers, dentists, teachers, accountants, even advertising copywriters. All of these people are served by professional publications, and the pages of these publications are filled with advertising for products that will help them do their job better.

There are two types of advertising messages directed to professionals. First, there are messages to them as consumers. In other words, they use things in their work such as drafting tables, calculators and computers, briefcases, and surgical tools. Advertisements for those products address them as consumers.

Second, they function as influencers and recommend things to buy in the corporate decision process. Purchasing agents, of course, are the primary professionals who buy things in behalf of the company but all professionals are involved in some way. An engineer, for example, may be the best source of information on what kind of gear is needed for a specific application. The supervisor or purchasing agent will seek this type of expert opinion and usually will get a recommendation on a supplier at the same time.

The decision process in business purchasing is complicated. It has been studied and modeled in an article in *Madison Avenue* by Sarah Lum.[4] This article outlines "buying centers" in industrial firms and the likelihood that various types of professionals will be involved. In a column in *Adweek*, Fred Messner makes the point that in business-to-business advertising it is important to understand the various steps in this purchasing sequence and to assign individual ads different responsibilities at the different steps.[5]

Professionals will be interested in your product if you can convince them it will help them do their work easier, faster, or with better quality. Appeals to convenience and time saving usually will be relevant to this audience. They are interested in anything that increases their professionalism. Sometimes an ego appeal may be appropriate. They may also appreciate any appeal that cuts costs and helps increase their personal profit.

Media Considerations

There are some distinctive characteristics of the media used in business-to-business advertising, and they affect how you develop the message. Primarily the media is print, either journals, direct mail, or product literature. That means the messages can be designed as a file filler for long-term reference. Typically, such messages will be long on copy and provide more information than you may normally see in consumer advertising.

Business advertising tends to be sought after by its audience and used as a reference to product innovation within the industry. Typically, business publications are read as much for their ads as they are for their articles. Most business publications contain reader service cards, where you can mark an advertiser by the number of the ad and send off easily for additional product literature. That's how this file filler function works.

Business journals are grouped into two categories: horizontal and vertical. These labels apply to the professional orientation of their readers. For example, a *horizontal* publication is one that serves all accountants across a broad band of industries. The focus is accounting.

A *vertical* publication, in contrast, serves a particular industry and all of the various professional categories associated with it. A publication on interactive computers, for example, might be read by accountants as well as by engineers, programmers, retailers, and teachers. The focus is on this particular narrow interest within the broader field of computers.

Personal Expertise

Advertising copy is written for experts, and you will have to become a technical expert too if you expect to tell them anything they don't already know. Most agencies that are involved in business advertising specialize in certain areas and their staffs will specialize even more. You can't write a pharmaceutical ad if you don't know anything about chemistry. You'll have a hard time writing agricultural ads if you have never been on a farm.

Most people working in business advertising have special education or experience to prepare them for these technical areas. If not, you will have to make a major effort to build your knowledge of a given technical area to the point that you can write about it without sounding foolish. Be prepared to do a lot of homework. You'll need to know everything you can about those who make it, those who buy it, those who use it, and those who sell it.

Creative Considerations

Approach.   The emphasis is factual, but the tone is hard hitting in most successful business ads. Business advertising is a very noisy environment, and people who specialize in that kind of advertising have to know how to break through the clutter. In a *Madison Avenue* interview, Peter Lubalin, creative director with Creamer Inc. in New York, says that their business advertising is designed to translate the product's strengths into "stopping power."[6]

In the same article William Foley, corporate services director for Marsteller, says their advertising philosophy is one of "confrontation." He explains, "We have determined that we need to land on the readers in the most surprising and/or intrusive way possible so that they will be compelled to pay attention."[7] Business advertising is strong, aggressive, and full of punch.

Business advertising is also image conscious. A company's reputation is the most important thing it has to sell to another company. Part of the door-opening responsibility of business advertising is to establish the reputation platform of the company, to develop a receptive climate for the salesperson. Foley describes the Marsteller approach, which he says is "to grab *mind-share* before market share."

Design.   Most of the "stopping power" of an ad is created in the graphics. Business advertising is not afraid to use attention-getting, provocative visuals. The strong visual is a recent trend in business advertising. Albert Molinaro, CEO for Klempner Advertising, a New York firm that specializes in business advertising, explained that "there is definite recognition in our specialized field on both the client's and agency's parts that the simpler and more dramatic presentation is more effective."[8]

Phil Burton includes a number of business ads in his book, *Which Ad Pulled Best.* A number of his "generalizations" derived from the analysis of research data deal with graphics. He concludes that higher-readership business ads tend to have big illustrations. He suggests using pictures of products in use rather than static tabletop shots and he also recommends using people in the pictures to humanize the gears and machinery. Symbolism is a problem in business advertising, and he warns that business readers are literal, fact seeking, and in a hurry. They may not take the time to puzzle out the symbolic meaning.[9]

Writing.   The most important thing to remember in business advertising is to use hard facts—no generalities, no flowery prose. *Prove* your point. Don't just state it. Burton has found that industrial readers want details. You may even want to try graphic details like "call outs," little pieces of copy around an illustration that point out significant details about the features. Specifications are essential, but don't just run the list. Even in business advertising you have to sell, rather than just list, the features.

The emphasis on facts doesn't eliminate emotion, however. People are technicians and specialists and professionals, but they are also human. The desire to succeed, to be respected, to have the best record, to make money is an emotional drive. Most of the facts have an emotional foundation, but the appeal to emotion should not be blatant. It's a delicate balance.

Burton warns that the headlines should be reader oriented rather than advertiser oriented. That's a fault he finds often in business advertising. He also suggests that headlines with all-encompassing claims do less well than specific claims. Burton suggests that general institutional copy is not as strong as case histories. He has also found that a disinterested third party is more believable proof for a claim than an obvious company claim. He notes that "brag and boast" copy is particularly repelling to business readers.

Professionals and technical experts have very well developed "crap detectors" and low tolerance for patronizing comments. Don't try to tell them something they already know. They are the professionals, after all. Be informative, be friendly, but don't be preachy.

9.4 DIRECT ADVERTISING

The short cut.   Direct advertising uses the shortest communication route to the consumer. The message is beamed directly to the consumer from the marketer bypassing any sales or retail staff. Its objective is to stimulate an immediate response to the message. The response may be in the form of actually buying the product, sending in for more literature, calling to place an order or a request for information, or visiting a sales location. The message is totally controlled by the advertiser, and it is addressed to a carefully defined audience who are thought to include primary prospects for this message.

What we are calling "direct advertising" is also known as direct response, direct mail, mail order, or direct marketing. *Direct marketing* is the broadest term and involves factors other than communication. *Direct mail* and *mail order* are not broad enough to be descriptive since other media are used besides mail. *Direct response* identifies a key characteristic of this form of communication and comes the closest to including all of the relevant media.

Media.   Direct advertising uses a variety of media. It may be found in magazines, television, newspaper, and radio. Its primary media, however, are printed pieces sent directly to the individual. The pieces may be letters, brochures, postcards, or catalogues. In all cases the messages contain some kind of device for facilitating a direct response by the consumer—a postcard, coupon, cutout and mail-in blank, or telephone number.

Advertisers.   Direct response is used for all kinds of advertising: consumer, business, or institutional. It is addressed to individuals at home and at work. It is also addressed to businesses and institutions. It may sell a product, service, or idea. It is becoming more common in business-to-business marketing, where the cost of a sales call may be more than $100 a contact.

Who uses direct response? Catalogues go back to the 1800s when the Montgomery Ward and Sears Roebuck catalogues brought a variety of merchandise to rural consumers. The early experimenters with this form of massive national marketing were the book clubs, record clubs, and magazine subscription services. In recent years, small manufacturers as well as retailing giants like Nieman Marcus are using direct response.

Associations also use direct response advertising. Membership campaigns and fund-raising drives are conducted primarily by direct response. The most effective appeal for either membership or money, of course, is from another member but personal appeals are difficult, time consuming, and expensive to run. A carefully developed mail appeal can be highly effective and cost effective as well.

Direct response can be used in all kinds of advertising situations but the critical characteristics include a carefully targeted audience, controlled communication from the advertiser to the prospect, a direct response, and no intermediate sales staff (although one of the responses may include getting prospects to visit a dealer or showroom). The advertising message is the primary communication with the consumer.

Growth Factors

Why is it such a growth area? For the marketer, it's cheap and it's dependable. All you have are the costs of advertising—no sales staff, no overhead. It's more profitable and totally under your control. For the consumer, the success of direct response advertising is a lifestyle phenomenon. It used to be a lot of fun to go downtown to go shopping. Now we climb into the car and drive to a shopping center, and we don't worry about changing out of our "grubbies." And with the parking problems, crowded stores, lack of sales staff, or the surliness of the ones we often encounter, going shopping has become more of a hassle than a pleasure.

Furthermore, more women are working, and their time is too precious to spend on a shopping trip. People who work would rather spend their free time at home or in some kind of interesting leisure activity. That's true for men as well as women. In terms of lifestyle changes, direct response advertising is popular because it permits the convenience of armchair shopping. You can sit in front of your fireplace and buy all the gifts you need for Christmas. You can browse and compare and meditate without pushy sales clerks.

There are some other technical changes in marketing that have contributed to the growth of direct response advertising. One is the credit card explosion of the sixties. Credit cards are accepted by most direct marketers, making it extremely easy to purchase anything they want to offer. Another technological factor is the 800 number, which permits toll-free ordering. Direct response research has found that using a toll-free number will increase the response rate by as much as 20 percent.[10]

The last, and perhaps most important, technological factor is the computer. It is possible for marketers to select extremely small but tightly targeted audiences for their products, a type of search and select process that would be impossible to do by hand. The computer also makes it possible to further personalize the message by directly addressing the prospect by name. Personalized selling may again become possible, replacing the anonymity of the mall.

This "personal setting" is another of the direct response advantages. However, many professionals feel it has not been used to its full advantage. Alexander Kroll, president of Young & Rubicam, U.S.A., told a group of direct marketers that "in this most personal of all media . . . only a few direct marketers are engaged in truly personal selling." Kroll also pointed out that "direct marketing—by magazine, mail or TV—can fill the void of personal selling created by the extinction of the corner store."[11]

The Audience

Selectivity.   One of the advantages of direct response is that it uses a rifle rather than a shotgun. Lists of prospects are available in SRDS, although that is a limited service. A good list house will have considerably more choices.

For example, one major house has over 3,500 occupational classifications on file and over 6 million establishments.[12] With the power of computer sorting, lists can be cross-compiled, merged, and purged to create a list designed specifically for your needs.

Impulse. Direct response advertising is designed for the "split-second glance." Whether the consumer is reading through a magazine or sorting through mail, the decision to consider the message is made instantaneously. With direct mail letters, the prospect is mentally sorting the mail into two categories: stuff to be tossed without reading and letters to be opened and skimmed, then maybe tossed or maybe put in a pile for further consideration. The objective of every direct mail copywriter is to get into that second pile.

When the decision has been made to keep the letter, most people will give the message a substantial amount of reading time. If the product is of interest and the writing has captured their attention, people will read considerably longer messages than they will in general advertising. If they are being asked to make a decision to buy a product, then they will probably want as much information as you can provide them. That's why direct response magazine ads and direct mail letters use long copy. The initial interest may be impulse, but the decision to buy is a considered one.

Another problem is the "gatekeeper" effect. In business communication a direct response piece is usually opened by the secretary, who makes the decision whether or not to pass the mailing on to the boss. In this situation, you have to second-guess the secretary as well as batter through the indifference of the boss. It's a two-level sort, and that just doubles your chances of being tossed.

Clutter. Not only are your readers operating on impulse, they are also inundated. Most households get several pieces of direct response mail every day. Generally, they consider this "junk mail." Some find it offensive, others welcome it. Those who object to this mail can have their names taken off the lists. However, Sid Bernstein reported in his column in *Advertising Age* that there were more than twice as many people contacted who wished to be put on lists than to be taken off.[13]

The result of this overwhelming use of direct response advertising is clutter. In this case, advertising is a victim of its own success. In truth, most consumers see little and remember less. It may take several mailings to make an impression and thousands of impressions to generate one response.

Accountability

Direct response advertising is the most accountable of all because the effect of the ad is immediate sales. Every ad is its own test of pulling power. If you run the same ad with two different headlines or two different visuals, you get concrete information on which works best. There are no hunches, no guesswork about direct response advertising. And every direct response copywriter knows his or her work will be measured in the mail. It's not a business for the thin-skinned.

Because of the measuring power of direct response advertising, there are some fairly well established principles. While these findings are compiled from direct response advertising, they still represent the basics of good advertising in almost every situation. David Ogilvy, long a student of direct response, suggests that all creatives can improve their work by studying the techniques used in this area.[14]

One of the best direct response copywriters in the business, Bill Jayme, outlined his view of testing in Bob Stone's *Advertising Age* column.[15] Jayme says he likes to "go for broke." He packs everything into the initial advertisement and then "tests down." In other words, he might drop from four-color to two-color, from using a token to not using one, and keep testing until the economy begins to cut into the return. Most direct response pieces are designed to reach a breakeven point, and Jayme keeps his eye on that as he tries out alternative versions of the message design.

Another complication in planning a direct response piece is the need to estimate the total costs of the promotion as opposed to the total income from it. Every campaign is planned with a breakeven point. The original testing is done to determine if the pulling power of the piece is strong enough to meet and pass that breakeven point. This is fiscal planning, but it is still a reality that the creative staff has to keep in mind when planning direct response advertising.

Creative Considerations

Catalogues.   Catalogues are specific types of direct response advertising. The Sears and Ward catalogues pioneered the techniques in the field. Even now most creative directors will tell you the best training a copywriter can have is to work for Sears writing catalogue copy. More recently, the action in the catalogue field has been with special interest publications produced by such marketers as L. L. Bean (sporting goods), Horchow (expensive collectibles), Victoria's Secrets (lingerie), Nieman-Marcus (exotic gifts), Hammacher Schlemmer (unusual home items), and Caswell-Massey (apothecary).

These catalogues are nothing like salesmen's catalogues, which just carry a list of the inventory. These books are works of art, in some cases coffee table pieces. A Christmas lingerie publication by Bloomingdale's, called *Sighs and Whispers,* became a collector's item.

Bob Stone, in a column in *Advertising Age,* gave some suggestions on how to organize and design contemporary catalogues.[16] His first suggestion is that you develop a theme for the book. Sometimes fashion books will use an exotic location such as the Isle of Capri or Marrakesh as a visual theme.

Then he suggested that you "lead with your best." In other words, find the most fascinating item in your list of merchandise and play it front and center. Strong positions, called "the hot spots," include front and back cover, inside front and back cover, middle spread, and pages before and after the order blank.

Copy has to sell, not just describe. In general interest catalogs like the Sears book, the catalogue copy is written very tightly. In a few short lines you have to establish the attractiveness of the item, explain what it will do for the customer, and give all the relevant product feature details such as colors, sizes, and construction.

Catalogue copy is usually written to a character count. The typeface and size are established, and the layout artist simply rules in a block for the type. The copywriter measures the block and estimates how many characters will fit on a line and how many lines will fit in the block. The copy is then written to fit those specifications—no more, no less. The editing is ruthless; every word must pay its way.

Stone describes a catalogue writer who was given the task of selling a toy lie detector in a Christmas toy catalog. The space allowed four lines of 22 characters each, but two of the lines had to be used for article number, shipping weight, and price. That left two lines. The writer's very successful copy was: "It works! Measures emotions to spot fibs."

Direct mail.   Direct mail pieces can take several forms. They can be letters from a store to its customers or they can be from a major national marketer, like an insurance company, to anonymous names on a series of mailing lists. They can be postcards or eight typewritten pages. They can include samples, coupons, product literature, or any number of other inserted materials. In fact, direct mail may not use mail at all. Inserts can be used in newspapers and delivery services will use "door knockers" to leave brochures and samples right on a doorknob.

Direct mail uses a letter format, and the letters are written in a personal tone. The consumer is addressed personally and by name if possible. Informal address using lots of "yous" is also common. John Tighe, a specialist in direct mail copywriting, opened one letter for *Popular Mechanics* this way: "Good friend, this invitation isn't for deadbeats, rip-off artists or 'gentlemen' who hate to get their hands dirty. It's for the rest of us. It's for the guys who aren't afraid to get down under the sink with a pipe wrench. Guys who don't mind sticking their hands in the toilet tank to adjust the ball cock (because they know it's going to save a $16 plumber's bill).[17]

The message starts on the envelope with some kind of curiosity provoking thought. To give you some idea how important the envelope is, Bill Jayme reports that he spends one-third of his time working on the envelope message.[18] He uses big bold one-word teaser headlines that crystallize the sales appeal. For a *Business Week* mailing aimed at businessmen frustrated by better-informed associates, he used the word "DAMN." The word "MOUSETRAP" worked well for *Inc.,* a publication aimed at entrepreneurs. For over two decades, *Esquire* has been running one of Jayme's mailings with the word "PUZZLE" as a teaser on the envelope.

Short copy is a hallmark of catalogues but long copy is typical of direct mail. Letters will often be six or eight pages long, and research finds that people will read the entire letter. Another well-respected direct mail copywriter is Bob Jones. He wrote an eight-page letter offering reproductions of American pistols priced at $2,500 a pair. Sales from this letter hit $5 million.[19]

Bob Jones also prides himself on using hooks to jolt the reader into reading the letter. His approaches are often unorthodox. For example, he started a letter for the Committee to Impeach the President (Nixon) with the salutation: "Dear Fool." He then challenged the reader to get involved rather than to remain passive. The letter raised over $1 million.

The message revolves around something direct response writers call "The Offer." According to Bill Jayme, the offer is the reason-why theme that runs throughout the entire package. He suggests, when you are planning a direct mail piece, that you start with the envelope and then move to the order form. Those two pieces will force you to crystallize the offer. He says this sequence "helps us to review the offer, analyze the offer, understand the offer and verbalize it."[20]

Some other tried-and-true techniques have been outlined in direct response columns in *Folio* magazine written by Eliot DeY. Schein, president of Schein/Blattstein Advertising.[21] These techniques include always using a real stamp on the envelope rather than a printed indicia. An inner envelope, like those used with invitations, says this is an exclusive message. The signature should be handwritten and printed in blue ink; the more it looks like a real signature, the better. Include a free gift or some kind of incentive. Get them involved by having them insert a token or scratch off a number.

If you are asking them to buy something, specify that it is a no-risk offer, and that their money will be refunded if they don't like it. Include a P.S. at the bottom and use it to wrap up the appeal of the message and hit them again—no one can resist reading a P.S. If it's a donation, mention it's tax deductible.

Use inserts in the envelope as a way of reintroducing the selling point. A second letter can work like a testimony confirming what was in the first message. A separate brochure is a good way to present product facts. The order form should be separate and, once again, it should refer to the main selling point. This is your last chance to anchor your sales. Of course, you need to include either a business reply envelope or a business reply card with prepaid postage. Make it as easy as possible to place the order. If readers have to look for a stamp, you are likely to lose them.

Production.   The last creative consideration is sometimes the first. Since direct response advertising is highly accountable, it also has to work with a budget. The cost of a magazine ad is the space rate plus the production costs. That is fairly easy to evaluate.

Direct mail pieces, however, are much more difficult. Every creative decision will have impact on cost. If you use a signature on the letter in blue ink, then that means the letter will be printed in two colors rather than in one, significantly increasing the costs. Printing on the envelope is an additional expense. If you have a second insert, you may be doubling your costs.

And then there are the postal costs and regulations. The only thing you can count on in dealing with the post office is that you'll never get the same answer twice. The regulations are so complicated that they are totally dependent on the individual interpretation of each postmaster. The only way through the morass is to take a dummy of your piece to the postmaster and get an official reading on whether it qualifies for the category of mailing you want and what the mailing cost will be.

There are some things you can do to control postage costs. Third-class bulk mail is considerably cheaper than first class. Research has found that first class with a stamp will pull better but, if you don't use the stamp, you might as well use third class. In order to use bulk mail, you have to mail a minimum of 200 pieces.

There are lots of regulations regarding the design of the envelope in terms of making it readable by the post office's optical scanning equipment. Mailings are also cheaper if they are grouped by zip code. A good mailing service can help you sort out these difficulties.

Planning a direct response piece involves making initial decisions on the design, getting an estimate, going back and revising the design, getting an estimate on the revision, and so on. You rarely get to produce the ultimate piece and say, "Costs be damned."

9.5 INSTITUTIONAL ADVERTISING

Institutional advertising is advertising that focuses on the reputation of the corporation or organization. We are using the word "institutional" for this type of advertising because it includes activities by associations as well as companies. This category includes corporate advertising to the financial or investment community, the business community, customers, and consumers. In addition to corporate image, institutional advertising also includes public service and advocacy or issue advertising. (See Exhibit 9–3.)

Institutional advertising is one area where the professional concerns of public relations and advertising overlap. The corporate image is usually the concern of the public relations staff, but the advertising specifically oriented toward corporate image usually is prepared by the advertising staff or agency. Obviously, there is a need here for maximum coordination.

Image and product.   Corporate advertising also needs to be coordinated with the product advertising. There should be thematic integration and continuity between the two. It is extremely hard for a company to project an image of

Little Things

Most of us
miss out
on life's
big prizes.
The Pulitzer.
The Nobel.
Oscars.
Tonys.
Emmys.
But we're
all eligible
for life's
small pleasures.
A pat
on the back.
A kiss
behind the ear.
A four-pound bass.
A full moon.
An empty
parking space.
A crackling fire.
A great meal.
A glorious sunset.
Hot soup.
Cold beer.
Don't fret
about
copping life's
grand awards.
Enjoy its
tiny delights.
There are plenty
for all of us.

Why Does Everyone Hate Meetings?

Three kinds of people
attend meetings.
Those who want progress,
those who don't,
and those who want to
impress the chairman.
98% of the talk goes
to 2% of the problem.
Remember the story of
the board of trustees who
agreed unanimously to spend
millions for an atomic
reactor, then fell in wild
dissension over the
request by the freshman
basketball coach
for a new blackboard.
Maybe the air is too
soporific.
Maybe the carafes of ice
water tend to lubricate the
long-winded.
Maybe the chairs are too
comfortable.
(A fast food chain designed
its chairs to be purposely
uncomfortable so people
wouldn't linger over their
coffee.)
At your next meeting, remove
the chairs, empty the carafes,
turn the thermostat down to 55.
A stand-up meeting
could be a stand-out.

It's What You Do— Not When You Do It

Ted Williams, at age 42,
slammed a home run
in his last official
time at bat.
Mickey Mantle, age 20,
hit 23 home runs
his first full year
in the major leagues.
Golda Meir was 71 when
she became Prime Minister
of Israel.
William Pitt II was 24
when he became
Prime Minister of
Great Britain.
George Bernard Shaw was 94
when one of his plays
was first produced.
Mozart was just seven
when his first composition
was published.
Now, how about this?
Benjamin Franklin
was a newspaper columnist
at 16,
and a framer of The United
States Constitution
when he was 81.
You're never too young
or too old
if you've got talent.
Let's recognize
that age has little to do
with ability.

Let's Get Rid Of "The Girl"

Wouldn't 1979 be
a great year
to take one giant
step forward
for womankind
and get rid of
"the girl"?
Your attorney says,
"If I'm not here
just leave it with
the girl."
The purchasing agent
says, "Drop off your
bid with the girl."
A manager says,
"My girl will get
back to your girl."
What girl?
Do they mean
Miss Rose?
Do they mean
Ms. Torres?
Do they mean
Mrs. McCullough?
Do they mean
Joy Jackson?
"The girl"
is certainly
a woman when she's
out of her teens.
Like you,
she has a name.
Use it.

EXHIBIT 9-3:   One of the most exciting corporate advertising campaigns has been a series of think pieces produced for United Technologies. (Courtesy of United Technologies Corporation)

dynamic and innovative leadership in its institutional ads when the product ads are stuffy and predictable.

In general, most institutional advertising is more interested in ideas, images, and attitudes than in the sale of specific products. The objectives are different for institutional and product advertising. That doesn't mean there is no bottom line or return on investment for corporate advertising. It does mean that the measurement is different. Corporations using institutional advertising measure success in terms of opinion change rather than dollars.

Institutional advertising differs in another dimension: the time frame. Corporate campaigns run for decades rather than days. The advertising waves are often planned in terms of years. Research is conducted over long periods, using tracking methods to establish benchmarks and norms and to spot the changes. Corporate identity is a long-term investment.

Target audience.   The audience for the measure differs with the type of advertising. Some are tightly targeted—to legislators or stock analysts, for example. There are commercial research and direct mail companies that can provide lists for such specific groups.

There are also general approaches common to the various types of institutional campaigns. Most institutional advertising attempts to reach opinion leaders. The idea is that there are certain people in various industries and in politics who influence how other people think—company presidents (CEOs), for example.

Iain Woolward, president of a San Francisco corporate communications firm, believes that the traditional categories of opinion leaders do not lead opinion. The person with the original idea, the one who changes opinions, tends to be an intellectual loner.[22] It may be that CEOs are more inclined to defend and maintain traditional opinions, rather than to forge into new areas. The top executives may rely on information provided by subordinates, perhaps even adopting opinions of middle managers, if they are well founded.

The whole concept of executives as opinion leaders may even ignore the real audience for the institutional message: the general public. Woolward observes, "As Joe Public thinks, so thinks the nation." Woolward explains, "If he overextends on his credit, so will the nation; if his work ethic deteriorates, so will the nation's; if he fights against corporate profits because he does not believe he will benefit from reinvestment, we will not have seen the last of windfall profit taxes." According to Woolward, much corporate advertising is misdirected; it is just companies talking to themselves, the believers talking to the converted.

Objectives.   Identifying the proper target for institutional advertising depends upon the objective of the message. If the objective is to reinforce current opinion, then perhaps advertising to the entrenched, and often conservative, leadership makes sense. If you are attempting to change opinions, then there needs to be a different rationale for the identification of the target. Middle management and technical staff may be more receptive than top executives, for example. Perhaps they are the influential ones within a company and within an industry. They may be the ones who are making recommendations and developing innovative strategies.

In Woolward's article in *Madison Avenue,* he pinpoints people he calls "the convertibles." His strategy is to identify the people who are set in their opinions—either pro or con—and ignore them. It's much harder to change an opinion than to create one. Instead, he recommends that you find that body of people who are not sure, whose opinions are unfocused. They are the ones who can be most easily affected by institutional messages. It may be that the readers of *Sports Illustrated* or *People* are more easily moved than the readers of *Forbes* or *Mother Earth News*—it all depends upon the issue.

Media.   Obviously the target audience, objectives, and message strategy are all interrelated. Normally, institutional advertising is oriented toward the "thought" publications, the publications presumed to be read by the opinion leaders. These include such publications as *Wall Street Journal, Forbes, Business Week,* and the executive issues of *Newsweek, Time,* and *U.S. News & World Report.* Other quality publications such as *The Smithsonian, Omni, National Geographic,* and *Scientific American* are thought to reach this leadership audience.

If you decide to use a general interest strategy, the choice of publication depends upon how opinionated the typical readers are on certain issues. Therefore, if you have a nutrition or health care message, the readers of *Reader's Digest* or *Good Housekeeping* may be more appropriate than *U.S. News & World Report.* But it depends upon the orientation of those readers and how focused their opinions are.

Magazines are not the only media used in institutional advertising. Some campaigns also use television and newspapers. In order for television to make sense, you must have a message that relates to a large and diverse mass audience. In the lead article for a special issue of *Madison Avenue* on corporate advertising, Barbara Mehlman, the editor, reported that in two out of three cases woman are more concerned about issues than are men. Her suggestion is to "hit the soaps."[23]

Image Advertising

The most common type of corporate advertising is image. This can take several forms. A company may have changed its name or logo and need an identity campaign to register this change. Some companies also suffer from a general lack of awareness. A house ad by Ogilvy and Mather quotes the Opinion Research Corporation whose "numerous corporate image studies find that most companies are handicapped by invisibility and remoteness."[24]

All companies, like people, have personalities. Sometimes the company is quiet and unobtrusive and generally unknown. Some companies are brash and vocal. The image even may be inconsistent with the company's actual personality. A campaign is needed then to bring the image in line.

Another typical situation is a result of the mergers and complexities of the contemporary business scene. So many companies are into so many different areas that their identities are badly fragmented. An identity campaign may be undertaken to bring some coherence to the company's image.

Objectives.   In the first situation, the objective is simply recognition of the new name or logo. The target audience will be the business community, including suppliers and dealers as well as present and potential customers. In the case of an organization the audience will be the members, related associations and their members, as well as companies involved in the association's business.

Campaigns that seek to establish, refine, or revise a company's image can be as complicated as the nature of the change. Simply reinforcing an image is relatively easy; changing an image radically will involve an extensive media buy and elaborate explanation copy. One is reminder; the other is persuasion.

The objectives in the multiproduct situation are also complicated. On one level, you will need to pull everything together around some common thread. There needs to be something universal in the various products and categories represented by the company's activities. This may involve major self-study by the company, its management, and staff. Some companies have undertaken an identity campaign, only to find that they have to first go through major organizational streamlining. On another level, you need to communicate the diversity of the company product line and the distinctiveness of its offerings.

Hugh Wolff, director of corporate communications for Ingersoll-Rand, says that it is usually not advisable to try to do everything in one ad. "A complex company cannot be communicated in total."[25] He suggests that the messages be tightly focused or at best all you'll create is confusion.

Research.   Another characteristic of image advertising is that it needs to be built on a solid research base. You can't create a new corporate image if you don't know what the current image is. Without that information, you don't know if you are maintaining a well-established image, creating one from largely unfocused fragments, or overturning a negative impression and building a positive image in its place. Research is necessary to establish the benchmark.

Focus groups are useful for generating information about the perceptions of various types of audience groups. Other techniques used in image advertising include tracking studies based on rating scales. In an article in *Journal of Advertising Research*, Thomas Garbett, senior VP for Doyle Dane Bernbach, outlined a program for the kind of image research necessary for corporate advertising.[26] Perceptual mapping using multidimensional scaling also is used to locate positions for products; it's useful for identifying corporate positions and tracking them over time. An article in *Madison Avenue* by Herbert Krugman describes General Electric's tracking program, which has been in effect since the mid sixties.[27]

Slogans.   An example of classic image advertising in a difficult area is the E. F. Hutton campaign: "When E. F. Hutton talks, people listen." Ralph Nader, the consumer advocate, has described this campaign as "probably the deepest mental imprint image ad ever developed."[28] The campaign positioned E. F. Hutton as *the* most respected source for reliable investment information. What started out as a short-term advertising campaign has created a long-term image for the company, an image that has become difficult for the firm to maintain.

Company slogans and logos are the two most obvious factors in the overall institutional image. Both are designed for long-term use, perhaps the life of the institution—although there are times when it is necessary to update a slogan or logo. The problem with updating either is that the old slogan or logo then becomes your most serious competitor. For many people "the pause that refreshes" is still the slogan of Coca-Cola, even though it hasn't been used in years. The other Coke slogans that come and go are identified in the public's mind as short-term campaign slogans.

In an article in *Madison Avenue,* Herbert Krugman analyzed the history of General Electric's corporate slogans.[29] In the early seventies, GE used "Progress is our most important product." In the late seventies, the company changed to "Progress for people." He observed that the new slogan was never able to register more than 21–23 percent Starch noted scores while the old slogan continued on registering 34–40 percent, even though it hadn't been advertised for over 10 years.

The average rating for a successful slogan, according to Krugman, is around 50 percent. The "Progress for people" never reached that level, and it was replaced with "We bring good things to life." There was something magical about the "good things" slogan. Krugman reported that "it generated a steeply rising slope of awareness and recognition never seen before in our history." The slogan achieved over 50 percent levels within 12 months. He says "good things" was successful because it was "not just a slogan, which implies just words, but also a melody, and also an accompanying set of pictures or visual images." He says it was perfect for the multi-image of television advertising.

Financial Advertising

Many corporations undertake institutional advertising in order to make themselves more attractive to stock analysts and potential investors. This is a very tightly directed form of advertising to a clearly defined target.

In a scathing indictment, Terry Haller, chairman of Financial Communications Strategy Center, criticized most financial advertising as having the "intellectual content of baby talk."[30] He observed that most creatives don't understand security analysts or understand the thought that goes into investment decision making. He said, "So-called creatives don't care much for analytical types and probably hate them as much as their own research departments. This shows in their work." He concluded that most financial advertising was vapid and humdrum.

Financial advertising needs to be built on facts, solid information—not fluff, not vague copy extolling technological breakthroughs and glittering bottom lines. In a study of what financial analysts read, the Marsteller agency found that numbers are not necessarily grabbers.[31] Most analysts have access to tons of data from their own computer services, data they consider more reliable than the little charts that appear in ads. What they do want is interpretation of the numbers and the story behind the numbers.

Even more important, they want to know about the future—where the company is headed. Most corporate ads focus on what the company has done in the past. While track record may be important to some consumers, it is less important to the analyst who has that data available. The future is the unknown.

Advocacy Advertising

Advocacy, or issue, advertising is used when a company or organization wants to take a public stand on an issue. First Amendment tests have gone all the way to the Supreme Court on this issue, and the present thought is that companies have the right of free speech, too.

Advocacy advertising is used when an issue surfaces that is critical to the well-being of the company or organization. Usually, the institution has reason to believe that its side of the issue is not being covered adequately in the press and therefore it is necessary to buy space to guarantee that the company's position is presented. (See Exhibit 9–4.) Most editors and reporters try to be accurate and fair in their coverage of issues. Sometimes, however, a particular view is not expressed in the way you would like to see it. The only way to guarantee that it appears as you wish is to buy the space and run your viewpoint as a paid advertisement.

There are some built-in problems with issue advertising, particularly by corporations. The public automatically assumes bias and is less inclined to give the message a fair hearing. One way to overcome this problem is to try to make your message as unbiased and factual as possible. That means you need to present both sides of the issue. If you do that, then there is less negative response when you state your view and support it with facts.

One of the favorable things about advocacy advertising is that there is more of a chance that it will be read. Starch research has found that well-presented issue ads are seen as more interesting by the public and the copy tends to be better read than the copy in product advertising. The ads are seen to be especially interesting if they follow an "op ed" think piece format.

Public Service

Most companies want to be seen as good members of their community, and they use institutional advertising to outline their sense of social responsibility. Some are actively engaged in community betterment without heralding their activities in ads. Corning, for example, has spent more than $37.5 million in grants to communities where its employees live, as well as to higher education and special

EXHIBIT 9–4: The "monopoly" advertisement by Union Oil is an example of an advocacy ad that states a position on a controversial topic. (Courtesy of Union Oil Corp.)

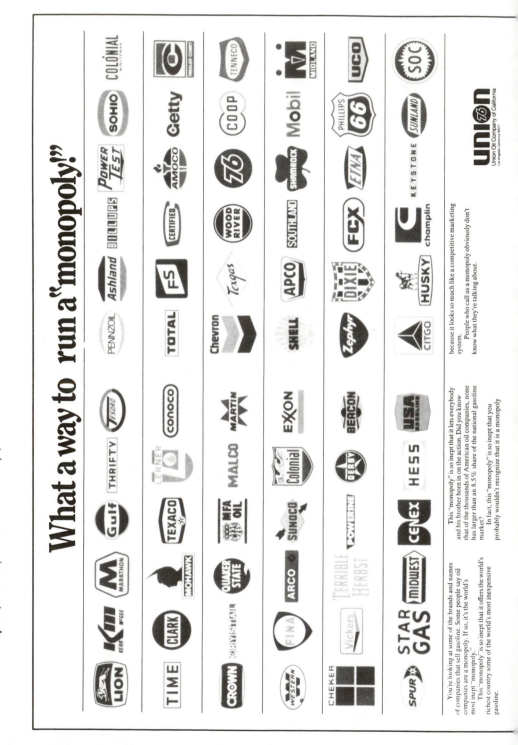

What a way to run a "monopoly!"

You're looking at some of the brands and names of companies that sell gasoline. Some people say oil companies are a monopoly. If so, it's the world's most inept "monopoly."

This "monopoly" is so inept that it offers the world's richest country some of the world's most inexpensive gasoline.

This "monopoly" is so inept that it lets everybody and his brother horn in on the action. Did you know that of the thousands of American oil companies, none has larger than an 8.5% share of the national gasoline market?

In fact, this "monopoly" is so inept that you probably wouldn't recognize that it is a monopoly

because it looks so much like a competitive marketing system.

People who call us a monopoly obviously don't know what they're talking about.

union 76
Union Oil Company of California
Los Angeles, California 90017

innovative social projects. Activities in this area are an important part of a long-term community relations program, usually administered by the company's public relations department. Advertising gets involved when there is a need to promote these programs to the public, business community, or industry.

Public service advertising is another aspect of social responsibility. The company, or a group of companies, will underwrite the advertising expenses of some good cause.

The Ad Council is an industry-wide program administered by a foundation with representatives from throughout the advertising industry. The Ad Council takes on clients representing such causes as child abuse, forest fires, crime prevention, and Negro youth college education programs, and organizes donated creative and media buying services from its member agencies. Arrangements are made with the media to provide free space and air time and the campaign runs with totally donated services. (See Exhibit 9–5.)

One of the most successful national public service campaigns by a company is the Shell "answer book" series developed by Ogilvy and Mather. This little "tip in" booklet gets consistently high magazine readership. Furthermore, the company has received more than 800,000 requests for copies.[32]

Creative Considerations

Self-interest.   The basic principle for writing institutional copy is the same as the basic product copy strategy: serve the reader's self-interest. Ron Hoff, director of FCB/Corporate, says this is violated every day by corporate advertising that is obviously self-serving.[33] There is a tremendous temptation in institutional advertising to write "we" copy rather than "you" copy. Give your reader some reason to read your message. If all you're doing is writing to the CEO or Board of Directors, you can do it cheaper and more effectively with a special mailing.

Style.   Writing style is another consideration. Institutional copy often sounds like it is either written with concrete blocks or wallpaper. It either bludgeons you to death or bores you to death. That probably reflects the attitude of the writers, who may very well dislike this assignment. It also tends to read like a tenth-grade essay and to be heavy with excess verbiage. Corporate stories should be just as interesting as product stories.

Ron Hoff criticizes the style of corporate ads that sound as if they were written in the "waiting room." Get inside the company, inside the offices, inside the factory and lines. He wants to see "hard hat copy" that makes the company come alive in whatever business it is in.[34] Hoff also suggests you use emotion: "companies marry, divorce, prosper, get sick and recover." There is high drama in corporate affairs, but it is rarely apparent in the company's ad copy.

9.6 PROMOTION

Promotion is a topic that wears many hats. Sometimes it is considered advertising, sometimes public relations; it may also be considered merchandising or sales promotion. Since this book focuses on the creative side of advertising, we will discuss various aspects of promotion, but from the viewpoint of what it can do to support an advertising program.

Publicity

Publicity is a very clear responsibility of the public relations staff. It involves getting media attention for the activities of your client in the form of news coverage in the mass media and announcements and articles in the trade press. The article is not paid for by the advertiser—in other words, it is a form of "free" communication. Not only is it free, but information that appears in the media as an article has more credibility than anything you can buy in a display ad. Publicity, therefore, should be a highly valued part of your promotional effort.

Most publicity efforts are oriented toward the total corporate or institutional communication program. Some publicity programs, however, are specifically designed to support advertising efforts. This is the type of publicity we will be concerned with in this chapter.

Many advertising campaigns need publicity support, either in the mass media or in, the trade press. Most campaigns are announced to the trade with press releases. If there are special events, then these are usually considered newsworthy and may receive coverage from mass media as well as trade media. Usually, coverage in the trade media is totally dependent upon press releases that are provided to the publications.

While getting press coverage is the goal, professionals acknowledge that they have no control over the media's decision to use or not to use the release. You are completely at the whim of the editor's sense of news judgment, as well as subject to the breaking news on that day that competes with your release.

As part of the publicity effort, you may want to consider planning special events. These create excitement among consumers as well as among any dealers, sales staff, wholesalers, or other resellers involved in merchandising your product. Special events such as grand openings, ribbon cuttings, recognition programs, celebrity appearances, and "stunts" of one kind or another demand a lot of planning—for participants as well as for press coverage. The more unusual the special event, the more likely it will be considered newsworthy and therefore merit press coverage.

The success of special event promotions depends upon your ability to identify activities relevant to your target. Coors, for example, has gotten national and international publicity from its Rocky Mountain bicycle races and, of course, that's an activity that appeals to its young western market. A number of major national companies sponsor such competitions in everything from marathons, golf, and tennis to ultimate frisbee, one-on-one beach volleyball, and darts. The objective of such special events is to associate the product with a valued lifestyle.

Support publications for special events include invitations, press releases, product literature, and press kits that include all of the above plus copies of speeches and photos of the participants as well as prizes. If the special event is in support of an advertising strategy, then it is important that all these collateral materials be planned to coordinate with the overall theme and message.

Sales Promotion

Sales promotion is on the front line of product sales. It provides the last and most direct stimulus to move the goods. There are several different categories of sales promotion, depending upon who is seen as the audience for the promotional effort.

The most direct sales promotion is to the consumer. This includes special price deals and incentives to get the consumer into the store to buy the product. This reflects a "pull" strategy, with consumer demand being used as a technique to pull the product through the distribution channel.

A second level of promotion is to the trade. Here the objective is to get the support of the relevant parts of the distribution chain such as wholesalers, brokers, dealers, sales representatives, even drivers. Finally there is the "reseller," the retailer who will be displaying your message in some form at the point of sales. Both types of promotion through the trade use a "push" strategy. We'll call these three categories consumer promotion, trade or channel promotion, and retailer promotion.

Consumer promotion.   The objective of consumer promotion is to create accelerated demand. While brand advertising is longterm, stimulating indirect action, sales promotion is shortterm and stimulates direct action. It creates sudden bumps in the sales curve and, while the sales increase with the use of sales promotion, they tend to fall when the promotion is over.

William Robinson, author of a column in *Ad Age* on sales promotion as well as the definitive textbook on the subject, identifies 12 basic sales promotion techniques for consumer as well as trade promotion.[35] Typical forms of consumer promotions he identifies include sampling, coupons, price deals, free-in-the-mail premiums, self-liquidating premiums, contests, games, sweepstakes, refunds and rebates, bonus packs, stamps, and other continuity programs.

There are a number of reasons for using these techniques in addition to the basic one of increasing product sales. Coupons and sampling can be used to encourage trial. This is particularly important with new product introduction, but it may also be important when you have a market where sales are low.

Loyalty can also be triggered with a careful use of promotional techniques. What you want to stimulate is repeat buying. Premiums that ask for multiple proof-of-purchase stickers are aimed at continuity of purchase. Coupons on the package also encourage repeat purchases.

Promotions are useful for image building too. For example, if you have an ad campaign running that tries to reposition a product, then you might use a related premium to build that association. The Marlboro country store is an example of an advertising campaign that uses self-liquidating western and outdoor premiums to reinforce image.

The whole category of "specialties" exists as image extenders. This category includes anything that can carry a message. If it's printable, inflatable, wearable, or edible, then it can be used in advertising. The matchbook covers and pens are still used, of course, but the excitement is in the novelty items that get attention and that are kept around because they are useful. For example, one company produces visors that are embedded with fragrances. If you are selling oranges, then give away visors that smell like oranges. Not to be outdone, another visor company has a line of visors with tiny built-in radios in the brim. Brass belt buckles, iron-on T-shirt transfers, calculators, and mugs are all competing with the standard calendars for the reminder advertising message.

Executive gifts are another type of specially advertising used for reminder advertising. These can include portfolios, decorator phones, office decorations, and leisure-related products such as tennis racket covers and golf club mittens.

Special offers are also useful to build ad readership. If you have a critical product announcement and you want maximum readership, then include a sweepstakes announcement. Starch scores consistently jump when a sweepstakes is included in the ad. Sweepstakes, of course, have legal restrictions. The prizes must be awarded strictly by chance, and there can be no purchase requirement. Entry blanks should be available, even to those who don't buy the product.

Involvement vehicles include puzzles and games and things that the target has to put together or construct in order to see the message. Busy people don't have much time for these kinds of activities, so there must be a strong curiosity angle or a built-in reward to make it worth their time. Simple games are used in the grocery industry to keep customers coming back to the same store. In this case, the game is also a loyalty trigger.

A Brass Pelican direct mail piece has an interesting special promotion used by a paper division of Kimberly-Clark. It was sent to art directors and people in public relations and advertising who might specify paper. The piece was a contest to locate the final resting place of an old treasure ship, The Brass Pelican. Three clues were sent out along with old maps of the Bahamas. The winner got an island vacation.

Trade or channel promotion.   Various products have different types of distribution channels. In some rare cases, the manufacturer may sell directly to the consumer or directly to the retailer. In other situations, the manufacturer sells to a wholesaler or a broker who then distributes the product to retailers.

The first problem is informing the various links in the distribution chain about any special advertising or promotion campaigns that you may be planning.

This kind of communication, typically, takes place through the trade press and direct mail.

The second problem is motivating key individuals to cooperate. It may come as a surprise to find that your campaign is not the most important thing on their minds. If you have to rely on the distribution chain for any help in your promotional effort, you must make it worth their while.

You may motivate them with trade allowances and discounts. Or you may try gifts and contests. Incentive programs need to relate to the advertising theme, but at the same time offer something of value to your target—in this case, the trade. When you plan incentive programs, you have to understand what turns these people on and the best way to do this is to copytest your promotional ideas.

Retailer promotion.   The last link in the distribution chain is the retailer, who is also the front line in sales. You need the support of the retailer whenever you undertake an advertising program that involves a special promotion. If you are producing point-of-purchase displays, counter racks, shelf talkers, and store banners, the success of your entire campaign depends upon the willingness of the retailer to use these materials. The problem is that he or she may be overwhelmed with such materials and that the majority of these merchandising materials may wind up unopened in the dumpster.

So how do you get cooperation? In a column on sales promotion in *Advertising Age*, Eugene Mahany identified some of the promotional goals that "turn on" grocers.[36] Primarily, "what turns on grocers is what turns their customers on." For example, he cites low prices and special price deals, anything that creates high-volume turnover, displays with built-in inventories, creative displays that capture impulse buyers, product tie-ins where the purchase of one leads to buying another, and anything that increases profit potential—such as trade allowances. In particular, they would like to know that there is substantial national advertising support that will create demand in their customers.

Some things don't build reseller cooperation. They won't use a display just because it's cute and they will avoid anything that is tacky or poorly constructed or that demands their time to assemble and maintain.

Many promotional techniques are subject to legal restrictions and many of the restrictions vary from state to state. It's a good idea to check such promotions with a legal advisor.

The Bottom Line

Sales promotion exists to stimulate short-term increases in the sales curve. That means it is easily measurable. In most advertising proposals that include sales promotion, there will be a section detailing return on investment. Using basic payout planning techniques, you will need to estimate the cost of the promotion—including every detail—and compare that against the expected sales increase. Is the promotion worth the effort? Keep in mind that there are no free promotions; even self-liquidating premiums demand advertising support and staff time.

Creative Considerations

There are four primary considerations to keep in mind when planning sales promotions. First, this is a highly creative area. A sales promotion works best when it is novel and attention getting. You won't win anyone's support with another handful of matchbooks and pens. Be creative.

Second, the sales promotion technique is usually utilized in support of some advertising program. It should be related thematically. If you are promoting a German beer, then it doesn't make sense to send sweepstakes winners to Hawaii. Give them a tour of the Black Forest.

Third, make it strategic. Sales promotion is not just a bag of gimmicks. Every idea you propose should be used to accomplish some specific objective— preferably an objective that can't be reached with conventional advertising. These techniques work to solve very specific marketing problems, but you have to identify the problem before you can come up with a viable promotional idea.

Fourth, research has shown that multiple sales promotion techniques have high readership and really pull consumers. In other words, if you can combine a coupon, plus a sweepstakes, and a premium, then your promotion will pull more than any one technique by itself. There is a synergistic effect to promotional activity that really heats up the marketplace.

NOTES

1. David Ogilvy, *Confessions of an Advertising Man* (New York: Dell, 1964).
2. Carl Hixon, "Leo," *Advertising Age*, February 8, 1982, p. M–8.
3. William Kinney, "Industrial's Hot New Creative," *Madison Avenue*, April 1982, pp. 72–76.
4. Sarah Lum, "Print Advertising in the Face of Adversity," *Madison Avenue*, May 1982, pp. 97–100.
5. Fred Messner, "Moving the Prospect One Step Closer," *Adweek*, April 26, 1982, p. 18.
6. Kinney, op. cit.
7. Ibid.
8. Verne Gay, "Special Report: Business to Business Advertising," *Marketing and Media Decisions*, May 1983, pp. 111–18.
9. Philip Ward Burton, *Which Ad Pulled Best?* 4th ed. (Chicago: Crain, 1981).
10. Bob Stone, "Twenty Questions Probe Top Concerns of Direct Marketers," *Advertising Age*, May 16, 1977, p. 77.
11. "Direct Mail Pieces Lack Creativity, Y&R President Claims," *Folio*, July 1978, p. 13.
12. Ed Burnett, "The Art of Using Industrial Direct Mail Lists," *Industrial Marketing*, May 1982, pp. 66–72.
13. Sidney Bernstein, "Mail Order Is Burgeoning Giant," Advertising Age, March 26, 1979.
14. Ogilvy, op. cit.

15. Bob Stone, "Leading Direct Response Writer Shares His Copywriting Secrets," *Advertising Age,* June 13, 1977, p. 53.

16. Bob Stone, "Hail the Catalog Copywriter: The Good Ones Make Every Word Sell," *Advertising Age,* March 5, 1979, pp. 52–54.

17. Jim Powell, "The Lucrative Trade of Crafting Junk Mail," *New York Times,* June 20, 1982, p. F7.

18. Stone, "Leading Direct Response Writer."

19. Powell, op. cit.

20. Ibid.

21. Eliot DeY. Schein, "BW's invitation," *Folio,* June 1978, pp. 40–41.

22. Iain Woolward, "Advertising to the Convertibles," *Madison Avenue,* May 1982, pp. 30–32.

23. Barbara Mehlman, "Corporate Advertising: From Image to Advocacy," *Madison Avenue,* February 1983, pp. 73–80.

24. Ogilvy and Mather house ad: "How to Create Corporate Advertising That Gets Results."

25. Hugh L. Wolff, "Is Corporate Advertising a Risk Worth Taking?" *Madison Avenue,* February 1983, pp. 73–80.

26. Thomas A. Garbett, "Researching Corporate Advertising," *Journal of Advertising Research,* 25:1 February/March 1983), pp. 33–37.

27. Herbert Krugman, "Tracking the Effects of Corporate Ads," *Madison Avenue,* April 1982, pp. 29–32.

28. Ralph Nader, "Challenging the Corporate Ad," *Advertising Age,* January 24, 1983, p. M–12.

29. Krugman, op. cit.

30. Terry Haller, "Corporate Ads Doomed," *Advertising Age,* January 25, 1982, p. 47.

31. Ed Zotti, "An Expert Weighs the Prose and Yawns," *Advertising Age,* January 24, 1982, p. M–11.

32. Ogilvy and Mather, op. cit.

33. Hoff, op. cit.

34. Ibid.

35. William A. Robinson, "12 Basic Promotion Techniques: Their Advantages—and Pitfalls," *Advertising Age,* January 10, 1977, pp. 50, 55.

36. Eugene Mahany, "Examine the 'Grocer Gestalt' to See What Turns Them On," *Advertising Age,* November 22, 1976, pp. 58–60.

The Creative
Side
of Campaigns

Chapter Ten

10.1 NATURE OF CAMPAIGNS

Many of the advertisements you have been studying and creating are "single-shot" ads. However, most advertising used by national advertisers is prepared as a campaign. An advertising campaign is a series of different ads in different media that are scheduled across a substantial time period. The different ads are all held together by a unifying campaign theme. A campaign may target one specific audience or it may address several different segments. It may focus on one specific product attribute or image, or it may cover all the attributes of the product. The essence of campaign planning, then, is theme and variation.

A campaign is more than just a series of ads, however. It is a way of thinking, of planning. It involves a long and serious process of analyzing your situation, identifying possible alternatives, deciding the best approach, and testing your decisions. A campaign represents the ultimate in strategic thinking by marketing experts, copywriters, art directors, producers, promotion specialists, researchers, and media buyers. It is a team effort and it pulls the best ideas from all different viewpoints and disciplines.

Objectives

One shot vs. repetition. Most national advertisers feel that a campaign works better than a one-shot ad. A campaign creates repetition. We know that it takes more than one impression to make an impression. We also know that you can repeat the same ad only a few times before the audience realizes that this is the same old message and tunes it out.

The secret to repetition, then, is to repeat the concept but vary the details of the execution. That way you can continue to repeat the essential information without boring your audience.

At the same time you are benefiting from repetition, you are also accruing interest. The more often the audience sees the message and its variations, the more likely it is to begin to develop some interest. The campaign can generate interest of its own more than an individual ad can. Of course, there are exceptions. There are boring campaigns that never catch fire and there are dynamic one-shot ads, like Wendy's "Where's the Beef." The Wendy's commercial was part of a campaign, but it took on a life of its own. The point is that, with a sustained campaign, the message itself can become a public event.

Most advertising planners feel that a campaign is especially important for small advertisers because it can create an awareness beyond the power of several single ads. The smaller the budget, the more you need a campaign to get maximum impact from repetition of your messages.

Attention and involvement.   Another benefit of a campaign is increased attention power. People select "familiar" messages to attend to because they are comfortable and no risk. A campaign can give a message a familiar face. Familiarity is also the foundation of closure. You can make familiar messages work for you by involving the audience in the completion of the message—but only if they have been exposed over a long period of time.

Repetition.   The primary purpose of repetition in advertising is retention. Repetition builds memorability. We know from learning theory that the more times you hear something, the more likely you are to remember it. Repetition is used to anchor a concept or an image in memory. Most advertisers say a minimum of three repetitions is necessary to make any impression—but that's just a minimum. You may remember seeing ads on television much more often than that. And jingles on radio may be repeated several times every hour.

So, how much repetition can an ad take? It's like fertilizer. We know that a little bit is good but, if you put a lot on the plant, you're likely to burn it up. If you repeat a message, you're likely to burn it out too. Media planners have elaborate formulas to predict the optimum level of repetition. Unfortunately, the critical factor in deciding on repetition is not media use but message strategy. Some messages can be repeated a lot; some can't.

Messages that can withstand lots of repetition have certain characteristics. They are simple, usually brand image or product identification messages. More likely than not, they are jingles. Like a verse in a song, anything that gets put to music can be repeated over and over. They are inoffensive and make few demands on the audience. In other words, they are easy to read, watch, or hear.

Some ads have an early point of diminishing returns. In other words, a lot of repetition builds wearout rather than retention. Ads that are particularly susceptible to this burnout problem are heavy dramatic or emotional, slice-of-life, humorous, or novelty approaches. You don't have to see talking chipmunks too many times before you would rather not see them again. The more effective an ad is at getting attention, the less it can stand a heavy repetition schedule.

Learning.   Our discussion of learning theory introduced the problem of teaching discrimination and generalization. Higher order abstractions are particularly hard to communicate in short, quick advertisements. Campaigns make it easier to form these general concepts by presenting the concept in numerous and varied situations.

Likewise, we know that multisensory learning aids retention. The more senses involved and the more the message is reinforced across channels, the more likely it will be attended to and understood. The visual and the verbal should be integrated and the messages across channels should be designed deliberately to reinforce each other. Campaigns are usually designed to be multichannel, with print as well as broadcast ads and sometimes direct mail and outdoor. The more media, the better.

Forgetting.   Establishing the message in memory is an important objective, but there's another factor to be considered. How do you keep the message anchored there? Obviously, this is another function of repetition. Certain types of messages are easier to forget (or harder to remember) than others. These messages need special care. They are lengthy or complex. The more involved the construction of the message, the harder it will be to anchor it. Simplify it as much as possible. Take the complex messages apart and express them in smaller chunks. And repeat them.

Telephone numbers illustrate the principle of "chunking" information so that it can be more easily remembered. Psychologists tell us that seven is the magic number, and you will note that the basic phone number is limited to seven numbers. When the area code was added on, it was treated as an entirely separate number, not as a part of the phone number. So you remember your area code, then you remember the phone number. The phone number itself is arranged in two groups of three and four numbers. That makes it easier to remember as well as to hear. If you want to foul someone up, give them the phone number with the pause somewhere other than between the third and fourth digit. It's almost impossible to remember.

The point is that complex, hard-to-remember information needs to be chunked and simplified in order to be remembered. That is another objective of campaigns. It provides a message structure that lets you present complicated information in small pieces.

Time frame.   Another supporting argument for the use of campaigns is the time factor. Repetition is important, but it is repetition over time that builds a sustained impression. Image building, in particular, is a long-term program. Reminder objectives need continuous messages over time. Generally, advertising over a long time is more effective than over concentrated short periods—at least for brand and national advertising. Even retail, when its objective turns to image building, uses long-term campaigns.

10.2 CAMPAIGN THEMES

The theme in an advertising campaign must be a strong concept that can hold together diverse efforts. The theme is like the creative concept we discussed in the sections on creative strategy. It is the "big idea" that makes the ad, or the campaign, distinctive. In campaign planning it is the thread that holds the fabric of the campaign together. You know that a campaign involves different ads for different audiences in different media at different times of the year. Now, what keeps those from being "one shots"? Only a strong theme can provide the necessary integration. The "Brother Dominic" character is a strong continuity device for the classic Xerox campaign. (See Exhibit 10–1).

When Pepsi moved to the classic "Pepsi Generation" theme, an entirely new type of lifestyle advertising was created. That theme continues to be expressed in subsequent campaigns through the years even though the specific campaigns change. The Virginia Slims campaign uses a contemporary, high-fashion woman juxtaposed against a turn-of-the-century woman in some kind of forbidding or dreary situation. This theme is expressed in the slogan: "You've come a long way, baby."

The theme for all of Hallmark Cards advertising is quality. The entire corporate philosophy is built on the concept of quality and quality control in production. The corporate slogan expresses that idea in the memorable phrase: "When you care enough to send the very best." Because of the universal identification of that slogan, it can be shortened to "When you care enough . . ." and the audience will complete the phrase.

As the Hallmark example illustrates, the slogan is not the same as the theme, although sometimes the only way to express the theme may be in the words of the slogan. Oftentimes, the theme statement will express a concept or position such as convenience, innovation, or money-saving. It's a handle for internal use by the people involved in creating and approving the campaign. The slogan puts that rather dry theme or concept into memorable, attention-getting words. It's the public statement of the concept or theme.

Variations

A campaign is a series of ads built around one central theme. The various ads are designed to be different for very specific reasons. As you plan a campaign, think about the logic behind these variations on your theme and be prepared to justify why you even need the various approaches.

Interest.   One reason for variation is simply to maintain interest. As has been mentioned, you can't repeat a message ad nauseum. Dick and Bert have developed some award-winning humorous radio campaigns for *Time* magazine. Listening to a humorous commercial is like listening to a funny joke. The first time it catches all your attention; the second time you listen to it with fondness remembering how funny it was. After that you get tired of hearing it. In order for the *Time* commercials to work, the comedy duo had to develop a series of little sitcoms focusing on different sections in the magazine. They were using variation because their particular messages would wear out in a hurry. Variation permitted more repetition of the central concept.

Media.   Another type of variation is by medium. Your review of the different media and their creative considerations should make it clear to you that the medium itself can affect the development and perception of the message. Each medium has its own peculiar strengths and weaknesses. You can't use ex-

EXHIBIT 10-1 The "it's a miracle" campaign for Xerox features the familiar character of Brother Dominic as a continuity device. Created by Needham, Harper, and Steers, the campaign involves print and broadcast advertising as well as merchandising support. (Courtesy of Xerox Corp.)

EXHIBIT 10-1 *(continued)*

The duplicators for those who appreciate the virtues of simplicity.

When you push a few buttons on a Xerox high-speed duplicator, a miracle occurs.

A multitude of complicated jobs are converted instantly into simple ones.

For example, you can get a Xerox duplicator that copies on both sides of a piece of paper, automatically.

That reduces, automatically. Collates, automatically. Feeds and cycles up to 200 originals, automatically.

And even makes two-sided 8-1/2″ x 11″ copies from unburst computer printouts, automatically.

But of all the virtues of simplicity, the greatest is this: It increaseth productivity.

Since Xerox duplicators are so easy to use, people can spend more time using them, and less time figuring out how. Anyone who can master the technology of pushing buttons can operate one of our duplicators.

So if you appreciate the virtues of simplicity, look into the virtues of a Xerox 9200 or 9400 duplicator.

We'll even arrange a simple demonstration at your convenience.

Just in case you don't accept miracles on faith alone.

XEROX

XEROX®, 9200® and 9400 are trademarks of XEROX CORPORATION.

EXHIBIT 10-1 *(continued)*

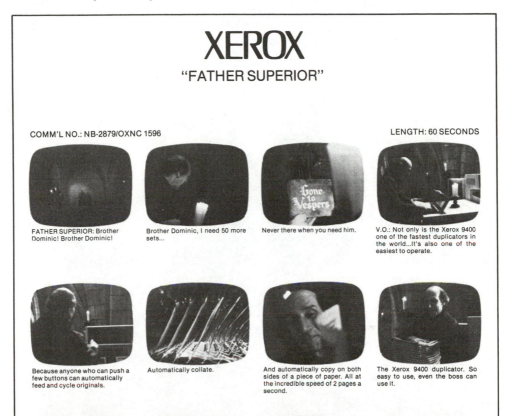

XEROX

"FATHER SUPERIOR"

COMM'L NO.: NB-2879/OXNC 1596

LENGTH: 60 SECONDS

FATHER SUPERIOR: Brother Dominic! Brother Dominic!

Brother Dominic, I need 50 more sets...

Never there when you need him.

V.O.: Not only is the Xerox 9400 one of the fastest duplicators in the world...It's also one of the easiest to operate.

Because anyone who can push a few buttons can automatically feed and cycle originals.

Automatically collate.

And automatically copy on both sides of a piece of paper. All at the incredible speed of 2 pages a second.

The Xerox 9400 duplicator. So easy to use, even the boss can use it.

BROTHER DOMINIC: Father!

FATHER SUPERIOR:
Yes, Brother Dominic.
BROTHER DOMINIC:
You did all this by yourself?
FATHER SUPERIOR:
Yes, Brother Dominic.

BROTHER DOMINIC: It's a miracle!

SUPER: XEROX.

EXHIBIT 10–1 *(continued)*

actly the same message in radio that you use on a billboard or in a brochure. Messages have to be designed specifically to take advantage of the media characteristics.

Schedule.   Time frame is another source of variation. If your campaign lasts an entire year, then you are advertising across all seasons and through all holidays. Every season and every holiday is a peg for your message.

Related to time frame is campaign scheduling. The campaign itself is planned against a calendar. There is a beginning, a middle, and an end to every campaign. Sometimes a campaign starts big and then winds down to the end. Sometimes it starts small and builds up to a big climax. This schedule is part of the campaign strategy, and should reflect what you know about the way the product is purchased and used. Special events may also affect the shape of this calendar, and you may use a media blitz at a particular point to reinforce a special promotion. Opening ads tend to be different from sustaining ads and from special event announcements. Variations in your ads may develop in response to the campaign calendar.

Attributes.   The product itself may structure your variations. You may want to develop special ads to explain different attributes or features. An automotive campaign, for example, may include separate ads on mileage, engineering and durability, comfort, style, and price. Each ad is single-minded and focuses on that specific feature.

Target.   You may need different ads depending upon how you have your audience targeted. You might have specified a business audience, for example, but within that market you may have engineers, accountants, and executives— all of whom are involved in the purchasing decision. That means you will need different ads for each target. Perhaps your campaign will need retail support, and in that case your dealers and distributors may be a separate audience whose interests are entirely different from those of the consumer groups.

There are probably other ways to break down the variations possible in advertising campaigns, but those are the major ones. The important thing to remember is that there should be a logic to your theme and variations. The variations are there for some reason. Make sure your strategy is clear in your own mind before you tackle presentation to a review board or client.

Continuity

Slogan.   The number one continuity device in an advertising campaign is the slogan. Since campaign planning is a military metaphor, you might say that a slogan is the "battle cry." The troops rally round, and the memorable phrase is on everyone's lips. A good slogan generates its own excitement. Some campaign themes continue for years, such as Bell Telephone's "Reach out and touch someone." When it works, stay with it.

Other campaigns change more frequently, sometimes because the market or the audience changes, sometimes because the campaign doesn't work as well as you might like, or sometimes because the campaign simply wears out.

In an active market where the competition is intense, the campaign slogans are on the frontline. Some of the memorable slogans used in the soft drink market recently include "Pepsi now," "Pepsi's got your taste for life," and "Catch the Pepsi spirit." Pepsi's chief competitor, the market leader, has kept the market alive with "Coke is it," "Have a Coke and a smile," "Look up America," and "It's the real thing." Other memorable soft drink slogans include "Be a Pepper" and "UnCola," which is a position as well as a slogan.

Another leader in its category is McDonald's. The McDonald's slogans have been particularly memorable. They include "Nobody can do it like McDonald's," "We do it all for you," "You, you're the one," and "You deserve a break today."

Obviously, the challenge in writing slogans is to come up with a phrase that sticks in the mind—something high in "shock value." It should reflect the character or personality of the product and the tone and atmosphere of the campaign. A slogan is designed to be repeated and remembered. Techniques used to increase this memorability factor include alliteration, rhyming cadence, and parallel construction.

The biggest problem with most slogans is that they don't identify the product or associate with the category. See how many products you can identify from the following list of slogans. As you move through the list, analyze the slogan in terms of its ability to trigger the product category and brand name. Some of them are much more effective than others. Why?

1. You're going to like us
2. Taste as good as they crunch
3. A powerful part of your life
4. Carry the big fresh flavor
5. A breed apart
6. Lets the good times roll
7. We circle the world
8. You deserve a break today
9. Always the leader
10. The closer you look, the better we look
11. A concern for the future
12. Gets the red out
13. Think what we can do for you
14. Strong enough for a man, but made for a woman

a. Merrill Lynch
b. Wrigley Spearmint
c. McDonald's
d. TWA
e. General Electric
f. Westinghouse
g. PPG Industries
h. American Airlines
i. Boeing
j. Johns-Manville
k. Bank of America
l. Eastman Kodak
m. MasterCard
n. Scott Paper
o. Mack Trucks
p. Doritos

15. Ideas to build on
16. Gentle enough to use every day
17. America's storyteller
18. Today is the first day of the rest of your life
19. Doing what we do best
20. The spray that does it all
21. A household name, at work
22. Has a lot more going for you
23. Getting people together
24. Stop babying yourself; eat hearty
25. We bring good things to life

q. Visine
r. Total
s. Kawasaki
t. Lysol
u. Ford
v. Poli-Grip
w. Secret
x. Allegheny
y. Johnson's Baby Shampoo

(answers on page 334)

Characters and situations.   In addition to slogans, characters may also be used as a continuity device. Mrs. Olson, Mr. Goodwrench, the Jolly Green Giant, Charlie the Tuna, Tony the Tiger, and the Marlboro Man have all maintained a distinctive image for their products. Hamms uses a bear, Schlitz Malt Liquor uses a bull.

The Virginia Slims commercials are built around a contemporary, high-fashion woman who is juxtaposed against a turn-of-the-century woman in some kind of degrading or dreary situation. The juxtaposition is the visual theme. The slogan expresses the concept: "You've come a long way, baby."

Graphics.   Johnnie Walker Red uses the color red as a visual theme. This long-running campaign, which is discussed in the chapter on color, has been built on all the warm positive associations we have for this color. It includes pictures of sunsets, embers dying down in the fireplace, red setters, red flowers, and red Christmas cards. It is not only the use of the color that holds this campaign together; there is also continuity in the mood of the ads. This is elusive, but when you see a Johnnie Walker ad, you know it is expressing the mellow feeling of relaxation.

The theme, then, can be expressed in the slogan as well as in some dominant visual—either art or photo. Continuity can be intensified in the use of a recognizable and distinctive layout. Type can even be a continuity device as in the antique, beat-up Cutty Sark typeface that is taken off the bottle label.

Broadcast.   In broadcast you have most of the same continuity devices—slogans, distinctive characters, use of colors, photos, artwork, or animated effects, and type. You also have continuity opportunities in the audio effects such as recognizable voices, music, or sound effects. Special visual effects in television sometimes are used as continuity devices.

Cross media considerations.   Continuity is enhanced by standardizing certain elements of the creative message and repeating them from ad to ad. It is relatively easy to maintain continuity within print or within broadcast. The real challenge is when you have to make major leaps across media. How can you maintain continuity when you move from newspaper to television and then to billboards? The features that will hold these messages together across media have to be deliberately planned.

You can't just pick up a still frame from a television spot and make it into a magazine ad—or a radio spot. If a print ad is tightly controlled and very formal, then the same feeling of enclosed space and formal movements should be retained in television. If the art is cartoon style in print, then animation using the same drawing style should be used on television. If the format of your message strategy is a testimonial, then carry that across all the media used in the campaign. If you use a slice-of-life in TV, then use it in print. Match the format across all the media and don't change it over time.

The difficult transition is from print to radio. Developing audio continuity is much more difficult without the picture. How do sound effects or music look in print? Likewise, what does crystal and china on a table sound like? Or an office?

10.3 THE CAMPAIGN PLAN

Campaign planning is involved and complicated. The end result of the planning process is a report, called a *Plans Book,* which is given to the client at the same time as the official *Client Presentation.* The end result of the campaign, of course, is produced ads that appear in the media.

The emphasis in this section is on the planning process, specifically the planning process that involves the creative side. However, since campaign plans are interwoven, everything that is done in research or media or marketing will also affect the creative side. In campaign planning, the specialists work side by side and the communication has to be very close and very direct.

Research.   It begins with extensive research into every aspect of the product: its past and present advertising, the competition and their past and present advertising, the users and the nonusers. The creative side needs to know everything that has ever been used and why it did or did not work—every ad, every jingle, every promotion.

At the same time the marketing and account management people are researching every question they can think to ask about the market. The media planners are doing the same with media use by this product as well as by the competition. Every member of the campaign team is up to his or her ears in research about respective areas of responsibility. And it all goes on simultaneously.

Analysis.   All of this is pulled together in a document known in campaign planning as the *Situation Analysis.* This report summarizes everything of significance that has been uncovered in the research effort. It leads up to an analysis of the basic *problems and opportunities* faced by the product and this campaign. What problems do you have to overcome with this advertising campaign? How can these problems be turned around to become opportunities?

Strategy.   The basic strategy decisions include positioning, targeting, and the development of a set of advertising objectives. These strategy decisions are the foundation for all the subsequent sections of the campaign plan, including the creative plan and the media plan. Everyone should be involved in the discussion and decision on these basic strategies since every one will guide all aspects of the campaign.

Creative plan.   The creative plan is next in the plans book, although it is developed simultaneously with the media and promotion plans. The creative section begins with an analysis of the underlying strategy of the campaign and the problems the message has to overcome. Message objectives are written to guide the specific details of the creative strategy.

The creative concept is presented, explained, and justified. Why does this approach make sense? Why is it better than any other approach? Concept testing is useful to justify these decisions.

The package of actual executions is then presented with additional explanations of the variations and their strategy. How do they tie in to the theme? Why are there different ads? What does each ad hope to accomplish? The explanations will normally be presented in a semicomp format. Print ads will have separate copy sheets. The television spots will be presented in a storyboard form. The radio commercials will be presented as scripts. Sometimes a "demo" tape will be produced for the client presentation for both radio and television. The storyboard may be shot in slides to be projected as the demo tape plays.

These semicomp executions can be copytested at this stage. Primarily, this level of copytesting is to determine if the ads work. Maybe you have a number of different alternatives, and what you want to know is which ones are the most effective. You may also want to test and see if a copy point is understood or if a graphic expresses the idea or association you intend. You may even take the competition's ads and reduce them to semicomp format and test them against your executions. That's a real moment of truth.

All of these executions are still in the proposal stage. The idea is to present them so the client understands what you are proposing without going to tremendous expense developing final versions. Most clients resent that kind of expense at this time. There is a tendency to try to make these proposals look finished, and that defeats the idea of review and approval. Clients may feel as if you are trying to do a "snow job" if these executions are overly finished.

Promotion.   The sales promotion and publicity proposals will vary with the nature of the campaign. Some campaigns need lots of promotional support; other campaigns are tightly focused on the traditional mediated advertisements. It will vary from client to client.

If you are doing a promotional plan, then the section will begin with a review of the campaign strategy and the implications of that strategy for promotion. You may also have specific sales promotion objectives to detail. Next is an explanation of the various promotions that you are recommending. Every promotional technique should be justified in terms of its contribution to the overall campaign objectives. This is no place to go crazy on hot air balloons and marathons, just because everyone else is doing them. Every promotional idea should also be tied in tightly to the theme. How does your great promotional idea reinforce the campaign theme? If it doesn't, dump it. The same thing is true for special events. They may be newsworthy, but if they don't support the campaign theme, then they are not part of this campaign.

Media plan.   The media plan is obviously not the responsibility of the creative side, but there are some aspects of the media plan that do affect your work. Obviously, creative and media have to talk to one another about the media vehicles. It doesn't make sense for the creative team to plan a campaign based on intensive use of television while the media planners are buying newspaper ads.

The decision on vehicles is determined by two things: the needs of the message and the limitations of the budget. Different kinds of campaigns need different types of media. Any good media plan will justify the media chosen first on the basis of the message being presented.

The budget, however, is always a restriction. Few planners ever have enough money to design the campaign of their dreams. If you have a small budget, then you have to plan your media accordingly. The creative people should be involved in this so that they understand the compromises made by the media planners.

Campaign evaluation.   The last major section in a campaign plan is a proposal for how the campaign will be evaluated. If your original campaign objectives made sense, then the campaign is evaluated on the basis of whether it achieved those objectives. Did you register a certain level of awareness? Does the target understand a copy point? Is the product associated with a need? This section explains what kind of research is necessary to determine if the objectives have been met. It is a proposal for an official, scientific research project.

Answers to Slogan Quiz: 1–d, 2–p, 3–f, 4–b, 5–a, 6–s, 7–m, 8–c, 9–o, 10–u, 11–g, 12–q, 13–k, 14–w, 15–j, 16–y, 17–l, 18–r, 19–h, 10–t, 21–n, 22–x, 23–i, 24–v, 25–e

Management
and the
Creative Side

Chapter Eleven

11.1 COPY EVALUATION

Process of Evaluation

Evaluation occurs throughout the process of developing an ad. Basically, there are two general categories of copytesting that concern the creatives: pre- and posttesting of the message. Pretesting is used in copy development; posttesting is used to evaluate the effectiveness of the ad after it has run. Pretesting often uses in-depth probing techniques of small groups of prospects; posttesting uses carefully constructed random samples and simpler questions. One is used to help in the development of the message and the other is used to test its success.

Pretesting happens continually in the copy development process. The writer and the artist do it constantly as they brainstorm for an approach. Hundreds of ideas may be generated and tossed out; it's a constant winnowing process. Research has proved that the more alternatives generated, the more likely you are to come up with a great idea. When an idea seems to have potential, then it will be tried out on colleagues and passers-by: "Hey, what do you think of this?" A lot of informal evaluation happens in the hall.

Creative strategy. The earliest type of official research involves testing and validating the strategy and translating the strategy decisions into creative ideas. In this early stage, tests are conducted to check the appeal, the promise, the benefit, and other strategic aspects of the approach. A lot of this testing uses convenience samples of the targeted audience—street corner surveys and mall intercepts, for example. The most common research technique used at this stage, however, is the focus group, since this is primarily a probing effort looking at motivations and the reasons behind the responses.

Concept.   When the creative team has a handful of potential ideas, then they are ready for concept testing. You can evaluate alternative concepts with a card test containing a couple of sentences of verbal description of the idea. That lets you get a reading without interference from execution details. For television, you can also include a key visual to accompany the verbal description.

The result of this concept evaluation is a final decision on the best approach. You can also test the strength of the idea in terms of its attention power and understandability. If you go back to your respondents a day or two later, you can also get a rough indication of memorability. If any one of the concepts appears to be outstanding, then you can move on and start developing the executions.

If none are outstanding, then it's time to start over again. It's easier to go back at this point and try for a new and stronger concept than it is to take a mediocre concept and try to make it great with dynamite execution. What separates great advertising from the rest (the other 99 percent) is the strength of the concept supported by dynamite execution. No amount of spit and polish will turn a tin concept into gold.

It's also a good idea not to get wedded to an idea early in the concept development stage. First attempts are rarely used. Occasionally, a winner will show up in the first batch of ideas but that is very unusual. Usually, the first batch of ideas contains all the clichés and obvious approaches, the tried and true, as well as a large group of halfway-there ideas. Most of the first ideas hit around the outside of the target. Pieces of them might be good, but none is perfect. Ten out of 100 will be possible, but only one out of 100 will be great. And you need the other 99 in order to appreciate the brilliance of your one winner. Don't give up too early.

When you do hit on a great idea, you'll know it—everyone on the team will know it. This may sound simplistic, but a really great idea is easy to spot. It jumps out at you. There will be no reservations in the minds of your team members. That's a way to test the brilliance of an idea—if anyone has reservations, then it probably isn't all that brilliant.

It isn't that the other ideas are wrong; they just don't have the *feel* of a great idea. Evaluate by consensus. It's kind of a magical thing. You may think it's impossible ever to find an idea that everyone agrees on. But that's the built-in "shlock" detector in the copy evaluation process. It's a question of how much do you really want to come up with a great idea.

Executions.   The next step in evaluation is execution testing. There are a thousand details in any execution, and every one of them could be handled in a dozen different ways. Artists rely on their professional judgment to sort out the best graphic treatment. Writers have an intuitive feel for the play of words.

Some of these decisions, however, are more a function of the audience response than of creative judgment and, in those situations, execution testing may be appropriate. For example, the creative team can do excellent versions of the ad using either a straight spokesperson, a common person testimonial, or a celebrity. The decision may best be made by trying out the different variations on the targeted audience in a focus group.

Likewise, you may want to know if there are any negative associations with a slogan, or if there is any problem with miscommunication for a headline. A quick set of intercept surveys can help answer those questions. Both concept testing and execution testing can be very helpful in the early development of the ad. Most of the testing at this point will use comprehensives or "roughs" for print and storyboards for television ideas.

Actual produced pieces are very expensive to develop for testing; however, they are produced and tested in those cases where an advertiser insists on research findings before committing the budget to a major media buy. A number of professional testing companies provide this service.

For these tests, the ads are prepared in as near to the final form as possible. Proofs and mockups of print ads and direct mail pieces are prepared. For magazines, the ads being tested may be in a portfolio with a number of other ads, or they may be "tipped in" to a magazine. Demo tapes are prepared for audio testing. Television commercials can be presented in several different ways. Photomatics are scenes shot from the storyboard and presented in a series of slides. An animatic is a videotape that has been shot from the storyboard with cuts, dissolves, zooms, and pans used to simulate action.

These tests are usually conducted in a formal interview or a controlled experimental setting. Sometimes focus groups may be used. Television can be tested in theater settings where participants are invited to watch a program with test commercials interspersed. Waiting room tests are also used. These are trailers parked in shopping mall parking lots. Participants are asked to wait in a waiting room environment, where there are magazines and other distractions as well as a television. Observers are able to watch and film the viewers' response to the various test commercials. Afterward, the participant is invited into a second room for an interview. Other research measures use more mechanistic methods that measure eye movement, the size of the pupil, brainwaves, and other psychological and biological reactions.

Evaluation at this stage compares alternative forms of an ad as well as how the ad compares to previous ads and the competition. The ads are also evaluated in terms of attention, miscommunication, and product identification. Follow-up studies can be used to measure memorability.

Postevaluation. This is the province of the commercial research services that monitor advertising effectiveness such as Starch, Burke, and Gallup and Robinson. There are more than 100 testing services, and they all have techniques that evaluate different aspects of an advertisement. For example, the Burke test evaluates television commercials in terms of "day after recall." The Starch scores measure print ads for "noted," "seen/associated," and "read most" using aided recall techniques. (See Exhibit 11–1.)

Day-after-recall (DAR) tests are primarily measures of attention and are criticized by many for both their validity as well as their reliability problems.[1] Affective responses created by emotional messages are ignored and few of the services measure miscommunication, attitude change, or behavior/action. The direct response industry, of course, is very good at measuring such factors as miscommunication and action, as well as attention, but that is the only area in the advertising industry that effectively tests a full range of communication effects.

Burke and Starch have evaluated thousands, perhaps even millions, of ads—and, because of this large comparative database, they have well-developed "norms" for the types of advertisements they test. These norms represent only the commercials performance on the limited types of effects measured by these services; however, these scores spell life and death for advertisements, as incomplete and imprecise as they may be.

A number of professionals, including David Ogilvy and most every copywriter who has been burned by a low Burke score, will point out that readership or viewership is not the same as salesmanship (persuasion). A study by the American Association of Advertising Agencies was reported in a research source book by Jack Haskins used at the University of Tennessee.[2] This study listed the factors that advertising professionals would like to see evaluated. The percentages in the following list indicate the percentage of the professionals rating the particular dimension as having the "highest value" in evaluating an individual ad.

Comprehension	80%
Behavior	63
Attitude	63
Recall	63
Buying preference	53
Believability	38
Recognition	15
Persuasiveness	13
Ad-liking	13

The problem is that different advertisements do different things. While it would be wonderful to be able to report an actual measure of effect on sales, we know that this is the one effect we can't measure very reliably, except in retail advertising and direct response. In most national advertising, there are simply too many other variables affecting the sale to be able to conclude the actual impact of the message. But there are effects we can measure, and these should be clearly spelled out in the advertisement's objectives.

EXHIBIT 11-1: The Amtrak "meant to fly" advertisement is an example of the kind of readership research available to magazine advertisers through the Starch service.
(Courtesy of Amtrak and Starch INRA Hooper, Inc.)

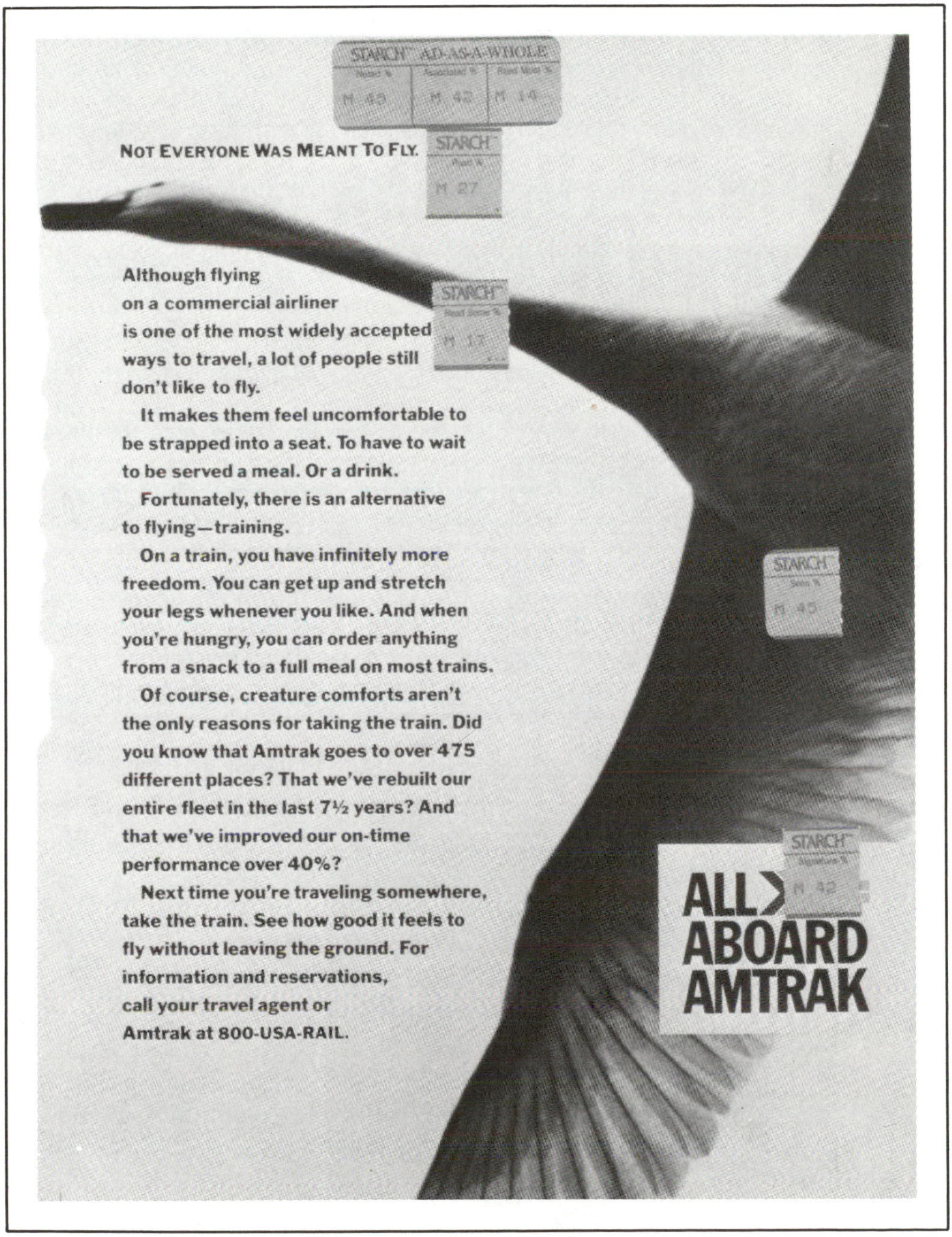

The problem with much copytesting is that the managers simply don't know what it is they want to measure; therefore, it is difficult to choose a testing service or design a study that tests the actual effectiveness of the ad. If the ad is designed to do things other than simply to get attention, then the Burke score, for example, will not give you much information on the effectiveness of the commercial. The only logical solution to the copytesting confusion is to state clearly communication objectives and then measure the ad, using tests that evaluate what that ad is supposed to accomplish rather than using some all-purpose bottom-line score that ignores or masks the effects you wanted to create.

An article in *Adweek* by David Ogilvy and Joel Raphaelson illustrates this difference between viewership and persuasion.[3] Ogilvy and Raphaelson describe a rating service by the Mapes and Ross research firm that rates a commercial's ability to *change* brand preference. One of the interesting things their study found is that 21 percent fewer consumers reported a change in preference influenced by a celebrity in a commercial when compared with the average change for all commericals. However, the celebrity commercials had a 22 percent higher recall. Why would there be a − 21 percent change in preference with a + 22 percent recall?

Ogilvy and Raphaelson explain that messages such as these focus attention on the celebrity rather than on the product. This is a phenomenon known as "vampire creativity." You can get high memorability of information that is only marginally related to the selling message while the product or brand gets lost. Good recall scores do not necessarily mean high persuasive effects.

Getting good scores.   An analysis of the Starch scores over hundreds of ads and a variety of product categories can give you some clues on how to get high Starch scores.[4] Some of the points are for the media buyers. For example, a double-page spread attracts 50 percent more readership. Second and third covers get about 30 percent more readership than a regular page. The back cover scores 60 percent higher. Other findings are clearly relevant to creative strategy:

- Color has 50 percent more readership than black and white
- Wordiness is not significant; readership decreases only slightly with an increase in text
- Photographs attract more interest than drawings
- Ads with people have higher readership
- Dogs, babies, and cute kids have high readership
- Men tend to give more attention to pictures of other men than to pictures of women
- Women give more attention to pictures of other women
- Food ads with recipes are better read than those without
- Food ads with appetite appeal are read more
- Ads with coupons are read more

Burke scores are used to evaluate television commercials, and there are truisms in the business about how to score high on this test. David Scott, creative director at Ogilvy and Mather, says it is easy to get a high Burke if you start off with something arresting. He calls it "the gorilla in a jock strap" technique.[5] Other commonly heard suggestings include:

- Use something irritating, exaggerated, or off-the-wall
- Introduce the product in the first five seconds
- Repeat the brand name five times
- Use a strong benefit approach (promise them the moon)
- Depict your target audience in the commercial
- Close with the name of the product and a visual that shows the name and package

Review Boards

Somewhere after the creative team has made its decision on the best approach and the best execution, but before the final presentation to the client, a meeting with the upper management of the agency is held. Called a *review board,* this group serves as the agency's sounding board and quality control center. The idea is to make the account team sell the approach to their peers and supervisors, admittedly the toughest critics of all. This serves as a practice presentation and a trial run on the explanation and justification techniques. Usually, review board members will ask tougher questions than the client, and that sharpens the team for the final client presentation. Review board presentations are also a way to keep upper management informed and that's very important in large agencies.

There is a lot of disagreement in the profession about review boards. The Leo Burnett agency lives by them. Creative people generally hate them; they see them as a medieval torture chamber that somehow has survived into contemporary times. In theory, review boards make lots of sense; in practice, they can be terribly destructive.

If the idea needs work, then a review board is a good way to force the creatives back into harness for the final all-night, last-ditch effort—and some of the best work comes out of those against-the-wall marathons. But what sometimes happens is that the executives pick and tear and homogenize. They can reduce an original idea to a mediocre cliché. Buxton has commented that the review board means "jeopardy for the fragile, fresh, or unique idea."[6] He explains, "The reviewers are likely to be the older, supposedly wiser, heads in an agency. They are also the more cautious and conservative." They can critique the essence out of originality. The success of a review board depends entirely upon the people who sit around the edge of the conference table and the biases, power politics, and hidden agendas that they bring along to the session with them.

Personal Judgment

Many people in advertising, managers as well as creatives, despise copytesting systems because they are so imprecise. Advertisers, however, want some assurance that an ad is a good one, and these numbers are considered better than nothing. In truth what is better than nothing, and better than a lot of copytesting services, is informed, educated personal judgment. Some researchers have even suggested that judgmental content analysis can predict day-after-recall scores as effectively as the testing services.[7] Of course, even if that were possible, one might ask why we would want to predict the scores rather than other, more relevant dimensions of message effectiveness. But the point is that informed judgment may be just as reliable an indicator of advertising effectiveness as the simplistic scores.

One of the most common activities in advertising is critiquing ads. Everyone does it—students and teachers do it, artists and writers do it, bosses and their barbers do it, women and blacks and other misunderstood and maligned groups do it. Everyone is an expert at it, and yet few are trained at it.

The "I response."   The mark of a novice in advertising is someone who critiques an ad by saying: "I like it" or "I don't like it." For most people in advertising, including the novices, this "I response" is inappropriate. To be exact, it's irrelevant. No one cares if you like it or not. What matters is whether the ad works and, in order to evaluate that, you have to consider the much more complicated questions of what is ineffective and effective in advertising and, in particular, what is good and bad for this ad in this situation.

Good and bad.   In advertising, they are situational bound. You can't evaluate an ad out of the context of both its strategic and aesthetic needs. Unfortunately, most of the award programs just appraise aesthetics—how artfully and distinctively the piece is executed. Those award programs are okay, but what they don't do is evaluate "good" advertising. What's needed is a program that considers both the strategic requirements as well as the aesthetic impact.

One thing you will discover by studying research scores is that "good" in advertising is a sliding scale. What works in one situation may be absolutely wrong in another. An advertisement that gets high recall scores can't be successful if the copy point recalled is wrong. That's similar to the "vampire video" problem where the commercial is recalled but the product is forgotten. The only way to evaluate a good advertisement is against its own problem situation and its own objectives.

There are some things that are universally wrong in advertising. One of the underlying premises of advertising is that an idea needs to be original to be attention getting so that borrowing ideas—creative plagiarism, in other words—is a universal (and ethical) wrong.

Advertising is a guest in people's homes, so insulting them is bad mannered and reflects poorly on the company, brand, and product being advertised.

Taste is a sliding scale, too, and levels of appropriateness will vary with the audience; however, it's hard to believe that the industry or anyone in it is well served by leers, sneers, and vulgarities.

Adese is another characteristic of bad advertising. Adese is described in detail in the chapter on advertising writing. It's hack writing and it's not good advertising, even if it sounds like what stereotyped ads are supposed to sound like. Everyone can develop a sense of copy aesthetics, whether you are a writer or not. Learn to recognize the various forms of adese.[8]

Guidelines.   To have truly educated judgment, you have to be a long-time student of advertising. That means you watch ads go through the development process, watch them run in magazines and on the screen, listen to the comments, and, yes, study the copytesting results. You develop judgment from experience. You can structure the experience by noting patterns. Certain patterns seem to happen and certain responses tend to follow.

You don't have to reinvent the wheel. Advertising professionals have been watching these same patterns and codifying them as checklists for years. The Thompson-Luce formula was developed in the forties and included some 35 factors. The Townsend system began with 27 points for national print advertising and was later shortened to nine critical points. David Ogilvy devised a scoring system for print advertising that highlighted 20 copy and layout factors. The purpose of a checklist is to give you a systematic way to review the ad to see if there are any glaring problems. With or without a checklist, we all go through this every time we look at a comp or storyboard.

The Ayer advertising agency has a little publication on *Evaluative Pretesting of Advertising.*[9] The booklet describes the functions of copytesting and, in so doing, it also states the agency's guidelines for good advertising. First, the ad should "produce the appropriate net impression on the target audience." Ayer defines an appropriate impression as one that makes "human contact." With that as the overriding objective, the booklet then states five auxiliary objectives:

- Accurately communicates its intended message
- Does so intrusively
- Is perceived to be personally relevant—something the prospects can identify with
- Engages the emotions in some positive way
- Is believable and not overly irritating

Ayer's philosophy of copytesting provides a set of guidelines for the evaluation of most advertisements. With experience, any professional in the field should be able to reliably exercise judgment on these factors. You might note that intrusiveness, attention power, is the only one of the factors that would be evaluated by the most frequently used copytesting services.

EXHIBIT 11-2:   The "Creative Code" was developed to outline acceptable industry standards for advertising. (Courtesy
of the American Association of Advertising
Agencies.)

CREATIVE CODE

American Association of Advertising Agencies

The members of the American Association of Advertising Agencies recognize:

1. That advertising bears a dual responsibility in the American economic system and way of life.

To the public it is a primary way of knowing about the goods and services which are the products of American free enterprise, goods and services which can be freely chosen to suit the desires and needs of the individual. The public is entitled to expect that advertising will be reliable in content and honest in presentation.

To the advertiser it is a primary way of persuading people to buy his goods or services, within the framework of a highly competitive economic system. He is entitled to regard advertising as a dynamic means of building his business and his profits.

2. That advertising enjoys a particularly intimate relationship to the American family. It enters the home as an integral part of television and radio programs, to speak to the individual and often to the entire family. It shares the pages of favorite newspapers and magazines. It presents itself to travelers and to readers of the daily mails. In all these forms, it bears a special responsibility to respect the tastes and self-interest of the public.

3. That advertising is directed to sizable groups or to the public at large, which is made up of many interests and many tastes. As is the case with all public enterprises, ranging from sports to education and even to religion, it is almost impossible to speak without finding someone in disagreement. Nonetheless, advertising people recognize their obligation to operate within the traditional American limitations: to serve the interests of the majority and to respect the rights of the minority.

Therefore we, the members of the American Association of Advertising Agencies, in addition to supporting and obeying the laws and legal regulations pertaining to advertising, undertake to extend and broaden the application of high ethical standards. Specifically, we will not knowingly produce advertising which contains:

a. False or misleading statements or exaggerations, visual or verbal.

b. Testimonials which do not reflect the real choice of a competent witness.

c. Price claims which are misleading.

d. Comparisons which unfairly disparage a competitive product or service.

e. Claims insufficiently supported, or which distort the true meaning or practicable application of statements made by professional or scientific authority.

f. Statements, suggestions or pictures offensive to public decency.

We recognize that there are areas which are subject to honestly different interpretations and judgment. Taste is subjective and may even vary from time to time as well as from individual to individual. Frequency of seeing or hearing advertising messages will necessarily vary greatly from person to person.

However, we agree not to recommend to an advertiser and to discourage the use of advertising which is in poor or questionable taste or which is deliberately irritating through content, presentation or excessive repetition.

Clear and willful violations of this Code shall be referred to the Board of Directors of the American Association of Advertising Agencies for appropriate action, including possible annulment of membership as provided in Article IV, Section 5, of the Constitution and By-Laws.

Conscientious adherence to the letter and the spirit of this Code will strengthen advertising and the free enterprise system of which it is part.   *Adopted April 26, 1962*

John Kiel, senior VP and creative director at Dancer, Fitzgerald, and Sample, wrote an article entitled "Can You Become a Creative Judge?"[10] In it, he developed eight rules to help the noninstinctively creative marketing person learn how to make creative judgments. His eight rules are as follows:

1. Make sure it adheres to strategy
2. Make sure it is directed to the right target
3. Make sure that it is single-minded
4. Make sure you know what the creative people have in mind
5. Make sure the advertising technique doesn't overpower the message ("vampire video")
6. Separate your personal prejudices from your judgment
7. Make sure the advertising doesn't change the product image
8. Have faith; let the creative people do their thing

Kiel's points include both "things to look for" and "ways to look at" advertising. He is obviously very conscious of the role interactions between creatives and account management.

Charles Frazer, a University of Colorado professor, has developed another set of criteria for evaluating ads.[11] His criteria is a list of things to "look at." He has two major categories: *concept* and *execution*. Under concept, he suggests you consider the following:

1. Strategy
2. The central idea
3. Addressed to prospect
4. Distinctive
5. Tasteful
6. Teamwork of all elements

Under execution, he lists the following areas:

1. Imaginative
2. Emphasize benefits
3. Aesthetically pleasing
4. Convincing argument
5. Simple and clear language
6. Strong opening and closing
7. Use medium to its fullest
8. Tie into theme

Both Kiel and Frazer's lists are useful guides to objective evaluation of copy.

The "Copy Chasers" is a long-running column that appears in *Industrial Marketing* magazine.[12] In this column, a panel of well-respected professional copywriters who specialize in business-to-business advertising evaluate other ads currently running in the trade press. After decades of such an exercise, the Copy Chasers have developed a set of 10 "Judgments" that they use to guide their evaluations. (See Exhibit 11–3.)

Harry Wayne McMahan, a long-time creative director and producer, has studied television commercials and developed a system for analyzing successful ones.[13] He has an extensive library of commercials that he considers successful because of their impact on the market. He has studied these commercials and described the ingredients of the ones he considers to be effective in terms of selling power. He has identified five key factors: 46 percent of the successful commercials use a Continuing Central Character (CCC), like the Jolly Green Giant; 41 percent use jingles; 29 percent use demonstrations; 29 percent tell an interesting story; and 21 percent use stars or celebrities.

He also noted that only 18 percent of these successful commercials registered a product name. He considers this better than normal. He cites Starch research that indicates one out of six or approximately 16 percent of the normal commercials will register a product name. Another 8 percent will misidentify the sponsor.

A well-researched area in advertising is direct response, and a number of the greats in advertising have looked to this body of literature for their personal philosophy of ad evaluation. David Ogilvy and John Caples are two well-known names who built their philosophies on direct mail techniques. The Direct Mail Marketing Association has summarized the results of their many years of research and published it in association newsletters and seminars.[14] The following points have been gathered from DMMA materials and, while they relate specifically to direct response, they still reflect basic and universal advertising techniques:

OPENING

- Develop a "hook"—something to mesmerize them during the first few dangerous seconds when they are trying to decide whether to read it or not
- If you have an offer, lead with it
- Use your most important benefit in the head—fire your biggest gun first

BODY

- The lead's function is to massage the interest; do that by enlarging on the benefit

EXHIBIT 11-3: Copy Chasers Criteria are used to evaluate copy.
(Copyright 1985 by Crain Communications, Inc.
Reprinted with permission.)

COPY CHASERS CRITERIA

I. THE SUCCESSFUL AD HAS A HIGH DEGREE OF VISUAL MAGNETISM

On average, only a small number of ads in an issue of a magazine will capture the attention of any one reader. Some ads will be passed by because the subject matter is of no concern. But others, even though they may have something to offer, fail the very first test of stopping the reader in his scanning of the pages.

Ads perish right at the start because, at one extreme, they just lie there on the page, flat and gray, and at the other extreme, they are cluttered and noisy and hard to read.

An ad should be constructed so that a single component dominates the area—a picture, the headline or the text— but not the company name or the logo.

Obviously, the more pertinent the picture, the more arresting the headline, the more informative the copy appears to be, the better.

II. THE SUCCESSFUL AD SELECTS THE RIGHT AUDIENCE

Often, an ad is the first meeting-place of two parties looking for each other.

So there should be something in the ad that at the reader's first glance will identify it as a source of information relating to *his* job interest—a problem he has or an opportunity he will welcome.

This is done by means either of a picture or a headline—preferably both—the ad should say to him, right away, "Hey, this is for you."

III. THE SUCCESSFUL AD INVITES THE READER INTO THE SCENE

Within the framework of the layout, the art director's job is to visualize, illuminate and dramatize the selling proposition.

And he must take into consideration the fact that the type of job a reader has dictates the selection of the illustrative material. Design engineers work with drawings. Construction engineers like to see products at work. Chemical engineers are comfortable with flow charts. Managers relate to pictures of people. And so on.

IV. THE SUCCESSFUL AD PROMISES A REWARD

An ad will survive the qualifying round only if the reader is given reason to expect that if he continues on, he will learn something of value. A brag-and-boast headline, a generalization, an advertising platitude will turn him off before he gets into the message.

The reward that the ad offers can be explicit or implicit, and can even be stated negatively, in the form of a warning of a possible loss.

The promise should be specific. The headline "Less maintenance cost" is not as effective as "You can cut maintenance costs 25%."

V. THE SUCCESSFUL AD BACKS UP THE PROMISE

To make the promise believable, the ad must provide hard evidence that the claim is valid.

Sometimes, a description of the product's design or operating characteristics will be enough to support the claim.

Comparisons with competition can be convincing. Case histories make the reward appear attainable. Best of all are testimonials; "They say" advertising carries more weight than "We say" advertising.

VI. THE SUCCESSFUL AD PRESENTS THE SELLING PROPOSITION IN LOGICAL SEQUENCE

The job of the art director is to organize the parts of an ad so that there is an unmistakable entry point (the single dominant component referred to earlier) and the reader is guided through the material in a sequence consistent with the logical development of the selling proposition.

A layout should not call attention to itself. It should be only a frame within which the various components are arranged.

VII. THE SUCCESSFUL AD TALKS "PERSON-TO-PERSON"

Much industrial advertising, unlike the advertising of consumer goods, is one company talking to another company—or even to an entire industry.

But copy is more persuasive when it speaks to the reader as an individual—as if it were one friend telling another friend about a good thing.

First, of course, the terms should be the terms of the reader's business, not the advertiser's business. But more than that, the writing style should be simple: short words, short sentences, short paragraphs, active rather than passive voice, no advertising cliches. Frequent use of the personal pronoun *you.*

A more friendly tone results when the copy refers to the advertiser in the first person: "we" rather than "the company name."

VIII. SUCCESSFUL ADVERTISING IS EASY TO READ

This is a principle that shouldn't need to be stated, but the fact is that typography is the least understood part of our business.

The business press is loaded with ads in which the most essential part of the advertiser's message—the copy—appears in type too small for easy reading or is squeezed into a corner or is printed over part of the illustration.

Text type should be no smaller than 9-point. It should appear black on white. It should stand clear of interference from any other part of the ad. Column width should not be more than half the width of the ad.

IX. SUCCESSFUL ADVERTISING EMPHASIZES THE SERVICE, NOT THE SOURCE

Many industrial advertisers insist that the company name or logo be the biggest thing in the ad, that the company name appear in the headline, that it be set in bold-face wherever it appears in the copy.

Too much.

An ad should make the reader want to buy—or at least consider buying—before telling him *where* to buy it.

Incidentally, many industrial ads are cluttered with lists of other products, factories and sales offices, name of parent company, names of subsidiaries or divisions, association memberships and other items, most of which are never looked at and which, if essential, could be set inside the copy area at the very end.

X. SUCCESSFUL ADVERTISING REFLECTS THE COMPANY'S CHARACTER

A company's advertising represents the best opportunity it has—better than the sales force—to portray the company's personality—the things that will make the company liked, respected, admired.

A messy ad tends to indicate a messy company. A brag-and-boast ad suggests the company is *maker*-oriented, not *user*-oriented. A dull-looking ad raises the possibility that the company has nothing to get excited about, is behind the times, is slowing down.

What we are talking about is a matter of subtleties, but the fact remains: like sex appeal (which is not easy to define), some companies have it, some don't. And whatever it is, it should be consistent over time and across the spectrum of corporate structure and product lines.

Of course, there has to be substance behind the picture. You can't—at least for very long—promise a silk purse and deliver a sow's ear.

Most successful companies have some sort of personality, and the advertising people should search for it and, finding it, transmit it to the people out there whom they want as friends.

- Copy should be benefit oriented
- Write "you" not "we" copy
- Paint a word picture of your promise; dramatize it
- Use conversational language, make it a letter to a friend
- Use captions under all pictures
- The closer you come to the tone of a personal letter, the higher the response
- Make sure the product is clearly defined and explained
- List and describe all special features
- The body is written like a chain; all the facts are assembled link by link
- Back every claim with proof
- Tell a success story
- Include testimonials and endorsements

CLOSING

- Make it clear how to order or buy
- Make a statement about the value to the purchaser—use comparison or metaphor to dramatize the value
- Close with some push to act immediately—what will they lose if they don't act now?
- Rephrase the dominant benefit somewhere in the closing
- In letters use a P.S. It can tie back to the headline, introduce another testimonial, or make an added inducement. Tremendously high readership
- In direct response use no obligation close (free trial), send no money, and money-back guarantee

Developing Copy Sense

The lists and points above can be summarized in a basic model that describes exactly what aspects of the advertising are being evaluated. There are two fundamental dimensions to every critique: strategy and aesthetics. Both are equally important, and both need to be evaluated by people with expertise in the respective areas.

A strong, highly memorable, and evocative ad may be totally off target. No matter how much you "love it," it's not a "good" ad. Likewise, a perfectly targeted and well-positioned ad that reads like a marketing manager's memo will not be successful because it's dull as dishwater. No matter how many times it restates the position, it still must get attention and be remembered. A good ad is one that is both strategically effective and aesthetically pleasing. That's the art and the science of advertising.

Creative strategy.   Does it speak to the right target? Does it select the right prospects? Does it tell them something they want to know? Does it identify the category, the product, and the brand clearly and immediately? Does it focus on one distinctive feature? Does it use a benefit or a promise? Are the benefits explained? If it uses a claim, is the claim supported?

After the ad has run, will the consumers be able to associate the product with the stated position? What will they think of when they think of your product or brand? Is the association strongly linked? And, finally, does it accomplish its objectives? If it's an introductory campaign, does it introduce and establish the product name, image, slogan, logo, package? If it is a reminder ad, does the new message continue to develop a constant image and position?

Aesthetics.   On the artistic dimension of the evaluation there are two things to consider: first is the concept, and second is the execution. The "Big Idea" is the theme or creative concept, the unusual approach that makes the advertisement distinctive and memorable. Ads may vary in their needs for a "glitzy" creative treatment, but they all need to get the attention of the targeted audience and be memorable to that audience. How well they succeed in terms of attention and retention is a measure of the aesthetic success of the creative concept.

The answer to the evaluation of the creative concept is usually yes or no. It either works (in terms of its audience) or it doesn't. And if it doesn't, start over. Rarely can you "fix" a problem with the creative concept by fiddling with it. As long as the creatives have done a successful job communicating, then the problem lies with the idea. If the idea comes across, but fails in terms of attention and retention, then it's back to the boards.

The second area in aesthetic evaluation is the execution, the thousands of details involved in making the concept come to life. In print advertising, you evaluate the words and the pictures and the layout. You'll consider the head and how it works with the illustration and how it leads in to the copy. You'll look at the development of the support in the body copy and the logic and story appeal of the body copy. You'll look at the clutter in the layout, the visual path, and the use of a dominant element.

In radio you'll consider the use of distinctive voices, appropriate sound effects, hummable music. Does the radio spot spur the imagination of the listener? Is the jingle unforgettable? With television you'll consider the use of motion and strong visual images, as well as the audio. Is there a strong opening and closing? Look also at the dramatic elements such as story development, characters, settings, lighting, costumes, and special effects.

In contrast to critiquing the creative concept, evaluating the execution involves looking at the pieces. If the creative idea doesn't fly, then everything is out the window. But if some of the execution details aren't right, it's still possible to "fix" the problem. It's important for people involved in critiquing to understand the difference between a fatal problem (the concept) and a fixable one (an execution detail).

It's also important to recognize the synergy of the details. An execution that works is one that works across all the details—the voices fit, the pacing is proper, the camera angles are precise—and it all works together. And when it does work, don't fuss with it. Only pick at it if there is some element that seems to spoil the effect. Tinkering with the pieces can be terribly destructive and, if the tinkerer lacks aesthetic judgment to appreciate this integration, the magic can be killed by changing a single word.

The schema.   Copy evaluation is complicated and problem oriented, rather than personal. A well-tuned critique is objective in a subjective area. That's why the "I response" is so inappropriate. The basic evaluation options can be summarized with a few simple statements:

1. It's great both strategically and aesthetically: **Let's run it.**
2. It's off strategically: **Better start over.**
3. It's off aesthetically:
   a. The creative concept doesn't work: **Better start over.**
   b. An execution detail doesn't work: **Let's fix it.**

If you are ever in a situation where you have to critique creative ideas, whether as a student or as a professional or manager, then you need to have a simple schema like this in mind. Knowing what it is you're evaluating depersonalizes the process. It's the structure that forces you to take an objective stance, to focus on the work rather than on the individual who did the work.

The procedure outline above guides the critiquing through a process and up to a point where someone has to say, "Yes, the strategy works" or "No, it doesn't." On that level, this critique becomes subjective. Evaluation of the strategy dimension is based on experience, good business sense, and, sometimes, research results. Copytesting may be important to the managers you have to work with who do not have a copy sense, but it shouldn't overpower business sense and experience.

Likewise, having sorted out the various types of aesthetic problems, someone at some point has to be able to say the creative concept does or doesn't work. Evaluation on this level now becomes a subjective one based on a well-developed sense of message needs and media aesthetics. Research can help a little but the heart of this type of evaluation is creative intuition, aesthetic sensitivity, and experience.

11.2 WORKING WITH CREATIVES

In administration science, which can be studied in business management or personnel, you will find an area of research and theory that deals with developing an organizational climate conducive to creativity. The supporting literature comes from psychology and education. This is an important topic for advertising because the entire industry is built on creativity, problem solving, and new ideas. Management style can nurture or destroy an individual's capacity for creative thinking.

Bill Marsteller in his book, *Creative Management*, said that "there is a worldwide myth that creative people are in short supply. If 'creative' is defined as producing unique ideas, then the myth is totally without foundation."[15] In advertising, creativity is everywhere. Everyone in the business is involved in generating ideas—from research to media buying to traffic and marketing strategy. Creative thinking is needed throughout the organization and not just on one side of the hall.

This chapter on how to work with creative people is addressed to those who have a career interest in the management side but its usefulness is much broader. Management is a universal skill. As Ed Buxton commented in his book, *Creative People at Work*,[16] "Everybody is somebody's boss." Even the creative people have to manage other creatives, and that may be the most difficult management situation of all since creatives are often the least prepared for the role of manager. So this section is dedicated to everyone in the business who has the opportunity to work with creatives—and that includes just about everyone—including creatives.

Organizational Climate

Organizations, regardless of their function and purpose, have some built-in problems. They tend to foster bureaucracy and to inhibit creativity. David Mars, a specialist on school administration, wrote in a paper published by the Creative Education Foundation[17] that our organizations—indeed, our society as a whole—is oriented toward producing conformity. He explains. "Conformity is seen by management as furthering the organization's goals and objectives. As a result, organization leaders tend to place emphasis on pleasing superiors in order to get ahead, not taking risks, supporting stability and keeping things the way they have always been."

That tends to be true of all organizations, including advertising agencies. Mars concludes, "In general, then, organizations lack creativity." In order for an organization to be creative, it has to break out of the mold. In order for leaders to foster creativity, they have to fight against the constant pressure for conformity and demand risk-taking.

Advertising agencies are battlegrounds. On the one hand, they are profit-making organizations, in many cases responsive to boards of directors and stockholders. On the other hand, their only product is creative thinking. Furthermore, you have management people who are responsible for maintaining the organizational functions, working elbow to elbow with creative people who have to break molds in order to be productive.

Attitudes and atmosphere.   Whether an organization is creative or not is a function of its overall personality. Creativity doesn't exist on one side of the hall, but not on the other. It trickles down from the top and affects the problem solving in all areas. Mars explains that "members of an organization in large measure take cues for their behavior within the organization from the behavioral patterns of the organization's leaders." Some organizations are creative, others aren't—and it depends upon the management strategy of the company's leaders.

In an article in the *Harvard Business Review*.[18] Frederick Randall discussed the "right atmosphere" for creativity and said that this is a "key management problem" He said that the "emotional atmosphere" is critical and cited five factors as important: availability of information, work pressure, rigidity of control, consequences of failure, and conditioned thinking.

Mars discussed the atmosphere and concluded that it needed to be "democratic."[19] He noted that there is more creativity in democratic organizations than in authoritarian ones. What he means by "democratic" is that "many persons participate in communication, decision making, and problem solving and everyone's input is valued."

The advertising industry, of course, tries to foster creativity, particularly for the creatives. There are a number of practices and viewpoints, however, that tend to violate the suggestions made by Mars and Randall.

Difference in Style

While everyone in advertising has to come up with ideas, the creative side does have a constant obligation to produce novel ideas under the heavy pressure of deadlines, budgets, client predispositions and strategy restrictions. It's the continual pressure to produce new ideas that makes the creative side the front line in the advertising business. People who work on the creative side have different ways to deal with this pressure. Some are stoical and quiet, but many are crazy and off the wall.

The other areas such as account management, research, and media also need creative thinking but they operate in a milieu that encourages more restrained and businesslike behavior. The real difference is that the business side generates numbers and the creative side generates images—words and pictures and music. Numbers have to balance; images have to move and excite.

An Australian Ogilvy and Mather executive, Renny Cunnard, describes the difference between the creatives and management as the difference between right-brain and left-brain people.[20] He says "the left brain works with letters, numbers, and words in an orderly, sequential, analytical, and logical fashion. It sticks to the facts from which only one single conclusion can be drawn. It works only with what is established, proven, real." In contrast, Cunnard describes the right brain as working "with images, dreams, and speculations in a disorderly, playful, and intuitive fashion. . . . It inhabits the world of the unorthodox, the unconventional, the improper, the unthinkable. It enjoys the mysterious, the bizarre, the fanciful, and the unknown."

The challenge is to create interaction and understanding between the right-brain people and the left-brain people. As Cunnard points out, this confrontation happens within many individuals who are both organized and creative but his description of the extremes mirrors the kind of confrontations found in many agencies.

He concludes that "you can see that agency managers are essentially left-brain types: creative people are essentially right-brain types." Is it any wonder that most agencies are battlegrounds? The "us versus them" syndrome that characterizes the interactions in many offices is furthered by management distrust and prejudice against creatives and the creatives' cynical disparagement of account executives.

According to the literature on organizational climate, this kind of tension, this tendency to break into warring camps, is not conducive to creativity. In an article on mismanaging creativity, Robert Licker observed that creatives "are damned by management's self-fulfilling prejudice against creative types—a prejudice that not only deprives individuals of a chance for growth and advancement, but dilutes the industry's greatest resource: people."[21]

The Creative Personality

One of the best copywriters in the business is a tall, quiet man with a humble and self-effacing style—silvering hair, soft spoken, a gentleman in the classical sense. His appearance and manner are scholarly, although he could never be a professor because he's too shy to get up in front of a class. This low-key man is Campbell Ewald's Clio-winning copywriter, Jim Hartzell, who is best known for Chevy's Bicentennial ad campaign: "Baseball, hotdogs, apple pie, and Chevrolet." Hartzell is one of the few in the business to carry the title: executive vice president/copywriter.

The stereotype.   He's good, but he may not fit your picture of the creative personality. You know the stereotype—the wildman running down the hall, throwing tantrums, ahead of what's in, disorganized office with bizarre decorations, erratic sometimes embarrassing behavior—particularly in client meetings, hypersensitive, moody, and overly emotional. Account managers have been overheard referring to such people as "children," the guys you keep "locked up" when someone important is visiting the office, and so on. These stereotypes are not conducive to creating respect and the productive, effective work you hope to generate.

Ego factors.   In fact, there's a wide range of personalities on the creative side, from the quiet and humble to the eccentric and crazy. But some general personality characteristics have been noted by researchers in creative behavior. Buxton mentions many of them in his book, *Creative People at Work.*[22] He says they have a strong sense of self, an ego factor that fuels a strong pride in authorship.

He notes that they also have a larger than normal need for praise and approval, and this is because the creative work they produce is mostly anonymous. He calls it "an exquisitely difficult role for a person with a superabundant sense of self." One of the many contradictions in the creative personality is that while they have strong egos, they also are constantly fighting self-doubt, a real "bundle of anxieties." He describes this as a constant state of "fear and doubt and misgivings," particularly for the young person new in the business.

Management savvy.   Not only is the wild and crazy stereotype inappropriate for most people on the creative side, many of them are well rounded and business sensitive. Many of the giants such as Bill Bernbach, Bill Marsteller, David Ogilvy, and John Caples, as well as the current leaders such as Mary Wells Lawrence, Keith Reinhard, John O'Toole, Hal Riney, Ed McCabe, Burt Manning, Jay Chiat, George Lois, Amil Gargano, and Jerry Della Femina, to name a few, all started out on the creative side. They not only moved into management, they built agencies and created philosophies.

Creatives can be brainwashed and bullied into believing that they have limited business skills, but they can just as easily broaden to fit into a management role. It's probably easier for creatives to become generalists and move into management than it is for MBAs and accountants, the numbers people who have never produced an ad. That's a difficult gap to fill, and it shows up in the insecurities of many management people who have no creative experience.

Some creatives move into management through the creative director's role. Creative directors most likely find themselves tied to management activities. Dick Wasserman explained the role in an *Advertising Age* column,[23] "In order that good work not be compromised out of existence, it must be shepherded through a rat's maze of timidity, inhibition, competition, group think, inertia, indifference, and just plain stupidity." He concluded, "That takes a leader who may or may not be a great creator."

On the other side of the issue, a lot of creatives aren't managers and don't want to be. Many writers suffer through the experience of being a copy supervisor. Normally to advance in the corporate structure, even people who have no management interests have to accept management responsibilities.

The point is that there are varieties of management talent and interests on the creative side. Some are good at it; some are terrible. We need both the Bill Bernbachs and the Jim Hartzells.

Work Habits

Hours.   One source of friction between the creative side and the rest of the agency is the difference in working styles. The creatives' job is to get ideas. Ideas come at all times of the day and night. Most creatives find it very difficult to turn off their minds when their working day is over. Sure, people in other areas take their work home with them, but that's not quite the same as being locked into a 24-hour problem-solving track.

Researchers on creative behavior know that the problems are never set aside, even when the person turns his or her attention to something else. The attention may be redirected, but the mind isn't. That's why the idea for a solution can "pop into the mind" at the most unlikely times—while commuting, while jogging, while meeting friends after work. True creatives never go anywhere without a notepad within reach at all times.

The creative person's working style just doesn't fit into nice segments like nine to five and coffee breaks at regular intervals. That's why many agencies provide some kind of flexibility in hours for creatives. They recognize that many creatives work best in a more open and unstructured environment.

Incubation.   The concept of incubation is particularly hard for accountants and business minded executives to understand. Incubation may mean getting away from it for awhile. When everyone is working against a deadline, bosses may not appreciate such truancy. Another aspect of the creative workstyle that others don't appreciate is that a lot of what creatives do is just sit and "think." Sure, they can pick up a pen and doodle while they are thinking, but still it appears to be "not working." There's a compulsion for others to wish the writer or artist would "get busy." It's important for people who work with creatives to remember that when an artist or writer is really working he or she is doing nothing visible. Putting an idea on paper is the last step in the process, what you do after the real work is done.

In reality, the quiet writer in the corner with feet on the desk may be in a state of complete panic with insides churning and wheels spraying gravel all over his or her mental office. The internal tension is producing enough electricity to power a thousand typewriters.

This is another source of friction between creatives and others in the agency. There is a point in the creative process when creatives need to be left alone. Don't disturb them while they are working on an idea. They may look as if they are not doing anything, but you can destroy the complicated edifice of ideas they are constructing in their minds if you interrupt them at the wrong time.

Blocks.   Creatives also have to develop a coping strategy for a professional malaise known as "blocking." Sometimes it's hard to get started and, when you stumble, you're sometimes inclined to "block." This means you can't get started again; the ideas just won't come. The "writer's block" phenomenon affects just about everyone who has to produce under intense pressure—the greater the pressure, the greater the chance of a mental block. Every creative person develops a different strategy for breaking the block, and some techniques are rather unconventional.

Deadlines.   While the working style may be open, the professional lifestyle is not undisciplined. Advertising is a business, and for creatives the fuel they run on is deadline pressure. The discipline comes from deadlines, and most creatives will admit they work the best and produce the greatest ideas when they are working against pressure. The blithe spirit who likes to dawdle over a design doesn't cut it in advertising. That characteristic separates commercial "creatives" from fine art "artists." It's not just the ability to produce under pressure, it's also a need for pressure to fuel the machine.

Atmosphere.   Another characteristic of many creatives is that they need mental stimulation. They don't tend to be happy in sterile modular cubes. They have a compulsive, and healthy, need to decorate and personalize their environment. That doesn't mean their offices need to look like pigpens, but it does mean the offices may be unconventional. It's better to encourage this spirit than to disparage it.

Teamwork

Every idea, ultimately, is a product of one mind—so producing an ad is an individual activity and sometimes a very lonely one. But groups and teams and buddies down the hall are very important in the process. It was noted in a preceding chapter that creatives need mental stimulation. They need to bounce their ideas off other people, preferably people who can play with the ideas and encourage the looseness that's essential to ideation.

There's nothing harder than being the only creative person in an office and having no one else to talk to. Fiction writers can go off to a cabin in the woods, but advertising writers need companions to recharge their batteries. Furthermore, originality means no one else has ever thought of it, and that's a little hard to evaluate when you are working by yourself.

There are times to work alone. During the immersion process you may want to go off somewhere and sort through lots of background information. Likewise, when it comes time to put the idea down on paper, then that's an individual activity. In betweeen, creatives need colleagues. Groups and teams and buddies are good for idea starting and idea testing. That can happen in the hall or in a creative "bullpen" or in a colleague's office where like-minded spirits happen to drop by at the same time.

Organization.   Office organization contributes to the atmosphere of an agency. Some agencies use creative bullpens, where the writers and artists are grouped in open-space office systems. Depending upon the system, these may work, but they probably won't be much appreciated by the creatives. If the space is totally open, then there needs to be some retreat where people can go when they need to think in quiet. A library, perhaps.

Some offices keep all the writers together and all the artists in another area. That's efficient in terms of use of supplies, but it impedes interaction. More recently, agencies have been experimenting with group "islands" bringing together writers, designers, and producers who work on the same accounts. Dick Wasserman, in his column in *Advertising Age,* talks about creative "family groups."[24] This seems to help integrate the functions and saves time and communication problems.

Meetings.   Most of the work done in agencies is a product of meetings. It's not a business for loners. The real medium of advertising is the meetings and they occupy a tremendous amount of everyone's time. The problem is that few people in advertising, especially the creatives, have any training in group interaction. In general, creatives are the type of people who are impatient with meetings. They weren't designed to be "meeting people." Good managers will keep formal meetings to a minimum and keep them short. Interaction is encouraged but in informal settings.

Management by Consensus

In dealing with creatives, decisions are best made by consensus. Unusual personalities, like Hal Riney, who are totally secure in their decision making and totally respected by their colleagues, may be able to operate in a more authoritarian manner, but that rarely works in most agencies.

Management by consensus means a decision is made when everyone involved feels it's the best way to go: it's not majority or authority rule. With majority or authority rule, you will have recalcitrant members who are uncooperative because they don't agree with the approach. The work may get done, but there's little excitement or pride.

Consensus management takes more discussion and candor, more leadership, and more time. If it's well handled, it also produces better work. The reason is that the group itself becomes a quality control factor. If several members can only give halfhearted support, then the idea probably isn't all that good. You can run with a so-so idea or keep working at it until you arrive at something that everyone loves. If you keep reaching for the idea that everyone loves, then chances are you will have a winner. You feel these ideas in your gut; everyone in the group knows they will work.

As mentioned in the beginning of this chapter, authoritarian management styles are probably the least effective. Intimidation and threats bring on mental blocks, and only make a difficult process even more difficult.

Buxton reported, in a survey of creative people, that 88 percent complained about a growing feeling of "uptightness" in management.[25] That may not be the same thing as authoritarian, but it stems from some of the same problems. Obviously, difficult financial times make agency managers more conservative, nervous, and less willing to gamble. Another problem is the growing number of people in management who have little rapport with creatives. These people may be particularly prone to "us versus them" thinking and their insecurities make them uneasy working with creatives.

Rewards

The biggest problem for management in its dealings with the creative side is developing a viable set of rewards. Incentives are very important in the advertising business. Most agencies, like other businesses, reward promising employees by advancing them up the ladder of titles and responsibilities. That's a typical reward scenario for management oriented people. Creatives, in a few cases, may respond to this traditional system. Usually, however, they could care less about titles and bossing someone.

Internal.   The greatest motivator of creatives is not external—it's not anything the agency can effect or stimulate—it's the pride and ego trip that comes from hearing your words over the air or seeing a four-color proof of your art. Like the runner's high, it's addictive and totally internalized. A *personal* pat on the back is what motivates most creative people.

That, however, doesn't keep them loyal to the agency. Management has a responsibility to reward good work if it wants to keep good workers. Because creatives tend to be internally driven, agency management has to be more creative in devising rewards for these people.

Recognition.   The most important reward is one that is the easiest for management to give—recognition and praise. As Ed Cooper wrote in an article in *Madison Avenue,* every creative is searching for recognition.[26] Creative people are always pushing themselves, and to do that they exist in a constant state of doubt about the quality of their work. Sure, some of them get arrogant and some put on arrogance to mask their doubts, but generally creative people are a bundle of insecurities. An "external" pat on the back is important, too. Next to self-congratulations, the greatest reward a creative person can get is for someone they respect to say, "Great work. I wish I had done that."

Salary.   Besides recognition and praise, there are some other rewards that count. Salary is probably the most important. Creatives use that to measure themselves against their peers—it's their number one way of evaluating their worth. When their salary slips behind someone they feel does equivalent work, then the doubts set in. They may want to be loved, but they also want to live well.

Offices.   Offices are another reward. The title on the door doesn't matter much, but the quality of the personal space provided is a visual symbol of their worth to the agency. Creatives pick up on that early in their careers.

As mentioned earlier, traditional business rewards—titles and promotions, and particularly management responsibilities—are not as important to many creatives.

Complaints

In a recent Michigan State University study of creatives and their interagency working relationships, the primary criticism of account managers is that they don't provide enough information or the right information.[27] Account management's biggest weakness in the eyes of the creatives is the communication side of their liaison role. It was mentioned that open communication is necessary for a creative atmosphere—so is complete communication.

Another big area of criticism, also related to communication, is the inability of some account executives to present a creative idea and sell it to the client. Ideas are abstract and the more fresh and original they are, the more challenging they are to sell. Many account executives are seen as lacking enthusiasm, which is critical to selling, and they seem to fear original ideas.

Another criticism that came out in the study is in the area of loyalty. Creatives often comment that the account executives function more as employees of the client than as employees of the agency. They lack the independent judgment that clients think they are hiring when they hire an agency. Not only are some account executives seen as lacking loyalty to the agency; they are seen as lacking the courage of their convictions (or the agency's convictions). For them, it's more important to placate the client than to do good advertising.

If you are on a management track and know that you will some day be working with creatives in an account executive position, then you might keep these comments in mind. There is a lot of friction and tension between creatives and management. Some is healthy, some is counterproductive.

As a manager, it will be your role to build the bridges and maintain the lines of communication. Avoid conditioned thinking that tends to use stereotypes and set up unnecessary friction between "us and them." Strive for a democratic style where everyone's viewpoint and input is valued.

Most of all, try to understand how creatives work and how the creative process works. Bruce Vanden Bergh and Keith Adler, two Michigan State University professors, call for "demythicizing the creative process" in order to make the management function more effective.[28] If you understand how creatives work and what you can do to support them or disappoint them, then you will be effective in your role. Most creatives admit that a top-notch account manager can make their jobs a thousand times easier, so they will appreciate your efforts.

NOTES

1. Lyman Ostlund, "Advertising Copy Testing: A Review of Current Practices, Problems and Prospects," Current Issues and Research in Advertising, University of Michigan Graduate School of Business, pp. 87–105.

2. William R. Swinyard and Charles H. Patti, "The Communications Hierarchy Framework for Evaluating Copytesting Techniques," Journal of Advertising, 8:3 (1979), pp. 29–36.

3. David Ogilvy and Joel Raphaelson, "Agency Boredom with Analysis Cripples Execution," Adweek, September 27, 1982, p. 72.

4. Edward Buxton, Creative People at Work (New York: Executive Communications, 1975), p. 143. Also, Daniel Starch, Measuring Product Sales Made by Advertising (Mamaroneck, N.Y.: Starch, 1961). Also, Philip Ward Burton, Which Ad Pulled Best, 4th ed. (Chicago: Crain, 1981).

5. Buxton, op. cit., p. 24.

6. Ibid., p. 25.

7. Terry P. Haller, "Predicting Recall of TV Commercials," *Journal of Advertising Research*, 12:5 (October 1972), pp. 43–45.

8. Sandra Moriarty, "The New Improved Never Before Offered EZ Copy System," *Industrial Marketing*, January 1983, pp. 50–51.

9. *Ayer Research Perspective: Evaluative Pre-Testing of Advertising* New York: Ayer Advertising, undated.

10. John Kiel, "Can You Become a Creative Judge?", *Journal of Advertising*, 4:1 (1975), pp. 29–31.

11. Charles Frazer, "Toward Some General Criteria for Evaluating Advertisements," American Academy of Advertising Conference, Minneapolis, 1977.

12. "Copy Chasers Seminar," *Ad Week*, sponsored by Crain Publishing Co., Chicago, August 1981.

13. Harry Wayne McMahan, *Communication and Persuasion: A Hard Look at Successful TV Commercials.* (Stephens Press, 1981).

14. Direct Mail Marketing Association. Collection of "Manual Releases" distributed annually at DMMA seminars.

15. Bill Marsteller, *Creative Management* (Chicago: Crain, 1981).

16. Buxton, op. cit.

17. David Mars, *Organizational Climate for Creativity* (Buffalo, N.Y.: Creative Education Foundation, 1969), p. 3.

18. Frederick D. Randall, "Stimulate Your Executives to Think Creatively," *Harvard Business Review*, July–August 1955, pp. 121–128.

19. Mars, op. cit., p. 23.

20. Renny Cunnard, "Creative People or Mangement. Does it Matter Who's Boss?", *Viewpoint*, a publication of Ogilvy and Mather, vol. 4, 1982.

21. Robert Licker, "The Mismanagement of Creativity," *Folio*, July 1975, pp. 44–49.

22. Buxton, op. cit.

23. Dick Wasserman, "Facing Up to Work Clans," *Advertising Age*, April 12, 1982, pp. M38–39.

24. Ibid.

25. Buxton, op. cit.

26. Ed Cooper, "I Wrote the Song," *Madison Avenue*, May 1983, pp. 97–98.

27. Sandra E. Moriarty and Bruce G. Vanden Bergh, "Creatives and Account Management: Their Working Relationship," Michigan State University, unpublished paper, 1984. Also, Bruce G. Vanden Bergh, "Improving the Working Relationship Between Account Executives and Creative Personnel: The Creative Viewpoint," 1983 Academy of Advertising Conference, Lawrence, Kans.

28. Bruce G. Vanden Bergh and Keith Adler, "Take This Ten Lesson Course on Managing Creatives Creatively," *Marketing News*, March 18, 1983, sect. 1, p. 22.

INDEX